Canadian Marketing Cases

Gordon H.G. McDougall
Wilfrid Laurier University

Charles B. Weinberg
University of British Columbia

Prentice
Hall

Toronto

National Library of Canada Cataloguing in Publication Data

Main entry under title : Canadian marketing cases

ISBN 0-13-087843-X

1.Marketing–Canada–Case studies. I. McDougall, Gordon H. G., 1942- II. Weinberg, Charles B.

HF5415.12.C3C289   2003   658.8'00971   C2002-900519-1

Copyright © 2003 Pearson Education Canada Inc., Toronto, Ontario

ISBN 0-13-087843-X

Vice President, Editorial Director: Michael J. Young
Acquisitions Editor: Kelly Torrance
Executive Marketing Manager: Deborah Meredith
Developmental Editor: Pam Voves
Production Editor: Julia Hubble
Copy Editor: Kelli Howey
Production Coordinator: Andrea Falkenberg
Page Layout: Heidi Palfrey
Art Direction: Julia Hall
Cover Design: Amy Harnden
Cover Image: Artville

2 3 4 DPC 05 04 03

Printed and bound in Canada.

Statistics Canada information is used with the permission of the Minister of Industry, as Minister responsible for Statistics Canada. Information on the availability of the wide range of data from Statistics Canada can be obtained from Statistic Canada's Regional Offices, its World Wide Web site at http://www.statcan.ca, and its toll-free access number 1-800-263-1136.

This book is dedicated to
Betty, Michael & Sandy;
and to Joanne, Beth, Geoff, Joshua, Amy & David

Contents

Part 2: Marketing Decisions

Part 3: Strategic Marketing

Preface

Canadian Marketing Cases is written with today's college and university students in mind. The book is designed to provide diverse challenges for the student—in line with the constantly expanding scope of marketing. No longer are marketing issues limited to the concerns of large companies selling manufactured goods in Canada. Today, Canadian companies need to think about global markets and to anticipate and meet threats from foreign competitors. In addition, more than half the economy is concerned with the marketing of services; the cases in this book contain many examples from services marketers in both the profit and nonprofit sectors. The New Economy and e-business marketing offer significant business opportunities; the cases provide many situations to consider the effective use of new technology. Students who are interested in a variety of careers want to know not only about large companies, but also about new ventures and small businesses. The cases in this book provide the diversity that students need and instructors want.

Our market research for this book indicated that students and instructors wanted both short but challenging cases and more comprehensive and integrative cases; we offer both. The demand was for cases that were more than illustrative examples. The desire was for cases where a range of management skills could be developed, tested, and improved. There was also a call for modern cases. We have tried to be responsive to those needs; for example, 80 percent of the cases are set within the past five years.

Marketing is a demanding and exciting field. In this book we've selected cases to capture the breadth and depth of Canadian marketing. The materials cover a broad cross-section of industries and types of organizations—large and small; international, national, regional, and local in scope—and include selling both to individual consumers and business or institutional purchasers. To reflect the growing global focus of Canadian business, a number of the cases have an international dimension. Canada's own diversity is represented by cases set in all regions of the country and by companies ranging from some of the best known marketers of nationally branded products to the newest startup enterprises serving a single market.

A key strength of the book, we believe, has been our ability to enlist the aid of marketing faculty throughout Canada in the preparation of cases. Not only have they told us what is needed in a new casebook, but also they have responded enthusiastically to our call by sending us their best and most recent cases. And they have been gracious in allowing us to edit their cases so that the book can follow a common format, making it more readable for students.

Many students using this book may be new to case analysis. While no universal formula for analyzing cases exists, we can help students learn to improve their case analysis skills. The introductory section, "Preparing and Learning from Cases," provides suggestions to the student new to case analysis. This section also includes a case, a student's written analysis of that case, and a critique of the student's report. These materials help a student become accustomed both to the demands of case analysis and the excitement generated from attempting to resolve difficult management problems.

To facilitate the teaching of this material, we have prepared a comprehensive *Instructor's Manual* that provides detailed notes on each of the cases in this book.

We have prepared more than half the materials in this book. The remaining cases have been primarily written by authors from a variety of Canadian academic institutions, including Alberta, British Columbia, Concordia, Guelph, Laurier, Manitoba, Ottawa, and Queen's. We want to thank the following case authors for graciously allowing us to use their cases in our book: Catherine Ace, Moya D. Brown, Lisa Callaghan, Delwyn N. Clark, John D. Claxton, Phil Connell, Grant Conrad, Peggy Cunningham, Darren W. Dahl, Lauren Dmytrenko, Keith Dorken, Thomas F. Funk, Gerald J. Gorn, Michael A. Guolla, Mark Haber, Eric J. Karson, Roger A. Kerin, Larry Lockshin, Geraldo Lopez, Christopher H. Lovelock, Hugh Munro, James E. Nelson, Hamid Noori, William A. Preshing, Robin J. B. Ritchie, Christopher A. Ross, Jeff Schulz, and Denise Walters. We also thank the copyright holders for giving us permission to reproduce their materials. We extend our appreciation to the managers of many organizations—sometimes disguised—that form the subjects of these cases, since it is only their willingness to share experience and data that makes case development possible.

We are particularly grateful for the "beyond-the-call-of-duty" secretarial service and word processing assistance of Rosalea Dennie and Michele Medford at the University of British Columbia and Margaret Dilworth and Elsie Grogan at Wilfrid Laurier University. We are also grateful to the following three instructors for providing formal reviews for this edition: Auleen Carson (Wilfrid Laurier University), Peggy H. Cunningham (Queen's University), and Keith J. Tuckwell (St. Lawrence College and Queen's University).

The financial support of the School of Business and Economics at Wilfrid Laurier University and the Faculty of Commerce and Business Administration at the University of British Columbia is gratefully acknowledged. We would also like to thank Andrew Firestone for his assistance. We're particularly appreciative of the important role played by the team at Pearson; Pam Voves, Maurice Esses, Julia Hubble, Andrea Falkenberg, and Kelli Howey.

Finally, we want to thank the many students we have had the privilege of teaching in Canada and around the world. Their enthusiastic response to case teaching has stimulated the development of this edition of our book. The fun and challenge of case teaching comes from the interaction between students and instructors.

Preparing and Learning from Cases

Unlike methods of instruction that use lectures and textbooks, the case method of instruction doesn't present students with a body of tried and true knowledge about how to be a successful manager. Instead, it provides an opportunity for students to learn by doing.

As a student, you may find that dealing with cases is very much like working with the actual problems that people encounter in their jobs as managers. In most instances, you'll be identifying and clarifying problems facing the management of an organization, analyzing qualitative information and quantitative data, evaluating alternative courses of action, and then making decisions about what strategy to pursue for the future. You may enjoy the process more—and probably will learn more—if you accept the role of an involved participant rather than that of a disinterested observer who has no stake or interest in resolving the problems in question.

The goal of case analysis is not to develop a set of "correct" facts, but to learn to reason well with available data. Cases reflect the uncertainty of the real world; the information presented is often imprecise and ambiguous. You may perhaps be frustrated that there is no one right answer or correct solution to any given case. Instead, there may be a number of feasible strategies management might adopt, each with somewhat different implications for the future of the business and each involving different tradeoffs.

PREPARING A CASE

Just as there's no one right solution to a case, there is also no single correct way of preparing a case. However, the following broad guidelines may help familiarize you with the job of case preparation (Exhibit 1). With practice, you should be able to establish a working style with which you feel comfortable. The guidelines on initial analysis and on developing recommendations should also serve you well for preparing written case reports or case-based exams.

Initial Analysis

First, it's important to gain a feel for the overall situation by skimming quickly through the case. Ask yourself,

- What sort of organization is the case about?
- What is the nature of the industry (broadly defined)?
- What is going on in the external environment?
- What problems does management appear to be facing?

An initial fast reading, without making notes or underlining, should provide a sense of what is going on and what information is being presented for analysis. Then you'll be ready for a very careful second reading. This time, try to identify key facts so that you can develop a situation analysis and understand the problem facing management. As you go along, try to make notes in response to such questions as:

- What decisions need to be made?
- What are the objectives of the organization itself and of each of the key players in the case? Are these objectives compatible? If not, can the problem be reconciled or will it be necessary to redefine the objectives?
- What resources and constraints are present that may help or hinder attempts by the organization to meet its objectives?

You should make a particular effort to understand the implications of any quantitative data presented in the text of the case; or, more often, in the exhibits. See if new insights may be gained by combining and manipulating data presented in different parts of the case. But don't accept the data blindly. In the cases, as in real life, not all the information is reliable or relevant. On the other hand, case writers won't deliberately misrepresent data or facts to try to trick you.

Developing Recommendations

At this point in the analysis, you should be ready to summarize your evaluation of the situation and to develop some recommendations for management. First, identify the alternative courses of action that the organization might take. Next, consider the implications of each alternative, including possible undesirable outcomes, such as provoking responses from stronger competitors. Ask yourself how short-term tactics fit with longer-term strategies. Relate each alternative to the objectives of the organization (as defined or implied in the case, or as redefined by you). Then, develop a set of recommendations for future action, making sure that these recommendations are supported by your analysis of the case data.

Your recommendations won't be complete unless you give some thought to how the proposed strategy should be implemented. Consider:

- What resources—human, financial, and other—will be required?
- Who should be responsible for the implementation?
- What time frame should be established for the various actions proposed?
- How should subsequent performance be measured?

Small-Group Discussions

The best results in the early stages of case preparation are generally achieved by working alone. But a useful step, prior to class discussion, is to discuss the case with a small group of classmates. (In some instances, you may find yourself assigned to a small discussion group or you may be required to work with others to develop a written report for possible group presentation.)

These small groups facilitate initial testing of ideas and help to focus discussion on the main points. Within such a discussion group, present your arguments and listen to those of other participants. Except in the case of group projects, the aim of such a meeting is not to reach a consensus, but to broaden, clarify, and redefine your own thinking—and to help others do likewise.

Effective marketing management involves adjusting corporate resources to the changing marketplace; this is different from just applying knowledge about what works and what doesn't work in marketing. Accordingly, the focus of small-group discussions should be on analysis and decision making: What are the facts? What do they mean? What alternatives are available? What specifically should management do? How and when?

RESPONSIBILITIES OF PARTICIPANTS

Instead of being a passive notetaker, as in lecture classes, you'll be expected to be an active participant in case discussions. Indeed, it's essential that you participate; if nobody participates, there can be no discussion! If you never join in the debate, you'll be denying other participants the insights that you may have to offer. Moreover, there's significant learning involved in presenting your own analysis and recommendations and debating them with your classmates. But don't be so eager to participate that you ignore what others have to say. Learning to be a good listener is also important in developing managerial skills.

Occasionally, you may know additional information not contained in the case, or perhaps you know what has happened since the time of the case decision. If so, keep this information to yourself unless, or until, the instructor requests it. (This advice also holds true for written reports and case exams.)

Learning comes through discussion and controversy. In the case method of instruction, participants must assume responsibility not only for their own learning, but also for that of others in the class. Thus, it's important for students to be well prepared, willing to commit themselves to a well reasoned set of analyses and recommendations, and receptive to constructive criticism. Students unwilling to accept this challenge are likely to find the case method aimless and confusing. On the other hand, if you do accept it, we're confident that you'll experience in the classroom that sense of excitement, challenge, and even exasperation that comes with being a manager in real-world situations.

EXAMPLE OF CASE ANALYSIS

There is no one way to analyze cases, but there *are* ways to learn how to do better case analyses. Moreover, you should remember that management problems don't come in neatly classified packages. Many cases raise multiple issues, and students should recognize that identifying problems and establishing priorities are the keys to case analysis.

To help you in case analysis, the following discussion includes a case (Gordon Power Tools), a student's written analysis of that case, and a critique of the student's report.

EXHIBIT 1	Preparing a Case: A Brief Outline

I. Initial Fast Reading

- no notes
- get a feel for what's going on
- think about major problems and forces present

II. A Second Careful Reading

- make notes identifying organized objectives, nature of problem(s), key facts, key decisions
- evaluate and analyze case data

III. Development of Recommendations

- identify alternative courses of action to meet objectives
- consider implications of each action
- provide recommendations, supported by analysis

Gordon Power Tools

Charles B. Weinberg

David Gordon, the owner of Gordon Power Tools Limited, faced an important decision. Should the company, for the first time in its 35-year history, begin a large advertising campaign?

The advertising campaign, if begun, would focus on the company's chainsaw products. In addition to chainsaws, the company marketed a variety of power tools (e.g., pneumatic drills, generators, and concrete vibrators) to the industrial and construction markets primarily in Ontario and Quebec. Chainsaws accounted for 32 percent of Gordon's sales and 38 percent of the company's profits.

MARKET BACKGROUND

While no precise data were available, Gordon estimated that it held a 15-percent market share in its market area for gasoline-powered chainsaws. It was the fourth largest manufacturer of these chainsaws in its region.

Gasoline-powered chainsaws were sold to loggers, farmers, large land owners (companies and institutions), and homeowners, who were primarily casual users with many trees on their property. The homeowner market appeared to be a growth area. The logger market, on the other hand, was quite cyclical, rising and falling with the boom-and-bust cycle that seemed to characterize the forestry industry.

At the time that the power saw company was purchased, half of its sales were made through a distributor, Excelsior Hardware Sales, which owned a number of large retail outlets and acted as a wholesaler to many other smaller retail outlets. All sales to Excelsior carried the distributor's own brand names. The Excelsior name was used for sales through its own stores and the Harter brand name for sales through other companies. (The Harter brand was solely owned and controlled by Excelsior.) In the most recent year, Excelsior accounted for 59 percent of Gordon's chainsaw sales; this percentage had been virtually constant over the past 15 years. David Gordon thought that his relationship with Excelsior was excellent.

HomeMart, which operated extremely large retail stores, accounted for about 10 percent of Gordon's sales. These chainsaws were sold under the HomeMart brand name.

David and his chief assistant, C.R. Croft, regularly called on all major forestry companies, other companies and institutions that were likely to be buyers of gasoline-powered chainsaws or involved in land-clearing operations, operators of lumber yards and building supply distributors, and occasionally large retailers. However, David and C.R. were not able to visit many of the dealers that sold chainsaws. For example, of the 53 dealers in northern Ontario that sold Gordon chainsaws, they had called on only 19 in the most recent year. Most dealers sold several brands of chainsaws, but many limited themselves to two or three brands. All sales in these markets (41% of the chainsaw business) were made under the Gordon brand name. The majority of these sales were made through wholesalers and retailers.

Gordon participated in a number of agricultural fairs each year and sponsored chainsaw cutting contests. However, the company had never advertised either in trade journals to reach dealers or in magazines that might directly reach the people who were the buyers and users of chainsaws.

Gordon manufactured a variety of chainsaw models, but they differed primarily in the length of their chainsaw blade and in horsepower. Trade association surveys showed that a number of other features were important to users. Weight of the chainsaw, ease of controls, whether it had a gas protector, and the warranty were important to consumers, with safety being a critical—although unspoken—concern to many. The Gordon chainsaws were at least as good as those of the major competitors on all these dimensions and had a slight advantage on weight. That is, for any given horsepower and blade length, the Gordon would weigh somewhat less than that of its major competitors. However, this advantage was very difficult to notice unless someone worked with a chainsaw for an extended period of time.

A typical gasoline-powered chainsaw had a retail price of $500. Excelsior and HomeMart received a 30-percent discount on this price, as did most other distributors and wholesalers to whom Gordon sold. On average, Excelsior or other wholesalers would take one-third of this discount (that is, $50), and the retailer would receive the remaining two-thirds (that is, $100).

Gordon's cost of goods sold for chainsaws was 70 percent of sales (48% represented materials including preassembled components, 22% represented labour) and the remainder was contributed to overhead and before-tax profit (Exhibit 1).

THE ADVERTISING PROPOSAL

Two years ago, David Gordon hired Kevin Towson as marketing manager for Gordon chainsaws. Kevin had worked for four years as a sales representative with Canadian Faucets, a major marketer of plumbing fixtures, and then spent three years as associate sales manager at a large consumer products company.

Kevin believed that Gordon could substantially increase sales of its own brand of gasoline-powered chainsaws if it achieved a greater presence in the marketplace. He felt that brand-name recognition would increase the company's sales both because dealers would be more inclined to mention the brand to their customers and because customers would be more inclined to specify—or at least recognize—the Gordon brand name.

Recently, a trade journal had published the results of a market survey that dealt with how individuals bought power tools. Although Kevin could not determine what portion of the buyers were professionals, such as loggers or carpenters, and what portion were home-owners, he still felt the results were helpful. The magazine had sent out a questionnaire to 1,200 recent buyers of power tools and had received 800 replies. The main results of the survey are shown in Exhibit 2. In brief, Kevin noted from the findings that 57 percent of buyers had a brand of power tool in mind before buying it and that 44 percent said that the dealer had considerable influence on the brand that was purchased. He felt that these results supported his contention that advertising could pay off for Gordon.

Kevin had interviewed a number of ad agencies about the possibility of handling the Gordon account. After extensive discussion, he hired the Summit Advertising Agency to represent the company and prepare an advertising plan. He negotiated a one-year contract with a flat fee of $5,000 to the agency. He had done this rather than pay a commission on advertising dollars spent because he didn't want the agency to have an incentive to recommend advertising expenditures just to increase their earnings.

Summit recommended that advertising would be an excellent investment for Gordon; however, if the Gordon brand name was to achieve recognition, Summit believed that a few small-space ads would not do much. Rather, the agency suggested that full-page ads should be used on a frequent basis. Summit had conducted some research and had identified a set of magazines and local papers that most loggers read, two trade journals that reached most retailers and wholesalers in Gordon's market area, and three magazines that targeted the "do-it-yourself" homeowner who might make use of a chainsaw. As shown in Exhibit 3, Summit proposed spending $45,000 on this campaign (of which 15%, the commission the media paid to Summit, would be rebated to Gordon). A key point in the advertising campaign would be the lighter weight of the Gordon chainsaw.

Kevin thought this was an excellent proposal and heartily endorsed it. An expenditure of this magnitude would require the approval of David Gordon, not only because of its size but also because of its novelty for this company.

Questions

1. What are the main issues Gordon Power Tools faces?
2. What alternatives should be considered?
3. What should Mr. Gordon do? Why?

EXHIBIT 1	Gordon Power Tools Limited Income Statement (in thousands of dollars)		
Sales			$4,233
Cost of Goods Sold (including shipping)			
Materials		$ 2,101	
Labour		1,040	3,141
Contribution		$1,092	
Manufacturing Overhead		$ 630	
Administrative Expenses		151	
Sales & Marketing		138	919
Net Profit (before tax)			$ 173

EXHIBIT 2	Excerpts from Survey of Recent Buyers of Power Tools Costing More Than $100

How much time did you spend thinking about the purchase?

- Less than 1 week   4%
- 1 week to 1 month   15%
- 1 month to 3 months   41%
- More than 3 months   40%

How familiar were you with the product before you bought it?

- Very familiar   28%
- Somewhat familiar   43%
- Not too familiar   29%

Did you have a brand in mind before your first visit to a dealer?

- Yes   57% (40% said they bought this brand)
- No   43%

How great was the dealer's influence on your purchase?

- Considerable   44%
- Some   18%
- Hardly any   15%
- None   23%

EXHIBIT 3	Summary of Summit Advertising Proposal		
Market Target	**Media Description**	**Intensity**	**Cost**
Retailers & Wholesalers	2 monthly trade journals: *Lumber Wholesaler & Retailer* and *Store Management*	6 ads per year in each magazine	$16,400
Homeowners	3 magazines aimed at do-it-yourselfers: *Popular Crafts, Homeowner,* and *Canadian Homes*	Ads in 2 issues of each magazine during heavy selling season	$18,500
Loggers	Local newspapers and magazines, e.g., *Forestry Workers' News*	1 to 4 ads in selected newspapers and magazines	$10,100

Student Analysis of Gordon Power Tools

ISSUE

Should Gordon begin a large advertising campaign for its chainsaw products?

DISCUSSION

Kevin Towson thinks that Gordon can substantially increase sales of chainsaws by undertaking a major advertising campaign. Although Kevin's work experience provided him with knowledge of marketing procedures, he has not fully considered the implications of his proposal. At his previous employer, he marketed products in which advertising was common and major branded firms competed directly against each other. At Gordon, Kevin is selling products in a market with direct and indirect competitors (including Excelsior, with its Excelsior and Harter brand names—see Exhibit 4). If the new advertising campaign is successful, Excelsior's chainsaw sales, under both their brand names, will likely suffer. (The effect on HomeMart, which emphasized price and breadth of selection, is likely to be minimal.) This could serve to tarnish the excellent relationship that currently exists between the two companies and that has apparently existed for 15 years, as evidenced by the fact that Excelsior has continually accounted for approximately 50 percent of Gordon-brand chainsaw sales over this period.

If this relationship does deteriorate, Gordon has more to lose than gain by operating independently of Excelsior. Excelsior's distribution channels allow Gordon to sell its products widely. Also, as indicated by the power tool buyer survey, many customers tend to purchase well-known, brand-name products. To capitalize on this fact, Gordon needs to have a

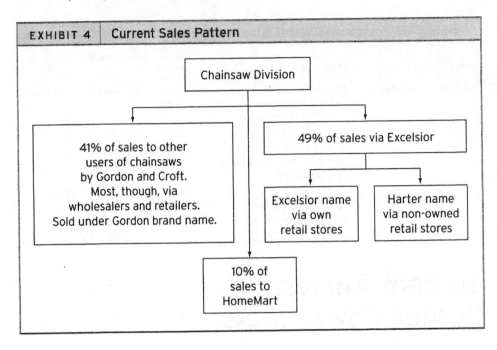

| EXHIBIT 4 | Current Sales Pattern |

well-established name through which to sell its products, something that Excelsior provides in its large distribution channels. Excelsior also has a strong influence on Gordon's sales because of the influence retailers have on purchases (also indicated by the survey). Finally, because most of Gordon's sales are currently through retailers and wholesalers, which require the same margins as Excelsior, Gordon saves nothing in terms of lower margins to dealers by not selling through Excelsior.

Therefore, assuming that there are currently no threats by Excelsior to stop selling Gordon-brand chainsaws under the Excelsior and Harter brand names, increasing advertising to improve Gordon-brand chainsaw sales could serve to cannibalize Excelsior's sales of Gordon-brand chainsaws. This would jeopardize the excellent relationship the two companies now have and, in the long run, cause Gordon to lose this powerful distribution channel that accounts for approximately three-fifths of its chainsaw sales.

ALTERNATIVES

1. Proceed with advertising plans.
2. Propose co-op advertising with Excelsior for Excelsior's brand names.
3. Increase sales in other ways (sales)

Analysis of Alternatives

1. Proceeding with advertising plans could weaken the relationship between Gordon and Excelsior and cause Gordon to lose or have its powerful distribution channels obstructed in the future.

EXHIBIT 5	Financial Analysis

Revenue to Gordon per Unit

Retail price		$500
Discount (30%)	$150	
Wholesaler margin (1/3 of 30%)	50	
Retail margin (2/3 of 30%)	100	150
Revenue to Commander/chainsaw		$350

Gordon's Current Unit Sales

Percentage of market	15%
Total dollar sales	$4,233,000
Percentage of revenue – chainsaws	32%
Chainsaw revenue	$1,354,560
Chainsaw price	$350
Approx. chainsaws sold (Commander total)	3,870
Chainsaws sold via Excelsior and HomeMart (59%)	2,280
Chainsaws sold direct	1,590
Total chainsaw market (3870 ÷ 0.15)	25,800 units

Contribution per chainsaw

Revenue/chainsaw		$350
Materials (48%)	$168	
Labour (22%)	77	
Cost/chainsaw	245	
Contribution/chainsaw		$105

Advertising Costs

Flat fee	$5,000
Proposed spending	$45,000
15% returned to Gordon	+6,750
Total advertising cost	$43,200

Extra Chainsaw Sales Required to Cover Advertising Costs

Contribution per chainsaw	$105
Chainsaws required to break even	$43,250/105 = 412
Required % of market:	412/25,800 units = 1.6%

2. Proposed co-op advertising with Excelsior for Excelsior's brand names would allow Gordon to magnify its advertising dollar and perhaps increase sales for chainsaws in areas in which David Gordon and C.R. Croft do not attempt strongly to sell Gordon-brand chainsaws.

Recommendation

Propose to Excelsior that co-op advertising for Excelsior-brand chainsaws be undertaken in areas in which Gordon does not heavily promote Gordon-brand chainsaws.

CLOSING NOTE

If Gordon does decide to advertise, either with or without Excelsior, the increase in sales of chainsaws required to pay for the advertising will give Gordon an idea of the feasibility of the proposal. As indicated in Exhibit 5, to pay for an advertising cost of $43,250 Gordon would have to have an incremental increase in chainsaw sales of 412. This would represent a 1.6-percent increase in market share (out of a total market of 25,800 chainsaws).

Critique of Student Analysis of Gordon Power Tools

OVERALL EVALUATION

Your analysis of the advertising campaign issue was thorough and clear. You should have widened the scope of your analysis, though, to capture some of the more subtle issues, such as: Is Gordon Power Tools too dependent on Excelsior? Can the relationship with HomeMart be enhanced? What are the relative merits of advertising and personal selling? What market segments should be pursued?

ISSUE IDENTIFICATION

Your statement of the issue was clear and concise. However, you didn't develop a statement of the broader problems facing the company. Remember that what people think is the problem is often only a symptom of the real problem. In this case, Kevin Towson was focusing on whether to advertise the Gordon brand of chainsaws. A situation analysis should help to identify other possible issues. Was the market changing, thereby making new forms of communication necessary? Did existing channels of distribution need to be supplemented? Was personal selling no longer feasible and/or effective?

Among the case facts to be considered in identifying key issues are

- Only 41 percent of sales are under the Gordon brand name
- David Gordon and C.R. Croft lacked the time to call on a majority of other dealers and distributors
- Brand preference is important to buyers
- Dealers exert considerable influence on buyers

Always question whether what *seems to be* the issue actually *is* the issue. Often, the problem goes deeper.

Your flow chart was very useful in clarifying the pattern of chainsaw sales and Gordon's relationship with Excelsior.

SITUATION ANALYSIS

You did not do a thorough situation analysis. It is usually a good idea to do one, because it helps you organize a lot of information and sheds light on the issues in the case. It also makes explicit the assumptions under which you are operating and lets you know what you don't know.

A situation analysis would have revealed, for example, that Gordon's relationship with Excelsior may be a mixed blessing. In your analysis, you did a very good job of explaining the advantages of the relationship, but you overlooked the associated threat. Gordon's dependence on a single major distributor puts it in a vulnerable position. That puts the advertising question in a different, more favourable light. Not only might an advertising campaign generate some "pull" demand, it might also reduce Gordon's vulnerability. However, you did a good job in recognizing that the impact of the ad campaign on relations with Excelsior must be considered in making a decision. How will the growth of major retailers like HomeMart affect Gordon?

ALTERNATIVES

Given your identification of issues, your list of alternative courses of action was fine. For completeness, it should have included the option, "Continue current policy." Maybe even more critical, however, was your not considering the alternative of hiring an additional salesperson. The case mentions that the executives don't have the time to call on all the accounts, and the market research data show that the dealer's influence is important in the purchase process.

The second alternative (co-op advertising) you proposed was particularly good because it went beyond what had been suggested in the case; a creative solution like this is a big plus.

ANALYSIS OF ALTERNATIVES

Your analysis of the alternatives you suggested was concise. It is important to state the criteria against which you are evaluating the alternatives. To a certain extent you did this, but only in your "closing note." You seemed to evaluate the alternatives against different criteria. For example, what is the incremental financial cost of each alternative? What are the incremental financial benefits? What are the nonfinancial costs and benefits? These criteria should have been the logical result of your situation analysis. You need to examine each alternative systematically, so that you can see exactly how well each one does on each criterion. Then, if new circumstances change the firm's priorities (for example, should the relationship with Excelsior sour), it is easier to see how the alternative stacks up.

Your economic analysis of the advertising alternative was good. You generally made reasonable assumptions in evaluating the financial impact of the proposed advertising plan. It's a good idea, as you did, to translate the numbers into a market share target. For a company with a current market share of 15 percent, an incremental market share gain of 1.7 percent is a considerable challenge.

In your analysis, you might note that the $5,000 fee to Summit Advertising is already committed for this year, so it is not an incremental cost and would not be appropriate for the break-even analysis. You were generally quite careful in your analysis, and it was correct to recognize the 15-percent rebate on media costs.

You should not be convinced too quickly that a particular alternative is superior. Avoid the temptation to try to find the one, "right" answer. Look at each possibility in as balanced a way as possible. For example, the alternative of co-op advertising still leaves Gordon quite dependent on Excelsior.

RECOMMENDATION

Your recommendation was clear and actionable. However, you could have been more specific by making recommendations that would have addressed such questions as, What rate should be used to share the co-op ad costs? What's the budget? What is the likely outcome?

ORGANIZATION OF REPORT

You might have used a more formal approach or framework in your "analysis" or "discussion" section. As mentioned earlier, you did not do a "Situation Analysis." Consider using subheadings, such as (a) consumer/buyer analysis, (b) market segmentation, (c) environmental analysis, and (d) company versus competition—strengths and weaknesses. While these categories may not always be appropriate, they help organize your thoughts and analysis. As an example, under "Buyer Analysis," you might consider, How important is advertising in the buying decision for a chainsaw? How important is personal selling? Are potential buyers aware of the Gordon brand name? The Excelsior brand name?

Lastly, the "Closing Note" catches the reader by surprise. This note should be presented earlier in the discussion so that the merits of your recommendations can be assessed.

TO RECAP

You have done a good job of examining one aspect of the case. If you had applied the same creativity to other issues and had approached the case more systematically, yours would have been a superior case analysis.

Part 1   Introducing Marketing

Stratford Festival of Canada

Gordon H. G. McDougall

Anita Gaffney, Marketing Director of the Stratford Festival of Canada (SFC), faced a challenging mandate for 2001: to sell 580,000 tickets and generate gross ticket sales of $30,127,000 for the Festival (April 25–November 4). The exciting playbill included Shakespeare's *The Merchant of Venice*, Noël Coward's *Private Lives*, Anton Chekhov's *The Seagull*, and four new Canadian plays including Robertson Davies's *Tempest-Tost* (Exhibit 1). With most of the marketing campaign developed, Anita's immediate focus was the customer relationship program. Started two years ago, this program took a new approach based on targeting five segments with different appeals and incentives. The segments ranged from the high-value Preferred patrons who came to Stratford every year to the Conversion patrons who had never attended Stratford but had asked for information within the past year.

While the customer relationship program was costly, results to date had been positive, based on the experiments and market research studies done in the past two years. The program appeared to offer the potential to generate revenue and solidify loyalty among valued patrons. However, Anita wanted to make sure that the strategy for the program was on target and effective. She also wanted to consider what role the Web site (www.stratfordfestival.ca) could play in the relationship program. The Web site provided extensive information on the SFC, accommodations, ticket prices, and so on. It also allowed individuals to book tickets online. She began to review the data in preparation for putting the relationship plan together.

BACKGROUND

In 1952, local journalist Tom Patterson enlisted the aid of Tyrone Guthrie, a well-known director, and Tanya Moiseiwitsch, a renowned stage designer, to establish a festival of Shakespearean theatre in the small southwestern Ontario city of Stratford. On July 13, 1953, Alec Guinness stepped onto the stage in a specially constructed tent to speak the opening words of *Richard III*. In the years since, the SFC has set benchmarks for the production of theatre, both classical and contemporary, on the North American continent.

Now in its 49th year, the SFC is a premier venue, offering world-class theatre to more than 640,000 patrons in a 28-week season in three theatres. Between 1993 and 2000, ticket revenue grew from $16.6 million to $26 million and ticket sales from 468,000 to 639,000 (Exhibit 2). With an estimated 2001 budget of $41 million, the SFC employs 875 people to deliver 14 productions and 668 performances at the three theatres to a projected audience of 580,000 (Exhibit 2). As in previous years, the hope was to exceed the projected target, which had been set for budgetary purposes. The SFC has a significant economic impact on the Stratford region (population of 30,000), generating approximately 150,000 room nights and creating overall economic benefits of about $170 million. As well, the SFC has created great citizen pride in Stratford, the "Festival City."

Research revealed that the SFC had a strong positive image. When asked what the SFC meant to them, respondents said Stratford was:

- traditional theatre, with Shakespeare at the core;
- great theatre—good plays, first class, a guaranteed success, enriching, variety, distinctive staging; and
- "Stratford Experience"—the town, river, swans, accommodations, dining, getaway.

However, some respondents also said the SFC was:

- not new or different, difficult to plan, lacking intriguing productions; and
- an attraction for older people, Americans, and students.

The SFC executive believed that the brand image encompassed three main areas:

- **Quality Theatre:** First and foremost, the Stratford Festival stands for quality theatre entertainment, and is differentiated from other theatrical experiences in that it presents a diverse variety of significant plays ranging from Shakespeare to contemporary selections in fresh, modern, and innovative styles that are playful and energetic and serve to enrich, inspire, and challenge.
- **Stratford Experience:** The Stratford Experience is a celebration of quality theatre set amidst a pastoral retreat, featuring beautiful parkland, fine dining, and rural diversions. Unlike most other experiences, a journey to Stratford is an event offering both beloved traditions and new discoveries.

- **Reputation & Influence:** The Festival is a highly successful and enduring company that attracts audiences of all ages and is a dominant landmark on the cultural landscape influencing professional theatres across the continent. The professional training and audience outreach offered by the Festival is unparalleled in the country.

As a non-profit charitable organization, the SFC relied on financial support from government, corporations, and individuals. While most of its revenue, 82 percent, came from ticket sales and ancillary services fundraising (14%), government grants (4%) also provided significant revenues. As well, governments at all levels have provided significant funds for infrastructure and capital programs, such as the past renovation of the Festival Theatre and the planned renovation of the Avon Theatre. Government funding was also important as it showed commitment to the SFC, which in turn could be helpful when the SFC approached the private sector for funding.

THE COMPETITION

In a broad sense, the SFC was in competition for the entertainment dollar of consumers. In comparison to many other entertainment choices, live theatre tended to be more expensive, with ticket prices ranging from $40 to more than $100. For the 2001 season, regular ticket prices at the SFC ranged from $48.90 to $79.15. As well, patrons of the SFC needed to travel some distance (Exhibit 3) to the Festival (e.g., 155 kilometres from Toronto; 260 kilometres from Detroit) and in many cases required accommodations. The consequence was that the majority of the SFC's patrons were higher-income and older individuals.

The most direct competitors were other live theatre companies, including the Shaw Festival. The Shaw Festival, in its 40th season, was one of the largest repertory companies in North America and the only theatre company in the world that specialized in plays written by George Bernard Shaw and his contemporaries. The Shaw Festival's 11 productions ran from April to November in three different theatres (Festival—861 seats; Court House—316 seats; and Royal George—328 seats). The 2001 playbill included *The Millionairess,* by George Bernard Shaw, and *Peter Pan,* by J. M. Barrie. The Shaw Festival benefited from its location in historic Niagara-on-the-Lake, a picturesque village 20 minutes from Niagara Falls. The area was one of the major tourist destinations in North America and was still considered a "honeymoon destination." Many theatre-goers, particularly from the United States, would see shows at both Stratford and Shaw (145 kilometres from Stratford), primarily during the summer months.

MARKETING & SALES DEPARTMENT

The Marketing & Sales Department brought together all functions within the Festival that interfaced with the public, from delineating and communicating image/brand, to facilitating ticket orders, to hosting patrons during their visit to the Festival. Specifically, the Marketing arm of the department, with 12 full-time employees and the help of two outside agencies, oversaw the advertising, publications, relationship marketing, Web site, travel trade, and media relations. The Sales arm of the department, with 11 full-time staff and 150 seasonal employees, undertook ticket and product sales, food and beverage sales, and event planning, the "front of house" hosting of patrons, and the management of the Friends of the

Festival, a group of 150 volunteers. The marketing and sales budget amounted to 12 percent of the overall operating budget, with the major expenditures being advertising, the *Visitors' Guide*, general office costs, and the call centre and ticket office (Exhibit 2). In addition to activities directly related to marketing and sales (e.g., the design, preparation, and mailing of the *Visitors' Guide*, advertising planning and placement, the call centre, and the ticket office), the department also handled media relations, photography, accommodations booking service, and "front of house." During the Festival, the "front of house" staff were responsible for ticket taking, ushering, car parking, and any other contact with theatre-goers at the performances.

The Web site was used to market and promote the season playbill and the ancillary programs that support it. Most visitors to the Web site sought information on the plays in the season, the price of tickets, and the season schedule. The Web site was launched in 1996 and substantially improved for the 2000 season. Web ticket sales for 2000 were forecast at $1.5 million, an increase of more than $500,000 compared to 1999. The SFC's goal was to increase Web usage, and specifically Web ticket sales, in order to lessen the burden and expense of serving the majority of its patrons over the phone. The target for Web sales was set at $5 million for the 2003 season.

Marketing Campaigns

Prior to 1998, the SFC marketing campaigns were broad-based, with heavy emphasis on television and newspaper advertising with the general goal of bringing theatre-goers to Stratford and boosting awareness of SFC's offerings. In 1999, the Festival adopted a much more focused approach to its marketing efforts, concentrating on stewarding existing patrons through a relationship marketing campaign and reaching out to new audiences through a media campaign, with a particular emphasis on newspaper and radio. This strategy took advantage of the extensive database of existing patrons and the need to continuously build new audiences for the Festival. An important marketing tool was the *Visitors' Guide* (an attractive booklet of more than 150 pages that included the plays to be performed and information on accommodations, dining, shopping, diversions, Festival merchandise, maps, theatre packages, group rates, how to order tickets, order forms, etc.). The *Visitors' Guide* was mailed to the more than 300,000 individuals listed in the SFC's database. The newspaper advertising was focused on the Toronto and Detroit markets as well as other large communities within 400 kilometres of Stratford.

Anita's major responsibility was the preparation and implementation of the annual sales and marketing plan (see Exhibit 4 for ticket sales statistics). Most of this work would be done prior to a given Festival season. This included setting the goals, budget, and ticket sales targets for sales via the call centre and sales to individuals, groups, and schools; the pricing strategy; the creative and media plan for advertising and media relations; and the relationship marketing plan.

Another significant responsibility for Anita was the constant monitoring of ticket sales, beginning in early December (the *Visitors' Guide* was mailed to members of the SFC in November) when members of the SFC (Exhibit 5) could purchase tickets in advance; non-members could purchase tickets beginning mid-January. Weekly targets were set in the marketing plan, and sales against targets were continually reported.

The SFC, and most other event marketers, sought to generate sales as quickly as possible. Early sales did two things: determined how well sales were going (and likely to go), and built momentum. Strong early sales could be used to create more excitement for an event (e.g., "Only a few tickets left!") and also motivated those involved in taking the ticket orders and those using telephone marketing to sell tickets. To generate early ticket sales and build momentum, the SFC, as noted above, mailed the *Visitors' Guide* well in advance of the Festival opening (previews began in late April and the official opening was May 28). Prior to 1999, the advertising campaign began in early April with quarter- to half-page newspaper ads (Exhibit 6), and in recent years advertising was begun in early January to coincide with the opening of the box office to the general public.

The Relationship Program

Over a number of years, the SFC had created and refined a customer database. Information was collected on all individuals who contacted Stratford for information, ticket purchases, requests for the *Visitors' Guide*, and so on. The information included name, mailing address, phone number, and tickets purchased. In early 1998, Anita had a customer value analysis conducted on the database, using frequency of visits to the SFC in the past five years and amount spent on ticket purchases. Based on the analysis of the 215,000 individuals in the database, five segments were developed:

- **Preferred:** Patrons who have attended in at least three of the last four years and are found in the 10th decile or highest spending group.
- **Loyal:** Patrons who have attended in at least three of the last four years and are found in the 1st to 9th decile group.
- **Upsell:** Patrons who have attended at least once in the last two years.
- **Reactivation:** Patrons who have attended for the first time in the past year, patrons who have not attended in the last two years, and patrons who did not attend last year but did attend the year prior for the first time.
- **Conversion:** People who have never attended but have requested information.

The value analysis to split the two top groups into Preferred and Loyal was as follows: all patrons who had attended in at least three of the last four years were selected, then ranked in order of how much they spent (dollars spent on tickets). The top 10 percent in terms of spending (10th decile) were placed in the Preferred group, the remaining (9th to 1st decile) were placed in the Loyal group. The three remaining groups were defined by attendance and purchase behaviour.

The results of the value analysis were enlightening: the Preferred and Loyal segments constituted approximately 11 percent of the database but generated more than 30 percent of the ticket revenues. The results changed Anita's way of thinking. She realized that the broad-based marketing campaigns might not be the most effective strategy and that devoting some resources to a segmented approach might be better. She decided to focus more on retaining current customers and encouraging them to buy more, and also on moving the segments up the value scale. Anita decided to conduct further research, which included an experiment to better understand the five segments.

First Relationship Program

The first program and study was conducted in the spring of 1999 by an external marketing research firm. The overall objective of the study was to determine the relative response in terms of ticket sales, by each of the five segments, to a customized package that included a personalized letter, an incentive, and a survey (see Exhibit 7 for more details). Each segment would be compared to a control group that was not contacted (except that the entire Preferred segment was sent the incentive). The package was sent to 50,000 individuals in the database (Exhibit 7). As Anita reviewed the results at the end of the campaign, she made the following observations:

The incremental revenue was calculated at $670,000 (Exhibit 7). This needed to be compared against the cost of the study, $300,000, and the distinct possibility that the program had just accelerated purchase decisions that would have been made later. However, this acceleration was still of benefit, because it was important to generate sales as quickly as possible.

The response in terms of ticket sales differed dramatically. Sales generated per package sent were highest for Preferred ($97.00) and lowest for Reactivation/Conversion ($9.00) (Exhibit 7).

The survey response rates, particularly among the Preferred and Loyal segments, were very high and suggested that these segments had a positive attitude toward Stratford. This was strongly reinforced by their plans to attend Stratford this year (Exhibit 8).

The information from the survey (Exhibit 8) was very helpful in building a more detailed profile of each segment. Aside from the demographic data, which showed that the Preferred and Loyal segments comprised older, more affluent patrons, these two segments had a very high rate of theatre-going, attending the SFC, and planning to attend Stratford this year. Across all the segments, the plan to attend Stratford this year was high.

While encouraged by the results, Anita was concerned about the cost of the campaign. She felt that there might be a more effective way of reaching each of the segments and that more frequent contact with the segments, particularly the Preferred and Loyal, might be beneficial. Overall, she believed that a relationship approach was the right way to go.

Second Relationship Program

Prior to the 2000 season Anita developed a relationship program with the SFC's advertising firm, which also conducted research studies. The overall goals were to help achieve increased ticket sales for the SFC, to build on the 1999 relationship program with targeted, meaningful communications in 2000, and to build new relationships with the lower-value segments. To accomplish the goal, patrons would be contacted more frequently, different programs would be established by segment, and the mailings to the Canadian and U.S. markets would be customized.

The 2000 relationship program contained three major initiatives. First, in November/December 1999, the *Visitors' Guide* was mailed in an upscale envelope to the Preferred, Loyal, and Upsell segments. Each segment received a personalized letter (Preferred and Loyal: welcoming them back and encouraging early bookings; Upsell: hard selling the Festival). For the Reactivation and Conversion segments, a *Visitors' Guide* was sent in January/February. In March 2000, the direct mail component of the program was launched (see Exhibits 9 through 11 for details and results). In November 2000 the Winter Relationship Study was conducted (see Exhibits 12 and 13). The estimated incremental cost of the program was $272,000, which included $35,000 for the November 1999 letter and envelope; $120,000 for the March 2000 direct mail campaign; and $47,000 for the Winter Relationship Study.

As Anita reviewed these results, she made the following notes:

- The top three segments all had three points of contact from the SFC during the year in addition to any advertising or other media that mentioned Stratford. This helped to remind them of the SFC and, it was hoped, encouraged them to maintain their ties.

- In the past the *Visitors' Guide* had been sent to everyone in the database, with an address printed on the back of the guide. By sending the *Visitors' Guide* in an envelope with a letter to the top three segments, the SFC was acknowledging that it valued their patronage.

- The direct mail component (Exhibits 10 and 11) had an impact in generating buyers and ticket sales. While many of those sales would probably have occurred without the mailing, the overall impact was very positive.

The most important result, which confirmed the previous study, was the sales generated by the Preferred and Loyal segments (Exhibit 9). These two segments were less than 30 percent of the database but purchased more than 70 percent of the tickets. The challenge was to maintain their loyalty to the SFC and to move the Upsell segment into the Loyal segment.

The Winter 2000 Relationship Study (Exhibits 12 and 13) was very positive, with high response rates and a very high percentage of respondents who planned to attend the SFC in 2001.

The Web Site

Statistics revealed that the Web site had more than 45,000 unique visits (number of different users) each month for May through July 2000 and, on average, each visitor had nine page views (number of different pages looked at by a visitor). Anita felt that the Web site might be beneficial to the relationship program but had only ideas at this stage. Her initial idea was that e-mail campaigns would be a cost-effective way of reaching various segments, but to date only 15,000 e-mail addresses had been collected on the database. Another idea was to include an offer to the Reactivation and/or Conversion segments to book tickets online at a reduced handling charge of $3.00. The current handling charge was $6.00 per order, whether tickets were booked online or through the call centre. For SFC, the actual cost of booking tickets online was $3.00 per order, whereas the cost through the box office/call centre was between $4.00 and $5.00 per order. A possibility for the Preferred and Loyal segments was a special section on the Web site that allowed them early booking for the season. Anita wondered if the idea could effectively encourage an increase in Web ticket sales and assist in relationship building.

The Decision

Armed with her review, Anita began to consider the relationship marketing options for the 2001 season. Anita wanted the program to help build momentum for sales, and the Preferred and Loyal segments were key to early sales and to a significant portion of individual ticket sales. Individual mailings and early advertising helped build momentum that she didn't want to lose, so there was a timing issue. As well, she wanted to acknowledge and/or reward the Preferred and Loyal segments in some way that would strengthen their ties to the SFC. This option had to be designed to ensure that it complemented the Membership Program (Exhibit 5), which was run by a separate department. There were more than 22,000 members of the SFC at different levels (Exhibit 5), some of whom were in the Preferred and Loyal segments (Exhibit 7). In total the members contributed a substantial portion of the 15 percent of revenues in the "Fundraising" category (Exhibit 2). Any option could not overlap the benefits the members currently received and could not conflict in any way with the membership program. In addition, Anita wanted to move the segments up the value chain—encouraging Upsell to become Loyal, and Reactivation to become Upsell. She was concerned that only a very small percentage of both the Upsell segment and the Reactivate segment moved up the value chain (Exhibit 14). The majority for both segments moved down. She also wanted to ensure that she reached each segment in a cost-effective manner and with more points of contact.

Anita also considered the possibility that there might be better ways to segment the database that could offer greater insights, improve the targeting, and increase the effectiveness of the relationship program. She believed the concept of value segments was an appropriate approach and that the Canadian and U.S. patrons should probably receive different packages. One consideration was to create a U.S. version of the *Visitors' Guide* with ticket prices in U.S. dollars. However, the more closely she matched the benefits offered with the segments' needs, the more effective the campaign would be.

Among the options Anita was considering were:

- Some way to thank the Preferred and Loyal segments, which purchase more than 70 percent of the tickets. One idea was to send them a poster that was custom designed and not available for sale. Another idea was a set of six special-edition postcards that would be designed in-house (total cost of $2.00 per set: $.50 for the cards and $1.50 for mailing). Other options included an SFC calendar ($.80 per calendar plus $1.50 for mailing), a Christmas card ($.52 per card plus $.80 for mailing), and an SFC pen ($.55 per pen plus $.90 for mailing). A personalized "thank you" letter for their support would cost $.50 per letter plus $.80 for mailing). The goal was to recognize these segments, strengthen their connection to the SFC, and accomplish this in a cost-effective manner.

- For the Upsell segment, an offer giving them a discount that would increase based on the number of tickets purchased. Another possibility was to "package the experience": to offer packages that would include tickets, accommodations, dinner, and so on, with the SFC responsible for making all the bookings. This would make it easy for those in the Upsell segment to attend multiple performances over two or three days. Anita felt that the Upsell segment offered considerable potential for growth.

- For the Reactivation and Conversion segments the options were not really developed, but Anita wanted to determine less expensive ways of reaching these segments. She considered sending them a smaller version of the *Visitors' Guide* that contained just information on the plays, or just a list of the shows. A *Visitors' Guide* cost $2.00, and mailing costs were another $2.00. A single-page promotion that could include all of the plays would cost $.10 with mailing costs of $.60. As well, the Web site might be helpful in reaching these segments by encouraging them to visit the site and send for more information via e-mail. However, although the Reactivation segment purchased few tickets per person, it was still the largest of the five.

Any of the relationship program activities of the previous two years could also be considered.

As Anita reviewed her notes, she knew that with the "right" relationship campaign the goals of the SFC could be met. She was determined to build that campaign.

EXHIBIT 1	Message from the Artistic Director

A Season Fit for a King

This is a historic season for the Stratford Festival of Canada—in more ways than one. Under the overall title "The Making of a King," we proudly present a three-play cycle of Shakespeare's histories—*Henry IV*, Part 1, *Falstaff* (*Henry IV*, Part 2), and *Henry V*—that has never before been mounted in a single Festival season. While each of these plays stands alone as a masterpiece of exciting action, political intrigue, and psychological insight, together they continue the sweeping epic saga that began with *Richard II* (presented in our 1999 season) and that will conclude, in our 50th season in 2002, with *Henry VI* and *Richard III*.

Our 2001 playbill also includes the premières of four new Canadian plays: Robertson Davies's *Tempest-Tost*, adapted by Richard Rose; Timothy Findley's *The Trials of Ezra Pound*; Dan Needles's *Wingfield on Ice*; and *Good Mother*, by Stratford Festival company member Damien Atkins.

Add to this Shakespeare's comedies *The Merchant of Venice* and *Twelfth Night*, Anton Chekhov's *The Seagull*, the brilliantly witty *Private Lives* of Noël Coward (born just a little over a century ago, in 1899), Edward Albee's *Who's Afraid of Virginia Woolf?*, the Jerome Lawrence and Robert E. Lee courtroom drama *Inherit the Wind*, and the beloved Rodgers and Hammerstein musical *The Sound of Music*, and you have a season fit not just for a king but for everyone who loves great theatre. I hope you will enjoy it!

Richard Monette, CM
Artistic Director
Stratford Festival of Canada

EXHIBIT 2	Budget and Performance Information, 2001

Budget

TOTAL BUDGET	**$40,820,000**
REVENUES	
Ticket sales (67%)	
Gross ticket sales	$ 30,127,000
Less discounts provided	$ 2,982,500
Net ticket sales	**$ 27,144,500**
Ancillary revenues (14%)	**$ 5,837,000**
Grants (4%)	
Canada Council	$ 710,000
Ontario Arts Council	$ 778,500
Total	$ 1,638,500
Fundraising (15%)	**$ 6,200,000**
	(continued over)

EXHIBIT 2	Budget and Performance Information, 2001 (continued)

SALARIES

Actors and musicians	$ 7,066,000
Artisans and craftspeople	$ 12,290,000
Other	$ 5,165,000
Total	**$ 24,521,000**

Total employees: 875

Year-round Stratford residents employed: 552

Performance

PRODUCTIONS AND PERFORMANCES

FESTIVAL THEATRE
1,824 seats − 4 productions − 261 performances

AVON THEATRE
1,117 seats − 5 productions − 243 performances

TOM PATTERSON THEATRE
487 seats − 5 productions − 164 performances

Total: 14 productions, 668 performances

Projected attendance: 580,000

41% of box-office dollar volume is from the United States

Source: *Visitors' Guide 2001*, Stratford Festival of Canada

Ticket Revenue and Attendance, Goal and Actual 1993 to 2000

		Goal	Actual
1993	Revenue	$18,308,000	$16,563,442*
	Tickets	468,458	447,838
1994	Revenue	$17,266,000	$17,261,020
	Tickets	454,000	466,091
1995	Revenue	$17,981,000	$18,261,020
	Tickets	450,000	460,847
1996	Revenue	$18,720,000	$20,085,272
	Tickets	480,200	502,105
1997	Revenue	$21,000,000	$21,889,836
	Tickets	497,000	504,707
1998	Revenue	$22,695,000	$23,591,730
	Tickets	506,000	523,015
1999	Revenue	$22,978,000	$25,594,500
	Tickets	484,000	565,086
2000	Revenue	$25,975,000	$28,262,026
	Tickets	523,000	639,141

* Gross Revenue, not including discounts.

EXHIBIT 2	Budget and Performance Information, 2001 (continued)

Marketing & Sales Budget 2000

General Office Costs (Sales) Salaries, telephone, data processing, postage, office supplies, open house	$ 586,860
General Office Costs (Marketing) Salaries, press clipping service, travel & entertainment, telephone, courier, subscriptions, photocopying, office supplies, leases	$ 768,585
Advertising Newspaper, radio, outdoor & magazine placement, advertising production, disbursements & fees	$ 1,230,000
Education Pre-show chats & fringe activities, Shakespeare on Wheels, Teaching Shakespeare School	$ 132,800
Group Sales & Schools Travel & entertainment, advertising, displays	$ 36,500
Media Relations Hospitality, TV Day, travel & entertainment, comp tickets, fees	$ 133,000
Advertising and Promotions Promotional servicing, local advertising, travel, promotional tickets, surveys, parade	$ 85,000
Photography Lobby photos, photocall fees, photo prints & slides	$ 66,500
Postage	$ 245,000
Distribution Mail house processing–*Visitors' Guide* & rack brochure	$ 30,000
Publications & Marketing Materials *Visitors' Guide*, signage, mid-season brochure, fanfares, fringe, letters & envelopes, advance brochures, Stratford for Students, STAR program, Internet, rack brochure	$ 841,615
Relationship Marketing Data analysis, creative, fees, programs	$ 272,000
Archives and Exhibits Salaries, supplies, telephone, fees	$ 125,000
Call Centre Expense Salaries and wages	$ 465,000
Accommodation Booking Service Salaries, printing, postage	$ 104,700
Ticket Office Salaries, wages, printing, postage	$ 217,540
Front of House – Festival Theatre Salaries, wages	$ 212,000
Front of House – Avon Theatre Salaries, wages	$ 94,400
Front of House – Tom Patterson Theatre Salaries, wages	$ 42,500
TOTAL MARKETING & SALES	**$5,689,000**

| EXHIBIT 3 | Stratford Location Map |

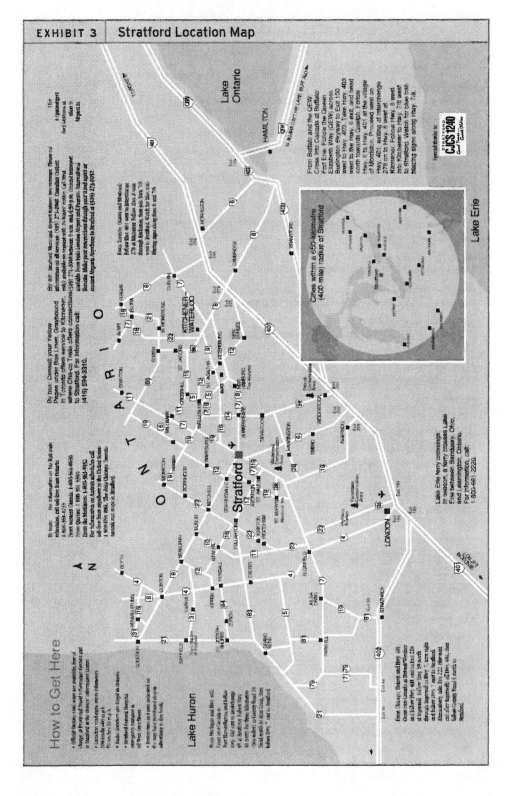

EXHIBIT 4	Total Ticket Sales—Selected Statistics, 2000		

Type of Buyer

Schools	12%	Individuals	77%
Groups	10%	Benefits & Lectures	1%

Geographic Area (Distance from Stratford in kilometres)

Toronto (155)	28%	Michigan (Detroit 260)	20%
Southwestern Ontario (10-145)	22%	New York (Buffalo 290)	4%
Rest of Ontario	6%	Ohio	4%
Rest of Canada	5%	Illinois (Chicago 680)	3%
Total Canada	61%	Rest of U.S.	8%
		Total U.S.	39%

Capacity by Month

May	83%	September	76%
June	78%	October	75%
July	80%	November	60%
August	84%		
Special Savings Programs	22%		
New Patrons	21%		

EXHIBIT 5	SFC Membership Information

Invest in the heart and soul of great theatre. Become a Member.

Friend Member $50-$99

- Priority ticket ordering before the general public
- One-year subscription to *Fanfares*
- Vote at the Annual General Meeting
- Priority Booking for Open House tours and demonstrations
- Tax receipt

Supporting Member $100-$174

Enjoy all Friend Member benefits plus:

- VIP Members' event—An opportunity to enjoy an interesting event and a specially priced preview for Supporting and Sustaining Members only
- The Eaton Lounge—Enjoy the VIP Members' lounge and the adjoining Seagram Terrace during the interval at the Festival Theatre

Sustaining Member $175-$249

Enjoy all Supporting Member benefits plus:

- Special Orders Service—Receive special ticket priority and personal attention from our Special Orders Department when ordering your tickets

Benefactor Member $250-$499

Enjoy all Sustaining Member benefits plus:

- One Bring-A-Friend ticket with our compliments for a guest to accompany you to a pre-selected performance (*in place of the VIP Members' Event*)
- Guaranteed Season Opening Night tickets if ordered by March 1

Associate Member $500-$999

Enjoy all Benefactor Member benefits plus:

- One Bring-A-Friend ticket with our compliments for a guest to accompany you to the performance of your choice, except for the Season Opening Night (*in place of the pre-selected dates*)
- Acknowledgement of your generous gift in the Festival's house programs
- A complimentary copy of the Souvenir Program
- Join Playwright's Circle Members and Festival Artists at a special behind-the-scenes event

Playwright's Circle $1,000+

For more information about this very special membership group, please call the Development Office at (416) 363-4711

The Fine Print: Memberships are valid for one year from the date of joining. All priority ticket benefits exclude the Student/Senior performances. Membership benefits are personal and non-transferable.

Note: Donors to the Festival receive a charitable tax receipt.

EXHIBIT 6	Example of Newspaper Advertisements

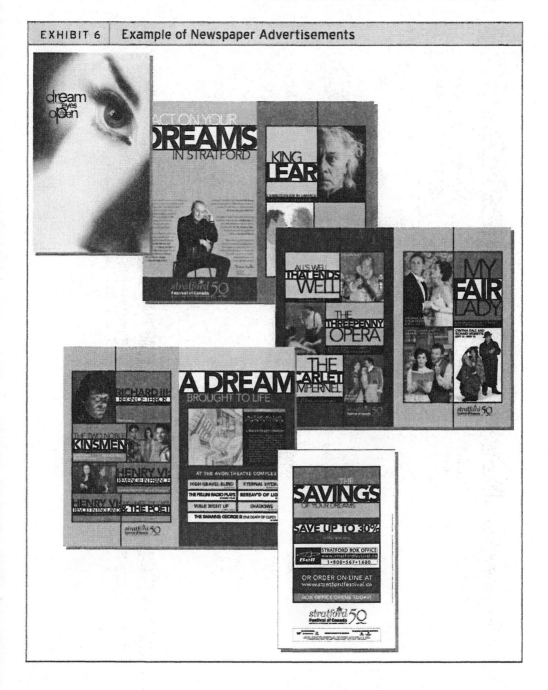

EXHIBIT 7	Relationship Study Spring 1999 Program Results					
	Preferred	Loyal	Upsell	Reactivation	Conversion	Total
Total Size	9,000*	15,000*	24,000*	124,000*	40,000*	212,000
Package Sent*	9,000	9,000	10,000	22,000 (Reactivation & Conversion)		50,000
Surveys Returned	43%	32%	17%	8%	6%	20%
Incentive Group:						
tickets sold	18,000	10,000	8,000	3,000	1,500	40,500
$ sales	$875,000	$470,000	$395,000	$150,000	$50,000	$1,940,000
Control Group:						
tickets sold	N/A	3,000	2,500	2,000	500	8,000
$ sales	N/A	$175,000	$125,000	$70,000	$25,000	$395,000
Incremental Sales						
tickets	N/A	7,000	5,500	1,000	1,000	14,500
$ sales	N/A	$295,000	$270,000	$80,000	$25,000	$670,000
Sales/Sent	$97.00	$52.00	$39.50	$9.00 (Reactivation & Conversion)		

* 75% of the Preferred segment, 22% of the Loyal segment, 12% of the Upsell segment, 3% of the Reactivation segment, and 1% of the Conversion segment were Members of the SFC. Membership ranged from "Friend" ($50–$99) to Artist Director's Cache (Gifts of over $20,000).

** A survey was sent along with the package to the 50,000 individuals. See Exhibit 8 for a summary of the survey results.

EXHIBIT 7	Relationship Study Spring 1999 Program Results (continued)

Notes

A relationship marketing program was conducted in the spring of 1999. Five distinct patron groups were identified from the Festival's database. The five groups were:

Preferred:	Patrons who have attended in at least three of the last four years and are found in the 10th decile or highest spending group.
Loyal:	Patrons who have attended in at least three of the last four years and are found in the 1st to 9th decile.
Upsell:	Patrons who have attended at least once in the last two years.
Reactivation:	Patrons who have attended for the first time last year;
	Patrons who have not attended in the last two years; and
	Patrons who did not attend last year, but did attend the year prior for the first time.
Conversion:	People who have never attended the Festival, but have requested information.

Each of the five groups was mailed a customized package in April that contained a personalized letter, a survey, a playbill, and a coupon for 15% off at a local Stratford restaurant. This mailing arrived in homes shortly after the SFC advertising campaign ramped up with increased placement size and frequency.

The control group for each segment was not sent anything. Since the entire Preferred Group received the incentive, there was no control group. All tickets and sales for the Preferred Group were excluded from Incremental Sales.

The incremental sales were $670,000; the cost of the test program was $300,000; the net revenue from the test program was $370,000.

EXHIBIT 1-8	Relationship Study Spring 1999 Survey Results

	Preferred %	Loyal %	Upsell %	Reactivation %	Conversion %	Total %
Response Rate	43	32	17	8	6	20
Age						
65 and older	27	37	34	22	25	30
55–64	34	25	25	23	21	27
45–54	24	24	25	24	20	22
35–44	12	9	11	15	12	12
25–34	3	4	3	12	12	7
Under 25	0	1	2	4	7	2
Household Income						
$75K & over	59	48	49	45	40	40
$50–75K	22	30	29	28	26	27
Under $50K	19	24	22	27	34	23
Planning to Attend This Year? Yes	90	82	79	72	68	80

EXHIBIT 8	Relationship Study Spring 1999 Survey Results (continued)

	Preferred %	Loyal %	Upsell %	Reactivation %	Conversion %	Total %
How many live theatre performances attended in past year?						
5 or more	88	65	61	50	43	N/A
2 to 4	9	27	30	36	38	N/A
One	3	6	6	6	10	N/A
None	0	0	3	8	9	N/A
How many of those have been at Stratford?						
5 or more	47	8	11	5	N/A	N/A
2 to 4	48	69	55	42	N/A	N/A
One	3	16	16	27	N/A	N/A
None	2	7	18	26	N/A	N/A

EXHIBIT 9	The Relationship Marketing Program 2000–Direct Mail Component: Relative Importance of Each Customer Segment

	Preferred	Loyal	Upsell	Reactivation	Conversion	Total
CANADA						
Mailed	4,588	12,374	11,195	25,762	5,900	59,819
Percentage of Total	7.7%	20.7%	18.7%	43.0%	9.9%	100.0%
Tickets to July 31	41,219	30,438	12,466	19,728	1,726	105,577
Percentage of Total	39.1%	28.8%	11.8%	18.7%	1.6%	100.0%
U.S.						
Mailed	4,199	3,629	3,901	12,303	4,928	23,960
Percentage of Total	14.5%	12.5%	13.5%	42.5%	17.0%	100.0%
Tickets to July 31	44,368	9,068	6,024	15,736	2,068	77,264
Percentage of Total	57.4%	11.7%	7.8%	20.4%	2.7%	100.0%
TOTAL						
Mailed	8,787	16,003	15,096	38,065	10,828	88,779
Percentage of Total	9.9%	18.0%	17.0%	42.9%	12.2%	100.0%
Tickets to July 31	85,587	39,506	18,490	35,464	3,794	182,841
Percentage of Total	46.8%	21.6%	10.1%	19.4%	2.1%	100.0%

Note: The Preferred segments in both countries were important customers. In Canada, they represent only 7.7% of the mailed total but had produced almost 40% ($2,077,000) of total tickets sales to the end of July. In the U.S. the Preferred represented a much higher proportion of the U.S. mailing total (14.5% versus 7.7% in Canada) and this translated into a higher percentage-of-total ticket sales in the U.S. (57.4%) versus Canada (39.1%).

EXHIBIT 10	The Relationship Marketing Program 2000–Direct Mail Component: Executive Summary

- In March 2000, a personalized direct mail package was sent to 88,779 patrons (all five segments) in the database—67% to Canada, 33% to the U.S.

- The primary objective was to generate incremental ticket sales for the 2000 Season, with emphasis on the June/July period. The secondary objective was to test the response of patrons to three added-value offers [Package 1—Preferred and Loyal—20% off a picnic basket; Upsell, Reactivation, and Conversion—received either 20% off two tickets and a dinner package (Package 2) or 10% off dinner at selected restaurants (Package 3)].

- From April to July inclusive, mailed group ticket sales increased by $3,822,000 (+65%), with a $2,390,000 (+85%) increase from Canadian and $1,432,000 (+52%) increase from U.S. customers.

- In Canada, Preferred and Loyal patrons together accounted for 68% of total Canadian sales. However, it was the Upsell, Reactivation, and Conversion segments that showed the strongest ticket sales increases in this period, reconfirming the fact that these groups leave their purchasing until much later.

- In the U.S., Preferred and Loyal groups accounted for 69% of U.S. ticket sales. The Upsell, Reactivation, and Conversion group sales increases were not as strong as their Canadian counterparts. Surprisingly, the increase in the Loyal group's sales was higher in the U.S. than in Canada during this period in the U.S. versus Canada indicating that Loyal customers in the U.S. left their purchasing until much later than Loyal Canadians.

- Overall, the three added-value tests acted primarily as a communication device to enhance the "Stratford Experience."

- They were not core direct marketing offers as they did not relate directly to the product. The results: Percentage who took up the offer—Package 1—3%; Package 2—3%; Package 3—14%.

- Factors other than direct mail influenced the sales behaviour of these patrons during these months—including advertising, publicity, and reviews.

EXHIBIT 11	The Relationship Marketing Program 2000–Direct Mail Component: Results by Segment

	Preferred	Loyal	Upsell	Reactivation	Conversion	Total
Mailed						
Canada	4,588	12,374	11,195	25,762	5,900	59,819
U.S.	4,199	3,629	3,901	12,303	4,928	29,960
Total	8,787	16,003	13,096	38,065	10,828	89,779
CANADA						
Number of Buyers						
March*	2,422	3,591	1,043	1,771	126	8,853
July	3,521	6,207	2,711	4,380	394	17,213
Difference	1,099	2,616	1,668	2,609	268	8,260
%	+43.4	+72.8	+159.0	+147.3	+212.7	+93.3
Number of Tickets						
March**	26,745	18,121	5,079	8,694	576	59,215
July	41,210	30,438	12,466	19,728	1,726	105,577
Difference	14,474	12,317	7,387	11,034	1,150	46,362
%	+54.1	+68.0	+145.4	+126.9	+199.7	+78.3
U.S.						
Number of Buyers						
March	2,270	676	279	1,010	147	4,328
July	3,073	1,544	787	2,049	294	7,747
Difference	803	868	508	1,039	147	3,365
%	+35.4	+128.4	+182.1	+102.9	+100.0	+77.7
Number of Tickets						
March	33,948	4,108	2,712	8,723	1,159	60,650
July	44,368	9,068	6,024	15,736	2,068	77,264
Difference	10,420	4,960	3,312	7,013	909	26,614
%	+30.7	+120.7	+122.1	+80.4	+78.4	+52.5

*   As of the end of March 2000, 8,853 buyers in Canada had purchased 59,215 tickets. These buyers were included in the direct mail package sample.

** From April to the end of July 2000, 17,213 buyers in Canada who had received the direct mail package had purchased 105,577 tickets.

Note: The increases for Canadian buyers between April and July 2000 were significantly higher for the mailed groups versus equivalent numbers from the control groups, which did not receive the March mailing. Specifically: 40% more in Preferred, 11% more in Loyal, 6% more in Upsell, 3% more in Reactivation, and 30% more in the Conversion group. Although the total U.S. mailing was only 32.6% of total Stratford mailing list, the U.S. produced a disproportionately higher share (42.3%) of all ticket sales to the end of July, with a much higher tickets/customer average (10) than the Canadian mailings (6.1).

EXHIBIT 12	Relationship Study—Winter 2000			
	Preferred	**Loyal**	**Upsell**	**Total**
SURVEY – WINTER 2000*				
Response Rate				
Canada (%)	53	43	33	41
U.S. (%)	39	33	23	31
Average # of Performances Seen in Past Year				
Canada	3.4	1.8	1.4	2.1
U.S.	3.7	2.0	1.6	2.3
Plan to Attend Next Year				
Canada (%)	95	88	77	86
U.S. (%)	95	89	74	87

	Canada	**U.S.**
DEMOGRAPHICS OF RESPONDENTS		
Age		
18-34	5	2
35-44	36	29
45-64	24	29
Over 65	31	36
Children Under 18 Living at Home		
Yes	51	16
No	49	89
Marital Status		
Single	11	13
Married	72	71
Divorced/Separated/Widowed	13	12
Income		
Under $34,999	8	7
35,000-74,999	33	27
75,000-99,999	15	17
100,000+	29	29

* Mailed to 24,000 Stratford patrons (Preferred, Loyal, and Upsell) in early November 1999.

EXHIBIT 13	Relationship Study–Winter 2000: Further Findings

- The demographic profile of respondents was fairly comparable across the three segments.
- In addition to attending Stratford, Canadian respondents also attended the Shaw Festival (36%), Roy Thompson/Massey Hall in Toronto (26%), *Mamma Mia!* (25%), *The Lion King* (23%) (two shows playing in Toronto), and Other (46%). U.S. respondents also attended the Shaw Festival (33%), *The Lion King* (14%), and Other (27%).
- Why Stratford is an appealing entertainment choice: high-quality productions (55% for both Canada and U.S.), live theatre (10% Canada, 6% U.S.), great getaway (8% Canada, 11% U.S.), and the Shakespeare content (11% for both Canada and U.S.).
- Have seen advertising for Stratford: 74% Canada, 55% U.S.
- Where advertising seen: Canada—newspaper 72%, direct mail (primarily the *Visitors' Guide*) 69%, television 20%, radio 19%, magazine 19%, flyers 12%; U.S.—newspaper 53%, direct mail (primarily the *Visitors' Guide*) 73%, television 5%, radio 10%, magazine 8%, flyers 14%.

EXHIBIT 14	Segment Changes Year over Year (Percentages)

	1999-2000			1999-2001			2000-2001		
	Same	Down	Up	Same	Down	Up	Same	Down	Up
Preferred*	77	23	N/A	65	35	N/A	78	22	N/A
Loyal**	69	17	14	51	33	16	66	27	7
Upsell***	19	62	19	29	54	17	21	63	16
Reactivate****	32	63	5	5	80	15	51	33	16

* Of the total Preferred segment in 1999, 77% were in the same segment in 2000; 23% moved down to another segment.

** Of the total Loyal segment in 1999, 69% were in the same segment in 2000, 14% moved up to the Preferred segment and 17% moved down to another segment.

*** Of the total Upsell segment in 1999, 19% were in the same segment in 2000, 19% moved up to another segment and 62% moved down to another segment.

**** Of the total Reactivate segment in 1999, 32% were in the same segment in 2000, 5% moved up to another segment and 63% moved down.

Arkan Inc.

Gordon H. G. McDougall
and Charles B. Weinberg

I'll have to make this decision by Friday so that we know where we're going, thought Jason Nelson, President of Arkan Inc., as he began reviewing the merits of two dramatically different new-product proposals. The first proposal was to modify and add new features to Arkan's best-selling scanner, the A-2880, which would further strengthen Arkan's position in the small office/home office (SOHO) market. The second proposal was to market a substantially different scanner based on emerging technology. It also involved tackling new markets. Jason Nelson felt that the success of Arkan was quite dependent on this new-product decision.

Jason was familiar with such high-risk decisions. He had long recognized that if Arkan were to grow and prosper in a fast-changing market, then continual revision to the product line was needed. He also knew that growth demanded a constant reassessment of technological possibilities and market needs. Success required anticipating market needs; however, being too far in front of the customer could lead to technological advances that appealed to few people other than the developers of the new product. However, having faced this decision many times before didn't make it any easier to find the correct path.

BACKGROUND

Some people were surprised that Canadian companies could compete effectively as producers of high-technology equipment. However, Canada was home to a number of successful, state-of-the-art hardware and software firms. The president of a leading software company had recently said: "We would never think of moving to the U.S. There, the best young talent is drawn to the major players. Here we can attract some of the brightest people to work for and stay with our firm."

In 1987, Jason Nelson, an award-winning computer optics specialist, left Hewlett-Packard Canada to form his own company. He had a strong desire to design, manufacture, and market his own scanner (a product just in its infancy). His vision, which led to Arkan Inc., was to produce a user-friendly scanner designed primarily for managers in SOHOs who needed a high-resolution unit. The product, branded A-2800, provided the user with an easily understood menu, a large memory, a resolution dpi (dots per inch) of 1200 x 2400, and a one-button operation that allowed for easy scanning and copying.

Since the A-2800 was introduced in 1989, it and its updated versions had captured a substantial share of the designated target market. While the firm had incurred losses in its early years, the last four years had seen steadily rising sales and profits. For 2000, Arkan Inc. had sales of $24,000,000 and profits of $1,890,000. In part, this was due to Arkan's ability to design systems that could be manufactured efficiently and also to the use of outside suppliers. Arkan had continually been able to stay abreast of the industry cost curve and successfully reduce its prices and costs over time. Its manufacturing facility produced four different scanners, two (the A-2880 and A-2890) that were targeted at the SOHO market and two that were targeted at two other markets: (1) home users who were photo buffs, and (2) small photo-finishing retailers who offered photo scanning for their customers.

THE TWO PROPOSALS

For the past three months work had proceeded on two separate fronts; one emphasizing an advance in the current product, the other incorporating a major technological change. Reports on both products had been circulated to management, and numerous meetings had taken place. Financially, Arkan could not afford to proceed with both developments. Finally, early in 2001, meetings were held on consecutive days to hear the two new-product proposals.

The A-3880 Proposal

At the first meeting, Linda Muir, vice-president Marketing, presented a report to the management committee (Jason Nelson; John Linder, vice-president Manufacturing; and Terry Lui, vice-president Research and Development; Linda Muir was also a committee member) in which she proposed that Arkan launch the A-3880, a new, updated version of the A-2880. She had stressed the following points in her presentation:

The A-3880 was based on proven technology that the target market valued because they were interested in reliability, high resolution, and continuity.

Arkan Inc. had a strong reputation with the SOHO market and held an estimated 35-percent share of that market.

The new features offered on the A-3880 (higher resolution at dpi 1600 x 3200; 36-bit colour; easy scanning, copying, e-mailing, faxing, and uploading to the Web) are benefits that the target market wanted. (This had been established in a survey conducted in the previous year.)

The new features would allow Arkan to develop a future version specifically targeted at Internet-linked home users wishing to share their photo files with other users.

After she made her presentation, a lively discussion followed debating the merits of the A-3880 proposal. As Jason Nelson reviewed his notes of the meeting, he recalled the major points of opposition. Terry Lui had raised several objections, including the following:

- The A-3880 offers only minor improvements that won't have much impact in the market.
- The B-4000, the new product that would be proposed by R&D on the following day, was a major technological breakthrough and should be the focus of Arkan's efforts.

The other major points were that:

- Arkan had been losing market share in the SOHO market to low-cost manufacturers. Arkan competed with three other major competitors located in the United States and about 10 small "offshore" competitors that manufactured basic, low-cost units.
- Arkan had also been losing market share to the major competitor that produced a scanner targeted at the same market. This competitive scanner used a somewhat different technology than Arkan for its line of scanner products. In the past two years, Arkan had lost 10 percent of the market to clones and the U.S. competitor.

The meeting ended with the agreement that no decisions would be made until after the second proposal was heard the following day.

The B-4000 Proposal

In that meeting Terry Lui, with great enthusiasm, presented a proposal for a dramatically different scanner targeted at graphic designers in the integrated marketing communications industry (e.g., advertising agencies, public relations firms, and communication consultants). Mr. Lui made the following points during his presentation:

- The new product, tentatively branded B-4000, used the latest microchip technology to incorporate a built-in transparency unit, a suspension system that eliminates mechanical bias and vibration, dynamic range control, and dual focus that eliminates light refraction rings in transparency scans.
- B-4000, with its technology and new software, had a competitive advantage over existing products in the market.
- While designed for a professional market, the superior quality of the product might attract other users as well.
- With its existing research and development capability, the firm could maintain this competitive advantage for at least five years.

As Jason Nelson recalled the meeting, he reviewed the points made by Linda Muir:

- Arkan did not have much knowledge of the proposed target customers, graphic designers, and what criteria they used in their purchasing decision for scanners.

- The estimated size of the total market (based on Terry Lui's information) was only $10,000,000 per year, one-fifth the size of the small businessperson market. The "design" market was growing at only about 8 percent per year, whereas the SOHO market was growing at 30 percent per year.

- The current market leader, MicroMax Graphics, held about 70 percent of the total "design" market and had a good reputation in the field.

Terry Lui had countered those points by noting:

- The B-4000 is a better product than the one offered by MicroMax Graphics and it is Marketing's job to sell that product. Interviews with prospective customers should be conducted immediately to determine what features were critical to this market.

- The margin on the B-4000 is 25 percent higher than on the A-3880.

- Arkan's strength is in research and development, and the B-4000 is proof that R&D remains critical to the firm.

Linda Muir also thought that the graphic design market might put a higher emphasis on graphical capabilities than the B-4000 line encompassed. She wondered whether Arkan had the capacity to be competitive in such a technology.

Terry Lui agreed that the graphic design market was a new field for Arkan, but he noted that the B-4000 already scored better on tests for distortion elimination than the existing competitors. He felt confident that the firm's scientists could maintain that lead.

THE DECISION

Later that day, Jason Nelson reflected on the arguments. He believed that Arkan did not have the resources to pursue both alternatives. He was also concerned because he saw the broad mission of the company as a focused, growth-oriented firm dedicated to developing technically superior products. *Well, this decision must be made soon,* thought Jason, *and I want it to be right.*

Rescuing 911

Robin J. B. Ritchie and
Charles B. Weinberg

It was the fall of 2000 and the mayor of Brantville, Ontario was embroiled in scandal. Unable to get through to the police on regular telephone lines to ask for directions, she had simply dialed 911. "I only use it under duress," Sheila Swanson insisted, but telephone records indicated that she had called 911 at least a half-dozen times to request directions since taking office the previous October. Details of the incident had been uncovered by the press, and for the past week newspaper headlines and television reports had been awash with news and commentary on the mayor's abuse of the emergency response line.

"Obviously we have some real communication problems," said Brantville Emergency Response System Manager Tony Petersen with a sigh. "For the last decade we've been educating the public to reserve 911 for emergency calls and then something like this happens. It's a public relations nightmare."

Citizens dialing 911 for non-emergency purposes had been a serious problem for Brantville in recent years, representing an estimated 65 percent of all calls to the service. While most 911 calls were picked up within five seconds, someone phoning on a busy summer night might be on hold for half a minute or more. This was far slower than many other Canadian cities: Tony had found out from his colleagues in other cities that

Ottawa and Halifax answered their 911 calls in an average of two seconds, while Winnipeg averaged slightly over three seconds. What was worse, the delay showed signs of compromising public safety: over the last year, 7,067 Brantville 911 callers (some 8 percent of total call volumes) had hung up before an operator answered the line.

The nature of these non-emergency calls varied greatly. At one extreme were legitimate calls for assistance that were simply not urgent enough to require an immediate dispatch. At the other were frivolous and crank calls. For instance, commuters stuck in traffic would dial 911 from their car phones to find out whether there was an accident. Elderly people in retirement homes would call for someone to talk to. And, in a particularly memorable incident, someone had dialed 911 to report a damaged mailbox. When told by the emergency operator to contact his nearest post office, he responded, "Well, you have me on the line, so why don't you take the information anyway."

Pressure on the 911 service was growing. During the past dozen years, the volume of calls in Brantville had risen more than 70 percent, while the 911 operating budget had expanded by only 22 percent, to $750,000. Public outcry had led City Council to spend $60,000 for two backup operators in late 1998, and $300,000 had been spent on new computer and telecommunications systems two years earlier. However, these were considered band-aid measures that merely bought time until a more permanent solution could be found.

The problem of overwhelming demand due to non-emergency calls was not unique to Brantville. In nearby Toronto, for instance, non-emergency use of the 911 system was approximately 60 percent.[1] Other Canadian cities reported comparable figures. The nature of these calls was similar to those encountered in Brantville (see Exhibit 1).

In addition to causing problems at the dispatch centre, the enormous volume of dubious 911 calls was also keeping police officers tethered to their radio cars. An internal police review estimated that only 20 percent of the 911 calls they answered in 1999 were top-priority emergencies.

BACKGROUND: BRANTVILLE

Located in southwestern Ontario, Brantville was a modern and growing city of a quarter million people, with a surrounding population that raised the total to more than 300,000. Thanks to astute planning, the city had managed to keep ahead of its infrastructure needs into the early 1990s. Its 911 emergency system had been installed in 1985 to serve Brantville and its surrounding communities, and had worked well for the first decade of operation. However, call volumes had increased rapidly since then: computer logs showed that 88,700 calls were made to the Brantville 911 system in 1999, up from 69,400 in 1994 and 49,300 in 1986, the first full year of operation. Significantly, recent strength in the technology sector had led to a period of strong growth for the local economy and heavy in-migration, placing additional demands on city services.

The nerve centre of the Brantville 911 emergency telephone system was a small, overcrowded office located on the eastern edge of downtown, across from City Hall and the central police station. There, a professional but understaffed team of dispatchers struggled to answer the growing number of calls. Turnover had been high recently, thanks largely to the growing workload and rising level of frustration. In addition, many operators were lured away by attractive job opportunities at a new Bell Canada call centre.

[1.] Alan Ferguson (1995), "Technology keeps 911 state-of-the-alert," *Toronto Star* (Metro Edition), February 24, p. A1.

When discussing current 911 problems, Brantville police acknowledged that they were largely victims of their own success. To encourage its use, 911 had been aggressively marketed for several years after being introduced, yet little effort had been made to teach the public how to use it properly. Moreover, during the early years of the service city policy had been to respond to all calls, emergency or not.[2] This had created a public appetite for 911 that recent efforts had not managed to dissuade. "Nine-one-one is like heroin," observed Tony Petersen. "It's easier to get people on it than off."

THE SITUATION PRIOR TO 911

Despite its current difficulties, 911 had begun as a practical solution to a serious problem.[3] Until the late 1960s, most Canadian municipalities had different telephone numbers for fire, police, and ambulance services. In the United States, where cities were larger and jurisdictional boundaries more complex, the problem had been even worse: The St. Louis telephone directory, for example, listed 161 emergency numbers prior to the introduction of 911 there. Moreover, the emergency numbers were typically hard to memorize. Callers who mistakenly called the wrong number would have to hang up and start again.

Other countries had solved the problem by adopting a simple, universal number for emergency services. In the United Kingdom, for example, residents had used 999 to summon police, fire, and ambulance since 1937. North American cities had tried something similar with seven-digit universal police access numbers, but experience showed these were not easily remembered and could be difficult to dial in an emergency.

By 1967, the problem in the United States had become so severe that the President's Commission on Law Enforcement and Administration of Justice recommended that "Wherever practical, a single [emergency] number should be established" nationwide for reporting emergencies. AT&T soon announced its choice of 911, and the first 911 call was made in Haleyville, Alabama in February 1968. Large U.S. cities rolled out the new service almost immediately, while smaller and more rural municipalities took several years to marshal the necessary funding. Canada followed a decade later, with the introduction of 911 service in Metropolitan Toronto in 1981.

The launch of the Brantville system in September 1985 had occurred with great fanfare and optimism. Although the number offered access to all emergency services, civic officials were most excited about its potential to improve the quality of policing. Since anybody could call 911, crimes could be reported in-progress, increasing the odds of making an arrest and discouraging many would-be felons from breaking the law in the first place. And because there would be no back door to police help, all citizens would receive equal protection. Experience in other jurisdictions suggested that Brantville police could expect greater community support and confidence, as well as increased citizen participation in crime detection.

Although this held true for the first several years of the system, the effectiveness of 911 as a law enforcement tool was now being called into question. Research conducted in several large American cities had found that fewer than 5 percent of total dispatched calls were

---

[2] Although this remained the policy in some municipalities, Brantville had since moved to a system where 911 operators would screen calls to assess whether an emergency response was needed.

[3] See Christopher H. Lovelock "The 911 Emergency Number in New York" in Lovelock, C.H. and Weinberg, C.B. *Public and Nonprofit Marketing: Cases and Readings* (New York: John Wiley, 1984) for a discussion of the need for and introduction of 911.

made quickly enough for officers to intervene or make an arrest.[4] Moreover, while a well-funded 911 system ensured rapid emergency response, critics pointed out that it left fewer resources for other elements of policing, such as foot patrol, community relations, and crime prevention. Despite these concerns, the public still considered response time a key test of their police department's effectiveness. As a result, 911 remained a key part of the Brantville policing strategy.

THE 311 ALTERNATIVE

One solution to the 911 problem that had been tried with some success was a 311 system. First proposed in 1995, 311 was developed as a means to divert non-emergency calls from 911. It provided callers with a single, easily remembered three-digit number that could be dialed from anywhere served by the system. The system was intended for non-life-threatening situations and to report crimes such as thefts, vandalism, graffiti, property damage, bad cheques, and lost or found property.

In Baltimore, Maryland, where 311 was introduced on a trial basis in October 1996, the system worked by connecting callers to a voice-mail system that directed the call to one of seven divisions within the Police Department. Callers would be told to hang up and call 911 if they were trying to report an emergency, and were allowed to bypass the system and talk to an operator if they wished. The idea of 311 had recently received the endorsement of federal authorities in the United States, and was gaining favour among several major cities. San Jose and Baltimore inaugurated their systems in late 1997, followed by Dallas, Chicago, and Washington, D.C. Although detailed cost figures were not available, the company hired to manage the 311 service in San Jose (a city approximately four times the size of Brantville) claimed that a basic system could be run at an annual cost of $150,000 (Canadian).

Based on the experience in these other cities, it appeared that 311 would reduce the number of 911 calls by somewhere between 10 and 30 percent (see Exhibit 2).

After two years of operation, officials in Baltimore were proclaiming their system a success: "911 was threatening to drown us in calls, and this has resuscitated it," proclaimed John Reintzell, director of communications for the Baltimore Police Department. "It's designed to allow 911 to do what it's supposed to do—handle emergency calls." Most 311 users also seemed to be pleased: more than 99 percent of those who called the number in Baltimore described themselves as satisfied with the service.

The 311 concept had its detractors, however. Chief among them was the National Emergency Number Association (NENA), a group of emergency-system professionals that had recently launched a media campaign against the establishment of new three-digit phone numbers. "We think it's confusing to the public," explained William Stanton, NENA's executive director. "A service like 311 eliminates one of the great strengths of the 911 emergency system—a single number that everyone remembers in a crisis." Stanton added that the option of dialing 311 placed callers in the unenviable position of having to assess the gravity of their own situation. In a true emergency, he explained, this could slow down the arrival of help by as much as several minutes: "We're talking about delay, and delay is what causes people to die."

[4.] George L. Kelling and Catherine M. Coles (1996). *Fixing Broken Windows: Restoring Order and Reducing Crime in Our Communities.* New York: Martin Kessler Books. Cities included in the study were San Diego; Kansas City, Missouri; Jacksonville, Florida; Peoria, Illinois; and Rochester, New York.

Another problem was how to pay for 311. Critics pointed out that the likely solution would be to redirect funding that had previously been earmarked for 911. They claimed that the resources needed to launch 311 programs would be better spent improving the current 911 system: enhancing network capacity, training telephone operators, and educating citizens about when to call 911.

While some people cautioned against spending any money on 311, cities that had introduced the system warned against not spending enough. In Washington, D.C. the 311 call centre averaged 2,000 calls a day during its first year, yet non-emergency calls to 911 continued to grow. In response, district officials had to expand their 311 marketing campaign to increase awareness of the new number and encourage its use. Meanwhile, in Baltimore, 23 percent of calls to the non-emergency system were being abandoned before operators could answer them. While there was no way to be sure, it was believed that most of those callers were hanging up in frustration and dialing 911 instead. "That should not be acceptable," said a high-ranking Baltimore city official, who spoke on condition of anonymity. "That means it's not working." At the very least, the problem suggested that 311, like 911, would have to be properly staffed if it were to be effective.

Finally, there were questions involving just what kind of problems 311 should address, and how to make this clear to system operators and to the public. The costs of failing to do so had recently been made painfully clear: In August of 1998, a motorist in San Jose, California had called 311 to report a mattress lying on a highway, but was told to call the California Highway Patrol. The exasperated motorist said, "Never mind. I'll just let somebody get killed." Some 25 minutes later, a car swerved to avoid the mattress and rolled over, killing a 75-year-old passenger.

OTHER OPTIONS

While a 311 system was a popular option, it was hardly the only one. A task force assembled by the Brantville City Council had identified four other options.

Seven-Digit Non-Emergency Number

Sensitive to concerns about the unique role of the 911 emergency number, many municipalities were opting for a seven-digit non-emergency number. The nearby city of Buffalo, New York launched its service in 1996 with a splashy advertising campaign featuring a sequence of rhyming slogans: "For a real emergency, call 911; we'll quickly send someone! Non-emergencies, it's 853-2222, and we'll tell you what to do." Apart from minimizing confusion with 911, Buffalo officials felt that a seven-digit number more clearly signalled the number's non-emergency status.

De-Marketing 911

Another approach, which could be used on its own or in conjunction with a new non-emergency number, was to "de-market" the 911 service. Just as advertisements had been used to inaugurate the system in the 1960s and 1970s, similar campaigns could be used to explain when a 911 call was appropriate and when it was not. Ads used in other cities focused on a number of themes. Some described how non-emergency calls created delays in responding to real emergencies, and reminded residents that they might someday be the one needing urgent assistance. Others focused on the cost to taxpayers of paying for a system that was overwhelmed by frivolous calls. Some municipalities tried an even more direct approach: In Montreal, citizens who called ambulances for minor medical problems received a blunt letter asking them not to do it again.

Brantville already operated a modest 911 education program, which included speaking engagements, demonstrations, videos, and written materials to familiarize citizens with the 911 telephone system. As well, the inside front cover of the local telephone book included a list of frequently called numbers, and instructions on when to use 911 (see Exhibit 3). However, it was clear that these efforts would need to be greatly expanded if de-marketing were to form an important part of the city's response strategy.

Expansion of the 911 System

A third and more straightforward option was simply to construct a larger, more sophisticated emergency call centre, and redesign the response system to deal with non-emergency calls. This was the solution adopted in Vancouver. Calls that did not require an immediate response would be sent to special units that would take reports or arrange for a community-relations officer to meet with the complainant at a later time. These included situations of larceny, animal disturbances, loitering, gambling, or indecent exposure, where the incidents were no longer in progress, the suspect had left the scene, no one was hurt, and no evidence or additional witnesses were available.

Expansion of 911 was the favoured option among Brantville beat cops, who feared that separate emergency and non-emergency numbers would serve only to create public confusion. They felt that 911 operators were well qualified to assess the seriousness of a situation, and wanted to receive dispatch orders from a single location.

Community Policing

An entirely different approach to the 911 problem had been developed by officials in Edmonton. In 1992, they reworked the city's policing system to revolve around community police stations where citizens are encouraged to report non-emergency incidents in person. To help the public adapt to the changes, the Police Service created "red pages" in the local telephone book with a comprehensive listing of station locations, phone numbers, hours of operation, and types of services offered. Four years after the change, Edmonton's yearly 911 calls had dropped from 84,431 in 1991 to 53,191. As the program gained acceptance, it was hoped that citizens would embrace the idea of community policing, and get in the habit of seeking out a neighbourhood police officer to deal with minor and less urgent problems.

Police associations from across North America were hailing the Edmonton model as an innovative and sensible approach to the 911 problem. "It goes beyond addressing symptoms and tackles the problem at a fundamental level," observed Frank Cioppetti, Deputy Commissioner of Operations with the New York City Police Department. Since Edmonton's population was roughly three times that of Brantville, it was felt that this approach was achievable locally. However, it would require a reorganization of the police service, and was thus more complex. Moreover, some cities that had introduced community policing had found it to be somewhat more expensive than traditional policing methods.

EXTENSION OF THE *N*11 TELEPHONE SYSTEM

Recent regulatory developments in the United States also seemed to have some bearing on the Brantford decision. In July 2000, the U.S. Federal Communications Commission announced that it had reserved 511 as a hotline for up-to-the-minute road conditions, and 211 for one-stop information on social services. In addition, local telephone companies would be required to implement 711 for a text telephone relay service where operators would help the hearing- and speech-impaired make calls.

The new 511 service would provide callers with customized traffic and road reports through a menu of choices, and contain 10 times as much traffic information as could fit into a 30-second radio spot. It was primarily expected to benefit travellers and others unfamiliar with local radio stations. Meanwhile, 211 was to serve as a one-stop resource for information on social services such as food banks, job and education programs, assistance for seniors, and volunteer opportunities. It had been proposed by the United Way of America, which had long sought a way to help people navigate the complex maze of human services agencies and programs.

Despite the FCC's announcement, however, it was far from clear that 511 and 211 would be widely adopted, at least in the foreseeable future. The decision of whether to implement the new numbers was the responsibility of individual state and local governments, which would also decide how to pay for the services and who should operate them. Across the country, legislators were expressing the same concerns that had been raised over 311—namely, that the new *N*11 numbers would detract from the uniqueness of 911 and make the emergency service less effective. Although supporters of 511 and 211 argued that a 711 service had already been launched in some jurisdictions with minimal impact on 911, critics noted that the hearing-impaired number was targeted at a small and well-defined group, while the new numbers would be widely promoted.

ADDITIONAL PROBLEMS: THE CELLPHONE QUANDARY

In addition to the overwhelming call volumes and frivolous calls, another major challenge for the Brantville 911 system was the proliferation of cellular phones. Across Canada, nearly 30 percent of all emergency calls were from cellular units, and in Brantville alone nearly 100 people dialed 911 from their wireless telephone every day. Yet these calls did not provide the location and number of the caller, and panicked callers often had trouble describing where they were. In addition, disconnected calls could not be re-located, and the routing technologies of cellular systems often sent wireless 911 calls to the wrong dispatching centre.

The problem was being tackled across the continent with a service known as Enhanced 911 (E911). In 1996, the U.S. Federal Communications Commission (FCC) ordered wireless carriers to install technologies able to locate callers to within 125 metres when they dialed 911 from a wireless telephone. By 1999, 911 had been approved as the universal emergency cell number in both the United States and Canada. A number of Brantville city councillors, led by the mayor, had expressed interest in adopting the E911 system as soon as possible. They argued that the number of wireless phones was growing and that the system would "help Brantville blaze a path of citizen-led public safety into the future." In addition, it seemed likely that a new system would include advanced computer dispatching software that would improve 911 operators' ability to handle existing calls.

But while 911 managers publicly proclaimed themselves pleased by the added capabilities of an enhanced system, they also harboured fears that its huge capital cost might draw resources away from the day-to-day operations of the existing dispatch centre. "It sounds great," said one unnamed official. "But we don't have a cost figure, and we need that new money for our operating budget."

THE CHALLENGE

The question of what to do next loomed large over the Brantville Emergency Response System, and particularly over Tony Petersen. First and foremost, he had to draft a plan for City Council to address the problem of 911 call volumes. Should he recommend the adoption of 311, as Baltimore, Washington, D.C., and San Jose had done? Or was Buffalo's answer of a seven-digit number a better solution? Alternatively, the city could try to manage the problem internally by establishing better procedures for non-emergency calls to 911. Yet this might attract even more frivolous calls to 911, and it would be difficult to change course and establish a separate non-emergency service once people had gotten into the habit of dialing a single number. And then there was the Edmonton solution, which seemed to be producing excellent results but was considerably more complex. Regardless of the solution he chose, Petersen knew that immediate action was needed. As a local newspaper had observed, "The current 911 situation in Brantville creates unacceptable risks for its citizens. City managers must implement an effective solution quickly, and at the lowest possible cost to the taxpayer."

EXHIBIT 1	Examples of Misuse of the 911 System

Purpose of Call	
Calgary	Neighbour's dog barking
	Seeking information on how to retrieve towed car
Halifax	Confirming schools were open following snowstorm
	Pet kitten missing
Toronto	Fire trucks battling blaze next door were "too noisy"
	Shortchanged by convenience store clerk
Vancouver	Verifying telephone had been connected
	Neighbour seen smoking marijuana
Winnipeg	"Urgently" needed a taxicab
	Wondering when garbage would be collected

EXHIBIT 2	Impact of 311 Implementation on 911 Emergency System	
	Reduction in Number of 911 Calls	Reduction in Average 911 Answer Time
Baltimore	25%	66%
San Jose	11%	16%
Dallas	10%	50%

| EXHIBIT 3 | Brantville Emergency Number Information Sheet (from Front Cover of Telephone Directory) |

Emergency

Police 9-1-1 **Fire** 9-1-1 **Ambulance** 9-1-1

9-1-1 Includes TTY Users
Dial 9-1-1 and continue to press the space bar of your TTY until answered

Other Emergency Numbers

Call Before You Dig

| (Call No Charge) | 1-800-567-5111 |
| or Cellular | *678 |

Crime Stoppers   669-8477

Crisis Centre for persons in emotional crisis: like depression, physical and mental abuse, marital and family upset and suicide

872-3322

Flood, Hurricane, Tornado, Toxic Spills

| 24hrs | 1-800-663-6553 |

Provincial Emergency Program (PEP) Information

538-3939

Gang & Youth Contact Line   775-3263

Helpline for Children

Reporting of Child Abuse & Neglect   333-4567

Hospitals   See Yellow Pages under "Hospitals"

Poison Control Centre   1-877-455-3433

Power Outages & Emergencies   324-5555

Sexual Assault Centre for Victims

| Rape Crisis Centre | 674-6868 |

| Rape Relief | 343-4477 |

Financial Analysis for Marketing Decisions, with Exercises

Charles B. Weinberg and
Gordon H. G. McDougall

A financial or economic analysis is necessary to evaluate all major courses of action in marketing. Introducing a new product, entering a new market, changing a price, or increasing the size of a salesforce are all decisions that can have significant financial consequences.

In this section, we review some of the basic concepts of financial and economic analysis as applied to marketing decision making. We concentrate on simplified situations in order to focus on the key issues. A set of exercises is provided to allow practise using these concepts.

COST, PRICE, AND CONTRIBUTION

Variable costs (VC) change with the volume of the product produced or sold. For a manufacturer, variable costs typically would include the costs of materials and labour; as more units are manufactured, total variable costs increase. Variable costs are usually expressed as VC per unit. This is often a good representation of the way such costs vary over the relevant range of sales for marketing decision making.

Fixed costs (FC) do not change with the volume and are those that would still be incurred, at least in the short run, even if no products were manufactured or sold. Fixed costs can include the rental of a building, the cost of display cases, the advertising budget, and other expenses that would not change, once committed, irrespective of the volume sold or produced.

Although in many analyses the two major cost categories are fixed and variable, in some situations a third type of cost, *semi-variable costs* (SVC), is important. Semi-variable costs tend to vary with the capacity to provide volume (often in stepwise fashion) as opposed to directly with volume itself. Such costs are particularly prevalent in service industries; for instance, an airline might incur a semi-variable cost of $300 per flight (for fuel, salaries, and landing fees) when adding an extra flight a day on its Toronto to New York schedule; its variable cost might be only $6 per passenger boarded (for refreshments and ticketing costs). For theatre companies, the cost of running another performance of a show, and for a retail store, the cost of opening an additional day are semi-variable costs. For a manufacturer, the decision to add an overtime shift to meet anticipated demand can involve semi-variable costs. Although we will not consider semi-variable costs explicitly here, they are often quite important and need to be considered in an economic analysis of alternatives.

Price (P) per unit is the revenue obtained per unit, net of any discount offered to others in the distribution channel. Price per unit times *volume* (V) sold gives the total (or gross) revenue realized by the seller.

Contribution or margin per unit is the difference between price per unit and variable cost per unit; that is,

Unit Contribution = P (per unit) − VC (per unit).

Similarly, total (or gross) contribution is the product of unit contribution times volume. Net contribution is equal to unit contribution times volume less fixed cost; that is,

Net Contribution = [(P − VC) × (V)] − FC.

To illustrate these concepts, consider the example of a British Columbia fruit packer who is thinking of setting up a small factory to produce frozen raspberry juice. Rental costs for the factory and facilities, including such factors as utilities, insurance, and property taxes, are $150,000 annually. Salesforce, advertising, marketing, and other management operating costs are $200,000 per year. The cost of leasing specialized packing and freezing machinery, which has a useful life of five years, is $100,000 annually. The cost of raw materials and labour is $15 per case (12 large cans) of frozen raspberry juice. If the selling price of frozen raspberry juice is $37.50 per case, then we could calculate the following:

$$\text{Fixed Costs} = \$150,000 + \$200,000 + \$100,000$$
$$= \$450,000$$
$$\text{Variable Costs per Case} = \$15$$
$$\text{Selling Price per Unit} = \$37.50$$
$$\text{Unit Contribution} = \$37.50 - \$15.00$$
$$= \$22.50$$

If the company expects to sell 24,000 cases in a year, then estimated costs and revenues would be as follows:

$$\text{Total VC} = 24{,}000 \times \$15 = \$360{,}000$$
$$\text{Total Revenue} = 24{,}000 \times \$37.50$$
$$= \$900{,}000$$
$$\text{Total Contribution} = \$540{,}000$$
$$\text{Net Contribution} = \$540{,}000 - \$450{,}000$$
$$= \$90{,}000$$

Next we shall examine some concepts that can be used to help evaluate the economics of deciding whether to set up the frozen raspberry juice factory.

BREAK-EVEN ANALYSIS AND PROFITABILITY

Break-even analysis allows management to calculate the level of sales required to cover the fixed costs of making any significant marketing change (Exhibit 1).

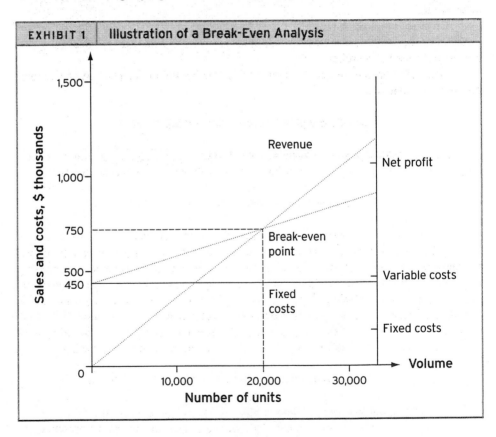

EXHIBIT 1 | Illustration of a Break-Even Analysis

The break-even volume is found by dividing the fixed costs by the unit contribution; that is,

$$\text{Break-Even Volume (in units)} = \frac{\text{Fixed Costs}}{\text{Unit Contribution}}$$

In the case of the raspberry juice packer, the break-even volume is

$$\frac{\$450{,}000}{\$22.50} = 20{,}000 \text{ cases}$$

If the alternative being examined involves a change from a current one, then the fixed-cost component of the break-even calculation is replaced by the amount of the change in the fixed costs. The importance of the break-even calculation is that it puts the focus on the profitability of a product, not just its sales volume.

One test of a marketing initiative is the feasibility of attaining the break-even volume. If the current market size is 50,000 cases, then selling 20,000 cases means getting a 40-percent market share unless the market is expected to grow rapidly. If high market share is necessary for success, then competitive reaction must be carefully considered.

For many marketing alternatives, such as the introduction of a new product, it would be unreasonable to expect the project to achieve break-even in its first year. In such a case management may look at the feasibility of attaining break-even within two, three, or more years.

While public and non-profit organizations may seek to obtain only a break-even volume, most businesses would not go ahead with a project unless a profit were likely. While the profit required can be set in many ways, one alternative is to specify it as a percentage of the investment required. Target profitability volume in units can be calculated as follows:

$$\text{Target Profitability Volume (in units)} = \frac{\text{Fixed Costs} + \text{Target Profit}}{\text{Unit Contribution}}$$

For example, if the raspberry juice producer had to invest $1 million to establish this business and set a target profit of 18 percent on the investment, then the number of units it would need to sell to achieve target profitability is calculated as follows:

$$\frac{\$450{,}000 + \$180{,}000}{\$22.50} = 28{,}000 \text{ cases}$$

CONDITIONAL SALES FORECASTS AND RESPONSE FUNCTIONS

In many ways, a break-even analysis evaluates a marketing program from a different perspective than that used in formulating the plan itself. The break-even analysis produces a target volume and asks how feasible its accomplishment is. In contrast, the development of a marketing plan forecasts that a certain level of sales is expected if the specified plan is implemented. In other words, sales are a function of a specific marketing plan. More succinctly, and in the context of the marketing mix, we can say that the plan represents a *conditional sales forecast* in that the sales are conditional on a particular marketing mix. A response function is the part of the conditional sales forecast that explicitly links a sales response to one or more elements of the marketing mix.

Take, for instance, the example of advertising expenditure level for the management of a regional movie chain. In the present marketing plan, a monthly advertising expenditure of $20,000 is expected to result in attendance of 60,000 people. However, increasing the ad budget by 50 percent to $30,000 is expected to increase the number of attendees to 66,000; increasing advertising by another $10,000 is expected, based on tests in other regions of the country, to raise attendance to 68,000 people. On the other hand, reducing advertising by $10,000 from the present budget of $20,000 is expected to reduce admissions to 50,000 people. Given these estimates, then, a forecast of sales conditional on advertising would be as follows:

Advertising Budget ($)	Estimated Attendance
10,000	50,000
20,000	60,000
30,000	66,000
40,000	68,000

As shown in Exhibit 2, attendance is much more sensitive to decreases than to increases in advertising.

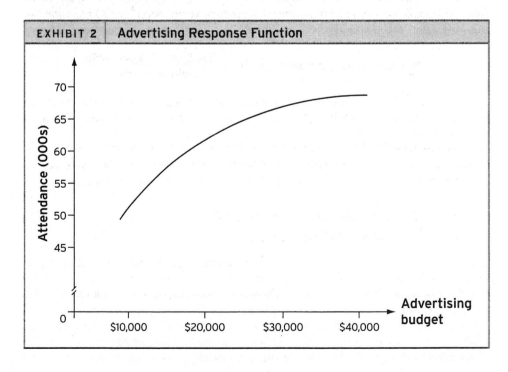

EXHIBIT 2 | Advertising Response Function

The profitability of changing the advertising level depends upon the contribution per ticket sold. If in this case the contribution were $3 per ticket sold, the following profitability analysis would help management to make a decision about the advertising budget:

(1) Advertising Budget	(2) Estimated Attendance	(3) = $3 × (2) Contribution Before Advertising	(4) = (3) − (1) Contribution After Advertising
$10,000	50,000	$150,000	$140,000
20,000	60,000	180,000	160,000
30,000	66,000	198,000	168,000
40,000	68,000	204,000	164,000

The most profitable level of sales is obtained when advertising spending is $30,000 for a contribution, after allowing for the expense of advertising, of $168,000. It is evident from looking at the data that the highest level of sales is not the most profitable level in this case.

This section has illustrated one form of profitability analysis. At times, more complex techniques may be needed to adjust for the time value of money, to allow for risk and uncertainty, and to account for possible competitive response.

UNCERTAINTY

Marketing managers develop marketing plans with the expectation that certain sales outcomes will be achieved. But they cannot be certain of those outcomes. A furniture manufacturer may find that a particular advertising campaign was not as effective as anticipated, or an amusement park operator may do better than planned due to unusually pleasant weather. Competitors may also take actions that keep firms from reaching their goals. Thus, a new brand of shampoo may achieve a promising 10-percent market share in its test markets, but only a 4-percent share when an established competitor engages in extensive promotional activity during the new brand's national launch.

There is no simple way to account for uncertainty. A good first step, however, is to identify the major sources of uncertainty in the marketing plan. In general, any uncertainties that have a significant impact on the final outcome need to be considered in depth. While no risk factor can be totally ignored, concentration should be placed on the critical ones. Market research may help narrow the range of uncertainty.

One test of a marketing strategy is to examine its robustness in the face of difficulties. Consider, for example, an airline opening a new route using jumbo jets. The strategy would be robust if the airline could profitably substitute a smaller plane on the new route, using the jumbo jet on the charter market if traffic were not to develop as expected.

All risk cannot be eliminated from marketing decisions, but it can be reduced. While many approaches are available to deal with uncertainty, we will mention just two here. The first is to estimate a range of possible outcomes of a particular decision and determine if management is willing to live with the resulting risk. A typical approach is to construct three scenarios—optimistic, expected or most likely, and pessimistic. For example, suppose a shampoo marketer has developed a new line of shampoos to appeal to men whose hair is greying. To market the line, the company will need to invest in advertising and promotion. The company thinks it will sell 50,000 tubes annually, with a contribution margin of $2 per unit. However, if the product catches on, sales could go as high as 100,000 tubes. On the other hand, the product could make no headway at all in the market and sell only 10,000 units. Profitability under these three scenarios would be as follows:

	Optimistic	Most Likely	Pessimistic
Sales (Units)	100,000	50,000	10,000
Contribution	$200,000	$100,000	$ 20,000
Fixed Costs	$ 75,000	$ 75,000	$ 75,000
Net Profit (Loss)	$ 125,000	$ 25,000	$(55,000)

The company might look at these data and conclude that it could not afford a loss of $55,000 and reject the project, at least in its present form, or it might feel that the chances of a profit are so much greater than the chances of a loss that the new shampoo should be launched. If it were to pursue this second course of action, the company would, of course, do whatever it could to prevent the pessimistic scenario.

A second approach to dealing with uncertainty is to try to estimate the probability of each outcome and then calculate an expected value. If the expected value is positive, then the company goes ahead with the project; assuming, naturally, that the firm has the funds required to invest in the project and that no better opportunities are available. While many pages could be devoted to a discussion of expected value, a common-sense example is sufficient, for our purposes, to convey its meaning and illustrate its calculation. Suppose you make a bet with a somewhat naïve friend, saying that you will pay him $1 if a tossed coin comes out heads, but he will pay you $2 if the coin is tails. In the long run, half the coin tosses will result in heads and half in tails (assuming the coin is fair). So half the time you will pay a dollar and half the time you will win $2. Your expected value is, therefore, $0.50, calculated as follows:

$$\tfrac{1}{2}(-\$1) + \tfrac{1}{2}(\$2) = -\$0.50 + \$1$$
$$= \$0.50$$

Probabilities are not so easy to determine for management decisions, but market research and test marketing do help. To return to the shampoo marketer, suppose the company estimated that there was a 10-percent chance of the optimistic scenario, a 10-percent chance of the pessimistic scenario, and an 80-percent chance of the most likely sales outcome. Then the expected profit from the new shampoo would be

$$.10(\$125,000) + .80(25,000) + .10(-\$55,000) = \$27,000.$$

In this case, the new product launch has a positive expected value, so it looks like the firm should go ahead with its plans.

Uncertainty is a reality for a manager. To consider only the most optimistic outcomes would be foolhardy, but to consider only the worst results would paralyze a company into inaction. Approaches such as those discussed here, which try to balance risk against profit, help managers make decisions in the face of an uncertain environment.

LONGER TIME HORIZONS

For some marketers, the time between taking an action and its impact on sales is very short. For example, when a fast-food chain advertises a special free drink with each hamburger ordered for one week only, the company's return is almost immediate. Other actions, however, involve a longer time frame, and it may be years before an investment earns its full return. For example, if the fast-food chain opened a new store, it might take several years before the store became profitable and even longer before the store's full potential was realized. To be more concrete, suppose opening the new store involved an investment of $90,000 on the company's part and produced a loss of $10,000 for the first year and an expected profit of $60,000 in each of the next two years. The company treasurer insists that all projects must pay for themselves within three years. Should the company open this new store?

The problem in answering this question is that money received a year or two from now is worth less than money available now. If you have money now, you can invest it and earn interest. If you do not have it now, you can try to borrow it from the bank and pay the banker interest. Suppose you go to a bank and the loan officer offers to lend $90,000 now if you pay the bank $100,000 a year from now. Then, in financial terms, the "present value discount factor" is .90, and a dollar a year from now is equivalent to $0.90 now. Similarly, a dollar paid two years from now is worth $0.81; calculated as (.90)(.90) = $0.81. Using this notion of "present value," here is how we might calculate the return on the $90,000 investment in a new store:

Years from Now	Profit	Discount Factor	Value Now
1	-$10,000	.90	-$ 9,000
2	60,000	(.90)(.90) = .81	48,600
3	60,000	(.90)(.90)(.90) = .729	43,740
			$83,340

The return of $83,340 is less than the required investment of $90,000, so on economic grounds the company should not proceed with the investment.

How could the company change this outcome? If a longer time horizon for cost recovery were permitted, then perhaps the project would be viable. Another alternative would be to upgrade the value of future returns by attempting, for example, to borrow money more cheaply.

These actions require a careful consideration of the company's financial policies, particularly with regard to setting the terms for judging marketing plans that involve both expenditures and returns over several years. In this brief discussion we can only suggest the need for considering both the short- and long-term effects of marketing actions and point out that some way of placing a value on future returns needs to be established. Such policies generally involve deciding on a time horizon over which to measure returns and a means to discount the value of future returns.

CONCLUSION

Financial and economic analysis is an important part of the evaluation of all significant marketing alternatives. This note provides an introduction to some of the basic approaches that will be helpful in case analysis. No one form of analysis, however, is sufficient to evaluate a course of action; the soundness of a plan must be judged against multiple criteria.

The following exercises provide an opportunity for you to apply the concepts of financial and economic analysis.

FINANCIAL EXERCISES FOR MARKETING DECISIONS

1. Computer Data Storage (CDS), located in Calgary, Alberta, holds a 4-percent share of the total annual market of 50,000 computer backup storage devices. CDS provides its retailers with a margin of 35 percent on a retail price of $2,000 per storage device.

   Brenda Ditner, CDS's controller, estimates that variable production costs amount to $825 per storage device and fixed manufacturing costs total $280,000 per year. In addition, shipping and packaging costs of $45 per unit are paid by CDS. Management costs are $95,000 per year, and the annual advertising budget is $120,000. The company employs one sales representative at a salary of $65,000.

   a) What are CDS's fixed costs?

   b) What are CDS's variable costs per unit?

   c) What is the unit contribution?

   d) What is the break-even volume for CDS (in units)?

   e) What market share is needed to achieve this volume?

   f) What are CDS's current profits?

   g) If establishing CDS involved an investment of $1,200,000 and the company requires a return of 16 percent on its capital, is the storage device line still profitable? Justify your answer.

   h) What are the profits after allowing for the required return on capital?

   i) Nick Wang, the firm's vice-president of marketing, estimates CDS can sell 6 percent more storage devices than it does currently by increasing its advertising budget from $120,000 to $140,000. Alternatively, if he reduces the advertising budget by $20,000, he expects to sell 95 fewer units. Should CDS raise or lower its advertising budget? Why?

   j) What would be the break-even level (in units) if the advertising budget were raised?

   k) What would be the break-even level (in units) if the advertising budget were lowered?

   l) As an alternative to the change in advertising, CDS is considering offering one free storage file sorter with every storage device sold. These sorters cost CDS $60 each. If this offer can increase storage device sales by 180 units, what would be the change in total profits?

2. Terri Holden, owner of Write For You Stationery, is preparing for a year-end performance review of her two stores. She opened the downtown store 15 years ago; the suburban store (located in a shopping mall) was opened 5 years ago. The following financial data have been collected.

	Downtown Store ($)	Suburban Store ($)
Purchases at Cost	1,383,000	1,869,000
Depreciation	12,000	18,000
Advertising	24,000	234,000
Returns and Allowances	102,000	228,000
Rent and Utilities	30,000	120,000
Beginning Inventory	309,000	846,000
Administrative Salaries	90,000	126,000
Telephone	4,500	4,500
Commissions	132,000	336,000
Salesforce Salaries	–	285,000
Office Expenses	24,000	33,000
Ending Inventory	393,000	660,000
Sales	1,908,000	3,750,000
Investment	1,260,000	2,400,000

a) Prepare operating statements for each store.

b) Using ratio analysis, compare the performance of the two stores. What are the implications of this analysis?

c) What shop would you close if forced to close one? Why?

3. Cool Gear Inc. has completed development of a new line of bicycle helmets for kids (ages 4 to 9). The helmets' fashion designs are based on comic book characters. Cool Gear expects to sell 30,000 helmets in the first year and 50,000 in the second year. The following financial and sales data have been assembled.

Retail selling price	$40
Retail margin	45%
Material cost/unit	$5.60
Labour cost/unit	$1.90
Packaging cost/unit	$.75
Salesforce salaries and expenses	$225,000
Manufacturing overhead	$114,000
Administrative expenses	$105,000
Sales promotion (first year only)	$60,000

Prepare a two-year financial summary for the helmets, including variable cost per unit, contribution per unit, total contribution, total fixed costs, break-even volume, gross margin, and net profit.

4. Laval Footwear (LF) is considering the addition of a new line of waterproof boots ("Water Smart") next year to its existing brand "Stay Dry." First-year sales of the new line are projected at 350,000 pairs. The table below provides price and cost data. The sources of these sales are expected to be 20 percent from new customers, 40 percent from competitors' customers, and 40 percent (of the 350,000) from previous buyers of LF's other brand, Stay Dry. Sales of Stay Dry totalled 230,000 pairs this year and are expected to remain at this level if the new line is not introduced. Michel Lafontaine, manager of the Boots Division, is concerned about the cannibalization of Stay Dry sales by the new line. Should the new line be introduced?

	Current Stay Dry	Year 1 with New Line	
		Stay Dry	Water Smart
Factory Selling Price	$22.00	$22.00	$26.50
Variable Costs	13.50	13.50	18.50
Fixed Costs	$840,000	$560,000	$2,800,000

5. Canadian Margarine Limited (CML) is a national producer of margarine. Last year, CML's research department completed the development of an innovative easy-to-spread, ultra-low-fat margarine to replace the company's current product.

The new CML easy-to-spread margarine offered the consumer a benefit not available from other products on the market—it contained aspin, which made the margarine taste very much like butter. "Blind" consumer taste tests indicated that the CML product had superior flavour and taste when compared with the current CML margarine and its competitors.

Hal Mira, New-Product Manager for CML, needs to develop a pricing plan for the new margarine. Market data have been collected (see the table "Competitive Market Data"). The product, promotion, and distribution components of the marketing plan have been tentatively set and are shown in the table "Product Data." Price is the only remaining consideration.

Competitive Market Data					
	Retail Price	Consumer Perceptions			Market
Company	(450 g pkg.)	Flavour	Taste	Value	Share
CML (current product)	$2.19	High	High	High	35%
Brand A	2.25	High	High	Medium	30%
Brand B	2.19	Medium	High	Medium	25%
No-Name	2.05	Medium	Low	Low	10%

Average retail price (weighted average): $2.19.

Total annual Canadian demand: 3 million packages.

Because of the "convenience" of this product, consumers are relatively price insensitive. Each $0.01 increase in the average price decreases total annual Canadian demand by only 50,000 packages.

Product Data	
Retail margin	20%
Wholesale margin	10%
CML Costs	
Raw materials	$0.46/pkg.
Packaging	$0.35/pkg.
Direct labour	$0.22/pkg.
Production overhead	$60,000/year
Administrative expenses	$80,000/year
Introductory advertising and promotion	$400,000
Second-year advertising and promotion	$250,000

a) Outline the factors that Hal Mira should consider in setting the price for CML's new margarine.

b) What pricing methods should be considered for the new margarine? What method do you recommend? Why?

c) What retail price do you recommend for the new margarine? What market share do you estimate for the new product at this price? Justify your estimate.

d) What will the gross margin and net profit be for the new product in the first and second years, at your recommended price?

6. Northern Airways, one of the country's regional air carriers, was considering operating an airplane shuttle service between Toronto and New York. The airline was to be named Executive Airlines, and all necessary operating arrangements had been made. Operating the airline would cost $800,000 per month for leasing for airplanes, management, and marketing.

In addition, the incremental costs were as follows:

Per Flight	
Crew pay	$193.00
Fuel	182.46
Airport landing fees	24.24
Airport personnel	21.54*
Per Passenger	
Food and drinks	1.26
Commissions	1.80
Passenger liability insurance	.64
* Provided by Northern Airways at the stated cost per flight.	

Jackson McGuinn, the manager in charge of Executive Airlines, believes that at a ticket price of $50 per flight, he can run 12 flights daily (6 each way), five days per week (four weeks per month), at an average of 82 passengers per flight. The entire operation would depend on two jet airplanes being totally dedicated to the service.

a) Prepare a monthly income statement for Executive Airlines.

b) What should Jackson McGuinn do? Why?

7. Felice Kurma, the owner of the Kurma Hair Salon in downtown Halifax, has to decide whether to open a second shop in a suburban shopping mall. If she does so, she would incur a monthly cost of $3,000 for the rental of a fully equipped hair salon and would have to sign a minimum one-year lease. Since Felice pays her employees on a commission basis, she estimates that each customer who comes to the store will provide a net return (contribution) to her of $3. She thinks it is most likely (about a 75% chance) that the suburban store will attract 1,000 customers a month, but there is a 10-percent chance that demand could be as low as 600 customers. On the upbeat side, she thinks there is a 15-percent chance of demand as high as 2,000 customers a month. Based on the experience of other salon owners, she believes that demand would not reach its full level until the third month of operation. The first two months would likely produce about half the sales of the other months, but would not be a good predictor of ultimate sales.

Should Felice open the salon at the suburban mall?

The Coors Distributorship

James E. Nelson
and Eric J. Karson

Larry Brownlow was just beginning to realize the problem was more complex than he had thought. The problem, of course, was giving direction to Manson and Associates regarding which research should be completed by February 20, 1989, to determine market potential of a Coors beer distributorship for a two-county area in southern Delaware. With data from this research, Larry would be able to estimate the feasibility of such an operation before the March 5 application deadline. Larry knew his decision on whether or not to apply for the distributorship was the most important career choice he had ever faced.

LARRY BROWNLOW

Larry was just completing his M.B.A. and, from his standpoint, the Coors announcement of expansion into Delaware could hardly have been better timed. He had long ago decided the best opportunities and rewards were in smaller, self-owned businesses and not in the jungles of corporate giants. Because of a family tragedy some three years ago, Larry found himself in a position to consider small-business opportunities such as the Coors distributorship. Approximately $500,000 was held in trust for Larry, to be disbursed when he reached age 30. Until then, Larry and his family lived on an annual trust income of about $40,000. It was on the basis of this income that Larry decided to leave his sales engineering job and return to graduate school to obtain his M.B.A.

The decision to complete a graduate program and operate his own business had been easy to make. While he could have retired and lived on investment income, Larry knew such a life would not be to his liking. Working with people and the challenge of making it on his own, Larry thought, were far more preferable than enduring an early retirement.

Larry would be 30 in July, about the time money would actually be needed to start the business. In the meantime, he had access to about $15,000 for feasibility research. While there certainly were other places to spend the money, Larry and his wife agreed the opportunity to acquire the distributorship could not be overlooked.

COORS, INC.

Coors' history dated back to 1873, when Adolph Coors built a small brewery in Golden, Colorado. Since then, the brewery had prospered and become the fourth largest seller of beer in the country. Coors' operating philosophy could be summed up as "hard work, saving money, devotion to the quality of the product, caring about the environment, and giving people something to believe in." Company operation is consistent with this philosophy. Headquarters and most production facilities are still located in Golden, with a new Shenandoah, Virginia, facility aiding in nationwide distribution. Coors is still family operated and controlled. The company had issued its first public stock, $127 million worth of nonvoting shares, in 1975. The issue was enthusiastically received by the financial community despite its being offered during a recession.

Coors' unwillingness to compromise on the high quality of its product is well known both to its suppliers and to its consuming public. Coors beer requires constant refrigeration to maintain this quality, and wholesalers' facilities are closely controlled to ensure proper temperatures are maintained. Wholesalers are also required to install and use aluminum can recycling equipment. Coors was one of the first breweries in the industry to recycle its cans.

Larry was aware of Coors' popularity with many consumers in adjacent states. However, Coors' corporate management was seen by some consumers to hold anti-union beliefs (because of a labour disagreement at the brewery some ten years ago and the brewery's current use of a non-union labour force). Some other consumers perceived the brewery to be somewhat insensitive to minority issues, primarily in employment and distribution. These attitudes—plus many other aspects of consumer behaviour—meant that Coors' sales in Delaware would depend greatly on the efforts of the two wholesalers planned for the state.

MANSON RESEARCH PROPOSAL

Because of the pressure of his studies, Larry had contacted Manson and Associates in January for their assistance. The firm was a Wilmington-based general research supplier that had conducted other feasibility studies in the mid-Atlantic region. Manson was well known for the quality of its work, particularly with respect to computer modelling. The firm had developed special expertise in modelling such things as population and employment levels for cities, counties, and other units of area for periods of up to ten years into the future.

Larry had met John Rome, senior research analyst for Manson, in January and discussed the Coors opportunity and appropriate research extensively. Rome promised a formal research proposal (Appendix 1) for the project, which Larry now held in his hand. It certainly was extensive, Larry thought, and reflected the professionalism he expected. Now came the hard part—choosing the more relevant research from the proposal, because he certainly couldn't afford to pay for it all. Rome had suggested a meeting for Friday, which gave Larry only three more days to decide.

Larry was at first overwhelmed. All the research would certainly be useful. He was sure he needed estimates of sales and costs in a form allowing managerial analysis, but what data in what form? Knowledge of competing operations' experience, retailer support, and consumer acceptance also seemed important for feasibility analysis. For example, what if consumers were excited about Coors and retailers indifferent, or the other way around? Finally, several of the studies would provide information that could be useful in later months of operation, in the areas of promotion and pricing, for example. The problem now appeared more difficult than before!

It would have been nice, Larry thought, if he only had some time to perform part of the suggested research himself. However, there just was too much in the way of class assignments and other matters to allow him that luxury. Besides, using Manson and Associates would give him research results from an unbiased source. There would be plenty for him to do once he received the results anyway.

INVESTING AND OPERATING DATA

Larry was not completely in the dark regarding investment and operating data for the distributorship. In the past two weeks he had visited two beer wholesalers in his hometown of Chester, Pennsylvania, who handled Anheuser Busch and Miller beer, to get a feel for their operation and marketing experience. It would have been nice to interview a Coors wholesaler, but Coors management had instructed all their distributors to provide no information to prospective applicants.

Although no specific financial data had been discussed, general information had been provided in a cordial fashion because of the noncompetitive nature of Larry's plans. Based on his conversations, Larry had made the following estimates:

Inventory		$240,000
Equipment:		
Delivery trucks	$150,000	
Forklift	20,000	
Recycling and miscellaneous equipment	20,000	
Office equipment	10,000	
Total equipment		200,000
Warehouse		320,000
Land		40,000
Total investment		$800,000

Balance Sheet

A local banker had reviewed Larry's financial capabilities and saw no problem in extending a line of credit on the order of $400,000. Other family sources also might loan as much as $400,000 to the business.

To get a rough estimate of fixed expenses, Larry decided to plan on having four route salespeople, a secretary, and a warehouse manager. Salaries for these people and himself would run about $160,000 annually plus some form of incentive compensation he had yet to determine. Other fixed or semi-fixed expenses were estimated as follows:

Equipment depreciation	$35,000
Warehouse depreciation	15,000
Utilities and telephone	12,000
Insurance	10,000
Personal property taxes	10,000
Maintenance and janitorial service	5,600
Miscellaneous	2,400
	$90,000

According to the two wholesalers, beer in bottles and cans outsold keg beer by a three-to-one margin. Keg beer prices at the wholesale level were about 45 percent of prices for beer in bottles and cans.

MEETING

The entire matter deserved much thought. Maybe it was a golden opportunity, maybe not. The only thing certain was that research was needed. Manson and Associates was ready, and Larry needed time to think. Today is Tuesday, thought Larry—only three days until he and John Rome would get together for direction.

Appendix 1

Manson and Associates Research Proposal

January 16, 1989

Mr. Larry Brownlow
1198 West Lamar
Chester, PA 19345

Dear Larry:

It was a pleasure meeting you last week and discussing your business and research interests in Coors wholesaling.

After further thought and discussion with my colleagues, the Coors opportunity appears even more attractive than when we met.

Appearances can be deceiving, as you know, and I fully agree some formal research is needed before you make application. Research that we recommend would proceed in two distinct stages and is described below:

Stage One Research, Based on Secondary Data and Manson Computer Models:
Study A: National and Delaware per Capita Beer Consumption for 1988–1992.

Description: Per capita annual consumption of beer for the total population and for population age 21 and over in gallons is provided.

Source: Various publications, Manson Computer Model

Cost: $1,000

Study B: Population Estimates for 1986–1996 for Two Delaware Counties in Market Area.

Description: Annual estimates of total population and population age 21 and over are provided for the period 1986–1996.

Source: U.S. Bureau of Census, Sales Management Annual Survey of Buying Power, Manson Computer Model

Cost: $1,500

Study C: Estimates of Coors' Market Share for 1990–1995,

Description: Coors' market share for the two-county market area based on total gallons consumed is estimated for each year in the period 1990–1995. This data will be projected from Coors' nationwide experience.

Source: Various publications, Manson computer model

Cost: $2,000

Study D: Estimated Liquor and Beer Licences for the Market Area 1990–1995.

Description: Projections of the number of on-premise sale operations and off-premise sale operations are provided.

Source: Delaware Department of Revenue, Manson computer model

Cost: $1,000

Study E: Beer Taxes Paid by Delaware Wholesalers for 1987 and 1988 in the Market Area.

Description: Beer taxes paid by each of the six currently operating competing beer wholesalers are provided. These can be converted to gallons sold by applying the state gallonage tax rate ($0.06 per gallon).

Source: Delaware Department of Revenue

Cost: $200

Study F: Financial Statement Summary of Wine, Liquor, and Beer Wholesalers for Fiscal Year 1986.

Description: Composite balance sheets, income statements, and relevant measures of performance provided for 510 similar wholesaling operations in the United States are provided.

Source: Robert Morris Associates Annual Statement Studies, 1987 ed.

Cost: $49.50

Stage Two Research, Based on Primary Data:
Study G: Consumer Study

Description: Study G involves focus-group interviews and a mail questionnaire to determine consumers' past experience, acceptance, and intention to buy Coors beer. Three focus-group interviews would be conducted in the two counties in the market area. From these data, a mail questionnaire would be developed and sent to 300 adult residents in the market area, utilizing direct questions and a semantic differential scale to measure attitudes toward Coors beer, competing beers, and an ideal beer.

Source: Manson and Associates

Cost: $6,000

Study H: Retailer Study

Description: Group interviews would be conducted with six potential retailers of Coors beer in one county in the market area to determine their past beer sales and experience and their intention to stock and sell Coors. From these data, a personal-interview questionnaire would be developed and executed at all appropriate retailers in the market area to determine similar data.

Source: Manson and Associates

Cost: $4,800

Study I: Survey of Retail and Wholesale Beer Prices

Description: In-store interviews would be conducted with a sample of 50 retailers in the market area to estimate retail and wholesale prices for Budweiser, Miller Lite, Miller, Busch, Bud Light, Old Milwaukee and Michelob.

Source: Manson and Associates

Cost: $2,000

Examples of the final report tables are attached (Appendix 2). This should give you a better idea of the data you will receive.

As you can see, the research is extensive and, I might add, not cheap. However, the research as outlined will supply you with sufficient information to make an estimate of the feasibility of a Coors distributorship, the investment for which is substantial.

I have scheduled 9:00 a.m. next Friday as a time to meet with you to discuss the proposal in more detail. Time is short, but we firmly feel the study can be completed by February 20, 1989. If you need more information in the meantime, please feel free to call.

Sincerely,

John Rome
Senior Research Analyst

Appendix 2

Examples of Final Research Report Tables

Table A	National and Delaware Residents' Annual Beer Consumption, per Capita 1988-1992 (gallons)				
		U.S. Consumption		Delaware Consumption	
	Year	Based on Entire Population	Based on Population Age 21 and Over	Based on Entire Population	Based on Population Age 21 and Over
1988					
1989					
1990					
1991					
1992					
Source: Study A					

Table B	Population Estimates for 1986-1996 for Two Delaware Counties in Market Area					
	Entire Population					
	1986	1988	1990	1992	1994	1996
County						
Kent						
Sussex						
	Population Age 21 and Over					
	1986	1988	1990	1992	1994	1996
County						
Kent						
Sussex						
Source: Study B						

Table C	Estimates of Coors' Market Share for 1990-1995
Year	Market Share (%)
1990	
1991	
1992	
1993	
1994	
1995	
Source: Study C	

Table D	Estimates of Number of Liquor and Beer Licences for the Market Area, 1990-1995						
Type of Licence		1990	1991	1992	1993	1994	1995
All beverages							
Retail beer and wine							
Off-premise beer only							
Veterans beer and liquor							
Fraternal							
Resort beer and liquor							
Source: Study D							

Table E	Beer Taxes Paid by Beer Wholesalers in the Market Area, 1987 and 1988	
Wholesaler	1987 Tax Paid ($)	1988 Tax Paid ($)
A		
B		
C		
D		
E		
F		

Source: Study E

Note: Delaware beer tax is $0.06 per gallon.

Table F	Financial Statement Summary for 510 Wholesalers of Wine, Liquor, and Beer in Fiscal Year 1986.

	Percentage
Assets	
Cash and equivalents	
Accounts and notes receivable, net	
Inventory	
All other current	
Total current	
Fixed Assets, net	
Intangibles, net	
All other noncurrent	
Total	100.00
Liabilities	
Notes payable, short term	
Current maturity long-term debt	
Accounts and notes payable, trade	
Accrued expenses	
All other current	
Total current	
Long-term debt	
All other noncurrent	
Net worth	
Total liabilities and net worth	100.00
Income Data	
Net sales	100.00
Cost of sales	
Gross profit	
Operating expenses	
Operating profit	
All other expenses, net	
Profit before taxes	
Ratios	
Quick	
Current	
Debts/worth	
Sales/receivables	
Cost of sales/inventory	
Percentage profit before taxes, based on total assets	

Source: Study F (Robert Morris Associates, #1987)

Table F	Financial Statement Summary for 510 Wholesalers of Wine, Liquor, and Beer in Fiscal Year 1986 (continued)

Interpretation of Statement Studies Figures

RMA recommends that Statement Studies data be regarded only as general guidelines and not as absolute industry norms. There are several reasons why the data may not be fully representative of a given industry.

1. The financial statements used in the Statement Studies are not selected by any random or statistically reliable method. RMA member banks voluntarily submit the raw data they have available each year, with these being the only constraints: (a) The fiscal year-ends of the companies reported may not be from April 1 through June 29, and (b) their total assets must be less than $100 million.

2. Many companies have varied product lines; however, the Statement Studies categorize them by their primary product Standard Industrial Classification (SIC) number only.

3. Some of our industry samples are rather small in relation to the total number of firms in a given industry. A relatively small sample can increase the chances that some of our composites do not fully represent our industry.

4. There is the chance that an extreme statement can be present in a sample, causing a disproportionate influence on the industry composite. This is particularly true in a relatively small sample.

5. Companies within the same industry may differ in the method of operations, which in turn can directly influence their statements. Since they are included in our sample, too, these statements can significantly affect our composite calculations.

6. Other considerations that can result in variations among different companies engaged in the same general line of business are different labour markets, geographical location, different accounting methods, quality of products handled, sources and methods of financing, and terms of sale.

For these reasons, RMA does not recommend that Statement Studies figures be considered as absolute norms for a given industry. Rather, the figures should be used only as general guidelines and in addition to the other methods of financial analysis. RMA makes no claim as to the representativeness of the figures printed in this book.

Table G	Consumer Questionnaire Results		

	Percentage		Percentage
Consumed Coors in the past:	Yes _____	No _____	

Attitudes toward Coors:	%	Usually buy beer at:	
Strongly like		Liquor stores	
Like		Taverns and bars	
Indifferent/no opinion		Supermarkets	
Dislike		Corner grocery	
Strongly dislike			
Total	100.0	Total	100.0

Weekly beer consumption:		Features considered important when buying beer:	
Less than 1 can		Taste	
1-2 cans		Brand name	
3-4 cans		Price	
5-6 cans		Store location	
7-8 cans		Advertising	
9 cans and over		Carbonation	
		Other	
Total	100.0		100.0

Intention to buy Coors:	
Certainly will	
Maybe will	
Not sure	
Maybe will not	
Certainly will not	
Total	100.0

Semantic Differential Scale, Consumers*

	Extremely	Very	Somewhat	Somewhat	Very	Extremely	
Masculine	_____	_____	_____	_____	_____	_____	Feminine
Healthful	_____	_____	_____	_____	_____	_____	Unhealthful
Cheap	_____	_____	_____	_____	_____	_____	Expensive
Strong	_____	_____	_____	_____	_____	_____	Weak
Old-fashioned	_____	_____	_____	_____	_____	_____	New
Upper-class	_____	_____	_____	_____	_____	_____	Lower-class
Good taste	_____	_____	_____	_____	_____	_____	Bad taste

Source: Study G

* Profiles would be provided for Coors, three competing beers, and an ideal beer.

Table H	Retail Questionnaire Results					

	Percentage		Percentage
Brands of Beer Carried:		**Beer Sales:**	
Budweiser		Budweiser	
Miller Lite		Miller Lite	
Miller		Miller	
Busch		Busch	
Bud Light		Bud Light	
Old Milwaukee		Old Milwaukee	
Michelob		Michelob	
		Others	
Total	100.0	Total	100.0
Intention to buy Coors:			
Certainly will			
Maybe will			
Not sure			
Maybe will not			
Certainly will not			
Total	100.0		

Semantic Differential Scale, Consumers*							
	Extremely	Very	Somewhat	Somewhat	Very	Extremely	
Masculine							Feminine
Healthful							Unhealthful
Cheap							Expensive
Strong							Weak
Old-fashioned							New
Upper-class							Lower-class
Good taste							Bad taste

Source: Study H

* Profiles would be provided for Coors, three competing beers, and an ideal beer.

Table I	Retail and Wholesale Prices for Selected Beers in the Market Area	
Beer	Wholesale Six-Pack Price[a] (Dollars)	Retail Six-Pack Price[b] (Dollars)
Budweiser		
Miller Lite		
Miller		
Busch		
Bud Light		
Old Milwaukee		
Michelob		

Source: Study I

[a] Price at which the wholesaler sold to retailers.

[b] Price at which the retailer sold to consumers.

Ethical Problems in Marketing Research

Charles B. Weinberg

Marketing managers and marketing researchers are frequently confronted by ethical problems and dilemmas. Gathering, analyzing, and presenting information raises a number of important ethical questions in which the manager's need to know and understand the market in order to develop effective marketing programs must be balanced against an individual's right to privacy. The interpretation and use of data can also raise ethical questions.

ASSIGNMENT

The following scenarios present ethical problems that might arise in marketing research. For each problem two possible responses are suggested. There may be other alternatives available, but for the purposes of this assignment only these two alternatives are to be considered. Your instructor will either assign you one of the specified positions or allow you to choose one of the two positions. Your assignment is to prepare arguments to defend your assigned or chosen position. Bear in mind that there are no uniquely right answers; reasonable people may choose different courses of action.

Prepared with the assistance of Freddy Lee.

1. A pharmaceutical company is conducting a telephone survey of physicians to assess their perception of the quality of the company's products. The marketing vice-president wants the interviews to be conducted by the company's marketing research department under the name of a fictitious market research agency. The vice-president feels that this procedure will result in more objective responses than if the company's name were revealed.

   A. As the market research director, you think it is neither necessary nor appropriate to use the name of a fictitious market research agency. Convince the vice-president of your position.

   B. As the vice-president, you know you can always hire an outside firm to do the work, but you don't want to spend the extra money to do so. You believe that any deception is harmless in this situation. Be prepared to persuade others of this position.

2. You are the Vice-President of Browser Software Development for Exploscape Corporation (EC). Many online companies are willing to purchase and promote your browser as their feature online browser if they can extract information on consumer surfing behaviour via cookies. Your software engineering department says that this is readily done and cookies can be embedded in the browser to track visited sites via the consumer's access log. In this way, each computer's unique IP will be tagged, and companies will have information about the consumer's surfing patterns. The engineers can do this using "Trojan" cookies, in which case consumers do not know, unless they ask, that their surfing behaviour is being tracked.

   A. You decide to have your engineers develop the Trojan cookies. How would you support this decision?

   B. You decide that it is not appropriate to extract information online via a Trojan cookie and opt to ask permission from the consumer before a cookie can be installed on the browser. If too many consumers refuse permission, this will seriously damage the potential revenue stream. How would you support this decision?

3. Your market research company is supervising a study of restaurants conducted for the Department of Consumer Affairs (DCA). The data, which have already been collected, include specific buying information and prices paid. The restaurants that participated in the study have been promised confidentiality. DCA demands that all responses be identified by business name; its rationale is that it plans to repeat the study and wishes to limit sampling error by interviewing the same respondents. Because the next study might be done by another market research company (based on an open bid), DCA requires that it maintain control of the sample.

   A. As the ministry official in charge of the project, you insist on having the names of the participating organizations. Prepare an argument to support this position to an impartial arbitrator.

   B. As the head of the market research company, you have decided not to provide the requested information. Prepare an argument to support this position to an impartial arbitrator.

4. A magazine publisher is planning a mail survey of its readers. The project director requests permission to use ultraviolet ink in precoding questionnaires in the survey. He points out that the accompanying letter refers to a confidential survey, but he needs to

be able to identify respondents to permit adequate cross-tabulation of the data and to save on postage costs if a second mailing is required.

A. As the market research director, you have decided not to allow the precoding of the questionnaires with ultraviolet ink. You will only allow precoding that is highly visible to respondents. Explain to the project director why you have taken this course of action.

B. The market research director has told you, as the project director, that he will allow the ultraviolet coding of the questionnaires if you can ensure that it will not cause any problems. Provide these assurances.

5. An independent market research firm is about to conduct a study funded by a somewhat unpopular federal policing agency. The study is on marijuana use among young people in a community and its relationship, if any, to crime. A structured questionnaire will be used to gather data for the agency on marijuana use and criminal activities. There is a concern that if the name of the funding agency and/or the actual purposes of the study are revealed to respondents response rates will be seriously reduced, thereby increasing non-response bias.

A. As the project director, you have decided to tell respondents about the sponsor of the study and its purposes right at the start of the questionnaire. Justify this decision.

B. As the project director, you will tell respondents who the sponsor is only if they ask. Justify this decision.

6. You are a market researcher undertaking a project for a regular client of your firm. A study you are working on is about to go into the field when the questionnaire you sent to the client for final approval comes back drastically modified. The client has rewritten it, introducing leading questions and biased scales. An accompanying letter indicates that the questionnaire must be sent out as revised. You do not believe that valid information can be gathered using the revised instrument.

A. As the market researcher, you decide to telephone the client and explain why the questionnaire should not be run as the client rewrote it. If the client insists on running the questionnaire as written, then you will implement the study. What will you tell the client? Justify your course of action.

B. As the market researcher, you decide to telephone the client and explain why the questionnaire should not be run as the client rewrote it. If the client insists on running the questionnaire as written, then you will refuse to implement the study. What will you tell the client? Justify your course of action.

7. You are the CEO of an Internet market research firm. A major online retailer of books and toys has offered to sell you access to its complete customer database for market research purposes. This would be an invaluable resource for your firm, as the retailer's records are quite detailed. Customers of the retailer have been told that their names will not be sold to any other retailer—"no other marketer will ever know your name" is prominently displayed on the retailer's Web site. The retailer has contacted a few other research agencies regarding the sale of the customer information.

A. You decide to buy the information from the retailer. Justify this decision. Would you insist on being the only market research firm to have access to this information?

B. You decide not to buy the information. Justify this decision.

8. A well-known public figure is going to face trial on a charge of failing to report his part ownership of certain regulated companies while serving as a provincial minister. The defence lawyers have asked you, as a market research specialist, to do a research study to determine the characteristics of people most likely to sympathize with the defendant and hence to vote for acquittal. The defence lawyers have read newspaper accounts of how this approach has been used in a number of similar situations.

    A. You have decided to accept the offer and will work aggressively for the client. A newspaper reporter telephones you to ask why you decided to work for this now discredited official. What do you answer?

    B. You refuse to work for the defence lawyers. Provide an explanation to the partners in your firm why you decided not to accept this business.

9. You are the market research director for a large chemical company. Recent research indicates that many of your company's customers are misusing one of its main products. There is no danger resulting from this misuse, though the customers are wasting money by using too much of the product at one time. You are shown the new advertising campaign by the advertising agency. The ads not only ignore this problem of misuse, but also actually seem to encourage it.

    A. As the market research director, you have decided to telephone the ad agency and suggest that the advertising be revised. If the ad agency does not agree, then you plan to raise the issue with senior management in your own firm. What will you tell the agency people and what will you tell management? Justify your course of action.

    B. As the market research director, you have decided to telephone the ad agency and make them aware of the problem. Any further action will be up to them. What will you tell the agency people? Justify your course of action.

10. Your market research company specializes in conducting surveys about health-related issues on the Internet. Often you would like to contact respondents to do additional surveys. To test people's likelihood of participating in a second study, you ask for their willingness to respond in two ways:

"Notify me about more health surveys," followed by two blank radio buttons with neither filled in:

Yes ◯   No ◯

"Notify me about more health surveys," followed by two radio buttons with the Yes button filled in:

Yes ◉   No ◯

Respondents can fill in either button in both cases; 59 percent of respondents to version A and 76 percent of respondents to version B indicated that they wanted to be notified of a second survey. (If only the No button were filled in, 38 percent of respondents indicated they wanted to be notified of a second survey.) In a subsequent Web survey, the response rate of people who responded Yes to version B was only 5 percent less than the response rate of people who responded Yes to version A.

    A. As manager of client services, you recommend to clients that they use version A. Justify this decision.

B. As manager of client services, you recommend to clients that they use version B. Justify this decision.

11. You are the owner of a small market research firm that specializes in the in-depth interviewing of teenagers. You started the firm three years ago, but your firm's reputation has grown and you now employ eight full-time professional staff; your clients include retailers, entertainment companies, and restaurants. Just after you made a major investment in computerized testing systems, the economy weakened and your business declined to such an extent that you may need to lay off several of your staff. A major tobacco company, which employs a number of market research firms, has invited you to join their team of market research suppliers and has offered you a lucrative contract.

A. As a non-smoker and the parent of three young children, you decide not to accept this business. Justify this decision.

B. Despite your personal concerns about smoking, you decide to accept this business. Justify this decision.

www.wlu.ca

Gordon H. G. McDougall

Tony Frost, Web Coordinator at Wilfrid Laurier University, had just received the survey results on Internet usage of Laurier's current and prospective students. As he reviewed the information in May 2001, he thought, *What have I learned about student usage of the Internet that would help me with our Web site? More importantly, what changes should be made to effectively target prospective students for Laurier?*

Hired in the fall of 2000 by Laurier's Public Affairs Department, Tony's primary responsibilities were to develop and advise on University-wide Internet strategies, to establish standards for the Laurier Web site, and to determine the use of appropriate technologies and training for individuals using the site. In his first six months his top priority was the redesign of Laurier's Web site, which was difficult to navigate and was visually uninteresting. The revised site (www.wlu.ca) was launched in March 2001.

Prior to joining Laurier, Tony had worked as a graphic designer (he had an honours diploma in graphic design) and then became webmaster at a regional municipality in Ontario. While working, he obtained a B.A., majoring in Communication Studies.

At the core of his objectives was to ensure that the Web site met the needs of Laurier's target audiences. As he stated: "Developing Web applications and a graphical interface for Laurier's Web site is difficult if no information is available on our target audiences. While we have information based on Canadian Internet use [Exhibit 1], it is not as specific as we require. We need to better understand the technical and human abilities as well as the behaviours of our own typical users."

WILFRID LAURIER UNIVERSITY

Wilfrid Laurier University is located in Waterloo, Ontario, approximately 100 kilometres southwest of Toronto. Laurier is regarded as one of the premier smaller universities in Canada. Competition for first-year placements is intense, and admission standards are among the highest in Canada. More than 70 percent of the 1,500-plus students entering the undergraduate program at Laurier are Ontario Scholars. Laurier has approximately 7,000 students enrolled in undergraduate (68%) and graduate (32%) programs.

A major goal at Laurier is to maintain or improve the quality of the high-school students who apply to Laurier and to encourage the top students to enroll at Laurier. The Web site (www.wlu.ca) plays an important role in providing information for this target audience. For example, students can book university visits online, take a virtual tour of the campus, and learn about the programs offered at Laurier.

TARGET AUDIENCES

Virtually all universities serve four main target audiences. Tony prepared descriptions of each segment at Laurier based on his assumptions of their Internet knowledge and usage:

- **High-quality prospective students:** Prospective students feel at ease with the Internet due to their early exposure to advanced computer technology. Studies indicate that teen use of the Internet has tripled since 1997 and that those under the age of 22 have accepted the Internet as a natural source of information and communication. Each new class of applicants will exert greater demand for instant, accurate information and services from Laurier's Web site.

- **Current students:** Generally, today's university students are sophisticated users of the Internet. Growing up with computers, they are comfortable with the Internet and prefer gathering their information online to more traditional sources.

- **Staff and faculty:** As knowledge workers in an institution of higher learning with an existing Web site and full Internet access, nearly all staff and faculty are comfortable in the use of the Internet. More research into their characteristics is required to ensure content is developed to meet their needs and abilities.

- **Alumni:** Although recent graduates would be similar to undergraduates in terms of Internet usage, the interests and behaviours of older graduates were less well understood. Moreover, while current students would have experience with www.wlu.ca (many courses had online materials), the Web site would be new to all but the most recent graduates (and many would be familiar with the older versions of the Web site). What would motivate alumni to use www.wlu.ca?

Tony wanted to gain a better understanding of each target audience so that his group could design and implement appropriate technologies/designs to provide a meaningful Web experience and enable the user's goals.

THE LAURIER DAY STUDY

As a first step, Tony decided to conduct a survey during Laurier Day, an "Open House" event held for prospective students who might be interested in coming to Laurier for their education. The Liaison Office estimated that approximately 1,400 high-school students would attend the event. Tony hoped to achieve a 20-percent participation rate (i.e., 280 students completing the questionnaire).

He designed the survey (see Exhibit 2, which includes the results of the study) with specific goals in mind. He wanted to establish a benchmark for how survey participants were using and accessing the Internet as well as how this had changed over the past year. This benchmark would allow an ongoing trend analysis to track changes in online behaviour. He had limited time to design the survey, so he concentrated on basic information. In the future he hoped to do more extensive surveys of both students and alumni.

The survey was conducted in April 2001 on Laurier Day (Laurier's open house) so as to be available to prospective students. It was conducted from a booth in a high-traffic area in the university concourse. While some faculty and staff members would complete the questionnaire, prospective and current students would be the primary respondents.

Appropriate signage was prepared to explain the purpose of the study. To stimulate participation in the survey, everyone who completed a survey was entered into a draw for one of two prizes (Laurier sweatshirts). The survey took place over a four-hour period and the booth was staffed by one person, who kept pens and surveys available. In total, 258 individuals completed the questionnaire: 140 high-school students (prospective students), 87 current students, and 18 faculty/staff.

Results

Tony decided to focus the analysis on prospective and current students, so he excluded the 18 faculty staff (7% of the respondents) from the analysis. As Tony suspected, both current and prospective students used the Internet (97%), the majority (66%) used the Internet more than five hours a week, and the majority (80%) rated their ability to use the Internet as excellent or good (Exhibit 2). He was a bit surprised that most (80%) accessed the Internet from home versus school (20%). However, further analysis revealed that the breakdown for prospective students was 93% home and 6% school; for current students it was 59% home and 41% school. In checking further, Tony felt that speed of Internet access might explain these results. He found that the faster the Internet connection, the more Internet usage. Prospective students were more likely to have faster Internet connections at home; current students were more likely to have faster Internet connections at Laurier.

The major reasons for using the Internet were e-mail (93%), obtain information/do research (85%), transfer/download files or software (39%), and obtain news/sports/weather (34%). "Content" and "Easy navigation" were important to the respondents in terms of effective Web sites, followed by "Fast download speeds."

Tony then ran a comparison between the prospective students and current students, looking for differences between the two. The most obvious difference was age: prospective students were younger (15% under 18, 85% 18–24) versus current students (1% under 18, 88% 18–24, 12% 25–34). Current students were spending more time on the Internet this year (71%) than prospective students (54%). Prospective students used the Internet more to play games (21% versus 9%) and go to chat rooms (22% versus 15%). Current students used the Internet more to look for jobs (43% versus 12%). In terms of effective Web sites, "Content" was ranked first by 44 percent of current students versus 34 percent by prospective students. For "Attractive graphics," 7 percent of prospective students ranked it first versus 1 percent for current students. No other major differences were found between the two groups.

While many of the comments provided by the students were positive (e.g., "like the virtual tour"), Tony was intrigued by a number of them, including, "would like to register and pay tuition on the site." He knew that Laurier was a long way from that possibility at the moment, but he also knew that students would value this option and that the Web site must meet the needs of its target audiences. The comments about "frustrating navigation," "faster access," and "outdated system" indicated that improvements could be made to the site.

More for curiosity than anything else (the sample size was too small to accurately interpret the data), Tony looked at differences between the 18 faculty/staff and the students. Faculty/staff were older and used the Internet more for research (100%), transferring files (61%), and obtaining news, etc. (56%). In terms of effective Web sites, 69 percent of faculty/staff ranked "Content" first, 0 percent ranked "Attractive graphics" first, 25 percent ranked "Easy navigation" first, and 6 percent ranked "Fast download speeds" first.

As he scanned the rest of the results, Tony began considering what inferences he could draw for improving the Web site. Specifically, what changes could be made in the short term? As well, what further analysis, if any, should be conducted on these data?

THE FUTURE

In the broader context, Tony saw this study as the first in an annual series of surveys that would track changes in the behaviours and capabilities of Laurier's Web users. He wanted to survey each of the four groups—prospective students, current students, faculty and staff, and alumni—and use the information to improve the Web site and meet their needs. His plan was to survey the alumni next. Laurier's administrators wanted to establish life-long relationships with their graduates and had been discussing the use of the Web site to assist in building these relationships. The proposed survey would definitely help in this regard.

First, Tony wanted to consider changes to the Web site based on the survey. In particular, what changes should be made to improve the site for prospective students? For current students? Then he would design the questionnaire for the alumni. Tony was particularly concerned about understanding how www.wlu.ca could serve the alumni.

As he began, Tony thought, *The Internet provides a tremendous opportunity to provide value to our students—past, present, and future. It's my job to identify that value, then deliver it.*

EXHIBIT 1	Internet Usage Information

* 84% of young adults said they prefer the Internet to the public library
* 47% of young adults would consider taking an educational course on the Web
* 90% of schools in Canada have access to the Internet for educational purposes
* 75% of Canadian teenagers have Internet access from home
* 93% of Canadian teenagers do their homework research on the Internet

Source: Various

EXHIBIT 2	Questionnaire and Results

Wilfrid Laurier University Internet Usage Study

Introduction

The information collected in this short survey will be used to improve
the Laurier Web site for people like yourself and your answers will be
kept confidential. We are sincerely interested in your honest opinions
and encourage you to be as accurate as possible. The survey will take 3 to 4 minutes to
complete. Remember to also fill out a ballot for a chance to win one of two Laurier
sweatshirts (winners to be drawn today). Thanks again for participating and good luck
in the draw.

Survey

1. Do you currently use the Internet?

    1a—Yes <u>97%</u> (IF YES, SKIP TO QUESTION 3).

    1b—No <u>3%</u> (IF NO, ANSWER QUESTION 2).

2. If you do not use the Internet, is it because…

    2a—You do not have access to a computer <u>0%</u>

    2b—You do not have Internet access <u>75%</u>

    2c—Not interested <u>12.5%</u>

    2d—No time <u>12.5%</u>

    2e—Other (SPECIFY) _____

    (SKIP TO QUESTION 11)

3. Approximately how many hours do you spend using the Internet in a typical week?

    3a—5 hours or less <u>34%</u>

    3b—6 to 10 hours <u>36%</u>

    3c—11 to 20 hours <u>18%</u>

    3d—21 to 30 hours <u>9%</u>

    3e—31 hours or more <u>3%</u>

4. Where do you access the Internet from the most?

    4a—home <u>80%</u>

    4b—work <u>0%</u>

    4c—school <u>20%</u>

    4d—other <u>0%</u>

5. On average, how does your usage of the Internet compare with one year ago?
   Are you…

    5a—Spending more time <u>61%</u>

    5b—Spending less time <u>16%</u>

EXHIBIT 2	Questionnaire and Results (continued)

5c—Spending the same amount of time 18%

5d—Did not use the Internet a year ago 4%

5e—Not sure 1%

6. When you use the Internet, what do you most frequently do? Check all that are applicable.

6a—E-mail 93%

6b—Obtain information/do research 85%

6c—Transfer/download files or software 39%

6d—Play games 17%

6e—Shop/make purchases 9%

6f—Look for jobs 24%

6g—Go to chat rooms/discussion forums 19%

6h—Obtain news/sports/weather 34%

6i—Other 10%

7. Would you say that your ability to use the Internet is...

7a—Excellent 29%

7b—Good 51%

7c—Average 17%

7d—Poor 2%

8. In the past year you have purchased goods over the Internet worth...

8a—Nothing, I have not made any purchases 70%

8b—Purchased less than $100 20%

8c—Purchased between $101 and $500 6%

8d—Purchased more than $500 2%

9. How do you primarily access the Internet?

9a—28.8 dial-up modem 4%

9b—36.6 dial-up modem 7%

9c—56.6 dial-up modem 31%

9d—Cable modem 29%

9e—DSL modem 7%

9f—T1 connection 1%

9g—Other 0%

9h—Not sure 21%

EXHIBIT 2	Questionnaire and Results (continued)

10. Using 1 for most important and 4 for least important, rank the following in order of importance for effective Web sites. (See below for responses)

10a—Good content ___

10b—Easy navigation ___

10c—Attractive graphics ___

10d—Fast download speeds ___

11. Please indicate which category best describes you:

11a—High-school student <u>61%</u>

11b—Laurier student <u>39%</u>

11c—Laurier employee <u>0%</u>

11d—Laurier faculty <u>0%</u>

11e—Laurier alumnus <u>0%</u>

12. In which age group are you?

12a—17 years old or younger <u>61%</u>

12b—18 to 24 years old <u>39%</u>

12c—25 to 34 years old <u>0%</u>

12d—35 to 44 years old <u>0%</u>

12e—34 to 54 years old <u>0%</u>

12f—55 years or older <u>0%</u>

13. What is your gender?

13a—Male <u>41%</u>

13b—Female <u>59%</u>

14. Using 1 for most important and 4 for least important, rank the following in order of importance for effective Web sites.

	Rank #1 (%)	Rank #2 (%)	Rank #3 (%)	Rank #4 (%)	Total (%)
Content	38	35	23	4	100
Easy navigation	31	33	26	10	100
Attractive graphics	5	9	19	67	100
Fast download speeds	32	22	31	15	100

Are there any comments you would like to make on using the Internet or on the Web site? _____

_____

_____

"Thanks for your help in this survey!"

| EXHIBIT 2 | Questionnaire and Results (continued) |

Laurier Internet Survey: All Comments

Comments on the Web site itself

Additional services on the Web site: registration, tuition, chat rooms, professor discussions

- Would like to register and pay tuition on WLU site
- Laurier needs a better Web page—more technologically advanced, better e-mail, perhaps Laurier chat rooms, discussion boards with professors, etc.

Positive comments: informative, easy to use

- Strive to be the best
- I enjoy your current Web site. It's informative.
- Web site was very easy to use, easy to find specific information, was attractive
- I like your virtual tour and your Web site is very informative

How it's designed and laid out:

- Better directions, update more frequently, more compelling to look at, more links
- The clearer directions to resources with individual departments (e.g., accessing notes, lectures online etc.)
- I enjoy the site now, but mach1 needs more space and I wish it would download quicker and have more links to other Laurier sites (like WLUSU.com)
- Summer, spring, part-time, and distance education Web site is terrible. Out of date, never works, pretty much useless.
- You need easier navigation for the student calendar
- Make the new home page something that gives us compelling reasons to look at it: news, announcements, etc.

General comments on WLU Internet access: *faster access*

- WLU needs better access, quicker and more terminals and printers
- The mach1 system is outdated and should be scrapped. Text-based e-mail was good in the '80s and early '90s, not in 2001. A system like McMaster's should be looked at.
- Getting thrown on a wild goose chase when trying to navigate is very frustrating
- Make Laurier's bandwidth wider for internal access
- Make your site faster
- Faster connections are needed at Laurier

Part 2　Marketing Decisions

case eight

Portable Heat Pad

*William A. Preshing
and Denise Walters*

In late 1999, Mark Tanner, a successful Canadian entrepreneur, purchased the Canadian rights to manufacture and distribute a reusable chemical heating pad named Portable Heat Pad. The product—a vinyl bag containing chemicals that produced a constant level of heat—had a variety of therapeutic uses, including treatment of muscle injuries and relief from arthritic pain. The task facing management was to develop a strategy for Portable Heat Pad in a market that had not changed in a number of years.

THE COMPANY

Mark Tanner owned the Tanner Company, which operated three businesses in western Canada—a peat-moss company, a mini-warehouse operation, and a landfill site. While attending a new-business seminar, he met the inventor of Portable Heat Pad and, after considerable investigation, paid $250,000 for the Canadian manufacturing and distribution rights. Mark also obtained a patent on the product in Canada, which would last 17 years.

THE PRODUCT

Portable Heat Pad consisted of a vinyl bag containing a sodium acetate solution and a small stainless steel trigger. Activating the trigger caused the solution to crystallize, producing a predictable and constant level of heat. Since the concentration of the sodium acetate solution could be varied, the pad was available in two temperature settings: 47 and 54 degrees Celsius (117 and 130 degrees Fahrenheit). The preset temperature could not be exceeded. The pad gave off heat at its present temperature for about 20 minutes, then started to cool but still produced enough heat to have therapeutic value for up to three hours. Use of the felt cover, which came with the pad, prevented rapid heat loss. The pad could be prepared for reuse by immersing it in boiling water for 15 minutes or autoclaving it in a chemical (but not a steam) autoclaving unit. An autoclaving unit acted in a similar manner to a pressure cooker. The pad could be reused hundreds of times until the vinyl wore out.

The Portable Heat Pad could be marketed in rectangles or squares of various sizes: 20 cm × 45 cm, 20 cm × 20 cm, and 10 cm × 10 cm (8 in. × 18 in., 8 in. × 8 in., and 4 in. × 4 in.), and in the shape of a mitt. The vinyl bags, which would be produced by an outside contractor, were stamped from a die and could be made in virtually any size and shape at an average cost per bag of $1.00. Each die costs about $2,000 (which would be paid for by the Tanner Company). It could be made in less than three weeks, enabling the company to respond quickly to changing market demand. The sodium acetate solution would be purchased from an Ontario supplier at an average cost of $2.00. Portable Heat Pad obtained an inventory of 150,000 triggers, on consignment from the inventor, which did not have to be paid for until the pads were sold. The triggers were required to "start" the Portable Heat Pad the first time it was used. The inventor had guaranteed to provide a future supply of triggers at a cost of $3.00 per unit. The felt covers and packaging were available from local suppliers at a cost per bag of $1.50.

The filling and sealing process was simple and neither labour- nor capital-intensive. This work would be done in the mini-warehouse to maintain quality control. One welder and three unskilled workers could produce 150 pads per hour or 22,000 per month. The combined wages of the welder and three workers would be $75.00 per hour. The company had purchased two welding machines, one as a backup in case of mechanical failures. As production needs increased, new welding machines could be purchased for approximately $15,000 each.

THE MARKET

Shortly after obtaining the rights to Portable Heat Pad, Mark Tanner hired Richard McKay as the marketing manager, at a salary of $80,000 per year. He had extensive sales experience including the introduction of a number of new products to the Canadian market. Richard's first assignment was to conduct an analysis of the market potential for Portable Heat Pad.

Because of Portable Heat Pad's versatility, it could be sold in three broad segments: (1) the medical treatment market, (2) personal warmth (for example, seat cushions, survival clothing, hand warmers), and (3) heating of inanimate objects (for example, food service, industrial equipment). After evaluating these market segments, Richard believed that the medical segment had the greatest potential for the immediate future, and he collected further information on this segment.

The Medical Treatment Market

The application of heat was a well-known treatment for relief from pain and decreased mobility in cases of arthritis and traumatic joint or muscle injury. This market can be divided into two segments: the institutional and the home market.

Within the institutional market there were a number of market subsegments including active treatment hospitals, auxiliary hospitals, nursing homes, and physiotherapy and chiropractic clinics. Richard estimated that the total annual usage for these facilities would be 29,332 units. He arrived at this estimate by phoning 20 hospitals in the Calgary and Edmonton areas and asking how many of these pads of all types would be ordered each year. On average, 24 pads were currently used by each hospital. Using Statistics Canada data he found there were 1,218 hospitals in Canada, and then projected the annual usage rate at 29,332.

Richard felt that the home market would be reached primarily through retail pharmacies and secondarily through medical and surgical supply stores. There are about 2,700 such outlets in Canada, and he estimated demand through them at 189,000. This estimate was based on a telephone survey of 25 retail pharmacies and 10 medical supply stores. He explained the product to each respondent and asked how many he or she might sell in one year. On average, the respondents said they would sell 70 units each year. Based on this information, Richard estimated that the total home-use market was 189,000 pads of all types annually.

As well, Richard believed that three market trends indicated a positive future for Portable Heat Pad. Heat had been under-utilized as a means of treatment because of problems with burns, electrical shocks from heating pads, inconvenience, and high cost. The Portable Heat Pad, with its unique design and features, could surmount these problems. Secondly, the mean age of the Canadian population was rising and the "baby boom" generation was approaching middle age. As people got older, the incidence of arthritis and other associated disorders would increase, leading to more extensive personal use of the Portable Heat Pad. Finally, as more people became fitness-conscious and participated in physical activities, athletic injuries that could be treated with heat would also increase.

Competition

No new products had been introduced in the industry in recent years and market shares were stable among competing firms. Portable Heat Pad would compete with four existing products: electric heating pads, hot water bottles, instant hot packs, and reusable hot packs. Richard prepared a competitive analysis for these products (Exhibit 1). The companies producing these competing products were divisions of large multi-product firms (such as 3M and Johnson & Johnson), fabricated rubber manufacturers, and electrical goods manufacturers.

Electrical heating pads applied controlled heat over large areas of the body. The pads could cause burns, especially in older patients with decreased skin sensitivity. There was a slight electrical shock hazard with the pads and, as they required electricity to operate, they were not truly portable.

Hot water bottles were portable and inexpensive but less convenient to use. The temperature was hard to regulate and heat was lost quickly, requiring frequent refilling. As with electrical heating pads, there was some danger of burns or scalding from hot water.

Instant hot packs worked on an exothermic chemical reaction principle. A larger bag contained water as well as a smaller bag full of chemicals. When the entire bag was crushed the chemicals were released and combined with water to produce heat. These packs were easy to use and were inexpensive. However, they gave off uneven heat that could cause burns and the chemicals were often toxic. They were not reusable.

Reusable hot packs were of two types: institutional and home use. The institutional market leader was the Hydropack, a canvas pack filled with gel that was heated in a steam or hot-water autoclave. The pack was wrapped in towels and applied to the patient. The main advantages of the pack were control (it was available in different sizes and the temperature could be regulated by proper heating) and long equipment life—in excess of 20 years. The disadvantages were the high initial cost, specialized heating equipment that was required, higher laundry bills (due to use of towels), and inability to produce "dry" rather than "moist" heat.

The home-use packs contained chemicals that were activated by hot water or steam. They were portable and provided a controlled temperature, but the heat output was lower and lasted a shorter time than Portable Heat Pad.

Portable Heat Pad had features that made it superior to all these products. It was truly portable, easy to use, and did not require specialized equipment. The temperature was absolutely controlled to reduce the possibility of burns, there were no toxic chemicals involved, and the pad produced therapeutic heat levels for up to three hours.

Based on his assessment of the competitive products, Richard believed that with a good marketing program Portable Heat Pad could achieve a market share of up to 50 percent. However, he knew that this was a guesstimate at best, and the actual market share obtained might be quite different. In particular, he was concerned about the need to change traditional patterns of use.

Focus Groups

To initiate some ideas as to how to market the product, Richard conducted five focus-group sessions. The five groups consisted of three groups of consumers who were likely users (for example, people suffering from arthritis, people in extended-care facilities, and physiotherapists). In each session, people were shown a sample of the product and asked about its uses, important features, suggested selling price, and where it should be sold. Selected results from the focus groups are provided in Exhibit 2.

INITIAL MARKETING IDEAS

Based on his analysis of the market, competition, and focus-group results, Richard developed a preliminary marketing plan for Portable Heat Pad. He felt that the product could have a retail price of $40, which was in line with the price consumers appeared willing to pay for a reusable pad with Portable Heat Pad's features. Retailers would probably expect a margin of 25 percent on retail selling price.

Successful marketing of Portable Heat Pad in both the institutional and home markets probably required acceptance by the medical profession. In the institutional market the physician must order the heat treatments before there would be a demand for the pads. The home user often bought products on the basis of a doctor's recommendation.

Existing competitive products were marketed through three distributors. Canadian Hospital Products was the only Canadian company that distributed to the institutional market. The company prided itself on carrying Canadian-made products. Northern Medical was a national distributor that would distribute the pad to pharmacies and surgical supply stores. In Quebec there was resistance to a product distributed from outside the province, and because of this, a Quebec distributor would be chosen. All three distributors would require margins of 15 percent on their selling price. Richard considered adding three salespeople to push the distribution of the product; each salesperson would be responsible for servicing either the home, institutional, or Quebec market. Salary and travel expenses for each salesperson were estimated at $60,000 per year.

Richard was uncertain about advertising but knew that the institutional market could be accessed on two levels: through the doctors and other medical personnel and through advertising aimed at purchasing agents for hospitals, nursing homes, and clinics. Considering the home market, promotional considerations would include the type of packaging and the product literature enclosed, as well as the type of advertising that would best reach the home market, which is composed primarily of older people.

Based on the information he had collected, Richard began preparing a marketing plan for Portable Heat Pad. He was optimistic about the success of the venture and looked forward to presenting the plan for approval to Mark Tanner.

EXHIBIT 1 | Competitive Analysis

Product type	Safety	Temperature Control	Selling Price	Heat Retention	Portability, Convenience	Weight Pliability
Electric Heat Pad	Burn and shock possible	Controlled, even	$20+	Indefinite	Fair, needs electricity	Fair
Hot Water Bottle	Burn possible	Uneven	$8+	15-25 min.	Fair, needs refilling	Poor
Instant Hot Pack	Burns, toxic	Uneven	$4+	10-20 min.	Good	Poor
Reusable Hot Pack	Good	Good	$60	35-40 min.	Fair, needs reheating	Fair
Home Pack	Good	Low heat	$3	15-25 min.	Good	Fair
Portable Heat Pad	Good	Good	$40	3 hours	Good	Very good

EXHIBIT 2 | Summary of Focus-Group Discussions

The summary is grouped into three categories: (1) consumers as users (particularly the arthritic and home market); (2) the institutional market (extended-care facilities and hospitals); and (3) the physiotherapy group (personal and sports-related use).

1. The Consumer Market

Key Uses

a. Substitution for other sources of heat.

b. Apply heat to ease the pain.

c. Arthritic users indicate that the pain is so substantial they will try anything on the market to seek relief.

(Continued on next page)

EXHIBIT 2	Summary of Focus-Group Discussions (continued)

    d. Arthritic users tend to be sensitive to the word "arthritic," thus anything that indicates relief will catch their attention. This is true with respect to advertisements, packages, discussions on talk shows, meetings with other arthritics, word of mouth, etc.

    e. Major use occurs at any time but there was substantial interest in the fact that the product could be used in the night without significant preparation.

Key Product Features

    a. Portability and controlled heat.

    b. Variable temperature at purchase time (product line question).

    c. Flat product—very useful when user is lying down.

    d. Product durability.

    e. Reusable, therefore only pennies per use.

    f. Length of time heat lasts, particularly when covered in a towel, was viewed to be very positive.

    g. Product could be packed in a suitcase or purse and used when travelling (in a car, plane, etc.).

    h. Product is safe to use (unlike the hot wax treatment for arthritis).

    i. Product is flexible and can be shaped to meet the user's needs.

    j. The product does not leak (unlike a hot water bottle).

Price

    a. Arthritics were prepared to spend in the order of $40 retail for the product.

    b. The group indicated a warranty would be critical to the initial purchase decision.

    c. Some felt a towel cover could be provided for an additional sum.

Outlet

The majority of the group felt the product would be best suited to availability in a drug store or a department store. The great advantage of the department store was the implicit guarantee provided by the store as part of its retail policy.

2. The Institutional Market

The discussion with people in the extended-care facilities indicated that they received treatment from the central physiotherapy units. In addition, many were arthritic and indicated they would like to have such a product in their room for use during the night. A major factor in the new product is safety and reliability with respect to temperature control. This is particularly significant for older people because of a reduction in sensitivity to temperature on their skin (they tend to like heat that is too strong and thus harmful to the skin).

(Continued on next page)

| EXHIBIT 2 | Summary of Focus-Group Discussions (continued) |

The major entry would be through the purchasing activity of the institutions. Individual pads may be acquired but payment would be personal. Price is thus a major factor for older people on restricted incomes.

Product acquisition varied greatly depending on whether the individual worked in a private clinic or in a hospital. Nurses who attended a focus group earlier also made the distinctions. That is, the staff who use the product are important to the decision, but the central purchasing group also assumes a key role. It was indicated that the major factor in the minds of central purchasing people in the institution was the ability to show cost effectiveness, and advice was given to use this part of the presentation to individual buyers for institutions. The private clinics indicated that they also consider cost-effectiveness and would look at the new product as the supply of existing heating pads was used up.

3. Physiotherapists

The focus group with physiotherapists indicated that they spend substantial amounts of money on heating pads and are looking for cost-effective products.

Use

a. Useful where heat is the treatment medium.

b. Use in emergency cases of hypothermia.

c. Do not use in cases of inflammation or where internal bleeding may be present.

d. Use in cases of inflammation after an initial treatment period where ice was used as the treatment medium.

e. Good potential for treatment of seniors because of temperature control, which is essential due to poor circulation.

f. Good potential for in-home use after physiotherapy treatment program.

Benefits

a. Convenient.

b. Cost-effective.

c. Safety due to constant temperature (point made was that heat is damaging; ice will not damage the skin because the person will stop using the ice due to the cold).

d. Warranty is essential to remove product liability from the user, particularly the user in private clinics. In essence they indicated a need to guarantee treatment time and product life.

HMV.com

Gordon H. G. McDougall

The Smashing Pumpkins promotion was in the back of her mind as Sara Ross, HMV.com's Internet Marketing Manager, reviewed the latest Web statistics with Jennifer Lipishan, HMV's Internet Marketing Coordinator. "Jennifer, what do you think about that Pumpkins promotion, you know we only sold four CDs online." "Yes," said Jennifer, "but we got over 16,000 hits and over 1,000 people entered the contest. And we sold a ton of CDs in the stores." Sara replied, "But we don't get paid for in-store sales. I know we generated a lot of publicity but how can I tell what's a successful promotion? We run at least five promotions every month. How can we tell which ones are successful?" "I agree," said Jennifer, "it's very difficult to sort out the impact of any particular promotion. We get too many reports, we deal with a lot of companies who measure traffic and create promotions for us, and it's hard to get an overall picture of what is going on."

Sara paused for a moment and then said, "I've got five promotions to sort out this week, we're planning a new affiliates program, we've got lots of data but it's hard to make sense of it. Jennifer, would you please pull some facts and figures together on what we have in the way of information and let's decide what are the key measures we should be looking at and where we should be going. The key statistics should help guide our strategy.

"We have some broad objectives here—driving traffic to the site, converting that traffic to sales, and helping HMV Canada maintain its leadership position in the retail music business. I know that a lot of customers use HMV.com for information then go to one of our stores and buy CDs. So we are getting sales in the end, I just don't know how many."

Jennifer replied, "I'll do that. It should take about a week." With that, Sara went to her second meeting of the day to discuss three promotions HMV.com and HMV were considering, and Jennifer went to talk to Dan Winkley, HMV.com's Content Manager, about some new banner ads they were planning for next week.

HMV

Beginning with one store in the United Kingdom more than 75 years ago, HMV now has more than 275 stores worldwide and is the world's premier music retailer. The first major period of growth came in the 1960s, culminating with the opening of HMV's 50,000-square-foot flagship store in London in 1986. At the time, this was the world's largest record store. The UK-based chain was able to successfully export the brand, and chains were established in eight other regions, principally in North America and Southeast Asia. Currently, HMV's international operations include stores in the United Kingdom, the United States, Ireland, Germany, Australia, Hong Kong, Japan, Singapore, and Canada.

For the past decade HMV had opened an average of ten new stores each year. Store sizes had generally been getting larger to accommodate the vast product range that HMV is known for stocking, while the advent of video sales served only to enhance the demand for increased trading space.

Until 1998, HMV was a part of the EMI Group, the world's third-largest music company (behind the Universal Music Group and Sony Music Entertainment). It markets its music through well-known record labels including Capitol Records, Chrysalis, and Virgin. EMI is also the world's largest music publisher, controlling more than one million copyrights. In March 1998, HMV was sold to form a new retail concern—the HMV Media Group—which also comprises the Waterstones and Dillons book chains in the United Kingdom. The EMI Group has a 42.6-percent investment in the HMV Media Group.

HMV Media Group is the world's largest specialist retailer of recorded music and the leading specialist retailer of books in the UK. By 2000 the Group operated 278 HMV music stores and 206 bookstores, with a combined annual revenue in excess of $2 billion (US). During 1999 HMV launched fully transactional Web sites in North America, the UK, and Japan.

HMV CANADA

In 1987, HMV began global expansion with a move into the Canadian marketplace, with the first store opening at Square One in Mississauga, Ontario. Since that time, HMV Canada has expanded to a current total of 96 stores and more than 2,000 employees from coast to coast. HMV Canada has a 20-percent share of the Canadian music market (the sixth largest in the world, with close to 50 million CDs shipped annually and total annual retail sales of more than $1 billion). Its major competitors include Sam the Record Man, A&B Sound, Music World, Virgin Records, and Tower Records.

As part of the HMV Group, HMV Canada is a leader in music retailing in terms of product selection, product knowledge, dedication to service quality, image and profile, style and design, and marketing and promotion. Every store offers a full range of titles, and the superstores are completely equipped for live performances. HMV's goal is to be the most successful retailer in the world by making sure that its stores offer the customer the same fun, energy, and excitement that is expressed in the music itself. As evidence of its leadership, HMV Canada has won "Music Retailer of the Year" for 12 consecutive years.

HMV.COM

With the development of the Internet and HMV's desire to be a revolutionary in the music retail industry, the decision was made in 1996 to go online. Over the next three years a substantial investment was made in infrastructure to build the online model. The site was developed in the United Kingdom with the plan that each country, including Canada, would use the "skeleton" and create a local interface.

The site was built in partnership with IBM using the existing AS/400 IBM platform at HMV. HMV had used the AS/400 for ten years, running business-critical applications such as stock and range management, catalogue management, product information, finance, fulfillment, and customer service. The main business challenge was to integrate e-commerce with its physical stores, to the benefit of both parts of the business. To achieve a truly effective Internet presence, HMV needed to have a secure, robust, and scalable solution, which they could also roll out worldwide. HMV used its existing infrastructure and its existing skills in AS/400 as much as possible to minimize the costs and workload.

Having customers order through the Internet allows HMV to better monitor its customers' view. "This is very important and it is a great advantage for HMV. Asking our customers what they think of our services through a simple form over the Internet and seeing how much they spend and on what helps us understand their requirement and expectations, and therefore [helps us] shape our future strategy," explained Duncan Bell, Business Technology Director at HMV Media Group.

HMV.COM CANADA

Canada was the first country to go online with HMV.com. HMV Canada had received approval in November 1998 and went online in July 1999. Among the challenges facing HMV.com was to ensure that a continuing synergy existed between HMV.com and the HMV stores. Both online and offline would support and "market" each other. As well, the gathering and analyzing of data to improve their Internet strategy was an important goal.

By September 2000 HMV.com had grown to a staff of 20 plus a Fulfillment Group of seven (all online orders were filled from a dedicated warehouse in Mississauga, Ontario). The HMV.com group was located in Etobicoke, a Toronto suburb. Reflecting the culture of HMV and the music world, many of the staff were young, enthusiastic, and innovative. The HMV.com Canada team received considerable support from the HMV Media Group (UK) in terms of coding and content. The Group also provided support for the HMV.com sites in Australia and Japan. As well, the sites for the UK, Australia, and Japan were launched based on knowledge gained from the Canadian experience.

As Internet Marketing Manager, Sara Ross helped launch the HMV.com site. Her background included a B.Comm. from McMaster University, brand management at Hershey Canada, Internet marketing and sales experience (working with companies that included Sony Music, MuchMusic, and CityTV), and Web development at Cyberplex (a software firm specializing in Web design). In broad terms, Sara has had experience in online promotions and has knowledge of e-commerce, traditional marketing, and the music industry.

Sara provided strategic direction in all aspects of marketing, advertising, promotions, and partner relations for HMV online. Part of her mandate was to drive traffic to the site, understand the consumers, and encourage purchases as well as integrate the online business with the bricks-and-mortar HMV stores. At times this was difficult, as some of the HMV retail group were not convinced that HMV.com resulted in extra business for HMV. They felt that HMV.com was cannibalizing some store sales.

Among the challenges faced by HMV.com Canada were limited resources, including a budget of less than $1 million for marketing. From Sara's view, this meant a reliance on co-op advertising as an important marketing component. The HMV.com team was constantly seeking to obtain co-op funds from record labels, like Warner Music, to promote specific artists or CDs online. It was a struggle because it was unfamiliar ground for many, including some record labels, who didn't see the value in banner ads or other online promotions. Further, the record labels saw HMV and HMV.com as one entity, so if a label, like Sony, had already invested in a promotion with HMV, it didn't perceive HMV.com as a separate entity with different needs and opportunities than a retail store.

Because of the budget, Sara didn't do a lot of offline marketing. One online tactic was permission-based marketing. A weekly newsletter called *HMV.communique*, which users signed up for, was e-mailed to roughly 70,000 registered users, providing them with alerts on special offers, contests, and events. Other tactics (see Exhibit 7) included Webcasts (using HMV3.web.com, a free Internet service provided to consumers who used HMV3.web.com as their home page), online specials, and contests.

HMV.com buyers were slightly older than those at the HMV stores; while the younger market used HMV.com for information, in general they preferred to buy at the stores. A recent exit survey of HMV retail customers found that while only 9 percent of respondents said they buy at HMV.com, 22 percent used the site to browse online and then buy in the store. Further, many young music-buying consumers did not have credit cards, a prerequisite for purchasing online.

As Internet Marketing Coordinator for HMV.com, Jennifer Lipishan coordinated the marketing, promotions, and advertising for HMV.com with the record labels, partner sites, and other HMV departments. After graduating from Wilfrid Laurier University with a B.B.A., Jennifer started her career at Microforum (a software and e-business solutions company) as a project coordinator focusing on the Ford of Canada account. She played an integral role in launching and implementing the Ford Dealer Web sites, as well as many dealer incentive programs, helping to boost overall Ford sales and push them one e-step forward into cyberspace. Since joining HMV.com in early 2000, one of Jennifer's goals was to make Internet shopping second nature to shoppers, introducing and exposing new and exciting music to music lovers while keeping HMV.com Canadian Music's E-tailer of the Year.

PREPARATION FOR THE MEETING

In preparation for the meeting with Jennifer, Sara made the following notes:

- The dynamics of the music industry (continual promotions—both on- and offline), the concept of HMV.com and HMV stores focusing on the same goal, and Web measurement issues made it difficult to sort out the effectiveness of an individual campaign or promotion.

- Given the many different creative approaches that can be used in the banner ads, the multitude of artists that could be promoted and the many different sites where the promotions/ads could be placed, is there a method, or at least an approach, to sorting out the effectiveness of any strategy or tactic?

- How should the budget be allocated among online, offline, and partnerships?

- What are the best ways of creating awareness of HMV.com?

- A primary objective is to drive traffic to the site. What are the most effective methods of doing that?

- What alliances/affiliates/advertising partners are most effective at driving traffic to the site?

- What are the most important Web statistics that we should use to answer these questions?

- What measures should we use to link traffic to sales?

In her preparation for the meeting, Jennifer first examined a number of the Web statistic reports that HMV.com received and made some observations. First, each of the affiliates/advertising partners used different reporting methods, thus making it difficult to compare the results of any given campaign or advertising partner. Second, because the banner ads were frequently changed to keep both the site and the look "fresh," it was difficult to track the impact of a specific banner ad. Third, because the format of the online ads varied (banners versus buttons, text versus graphics, top of page versus middle or bottom), determining campaign or tactic effectiveness was difficult. Fourth, the home page of HMV.com (Exhibit 2) was changed three times a day to keep it "fresh" and to encourage users to return to the site, which meant that any campaign could also be affected by the home page changes. Finally, because HMV and HMV.com jointly ran many of the promotions and campaigns, it was difficult to attribute the results to either group.

Jennifer also visited the sites of four Web-tracking services to review what types of information they provided. The sites were NetTracker (www.sane.com); Funnel Web (www.quest.com/funnel_web/); Nedstat Pro (www.nedstat.com/usa); and Webtrends (www.webtrends.com). While she believed one of these firms might provide more focused reports than those now used by HMV.com, she decided to put this idea on hold.

Jennifer then selected the reports she believed were important or representative of the information that HMV.com received:

- Sympatico.ca tracking report (Exhibit 1)—example of a monthly traffic report from Sympatico.ca (a major partner).

- HMV.com Weekly Statistics (Exhibit 3)—the main report that summarized the weekly activity at HMV.com (11-Dec-99 is included for comparison purposes).

- Referral Report (Exhibit 4)—where users of HMV.com come from.

- HMV.com's Major Partners/Affiliates (Exhibit 5)—the major partners that HMV.com used to drive traffic to the site. The contracts/fees with each partner varied; Sympatico.ca, Virtual Marketplace, and Telus (which included MyWinnipeg.com, MyBC.com, MyAlberta.com, and MyToronto.com) were based on a flat fee; Canadashop.com fees were based on number of impressions; and Norstar Mall was based on a performance fee per click-through.

- Smashing Pumpkins Promotion (Exhibit 6)—a report prepared by Tone Interactive (an Internet promotion firm that handled advertising placements, contests, and measurements), which assisted HMV.com in a promotion.

- Monthly Marketing Summary (Exhibit 7)—an example of the marketing activities for HMV.com in a month. Jennifer estimated that in an average week there would be eight changes to the site (e.g., changes to banner ads, new promotions, etc.). She calculated that from July to October 2000, 25 contests were run, at least one major campaign was run each month, and various partnerships were used to run contests, campaigns, or special ads.

- Affiliate Marketing Summary (Exhibit 8)—the proposed affiliate plan, prepared by Jason Stainton, on HMV.com's revised affiliate plans. Jason, the new affiliate coordinator, had prepared this plan in late October 2000.

In reviewing the Web tracking service reports Jennifer made the following notes:

- A one-month Christmas campaign run by Adsmart (an Internet service firm that placed ads on various sites for clients) that targeted financial Web sites (Toronto Stock Exchange, Small Cap Centre, Fund Library, etc.) generated 221,127 impressions and 319 clicks, for a click rate of .14 percent. A recent study of click-through rates in the U.S. showed the average click rate across a wide range of firms was .39 percent.

- On average, over a three-month period the click rate on MyWinnipeg.com was .29 percent.

- A report by Tone Interactive on a campaign (HMV 2 Hit Me) on five sites (including Yahoo.ca, Canoe.ca, Star.com, and Tribute.ca) generated 160,679 impressions and 1,067 clicks, for a click rate of .66 percent and 81 hits on HMV.com's home page.

- A report by DoubleClick showed a click rate of .42 percent, and a report by AltaVista showed a click rate of 1.28 percent.

- The Smashing Pumpkins contest (Exhibit 6) generated 16,190 hits to the home page, 1,275 hits to the order form, 43 hits to process an order, and 4 hits to complete an order. There were 1,285 hits to the contest entry and 202 hits to process the contest entry. There were 1,320 hits to download the song.

THE MEETING

A week later when Sara and Jennifer met, Sara presented her notes and then Jennifer discussed her observations and went through each of the reports (Exhibits 1 and 3–7). Sara said, "Okay, let's figure out what our main goals should be, what information we need to evaluate, whether or not we are achieving our goals, what information we have and what we need." "Agreed," said Jennifer, "and I think we should keep the goals straightforward to begin—how do we drive traffic to the site and who are the best affiliates to work with. I think that Jason's report [Exhibit 8] is a starting point for the affiliates issue." "Sounds good," replied Sara. "Let's get to it."

EXHIBIT 1	Tracking Report Prepared by Sympatico.ca for HMV.com

SYMPATICO
HMV
Campaign run dates: Mar 1 – Dec 31/00   Promotion Item = http://www.hmv.ca

Campaign Overview

	Week	Page	Page Impressions	Click-Throughs	Yield
Banners	Mar 1-Aug 8	Various	932,182	4,956	0.53%
Buttons/Links	Mar 1-Sep 5	Shopping	709,917	4,285	0.80%
Ad Box/Button	Mar 1-Sep 5	A&E	485,047	3,596	0.74%
Ad Box	May 5-June 6	Health	151,674	419	0.28%
Ad Box/Button	May 12-Aug 22	Kids & Teens	35,165	2,049	5.83%
Button	Mar 1-Sep 5	Home & Family	101,258	334	0.33%
Button	July 12-Aug 22	Food & Drink	24,447	132	0.54%
Button	July 12-Aug 22	Automotive	132,343	334	0.25%
Button	July 12-Sep 5	Travel	297,497	966	0.32%
Page	July 12-Aug 8	Summer Collection	83,840	974	1.16%
Ad Box	Aug 16-Sep 5	Personal Finance	117,968	188	0.16%
Ad Box	Aug 16-Sep 5	Sports	47,820	449	0.94%
Button	Aug 23-Sep 5	Computers	1,553	12	0.77%
Total Banners, Buttons/Links, Ad Boxes			**3,120,711**	**18,694**	**0.60%**

Page		Mar-00	Apr-00	May-00	Jun-00	Jul-00	Aug-00	TOTAL
Shopping Text Link	Impressions	74,287	62,648	61,491	48,457	61,776	74,744	383,403
	Click-throughs	433	430	327	245	229	317	1981
	Yield	0.58%	0.69%	0.53%	0.51%	0.37%	0.42%	0.52%
Shopping Button	Page impressions	101,969	–	93,380	72,513	89,345	95,027	452,234
	Click-throughs	25	–	78	564	966	521	2,154
	Yield	0.02%	–	0.08%	0.78%	1.08%	0.55%	0.50%
	Total page impressions	176,256	62,648	154,871	120,970	151,123	169,771	835,639
	Total click-throughs	458	430	405	809	1,195	838	4,135
	Total yield	0.26%	0.69%	0.25%	0.67%	0.79%	0.49%	0.52%

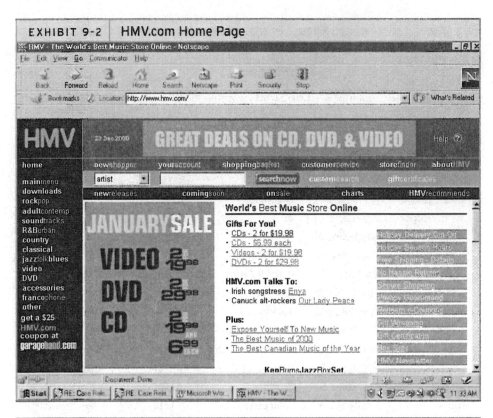

EXHIBIT 9-2 | HMV.com Home Page

EXHIBIT 3	HMV.com Weekly Statistics

HMV.COM

Week Ending:	11-Dec-99	02-Sep-00	09-Sep-00	16-Sep-00
Number of Hits for Home Page	113,723	129,060	128,455	146,009
Number of Successful Hits for Entire Site	4,221,514	5,349,517	5,054,489	5,697,323
Number of Page Views (Impressions)	1,708,962	1,953,497	1,901,093	2,165,986
Number of Document Views	1,302,126	1,501,742	1,462,931	1,614,579
Number of User Sessions	93,034	152,714	150,657	152,634
Average Number of Hits Per Day	603,073	764,216	722,069	813,903
Average Number of Page Views Per Day	244,353	279,109	271,617	309,466
Average Number of User Sessions Per Day	13,290	21,816	21,522	21,804
Average User Session Length	00:12:32	00:11:14	00:10:51	00:11:31
Number of Unique Users	41,860	72,844	70,986	77,086
Number of Users Who Visited Once	41,860	57,750	56,007	61,608
Number of Users Who Visited More Than Once in a Week	8,251	15,094	14,979	15,748
Number of Orders Placed	N/A	1,873	1,637	1,905
Conversion Rate	N/A	2.57%	2.31%	2.47%

EXHIBIT 3	HMV.com Weekly Statistics (continued)

Notes:

1. Number of hits for home page: The total number of visitors to HMV.com during the week– this was an unreliable measure as the hits counted include all the files that were loaded including text and graphics for a page; therefore one page could include 25 hits.

2. Number of successful hits for entire site: Successful hits are the number of times people have viewed a page or downloaded a file

3. Number of successful page views (impressions): Amount of time a user hits an HTML page (access to non-HTML documents are not counted)

4. Number of document views: Number of times a user hits a non-HTML page

5. Number of user sessions: Number of sessions of activity (all hits) for one user of a Web site

6. Average number of hits per day: Number of successful hits/7

7. Average number of page views per day: Number of successful page views/7

8. Average number of user sessions per day: Number of user sessions/7

9. Average user session length: Average time spent at site by user

10. Number of unique users: Number of different users

11. Number of users who visited once: Self-explanatory

12. Number of users who visited more than once: Self-explanatory

EXHIBIT 4	Weekly Referral Report[1]

	Site	Referrals		Site	Referrals
1	http://hmv.com/	34,718	13	http://www.sonymusic.ca/	30
2	http://www.myhmv3web.com/	8,030	14	http://www.canada.com/	75
3	http://www.telus.net/	2,613	15	http://members.home.net/	12
4	http://lw3fd.law3.hotmail.msn.com/	824	16	http://w1.111.telia.com/	161
5	http://lw8fd.law8.hotmail.msn.com/	708	17	http://www.listen.com/	92
6	http://lw7fd.law7.hotmail.msn.com/	700	18	http://artists.mp3s.com/	36
7	http://www.1.sympatico.ca/	648	19	http://ca.yahoo.com/	97
8	http://lw4fd.law4.hotmail.msn.com/	630	20	http://www.showbizz.net/	95
9	http://lw2fd.hotmail.msn.com/	620		Subtotal for the referring sites above	50,082
10	http://www.mybc.com/	591		Total for the Log File	64,046
11	http://www.alberta.com/	246			
12	http://lw1fd.hotmail.msn.com/	521			

[1] To be read: 34,178 users came directly to HMV.com; 2,613 users came from http://www.telus.net/. In any given week, the number of referrals from any given site could change significantly, depending on the promotions run that week. For example, if HMV.com was running a specific ad box on sympatico.ca, HMV.com would get more clicks from that site during the promotion period.

EXHIBIT 5	HMV.com Partner Specifications Summary

Site	Site Location	Ad Space
Telus – includes:		
MyWinnipeg.com	www.mywinnipeg.com	468×60 banners
MyBC.com	www.mybc.com	468×60 banners
MyAlberta.com	www.myalberta.com	468×60 banners
MyToronto.com	www.mytoronto.com	468×60 banners
Sympatico	www.sympatico.ca	468×60
		120×60
		120×90
		Text ads (280×22)
Virtual Market Place	www.vmp.com/browse.asp?top-category=10	HMV storefront
	www.vmp.com	120×30 HMV button
		5 80×80 featured products
Canadashop.com	www.canadashop.com	120×70 button
		486×60 banners
	www.canadashop.com/directory.htm?cat=9	HMV storefront
Norstar Mall	www.norstarmall.com	468×60 banners
Excite.ca	www.excite.ca	468×60 banners
		190×35 banners
		100×30 test box
		Text link
Virtuecast	www.virtuecast.com	468×60 banner
HMV3WEB	www.myhmv3web.com	5 featured product
		1 120×60 ad button
		1 perpetual link

Note: A 468×60 banner is approximately 12 centimetres by 2 centimetres and is defined as a full banner. Banners are measured in pixels. A pixel is the smallest part of the video screen that can be turned on or off or varied in intensity.

EXHIBIT 6	Tone Interactive–Smashing Pumpkins Campaign

Campaign Background

The Objective

HMV.com, a leading music retailer, approached Tone Interactive in order to build its brand awareness and equity through an interactive ad campaign targeting young adults. The specific means by which HMV wanted to obtain its campaign goals was by stimulating excitement around the much-anticipated Smashing Pumpkins CD prior to its retail release.

EXHIBIT 6	Tone Interactive–Smashing Pumpkins Campaign (continued)

The Solution

In conjunction with HMV, Tone Interactive developed an interactive campaign that integrated both the branding and the ad-based commerce efforts into one interactive ad. A popular Smashing Pumpkins sound clip was placed in the ad. This brief sound clip played once the ad loaded on its Web page, a tactic that attracted the attention of the campaign's desired demographic. When an interested user clicked on the ad (a mini Web site), it expanded to offer the options of listening to a preview of the track, pre-ordering the CD (which included an exclusive six-track CD sampler, all hand-picked by Billy Corgan, the leader of the Smashing Pumpkins), or entering an e-mail address to win tickets for a Smashing Pumpkins concert.

Tone Interactive's detailed campaign reporting also assisted HMV in tracking and researching their target demographic. When the consumer interacted with the rich media ad, Tone Interactive tracked user information such as state/province, media placement (which site the user was on when they saw the ad), time of day, and type of browser. This allowed HMV to develop a much richer and actionable demographic database.

The Results

Results of the campaign clearly met the objectives. HMV raised awareness of its presence on the Internet and positioned itself as an innovator via its use of this progressive media. Click-through rates were significantly higher than for standard gif banners. Excitement was also generated around the release of the new Smashing Pumpkins CD by allowing people to sample the album's music and enter a promotion. Finally, HMV was able to create an extensive database of permission-based profiles including the names, e-mail addresses, and phone numbers of consumers.

Source: www.ToneInteractive.com

EXHIBIT 7	HMV.com Marketing Summary for March 2000

Campaigns

Hit Me Campaign (Feb. 7–Mar. 12)

Advertising on: Canoe.ca, Thestar.com, tribute.ca, Norstar Mall, excite.ca, Canada.com

Contest: Win a trip for two to see Smashing Pumpkins live somewhere in North America; 2,329 entries

Testing java e-banners (Pumpkins) and audio-banners

Featured Artist

Joni Mitchell

Contest: Win a limited-edition *Classic Love Songs* box set; 152 entries

EXHIBIT 7	HMV.com Marketing Summary for March 2000 (continued)

Canadian Music Week (Mar. 1-5)

Sponsorship and $10 HMV.com coupon for 1,500 delegates in bag

Clicks and Mortar seminar sponsored by HMV.com

Panel Speakers: Andrew/Frank/Mike/Sara

Natalie MacMaster live Webcast from CMW, March 3, promoted on Rounders.com, to Natalie fan base and Natalie site

Signage in Clicks and Mortar room, Internet stage for Natalie, registration lobby, conference lobby

HMVexposed

Flyers in HMV.com customer shipments

Micro-site built, McMaster & James Tour Diary

March Campaign (Mar. 27-Apr. 23)

100 Titles $9.99 Sale

HMV.com centre spread in instore flyer

Contests

Oscar DVD Player Giveaway (Mar. 13-26)

386 contest entries/7 correct answers

Contest: Predict the Big 5 Oscar Winners on HMV.com

Grand Prize: DVD player; secondary prizes three sets of Oscar-winning soundtracks

Juno Awards Contest on HMV.com (Feb. 16-Mar. 7)

1,287 contest entries

Grand Prize: airfare from anywhere in Canada to Toronto, two-night stay at the Crowne Plaza, 1 set of Juno tickets, $200 HMV.com gift certificate, $100 gift certificate to Al Frisco's

Visa (Mar. 1-May 1)

2000 Olympic Promotion with five other online retailers

Award a prize of one/month on site for three months.

Visa picks a time and the consumer closest to that time gets their purchase free.

Marketing is free: statement insert (13.5 million card users), banners on site, TV support, advertising on statement

20th-Century Masters (Feb. 16-Mar. 16)

Contest with Autoguide.net; win an entire Masters collection from HMV.com

EXHIBIT 7	HMV.com Marketing Summary for March 2000 (continued)

Oasis/Athlete's World Contest (Feb. 29–Mar. 20)

HMV.com as entry point for instore contest

Kathy Smith Bag Giveaway (until Mar. 9)

Banners on MyWinnipeg.com and Sympatico.com (10,000 impressions)

26 sold

Mystery Tour (Mar. 15–Apr. 30)

Bruce Springsteen contest giveaway with Bell Mobility and Canada.com

Prizing—box for Springsteen at ACC, Canada.com leather jacket, HMV.com gift certificates

Promotion in Bell Mobility stores, site, Canada.com, HMV.com, and .com Direct to Customer packages

National Post ads in Ontario and Quebec: March 23, 30, April 4, 11, 18

Rogers AT&T (Mar. 20–Apr. 30)

Contest for each call made during the six weeks, customers receive one ballot in a $50,000 sweepstakes. First prize is three trips. Second prize is 10 home-electronics packages.

HMV.com provides 25 prizes of a free CD per month for a year (12 CDs total/winner)

Get tagged on direct mail (850,000)

Pre-orders

WWF "Aggression" Pre-order (Feb. 23–Mar. 28)

Value-add: Dog tag

WWF posters in *Toronto Sun*

5 pre-orders

NSYNC (Mar. 4–20)

Value-add: Trading cards

$5,000 for NSYNC Keyword Campaign

126 Pre-orders

Star Wars Episode 1

Value-add: Limited edition pins

141 WDS/50 PS pre-orders

Supergrass (Mar. 27–Apr. 4)

Value-add: 5 exclusive bonus tracks

EXHIBIT 7	HMV.com Marketing Summary for March 2000 (continued)

19 sold to date

Headstones (Mar. 29-...)
Value-add: Autographed copy of *Nickels for Your Nightmares*

17 sold to date

Direct-to-Customer Shipments
500 Soul Decision postcards

2,000 Bell Mobility Browse to Win flyers

HMV Exposed catalogue

Webcasts
McMaster & James Webcast from Square One—Mar. 13, 1:30
Handed out flyers at event to draw fans back to the archive

Liquid Audio track "Thank you" promo download free for 30 days, expires after 7 days

Webcast features pictures from Square One instore, performance, and Virtuecast fan-question-based interview and HMV.com ID

Banners running on Excite home page, Sympatico.ca, vmp.com, and Canada.com

Yonge and Eg Opening
Soul Decision Webcast—50 postcards and 400 stickers distributed at the event

Ivana Santilli Webcast

Advertising
CMW Tour & Session Guide Directory, full page 4-colour [trade ad]

RPM CMW issue, half page black + pink [trade ad]

CMW Consumer Guide, full page 4-colour [consumer ad]

2000 Official Juno Program, full page [page 3] 4-colour [consumer ad]

Chart magazine, March issue, full page 4-colour [consumer ad]

Sympatico, NetLife: March issue, Music and the Internet

Shift magazine—April/May Issue: Music on the Internet edition

Now magazine—Feb. 16 issue (Afro Cuban All Stars); Mar. 2 (CMW)

Now Magazine—Free Ad, congratulating Juno winners

National Post ads Ontario and Quebec: Mar. 23, 30, Apr. 4, 11, 18

EXHIBIT 7	HMV.com Marketing Summary for March 2000 (continued)

Speaking Engagements

Online to Profit Conference—Mar. 10

E-retail Conference—Mar. 1

Wilfrid Laurier MBA Class—Mar. 16

Partnerships and Sponsorships

Partnerships

Sympatico Lycos

Deal signed, press release needs to be written

Starting relationship March–May (banners, Top 10s and features, e.g., automotive)

May include new content and utility from Lycos (e.g., keyword searches, chat, etc.)

3WEB/HMV

Greater Toronto Area, HMV stores sell install CDs for $9.95, customers receive free Internet access

Branded with HMV.com irremovable banner, 5 feature spots on 3web.net, space for an HMV.com commercial.

Sponsorships

MyWinnipeg.com: Best of Winnipeg 3 CD giveaway

Campuskiss.com: Two $40 gift certificates; 8 prizes of $20 gift certificates

Sympatico.ca: Gift certificates for referring people—Employee Incentive Program

National Post Online: $100 Gift Certificate Prize for Information Highways 2000 Conference

Bizrate Surveys—Certified Gold Merchant

News Coverage and Press Releases

News Coverage

Venture re: Adpulse audio/Java partners for Pumpkins banner

BusinessNews: featuring Reciprocal and HMV.com, filmed in an HMV NY store

Press Releases

E-tailer of the Year

Soul Decision Webcast (distributed by Universal)

McMaster & James Webcast (distributed by BMG)

3 Web Partnership Announcement (distributed by Cybersurf)

EXHIBIT 8	Affiliate Marketing Summary

Affiliate Marketing Overview

Prepared by Jason Stainton, Affiliate Coordinator, HMV.com

Affiliate marketing is a very new yet effective way of directing traffic and sales to your site. The "pay for performance" method of marketing has opened new doors to building successful partnerships in the online community. Affiliate marketing has been measured as being one of the most effective online marketing techniques; it is rated equal to the effectiveness of e-mail marketing to a current customer base.

Given the relatively young age of affiliate marketing, many companies that have seen these statistics have jumped into the game fast and furious, thinking that by maximizing their affiliate numbers they will maximize their affiliated revenues. Yes and no... Forrester reported finding from the companies they interviewed that many had management headaches, with too few people to manage a large number of participants and an affiliate program where 80 percent of the revenue came from less than 20 percent of the affiliates. This type of information has prompted people in the industry to rethink affiliate marketing in a way that we can concentrate on raising conversion rates while keeping the program costs and management headaches to a minimum. The recommendation is good affiliate software that enables you to customize your relationship while providing a well-thought-out program. This program should cater to the affiliates that are best targeted to drive your sales and have all the tools available for affiliates to self-manage a portion of the relationship effectively.

E-Commerce Partners: HMV's Plan

It is HMV's plan to build a strategic network of e-commerce partners. We have invested in iMediation software that allows us the ability to customize and enhance the "affiliate relationship" with our selected partners. We have developed a competitive commission structure that pays between 7 and 15 percent dependent on the revenue generated. This structure has an equal or higher base percentage to revenue scale than our competitors. We will be issuing our commission cheques based on reaching a minimum monthly amount of $200 and will be sending the cheques no later than 30 days after the end of the month. This monthly cheque will also be an opportunity to promote upcoming events or provide rewards for our producing affiliates. The idea is to build the program slowly but strategically by selecting a small number of key partners that will drive targeted sales and have high traffic numbers. It is HMV.com's plan to build the program in two phases.

In the first phase we would like to test the program with our partners by setting up a small number of "affiliate relationships" and paying very close analytical attention to the tracking and recording. With this information we can better assess what works for HMV.com and make educated decisions on what areas, genres, formats, etc. drive the best sales and provide us a focus for the growth of our network. This initial testing phase should last until the first quarter of 2001, when our site will be upgraded and all linking codes, etc. will be changed from what exists now. With a small, manageable group of affiliates this change will

EXHIBIT 8	Affiliate Marketing Summary (continued)

not be as difficult to undergo. The site upgrade should give us the capability to put affiliate access links on the home page and link to affiliate information. Once signed in as an affiliate your user name and password will give you access to an information zone with affiliate-related graphics, news, and information.

The second phase will consist of a two-tiered program. One tier will continue to focus on the e-commerce partner relationship that began in the first phase; however, we will open the doors, promote and drive these strategic partnerships. These relationships will often include but also cross the barriers of affiliate marketing into the more traditional online marketing and promotions with HMV.com. The affiliate software will play a large role in these relationships by providing ways to infuse HMV.com into the partner-sites in a co-branded way. This creates the appearance to the user that the affiliate site (which they have learned to trust) and HMV.com are aggregated and thus create an enhanced-use experience, driving the conversion rates.

The second tier of this phase will consist of a larger number of affiliates; however, the average size of these affiliates will be much smaller, a traditional "affiliate network" relying more on a straight revenue-sharing relationship.

This tier will be self-managed by the majority, by providing the necessary tools, information, and instruction for the affiliate upon acceptance of their application. This will work using the lighter interface of the iMediation software, making the signup much simpler and more straightforward. Along with the lighter platform, the affiliates will have access to a selection of graphics (banners and buttons) linking information (including what works best, pros/cons of different links, success stories of other affiliates, promotions, events, etc.). This program will allow credit to accumulate in an individual affiliate HMV.com account that at any time can be used toward the purchase of CDs. This way the affiliate, which would probably not generate the minimum cheque amount each month, can take advantage of the sales immediately rather than waiting for a minimum payment amount to accumulate.

In addition to these plans we will continue to look at new information regarding affiliate marketing. It will remain a high priority to keep up on all the industry standards, competition, reports, and recommendations so that we can first become a leading-edge program model and then continue to break new ground in affiliate marketing in the years to come.

Vancouver Canucks

Catherine Ace

In July 2001, John Rizzardini, Senior VP of Sales and Marketing for the Vancouver Canucks, was preparing for a meeting with Chief Operating Officer (COO) Dave Cobb; at the meeting, John would lay out his marketing plans for the 2001/2002 hockey season.

The buzz at the Canucks' headquarters, General Motors (GM) Place, was great: the Canucks had played well enough in the past year to gain a playoff position, their business performance was improving steadily, and Brian Burke, President and General Manager, had just been awarded the Sporting News' Executive of the Year award. Furthermore, the Vancouver Grizzlies, an NBA franchise, had just left town, providing an opportunity to fill a void. In addition, John believed that more could be done with the Canucks' Web site (www.canucks.com), which had been successfully relaunched in January 2001 (Exhibit 1).

One challenge was to use the Internet to build a relationship with fans and the Vancouver business community. Another key challenge was to build a presence that would allow for business success not only when the team was winning, but also when it wasn't doing so well!

This case was prepared with the gracious assistance of John Rizzardini, Senior Vice President Sales & Marketing, and the Vancouver Canucks, and the Orca Bay organisation.

BACKGROUND

The NHL

The National Hockey League (NHL) is an unincorporated, non-profit association of members who are associated by mutual consent and contract. Each NHL member holds a franchise from the NHL for the operation of a hockey team. The NHL consists of two conferences: the Western Conference (15 teams) and the Eastern Conference (15 teams), with each conference divided into three divisions. The Vancouver Canucks play in the Northwest Division of the Western Conference, which also includes teams from Edmonton, Calgary, Colorado, and Minneapolis/St. Paul (Minnesota, which joined in the 2000/2001 season).

The Canucks have been a member of the NHL since the start of the 1970/1971 season. Membership of the NHL provides the Canucks certain rights, which include the right to operate a team in the NHL, protection of local territory, a share of revenues in the NHL, and the right to participate in player drafts.

Revenue Streams

The NHL regular season runs from the beginning of October through to mid-April each year, with each team playing a number of pre-season exhibition games (usually not more than nine) and 82 regular season games, of which half are played in the home team's arena. At the end of the regular season, the teams finishing first through eighth in each Conference engage in a series of playoff games, with the winners of each Conference play-off meeting in a best-of-seven series to determine the winner of the Stanley Cup, the symbol of professional hockey supremacy. Ticket revenues from all home games, including playoff games, are received by the home team. Reaching the playoffs leads not only to recognition, but also to financial rewards. Ticket sales are the most important revenue stream for an NHL team, accounting for approximately 40 to 60 percent of total revenue (about 45% in the case of the Canucks). Season tickets, game tickets, group sales, executive suites, and hospitality suites make up the ticket sales portfolio.

Income from national broadcasting reaches each NHL team based on an equal share of the revenue derived from agreements that are negotiated by the NHL on behalf of its members. The NHL entered into four-year agreements for both national broadcasts and national cablecasts in Canada beginning with the 1998/1999 season. The national broadcast agreement in Canada is with the CBC. Labatt Breweries of Canada is the major beer sponsor of the national broadcast package. The national cable agreement is with Sportsnet. In the United States, the NHL has entered into five-year network and cable agreements with ABC and ESPN, respectively, which commenced with the 1999/2000 season. Each member club has the right to broadcast its games in its own territory. The Canucks have television agreements with CTV for broadcast and Sportsnet for cable. Virtually all games are televised, as the following table shows:

Televised Home Games				Televised Away Games	
2000-2001	2001-2002			2000-2001	2001-2002
38	38*			39	32*

* Tentative

The Canucks have the right to retain all revenue from the sale of rinkside advertising and in-ice advertising. The club can also retain other income from sponsorship—where agreements might include a variety of items such as rinkside advertising, advertising time during Canucks broadcasts, program advertisements, and game-night sponsorships. Furthermore, the Canucks have the right to retail programs, hockey novelties, hockey clothing, and other major-league sports clothing.

The Vancouver Canucks play their home games at GM Place, which is owned and operated by the Orca Bay Arena Corp. (OBAC); the Canucks have a licence agreement with OBAC for 20 years, commencing with the 1995/1996 season. The arena and the rights and obligations of OBAC under the arena licence were transferred to Orca Bay Arena Limited Partnership (OBALP) in March 1996. OBAC and OBALP are affiliates of the Canucks. As a result of the agreement, the Canucks are entitled to the following:

a) all revenue from seating (approximate capacity is 18,400 seats) except as otherwise noted below: ticket prices ranged from $25 to $88 in 2000/2001 with an average price of $49. Food and beverage concession revenues averaged about $10 per fan and souvenirs/merchandise averaged another $8.

b) the use of office space, dressing room space, training room space, workout area, and coaches' offices;

c) a percentage of food and beverage concession income;

d) the exclusive use of space for a retail store in the arena;

e) all revenue from executive suite passes sold on a game-by-game basis. OBALP is entitled to receive all other revenue from multi-year executive-suite licence agreements;

f) all revenue from the sale of suite passes for playoff games; and

g) all broadcasting revenue.

The Canucks are obliged to pay a minimum licence fee each year, plus consumer price index increases applied cumulatively during each year of the lease term. OBALP is responsible for providing certain services, called "event services," during pre-season and regular season games.

BUILDING A TEAM, A DREAM, AND A TRADITION— WHO ARE THE CANUCKS?

From its inception, the team had built a considerable following in the area and had a number of successful runs to the playoffs, with the early 1980s and 1990s seeing some memorable moments on the ice. By the early 1990s the NHL was expanding, as were players' salaries. Frustrated with insufficient revenues at the Canucks' home arena, Pacific Coliseum, and the lack of corporate amenities that the site offered, Arthur Griffiths (son of

Canucks owner Frank Griffiths) initiated plans to build a $100-million arena for the Canucks at the former Expo site in downtown Vancouver. With actual construction costs coming in closer to $160 million, Arthur applied for an NBA franchise to help with the financing for the new arena. It was at this time that John E. McCaw, Jr. became Arthur's partner, and they established Orca Bay Sports & Entertainment to be the umbrella organization through which they would run their various sporting business concerns.

GM Place (popularly known as "The Garage") opened in September 1995, home to the Canucks and the Vancouver Grizzlies of the National Basketball Association. With 88 luxury suites, 2,200 club seats, three restaurants, and the latest in entertainment audio and video technology, it was a success with fans and the corporate community.

The 1995/1996 season saw the Canucks start with a season ticket fan base of 12,100, an all-time high, and ticket receipts for the season were excellent: average attendance was 17,795, the highest in franchise history (Exhibit 2). The team made the first-round playoffs in spite of not playing well at the start of the season and star player Pavel Bure's injury early in the season.

WHEN THE SPORT BECAME JUST A BUSINESS

The 1996/1997 season saw salaries continue to rise, an economic slowdown, a weakened Canadian dollar, and lower attendance. The team failed to make the playoffs and the general concern that the Canucks were distancing themselves from their fans was not helped by the media, who were becoming increasingly frustrated by what they saw as a corporate public relations machine getting between them, the owner, the players, and the game.

A further move during this season that was to receive a mixed reaction was the introduction of a new logo—an Orca, or stylized killer whale—which was seen by many to have more of a connection with the name of the Orca Bay corporation than the Canucks team. Some fans who had initially welcomed the new arena now felt nostalgic for their traditional arena, Pacific Coliseum, and the lower prices for food and parking that went with it.

The 1997/1998 season saw the arrival of marquee player Mark Messier, which immediately raised the fans' expectations of the team's performance—but the team started slowly. In mid-season, the coach and general manager were fired and replaced by a new, controversial coach who traded away players who were key fan favourites. Recognizing the marketing challenge facing the Canucks for the 1997/1998 season, the team embarked on a strategy that included holding ticket prices at the same level as the previous year and more aggressive sales tactics—including developing a number of new alternatives to full season-tickets packages (e.g., combination packages, half seasons) to maintain a season-ticket base. Tickets to the All-Star game, scheduled for February 1998, were used to leverage sales of season-ticket packages. A strong emphasis was placed on group ticket sales. Additional sales staff were added to call on companies to sell season tickets and suites face to face. Laptop presentations were developed for sales representatives to showcase the emotion of the game and the value of purchasing season tickets.

In addition, an intensive communication plan was developed to balance out the heavy attacks that local sports writers were launching against the team and the direction it seemed to be taking. Canucks team representatives were scheduled on weekly radio shows, players made frequent appearances at community functions, front-office staff made speeches, and content on the Web site focused on chats for fans and community relations news.

GETTING THE FANS AND THE TEAM SPIRIT BACK INTO THE BUSINESS OF SPORT

The 1998/1999 season saw the appointment of Brian Burke as President and General Manager of the Vancouver Canucks.[2] He brought the vision of building a stable team of young players who could learn and grow together and the stated aim of building a strong business based upon team success. Brian quickly brought in Marc Crawford as Head Coach.[3]

While the 1998/1999 and 1999/2000 seasons were seen as a time when the new plans could be put into place, the young team playing at the end of the 1999/2000 season had begun to rekindle the connection with the fans. A young squad of players brought up from the farm team[4] made a late-season run for a playoff position. Fans and the media began to take notice of the team due to some surprising wins, "come from behind" heroics, timely scoring from unknown players, the grit of the players, and the overall team effort each game. General Manager Brian Burke's vision to build a team of young prospects from the farm system—players who were "belligerent" in pursuit of the puck—was beginning to show results.

The questions asked by fans and the media at the end of the season were "Who are these young players?" and "Was the team success late in the season just a fluke, or was it a sign of future success?"

2000/2001: Marketing Plans and Results

Based on the new team attitude, the aims for 2000/2001 were to:

- Sell more tickets
- Give an emotional reminder of the late-season run
- Sell a team of youth and promise
- Remind fans why they love hockey
- Develop a personal touch with fans
- Promote likeable, down to earth, handsome, hardworking kids on the team versus the aloof NBA players[5]
- Promote the Canuck family and management with ties to Vancouver

---

[1.] Brian Burke had been Director of Hockey Operations for the Canucks (from 1987 to 1992). Brian joined the NHL front office in 1993 as Senior Vice-President and Director of Hockey Operations and stayed for five years before returning to Vancouver.

[2.] Crawford was the third youngest coach to win a Stanley Cup with the Colorado Avalanche in 1996 and came to the Canucks not only with a great coaching pedigree, but also with a local history: he played every game of his six-year NHL playing career for the Canucks, having been a rookie with the team that faced up to the NY Islanders in the 1982 Stanley Cup final.

[3.] Every NHL team typically has a minor-league affiliate that plays in either the International Hockey League (IHL) (disbanded at the conclusion of the 2000/2001 season) or the American Hockey League (AHL). These teams are generally independently owned and operated and typically have agreements with NHL teams under which the NHL team provides a certain number of players to the minor-league affiliate. These players are under contract to the NHL team and are effectively loaned to the minor-league affiliate. The main benefit of the system to the NHL teams is the ability to develop younger players.

[4.] The Vancouver Grizzlies NBA team was at the same time being vilified in the press for their inability to perform on the court and ownership/management miscues. They finally left Vancouver for Memphis at the end of the 2000/2001 season.

Grizzlies Average Attendance:	1995/1996	1996/1997	1997/1998	1998/1999	1999/2000	2000/2001
	16,490	14,359	14,129	8,869*	12,917	9,437

* Lock-out year

Sales Strategy

- Ticket prices were increased by about 5 percent over the previous year; price increases were positioned as "fair" and below the Canadian NHL average.
- The Canucks maintained a similar-sized sales staff supported by numerous direct sales initiatives, marketing promotions, and community programs.
- Aggressive ticket renewal follow-up was supported by ticket-holder breakfasts, and overall optimism associated with the team resulted in a strong renewal despite price increases.

Tactics

- Go back to those season-ticket holders and "ice pak" (mini-season packages of tickets for 10 to 20 games) holders who had severed ties with the team during the past five seasons and present them with a comeback offer.
- Focus products and promotions on desirable opponents and best nights of the week to generate sellouts.
- Stay with the same products, limit the number of discount offers.
- Promote urgency through scarcity of tickets for many games ("buy early").

Communications Plan

The communications plan consisted of three main components: media and customer relations, advertising strategy, and community relations.

Media and Customer Relations

Team management and the new COO hosted 12 breakfasts with season-ticket holders to outline the plan for the franchise both on and off the ice. The big feature here was the new COO himself, Dave Cobb. Dave, a Vancouver boy whose father drove the Zamboni[6] for the Canucks at the Pacific Coliseum, was a lifelong Canucks fan, adept at making finances work.

The Canucks continued to have team personnel and players on live radio shows (which provided unedited content and a sense of spontaneity to the fans). Head Coach Marc Crawford continuously delivered his team message of working hard to regain RESPECT— this theme was extended to the organization as a whole, turning the business around in the minds of the media and fans.

The practice of having interviews with selected players during live television coverage was continued, and the access to the team and the dressing room before and after games was managed for the convenience of the media.

---

[5] This is the machine that cleans and refinishes the ice on an ice rink—Zambonis are a feature of every interval at a hockey game.

Advertising Strategy

Television and radio commercials used opera music, emotional play-by-play calls, and key video clips to remind fans of the excitement of the late-season surge. These advertisements appealed directly to fans' hearts, encouraging them to open their wallets and buy a ticket or to at least listen to or watch the game on broadcast media. (An example of the Canucks advertising can be seen on their Web site, at www.canucks.com.)

Print advertising focused on building a connection with the fans and emphasized the young players with "spirit" (this was followed up right through the season with emotional print images, as shown in Exhibits 3 and 4). Newspaper and outdoor advertisements featured large images of the players, as well as a retail message, thereby reinforcing the young, "every mother's son" image of the team. Extended branding was carried out through bus signage, SkyTrain[7] transit boards, bathroom stalls, in arena signage, poster series in arena, and poster distribution throughout the community.

The primary retail product was an 11-game ice pak—this was the most affordable in price and time commitment to a mass audience, and took the lead in terms of being offered in advertisements (other than the encouragement to attend at least the specific game being promoted). It allows fans to choose either a weekday or weekend run of 11 (or 15) games. Prior to booking fans could even check out the view of the ice from their preferred-seating section via the Canucks' Web site.

Community Relations

The Vancouver Canucks recognized that success on the ice had to be mirrored in connections with the community off the ice. They had had an active community relations program for many years, but this was augmented and given a new importance for the 2000/2001 season. (See Exhibit 5 for a summary of the Canucks' community relations program.)

TICKET SALES RESULTS FOR 2000/2001

As shown in Exhibit 6, the results were very positive. In particular, the club was pleased that the 16-percent attendance gain was larger than that achieved by any NHL team in the past year and ran through all elements from single ticket sales to season and group packages.

Planning for 2001/2002

"The 2000/2001 season was certainly successful—both on and off the ice," stated John Rizzardini. "I'm glad I came back!"[8] Many of the question marks about the team from the previous season were answered by a consistent winning performance. The players were accepted as underdogs, perhaps not as well paid and skilled as the opponents but winning with grit, hustle, and character. The plan to build a young team with promise was working. A place in the playoffs led to an extended season of excitement, and there was an air of promise for the future. (See Exhibit 7 for an overview of results.)

[6.] SkyTrain is the Vancouver rapid transit system.

[7.] He'd first been with the Canucks in 1995 as Vice President of Customer Sales and Service, had then spent a year in Los Angeles as Executive VP of the LA Arena Corporation, parent company of the Staples Center, the Los Angeles Kings, Los Angeles Lakers and Los Angeles Galaxy, before returning to take up his new post.

The business side of the Canucks was a positive story, too. With 17 sellouts in 41 games, the media wrote of the return of Canucks fans to GM Place and the high energy of the crowds. Team spokespersons announced the improved financial condition of the team, lending further belief that the franchise was on solid ground.

"But where do we go from here?" John wondered. "With all this good buzz should we increase ticket prices, and if so, by how much? Should we be delivering more fan service, offering more merchandise and pushing e-business and eCustomer Relationship Management opportunities, or cutting back on costs and making sure that our financial results are good for next year? How can we make sure we get the most of the sporting dollar in the fans' pockets, especially now that there's no NBA basketball in Vancouver? Indeed, since there's no more basketball at GM Place, should we take real strides towards making the whole experience of visiting the rink a 'hockey only' experience? Should we alter the physical environment at all, and if so, how and how much?"

John sat down with a blank piece of paper and an open mind—no alternative was to be excluded from his list of possible paths. After a quick brainstorming session the following issues clearly emerged as needing serious consideration:

- *Personification/brand:* Who/what are we, the Canucks, to our fans? How do they see us? Do we have to make ourselves more obviously a physical part of the community? Do we have enough appeal for all the fans, whatever their age? We've taken a very definite step by introducing a cuddly Canuck mascot, the velvety Orca, between the 2000/2001 and 2001/2002 seasons.

    What if one player "becomes" the team? Are we leaving ourselves wide open to problems if that player is traded? How much should our players *be* the embodiment of the team? Is the whole truly greater than the sum of the parts? With the Canucks' star player, Markus Naslund, signing for three more years, we've got a strong, popular captain on board—how can we make the most of that off the ice?

- *Cost impact:* Given that we have real—and high—financial responsibilities, how far can we push the prices we charge to our customers? to attend? to view? to listen? to wear? to support? How can we add value and perceived value to all that we do? Should we increase prices, based upon improved perceived value? How do we approach local businesses to ask for more support?

- *E-presence:* Sports marketing and sports business do not exist in a vacuum, and with our audience and fan profile matching that of the heaviest users of the Internet we cannot ignore the potential advantages of having the best Web presence possible. We need to identify the best hockey (see NHL.com for a list of team Web sites), basketball (NBA.com), and football (NFL.com) Web sites and see what we can learn from them.

"If there's one thing I know about sports marketing," reflected John, "it's that the franchise isn't just the 22 players on the ice, it's the whole management and business team too. From the person selling you the ticket to the parking attendant who says 'thanks for coming' as you leave the game—every point of contact with the fan matters in building long-term fan support."

John only had a week to prepare for his meeting with Dave Cobb to present a preliminary marketing plan for the 2001/2002 season. While the success of the past season had created an optimistic feeling in the Canucks' offices, John knew that an effective marketing plan would be needed to build on that success and reach higher goals for the next year.

EXHIBIT 1	News Release from Vancouver Canucks

Revamped Canucks.com Reaches 7 Million Page Views

4/16/2001

VANCOUVER, B.C. The Vancouver Canucks are pleased to announce that their redesigned Web site, www.canucks.com, has been able to generate over 7 million page views in only three months of operation. This is an increase in page views of over 400% during the same time span as last year. Having achieved these numbers in the regular season, the Web sites' playoff plans are to take fans deeper into the games at GM Place than ever before.

Beginning on Monday, April 16, in conjunction with INSINC, its Webcast services company, the Canucks will be providing a service that high-speed Internet customers will be able to access before, during, and after the home games.

In addition to the usual unique coverage fans have come to expect, high-speed users will be able to see the pre-game skate from GM Place beginning with the teams hitting the ice shortly after 6:00 p.m. During the game, the Web site will provide fans with two streaming audio-video sources that will show the Canucks managerial box, the broadcast gondola, and the hallway in the Canucks dressing room area. Also, the site will show features of all the goals and highlights of each period as soon as it is completed. Following the game, live streaming cameras will show the Marc Crawford post-game press conference as well as all the interview action live in the dressing rooms.

The Canucks are excited to be able to provide the fans that have supported the team and the Web site with this unique experience.

EXHIBIT 2	Attendance Data

	Average attendance	Season base	Average NHL attendance
1995/1996	17,795	12,100	15,986
1996/1997	17,320	11,000	16,548
1997/1998	17,119	11,657	16,196
1998/1999	15,803	8,684	16,261
1999/2000	14,642	7,450	16,376
2000/2001	17,017	8,000	16,563

Is there a better game in the whole world?

The seat you can buy today... will be gone tomorrow.

SEASON TICKETS or our NEW ½ SEASON TICKETS

899-GOAL

EXHIBIT 4 | Canucks' "Can't Wait" Advertisement

We can't wait to play for you again.

"I can't express how much our fans mean to us. The standing ovation I got before the Kings game brought tears to my eyes.

The cheering when our team came out for our first playoff game gave me goosebumps.

The way you stood and cheered for us at the end of our last game shows what classy fans you are. You made a difference and we can't wait to play for you again."

—Markus NASLUND
Captain, Vancouver Canucks

The seat you can buy today... will be gone tomorrow.

SEASON TICKETS or our NEW ½ SEASON TICKETS

899-GOAL

EXHIBIT 5	The Canucks' Community Program

Education: Having stated that they are committed to supporting students as they strive to complete their educational goals, throughout the season Vancouver Canucks players visit local schools and communities to encourage children to stay in school. The Canuck organization also donates merchandise and tickets to local schools and educational centres, raising necessary funds to make improvements in their facilities. They were directly involved in the Seventh Generation Club, the Larry Ashley Scholarship, the Pacific Coast Amateur Hockey Scholarship, and the UBC Hockey Scholarship.

Grassroots: Believing it is important that children of all ages have exposure to the game of hockey, the Canucks, in conjunction with the BC Centre of Excellence, deliver a number of grassroots hockey programs and events to the community. These include the Mini/Minor Hockey Program, the Nike/NHL Street Hockey Program, NHL Breakout, and NHL Superskills.

Canuck Foundation and Charitable Initiatives: The Canuck Foundation was founded in 1986 and has since established a strong community presence in Vancouver and British Columbia. The Foundation provides much-needed support to children's charities, education, and grassroots hockey programs. With the ongoing help of individuals and corporate partners, the Foundation works with Canucks players and management to have a positive impact in the community. The primary focus of the Foundation's fundraising efforts has been Canuck Place, a hospice for terminally ill children and their families, which opened its doors in 1995. This unique healthcare facility focuses on the child and family as a unit and provides for their physical, emotional, and spiritual needs. Canuck Place provides palliative, respite, and bereavement care.

Other initiatives include donations in kind, the community ticket program, and the Christmas Campaign.

EXHIBIT 6	Ticket Sales Results for 2000/2001

Attendance: Ran at an average 17,017—up 16.2 percent from the previous season (14,642). This was the largest gain from the previous season among the 30 NHL teams.

Season-Ticket Base: 8,000; was 7,450 the previous season.

New Season-Ticket Equivalents: Sold 1,662; 270 percent increase over previous season.

Group Sales: Sold over 3,000 group tickets per game; record high resulting in income of $4.2 million.

Ticket Revenue: Up 27 percent from previous season.

Suite Sales: Up 5 percent from previous season.

Group Sales: Sold more than 3,000 group tickets per game, a record high, accounting for about 15 percent of ticket revenues.

Total Team Revenues: Up 22 percent from previous season.

EXHIBIT 7	Team Results					
Season	Games played	Won	Lost	Tied	Playoffs	Division finish
1995/1996	82	32	35	15	Y	2nd
1996/1997	82	35	40	7	N	4th
1997/1998	82	25	43	14	N	7th
1998/1999	82	23	47	12	N	4th
1999/2000	82	30	37	15 (8)	N	3rd
2000/2001	82	36	35	11 (7)	Y	3rd

Online Executive Training Inc.

Thomas F. Funk

"This could cost upward of $400,000 before I get my first customer," thought Tom Jackson, President and Owner of Executive Training Inc. (ETI). It was early September 2000, and he was reflecting on his idea of starting Online Executive Training Inc., a new service using online delivery of training programs. ETI was a successful firm providing marketing and sales training for agricultural companies, but Tom was wondering if the time was right to introduce a major new product line. Since ETI's inception in 1982, all training programs had been conducted in face-to-face, classroom-type settings. ETI was very good at this traditional method of delivery, and had a number of long-term, highly satisfied clients.

Given the rapid expansion of Internet use, Tom's idea was to add online program delivery to his existing business. To further explore the idea, he commissioned a market research study and prepared initial cost estimates of the product launch. As he reviewed this information, he was concerned about the high initial investment. He wondered whether the market was really ready for this approach and if and how he should proceed.

EXECUTIVE TRAINING INC.

Tom Jackson established ETI, located in Milton, Ontario, in 1982 to provide marketing and sales training programs for agribusiness firms. The agribusiness industry included those firms that provided farmers with products (e.g., equipment, fertilizer, seeds, etc.) and services (e.g., crop management practices, dairy herd management, etc.). Over the 17 years the company had been in business, revenues grew from just under $100,000 in the first year to $1,200,000 in 1999. In addition to Tom, ETI employed three full-time trainers and one full-time administrative assistant.

ETI's product line consisted of programs in marketing and sales. All the programs were custom designed and offered to clients in both Canada and the United States. Current clients consisted of both large and small agribusiness firms in the seed, chemical, machinery, animal health, and feed industries.

A typical ETI program was three days in duration and normally held at a central location such as a hotel or a company's training centre. Although participants included middle and senior management, most were sales representatives. The usual number of participants in a program varied from 15 to 25.

Although ETI programs were custom designed for individual clients, they were built around standard course modules. The customization usually consisted of changing the mix of course modules used and some cosmetic changes such as use of the company's logo on visual materials.

Two three-day ETI programs were very popular and accounted for nearly 75 percent of the company's revenue. The first program, Principles of Agri Marketing (PAM), was targeted at sales reps and was designed to provide basic marketing skills. As in all ETI programs, the method of instruction consisted of lecture/discussions and case studies. PAM topics normally included (1) Marketing Strategy Planning, (2) Financial Analysis for Marketing Decisions, (3) Marketing Products and Services, (4) Building a Marketing Mix, and (5) Customer Buying Behaviour.

The second program, Strategic Agri Selling (SAS), was also targeted at sales representatives and was designed to develop basic selling skills. In addition to lectures/discussions and case studies, this program involved role-playing sales situations. SAS topics normally included (1) Preparing for a Sales Call, (2) Opening a Sales Call, (3) Probing for Information, (4) Presenting Features and Benefits, (5) Handling Objections, (6) Closing the Sale, and (7) Follow-up Service.

THE ONLINE OPPORTUNITY

ETI had always relied heavily on computer technology in developing and presenting programs. It was one of the first training companies to adopt computer-generated graphics in the late 1980s when this technology was developed. More recently, Tom experimented with digital video in presentations. For years the company used analog video in taping role-plays for subsequent analysis and discussion.

In July 1999, Tom attended an American Marketing Association conference on the use of online educational programs. Although the conference was designed mainly for university people who might want to start teaching online, Tom immediately recognized that this approach might be appropriate for the type of training programs his company conducted.

Online educational programs used the Internet as a delivery mechanism. Instead of face-to-face lectures, narrated PowerPoint presentations were used to deliver conceptual material. Various conferences were designed in chat rooms to allow participants to discuss cases or exercises. Assignments were completed using word-processing programs and sent to the instructor as attachments. Tom was absolutely amazed at the versatility of this approach and began to think about how he might use this approach at ETI.

In October 1999 Tom signed up for a four-week online training program, Achieving Exceptional Customer Satisfaction, offered by the Ontario Agricultural Training Institute (OATI) (www.oati.com). During this course Tom really began to appreciate the power of online delivery. Although the course attracted only eight participants, that was a sufficient number for Tom to see the ability of online delivery to facilitate participant interaction. Each week the participants were given case studies to read and discuss, and it was common for a hundred or more interactions among the eight people. Not only were there numerous interactions but also, in Tom's opinion, the quality of the interactions was superb. In addition, Tom was very impressed with the quality and quantity of individual feedback provided by the instructor. Based on this experience, Tom became convinced that the online method of delivery was a viable alternative to more traditional methods.

After completing the OATI course, Tom began to investigate the feasibility of adopting this approach for ETI. He started to assemble information on the costs associated with online delivery as well as the potential market for this product. He began by reviewing what was currently available on the Internet.

THE ONLINE EDUCATION INDUSTRY

Based on the online education industry review, Tom was amazed at the number of Web sites and course offerings on the Internet. He made the following summary notes:

- eLearners.com (www.elearners.com) provided extensive information for people considering learning online. It listed more than 24,000 online and distance learning courses and 2,400 distance and e-learning degree and certificate programs offered by 2,400 firms, ranging from universities to community colleges to consulting firms to specialists in training in a variety of areas. He noted that no firm was focused on agribusiness.

- Global Network Academy (www.gnacademy.org) was a non-profit organization that listed distance learning opportunities throughout the world. Their catalogue contained 23,862 courses and 2,511 programs.

- World Wide Learn (www.worldwidelearn.com) provided a directory of online courses ranging from online MBA programs to art courses. There were more than 300 Marketing courses listed on the site from universities, community colleges, training firms and publishers such as Harcourt and McGraw-Hill.

- University of Phoenix (www.phoenix.edu) was probably one of the most recognized online universities and had considerable experience in the online education market.

- National Agri-Marketing Association (www.nama.org) provided current news, events, and company information for professionals in the North American agribusiness market. No online courses were listed on the site but various local chapters listed talks and seminars dealing with a wide range of topics, most of them technical in nature.

COST INFORMATION

Because online training was a new concept, cost information was difficult to estimate. Based on information gleaned from a number of sources, Tom developed the following cost estimates:

Course development costs could range anywhere from $30,000 to $50,000 for a single course. This included the development of teaching materials, software development, and programming. Once a course was developed it would cost at least $10,000 each year to update material and technology.

Getting involved in online training would require more administrative support than ETI currently had available and this would cost an additional $50,000 each year.

Because of the method of delivery, instructors for online courses could be retained on a per-course basis. Hiring the type of people required would probably cost ETI $150 per hour of instruction time. Tom estimated that it would take approximately 30 minutes per student per week of an instructor's time to provide basic instruction and feedback. Higher levels of individual feedback would require much greater instructor involvement, perhaps as much as one hour per student per week.

Several Internet providers were willing to support online training. Their fees for hosting a course were in the vicinity of $15 per week per participant. This included Internet access as well as some technical support for participants.

The cost of teaching materials varied a great deal depending upon the subject matter. Tom felt that $15 per participant per week would be a high estimate.

MARKET INFORMATION

Although Tom had been involved in the training business for many years, online training was so new that he did not have a feel for this market. Consequently, he retained the services of Kelso Marketing Research to conduct a telephone survey of 50 randomly selected agribusiness organizations in Canada and the U.S. The main objectives of this research were to:

- Determine the size of the market for training in general;
- Determine the type of training currently undertaken;
- Determine the likely demand for online training.

Summary results of this study are presented in Appendix A.

THE DECISION

Armed with the cost and market data, Tom started to think about how he might expand his business to include online training. It was apparent that the major short-term opportunity would be in sales training. Most agribusiness companies used sales training for their employees and there appeared to be some dissatisfaction with existing programs.

Tom thought his first product would be a six-week introductory sales training course targeted at new sales reps. This course could be offered on both a public and private basis. The public course would be scheduled to run eight times a year and people from any company could enroll. This would result in a group of participants from different companies. The private courses would be sold to individual companies and customized to some extent to meet their specific training needs.

Both the public and private courses would contain essentially the same content as the current three-day sales training course offered by ETI. Lectures would be in the form of narrated PowerPoint presentations. ETI would develop a number of video clips showing parts of sales calls that could be critiqued and discussed by participants in online conferences. An instructor who would monitor the discussion in the conferences would provide feedback. Participants would be expected to devote five hours a week to the course. This made one week of online experience more or less equal to a half day of face-to-face training.

Marketing the courses was a major consideration. ETI had not done much marketing in the past because there was a lot of repeat buying by satisfied clients. Moreover, word-of-mouth was an effective method in getting new clients. Tom knew he would have to develop an effective marketing program in order to be successful with the new online venture. Ideally, the online courses would be sold to new clients so as not to cannibalize clients from existing face-to-face courses.

The marketing program for the online product could be designed using one or more approaches. One method was to hire one or more full-time sales reps, who would use a combination of telephone and personal contact with prospects. A full-time sales rep would cost ETI approximately $100,000 annually including all benefits and expenses.

A second method was direct mail. A professionally prepared direct mail piece could be designed and mailed to prospects for approximately $20 a contact. This included all the design work as well as the costs of distribution. Tom noticed that many companies were using CDs in direct mail. The advantage of a CD was its ability to demonstrate how the online learning system actually worked. Adding a CD to the direct mail would increase distribution costs to approximately $25 a contact and would result in a one-time production cost of $30,000 for the CD.

A third method was to use media advertising. The most logical publication to use was *Agri Marketing* magazine (www.agrimarketing.com), a monthly publication. Sales and marketing executives in virtually all agribusiness companies received this magazine. One full-page colour ad in this publication costs $6,000.

Finally, the Internet was an obvious medium to use for the new product line. What should be done or how it should be done was not clear.

Regardless of the communication media used, a key issue was how to position the new product. Tom was not sure how to deal with this issue, but believed the marketing research would provide some insight.

In addition to developing a communication program for the online product, another key issue was to establish a price. Normal industry practice was to establish prices on a participant-per-day basis. Tom noted from the research results that the average price paid per day per participant was $500, or $1,500 for a three-day course. He felt that this might not be appropriate for online training, and other alternatives could be considered. While the research indicated that many respondents expected to pay a lower price for an online course, they also said that among the problems they faced with training were the time required for training, that people were away from their work, and the costs associated with travel and so on. Tom felt that the opportunity existed to price these courses higher to position them as a better alternative. He was considering a price of $2,000 or even $2,500 for the courses but needed to consider the whole pricing issue further.

With all this in mind, Tom wondered if this was the right move for ETI at the present time. Online training seemed like the way of the future, and if he could get established in the area before competition he would have a real advantage. On the other hand, was the time really right for this move? Was the market ready to accept a fairly radical departure from current practice? Given the initial investment of about $400,000 for marketing and course development, would it pay off?

Appendix A

Market Research Summary

The objectives of this research were to determine the size of the market for training in general, the type of training currently undertaken, and the likely demand for online training. In total, 50 companies representing different sectors of agribusiness were interviewed in Canada and the United States. Company names were randomly selected from a listing of 2,500 agribusiness firms found in the annual *Marketing Services Guide* published by *Agri Marketing* magazine. It was believed that the 2,500 companies encompassed virtually all agribusiness organizations in North America. The survey consisted of three sections: Section A focused on characteristics of the individual companies, Section B identified the various training programs currently used by these companies, and Section C was designed to gain information on how people perceived online training and whether or not they saw this as a viable alternative to more traditional methods.

SECTION A

The first section focused on the companies themselves in terms of what they did, how large they were, and the number of employees participating in training programs. The purpose of this section was to get some idea of market composition and size.

How many employees does your company have?

Each company was asked to provide data on the number of people they employed. The responses from the sample companies varied greatly, with the smallest having ten employees and the largest having 85,000 employees. The average company in the sample employed 410 people, with 10 percent being involved in sales and marketing. All sales and marketing employees receive some training over the course of a year.

What business is your company involved in?

Respondents were then asked to list the type of business they were involved in. Possible responses were feed, seed, fertilizer, agricultural chemicals, farm equipment, financial services, and grain handling. Tabulation of the results revealed a good distribution among all of these sectors.

Approximately how many sales and marketing employees have access to computers and the Internet at home and at work?

Respondents were asked to provide the number of sales and marketing employees that had computer access at home or at work. Results showed that 64 percent provide computer access to all of their sales and marketing employees, another 12 percent provide computer access to more than 50 percent of their sales and marketing employees, while the remaining 24 percent provide computer access to less than 50 percent of their sales and marketing employees. These statistics decreased slightly when respondents were asked to give the number of employees who also had access to the Internet at home or at work.

SECTION B

The purpose of this section was to identify the different training programs currently in use. Information such as the styles of teaching, length and frequency of the course, cost, amount of feedback provided, and level of satisfaction were explored.

What are some internal and external training programs that you have provided to your sales and marketing employees on either an individual or group basis over the last two years? What are some of the characteristics of these programs?

The main types of training programs used by companies, in order of popularity, were:

- Sales Training
- Product Training
- Marketing Training
- Time Management

The majority of programs appeared to be customized to the needs of the individual companies. Only a small percentage of the programs were generic. Almost all of the programs were purchased from external suppliers as opposed to being provided in-house. The sample companies listed a large number of external suppliers.

Respondents were also asked to state the methods of instruction used in training courses. The most common methods were:

- Lecture
- Video
- Case

Most of the training programs were one, two, or three days in length. The remaining programs were all less than one week in duration. Most of the courses were held either annually or biannually.

The range in the prices of these programs was $3,000 to nearly $30,000. The cost per participant per day varied from a low of $250 to a high of $600. The average was $500 per participant per day. These costs included:

- Fees and expenses paid to the training supplier
- Travel, food, and accommodations for participants
- Facilities for the program

The costs do not include the value of time away from work for program participants.

Not surprisingly, the number of participants in each course varied greatly. In most companies all sales and marketing people took some training each year. As a result, the number of potential participants can be directly linked to the number of people employed in sales and marketing.

Most respondents confirmed that their training courses provided some feedback. This feedback took many forms including individual follow-up by the trainer, tests, and role-play sessions. All respondents stated that feedback was something they valued a great deal and was an area that needed considerable improvement.

The data showed that while most respondents felt that training programs were effective, many stated that there was definitely room for improvement.

Are there other programs that you would like to see? How would they be structured?

When asked to list any training programs they would like to see, most people responded by saying that they would like to see more customized programs related to their company, products, and people. Virtually all respondents stressed the fact that sales training programs were the highest-priority training activities in their companies.

In your company, what are the biggest problems you have faced with the training of employees?

This question was asked to determine limitations with traditional methods of training. The most frequently cited responses to this question were:

- Time required to do training and have people away from their work
- Costs associated with travel, lost production, and the training program itself
- Finding training programs that meet the needs of the individual
- Identifying the skills that require improvement
- Finding time to complete the training and getting everyone into one central location
- Lack of ability to measure the impact of training on an individual or group basis
- Lack of individual feedback to participants during and after a training program

SECTION C

The last section of the questionnaire was designed to gain information on people's perceptions of online training. This information included awareness, benefits, concerns, and price.

Prior to this interview, had you ever heard of or had you used online training?

Two-thirds of the respondents confirmed they had heard of online training while 20 percent stated they had heard of and had actually investigated online training. Only 8 percent of the respondents stated they were currently using online training.

Where did you hear about online training?

The most common ways people had become aware of online training were:

- Internet
- Magazines and newspapers
- Universities
- Training suppliers
- Colleagues
- Other companies

List the benefits you think online training might provide your company.

The most significant benefits identified were:

- Lower costs
- Increased convenience
- Can learn at own pace
- Flexible to needs and schedule
- Superior feedback and interaction

List any concerns you think you might have with online training.

The most significant concerns identified were:

- Not enough interaction with other participants or the instructor
- Motivating trainees to actually do the program
- Participants may not have the required technology or feel comfortable with this technology
- Difficulties in monitoring performance
- May be hard to provide good feedback

Assuming that online training in sales and marketing were available at a reasonable price, would your company be interested in trying this method of delivery?

In response to this question

- 12% stated that they definitely would try online training
- 20% stated that they probably would try online training
- 36% stated that they may or may not try online training
- 28% stated that they probably would not use online training
- 4% stated that they definitely would not use online training

Would you expect this type of training to be less expensive, as expensive, or more expensive on a per-student basis than traditional training?

Nearly 72 percent of the respondents felt online training would be less expensive than traditional training; another 20 percent felt that online training would cost the same as traditional training; while the remaining 8 percent felt online training would be more expensive.

Sharratt Furniture Inc.

Roger A. Kerin

Late in the evening of January 18, 2002, Phillip Snyder, President of Sharratt Furniture Inc., called Dr. Sean Tallon, a marketing professor at an Ontario university and a consultant to the company. The conversation went as follows:

SNYDER: Hello, Sean. This is Phil Snyder. I'm sorry to call you this late, but I wanted to get your thoughts on the tentative 2002 advertising program proposed by Jack Dunn of Dunn and Taubner, our ad agency.

TALLON: No problem, Phil. What did they propose?

SNYDER: The crux of their proposal is that we should increase our advertising expenditures by $200,000. They suggested that we put the entire amount into our consumer advertising program for ads in several shelter magazines.[1] Dunn noted that the National Home Furnishings Foundation has recommended that furniture manufacturers spend 1 percent of their sales exclusively on consumer advertising.

TALLON: That increase appears to be slightly out of line with your policy of budgeting 5 percent of expected sales for total promotion expenditures, doesn't it? Hasn't Joan Seto [Vice-President of Sales] emphasized the need for more sales representatives?

[1.] Shelter magazines feature home improvement ideas, new ideas on home decorating, and so on. *Better Homes and Gardens* is an example of a shelter magazine.

SNYDER: Yes, Joan has requested additional funds. You're right about the 5-percent figure, too, and I'm not sure that our sales forecast isn't too optimistic. Your research has shown that our sales historically follow industry sales almost perfectly, and trade economists are predicting about a 4-percent increase for 2002. Yet, I'm not too sure.

TALLON: Well, Phil, you can't expect forecasts to be always on the button. The money is one thing, but what else can you tell me about Dunn's rationale for putting more dollars into consumer advertising?

SNYDER: He contends that we can increase our exposure and tell our quality and styling story to the buying public—increase brand awareness, enhance our image, that sort of thing. He also cited industry research data that showed that as baby boomers [consumers between the ages of 40 and 60] age they are becoming more home-oriented and are replacing older, cheaper furniture with more expensive, longer-lasting pieces. All I know is that my contribution margin will fall to 25 percent next year because of increased labour and material cost.

SNYDER: And one more issue. I've been talking with a small firm that designs Web sites. We're probably already a little behind the industry on this but we'd like to consider it. We see three objectives we could accomplish with a site. One objective would be consumer advertising/information—we would show our product offering on the site and tell consumers where they could buy our products in their town or city. Second, we could use the site for our retailers—we would have detailed product information and the selling features of each line. Third, we could also use the site for retail orders—we'd set up an online ordering system for them. To be frank, it's just in the idea stage. We've been throwing around these suggestions and I think we need do something but I'm not sure what.

The Web design firm estimates that the basic consumer site could be put up for about $25,000. Adding the retailer information would add about $10,000 to the basic cost, and adding online ordering would add another $10,000 to $25,000 to the cost. We'd also probably need to spend some money to maintain the site. I'd like your thoughts on this issue as well.

TALLON: I understand your concerns. Give me a few days to think about the proposal and the Web site. I'll get back to you soon.

After hanging up, Sean began to think about Phil's summary of the proposal, Sharratt's present position, and the furniture industry in general. He knew that Phil expected a well thought out recommendation on such issues and a step-by-step description of the logic used to arrive at that recommendation.

THE COMPANY

Sharratt Furniture is a manufacturer of medium- to high-priced wooden bedroom, living room, and dining room furniture. The company was formed at the turn of the century by Phillip Snyder's grandfather. Phil assumed the presidency of the company upon his father's retirement. Year-end net sales in 2001 were $75 million, with a before-tax profit of $3.7 million.

Sharratt sells its furniture through 1,000 high-quality department stores and independent furniture specialty stores across Canada and in several Midwestern states (primarily Michigan and Illinois), but all stores do not carry the company's entire line. The company is very selective in choosing retail outlets. As Phil often stated in company meetings, "Our distribution policy, hence our retailers, should mirror the high quality of our products." As a matter of policy, Sharratt does not sell to furniture chain stores or discount outlets.

The company employs ten full-time salespeople and two regional sales managers. Sales personnel receive a base salary and a small commission on sales. A company sales-force is atypical in the furniture industry; most furniture manufacturers use sales agents or representatives who carry a wide assortment of noncompeting furniture lines and receive a commission on sales. "Having our own sales group is a policy my father established years ago," noted Phil, "and we've been quite successful in having people who are committed to our company. Our people don't just take furniture orders. They are expected to motivate retail salespeople to sell our line, assist in setting up displays in stores, and give advice on a variety of matters to our retailers and their salespeople." He added, "It seems that my father was ahead of his time. I was just reading in the *Furniture Industry Outlook* for household furniture that the competition for retail floor space will require even more support, including store personnel sales training, innovative merchandising, inventory management, and advertising."

In early 2001, Sharratt allocated $3,675,000 for total promotional expenditures for the 2001 operating year, excluding the salary of the Vice-President of Sales. Promotion expenditures were categorized into four groups: (1) sales expense and administration, (2) co-operative advertising programs with retailers, (3) trade promotion, and (4) consumer advertising. Sales costs included salaries for sales personnel and sales managers, selling-expense reimbursements, fringe benefits, and clerical/office assistance, but did not include salespersons' commissions. Commissions were deducted from sales in the calculation of gross profit. The co-operative advertising budget is usually spent on newspaper advertising in a retailer's city. Co-operative advertising allowances are matched by funds provided by retailers on a dollar-for-dollar basis. Trade promotion, directed toward retailers, includes catalogues, trade magazine advertisements, booklets for consumers, point-of-purchase materials, such as displays, for use in retail stores, and technical booklets describing methods of construction and materials. Also included in this category is the expense of participating in trade shows. Sharratt is represented at two shows per year, one in Toronto and one in High Point, North Carolina. Consumer advertising is directed at potential consumers through shelter magazines. The typical format used in consumer advertising is to highlight new furniture and different bedroom, living room, and dining room arrangements. The typical vehicles used for consumer advertising are shelter magazines such as *Better Homes and Gardens* and *Canadian House & Home*. The dollar allocation for each of these programs in 2001 is shown in Exhibit 1.

EXHIBIT 1	Allocation of Promotion Dollars, 2001
Sales expense and administration	$ 995,500
Co-operative advertising allowance	1,650,000
Trade advertising	467,000
Consumer advertising	562,500
Total	$3,675,000

Source: Company records.

THE INDUSTRY

The household furniture industry in Canada is composed of more than 1,400 firms—down from 1,900 firms in 1989, the year the Free Trade Agreement between Canada and the United States was implemented. Between 1989 and 1994, the 15-percent tariff on furniture entering Canada from the U.S. was eliminated, as was the 2.5-percent tariff from the U.S. to Canada. By 1994, employment in the industry dropped by 25 percent. However, many of the firms that remained shifted to more specialized, higher value added segments of the market. As well, productivity and sales increased dramatically—value added per employee increased by 70 percent and average sales per factory by 75 percent between 1988 and 1996, as these firms were faced with intense competition from their U.S. counterparts. The most significant change was the international focus: Canadian furniture exports to the U.S. increased by 380 percent and now exports accounted for more than 55 percent of Canada's furniture output. Total household wood furniture industry sales (which were 50 percent of the total furniture industry sales) at manufacturers' prices were estimated to reach $17 billion in 2002 in the markets covered by Sharratt (Canada and the Midwestern states).

Because Sharratt had operated in the U.S. for more than 20 years, company executives saw the Free Trade Agreement as a greater opportunity than threat. The company expanded its marketing efforts in the U.S., and by 2001 more than 70 percent of its sales were to the U.S. Major well-known manufacturers of wood furniture in Canada include Bassett Furniture Industries, Drexel Heritage, Ethan Allen, Sklar Peppler, Sealy, and Kroehler. No one manufacturer accounts for more than 5 percent of the Canadian or 9 percent of the U.S. wood-furniture market.

The selling of furniture to retail outlets centres on manufacturers' expositions held at selected times and places. At these *marts,* as they are called in the furniture industry, retail buyers view manufacturers' lines and often make buying commitments for their stores. However, Sharratt's experience has shown that sales efforts in the retail store by company representatives account for as much as one-half of the company's sales in any given year. The salespeople were paid an annual salary of $50,000 plus 0.5-percent commission on sales they made in retail stores. The major manufacturer expositions for Sharratt occur in Toronto in October and High Point in April. Regional expositions are also scheduled during the June–August period in such locations as Vancouver and Detroit.

FURNITURE BUYING BEHAVIOUR

Even though industry research indicates many consumers consider the furniture shopping process to be enjoyable, consumers acknowledge that they lack the confidence to assess furniture construction, make judgments about quality, and accurately evaluate the price of furniture. Consumers also find it difficult to choose among the many styles available, fearing they will not like their choice several years later, or that their selection will not be appropriate for their home and they will be unable to return it.

Results of a consumer panel sponsored by *Better Homes and Gardens* and composed of its subscribers provide the most comprehensive information available on furniture-buying behaviour. Selected findings from the *Better Homes and Gardens* survey are reproduced in the Appendix. Other findings arising from this research are as follows:

- 94% (of the subscribers) enjoy buying furniture somewhat or very much.

- 84% believe "the higher the price, the higher the quality" when buying home furnishings.
- 72% browse or window-shop furniture stores even if they don't need furniture.
- 85% read furniture ads before they actually need furniture.
- 99% agree with the statement "When shopping for furniture and home furnishings, I like the salesperson to show me what alternatives are available, answer my questions, and let me alone so I can think about it and maybe browse around."
- 95% say they get redecorating ideas or guidance from magazines.
- 41% have written for a manufacturer's booklet.
- 63% say they need decorating advice to "put it all together."

THE BUDGET MEETING

At the January 10 meeting attended by Dunn and Taubner executives and Sharratt executives, Jack Dunn proposed that the expenditure for consumer advertising be increased by $200,000 for 2002. Co-operative advertising and trade advertising allowances would remain at 2001 levels. Jack further recommended that shelter magazines account for the bulk of the incremental expenditure for consumer advertising.

Joan Seto, Sharratt's Vice-President of Sales, disagreed with the budget allocation and noted that sales expenses and administration costs were expected to rise by $50,000 in 2002. Moreover, Joan believed that an additional sales representative was needed to service Sharratt's accounts, since 50 new accounts were being added. She estimated that the cost of the additional representative, including salary and expenses, would be at least $70,000 in 2002. "That's about $120,000 in additional sales expenses that have to be added into our promotional budget for 2002," Joan noted. She continued:

"We recorded sales of $75 million in 2001. If we assume a 4-percent increase in sales in 2002, that means our total budget will be about $3.9 million, if my figures are right—a $225,000 increase over our previous budget. And I need $120,000 of that. In other words, $105,000 is available for other kinds of promotion."

Jack's reply to Joan noted that the company planned to introduce several new styles of living room and dining room furniture in 2002 and that these new items would require consumer advertising in shelter magazines to be launched successfully. He agreed with Joan that increased funding of the sales effort might be necessary and thought that Sharratt might draw funds from co-operative advertising allowances and trade promotion.

Phil interrupted the dialogue between Joan and Jack to mention that the $200,000 increase in promotion was $25,000 less than the 5-percent "percentage-of-sales" policy limit. He pointed out, however, that higher material costs plus a recent wage increase were forecast to squeeze Sharratt's gross profit margin and threaten the company objective of achieving a 5-percent net profit margin before taxes. "Perhaps some juggling of the figures is necessary," he concluded. "Both of you have good points. Let me think about what's been said and then let's schedule a meeting for a week from today."

As Phil reviewed his notes from the meeting, he realized that the funds allocated to promotion were only part of the question. How the funds would be allocated within the budget was also crucial. A call to Sean Tallon might be helpful in this regard, too.

Appendix

Selected Findings from the *Better Homes and Gardens* Consumer Panel Report–Home Furnishings*

Question: If you were going to buy furniture in the near future, how important would the following factors be in selecting the store to buy furniture?

Factor	Very Important	Somewhat Important	Not too Important	Not at All Important	No Answer
Sells high-quality furnishings	63%	31%	4%	1%	1%
Has a wide range of different furniture styles	59	29	8	3	1
Gives you personal service	60	30	8	1	1
Is a highly dependable store	85	13	1	–	1
Offers decorating help from experienced home planners	27	36	25	11	1
Lets you "browse" all you want	77	18	3	1	1
Sells merchandise that's a good value for the money	82	16	1	–	1
Displays furniture in individual room settings	36	41	19	3	1
Has a relaxed, no-pressure atmosphere	80	17	2	–	1
Has well-informed salespeople	77	20	2	–	1
Has a very friendly atmosphere	68	28	3	–	1
Carries the style of furniture you like	88	10	1	–	1

*Reprinted courtesy of the *Better Homes and Gardens* Consumer Panel. Results are based on responses from 449 panel members.

Question: Below is a list of 15 criteria that may influence what furniture you buy. Please rank each from 1 as most important to 3 as least important.

	1	2	3
Guarantee or warranty	11%	11%	26%
Brand name	9	7	14
Comfort	35	28	15
Decorator suggestion	4	2	3
Material used	15	24	15
Delivery time	1	1	1
Size 8	11	14	
Styling and design	33	18	22
Construction	34	24	13
Fabric	4	26	25
Durability	37	19	14
Finish on wooden parts	6	15	17
Price	19	22	16
Manufacturer's reputation	4	9	15
Retailer's reputation	2	5	11

Note: Only first three rankings shown.

Question: Listed below are some statements others have made about their homes and the furniture pieces they particularly like. Please indicate, for each statement, how much you agree or disagree with each one.

Statement	Agree Completely	Agree Somewhat	Neither Agree nor Disagree	Disagree Somewhat	Disagree Completely	No Answer
I wish there were some way to be really sure of getting good quality in furniture	62%	25%	5%	4%	3%	1%
I really enjoy shopping for furniture	49	28	8	10	4	1
I would never buy any furniture without my husband's/wife's approval	47	23	11	10	7	2
I wish I had more confidence in my ability to decorate my home attractively	23	32	12	12	19	2

Question: Listed below are some factors that may influence your choice of furnishings. Please rate them with 1 being most important, 2 being second most important, and 3 being least important, until all factors have been ranked.

	1	2	3
Friends and/or neighbours	1%	17%	16%
Family or spouse	63	9	14
Magazine advertising	16	30	30
Television advertising	1	7	15
Store displays	19	37	22

Note: Only first three rankings shown.

Question: When you go shopping for a major piece of furniture or smaller pieces of furniture, who, if anyone, do you usually go with? (Multiple responses allowed.) Who, if anyone, helps you decide? (Multiple responses allowed.)

	Usually Go with		Helps Decide	
	Major Pieces	Other Pieces	Major Pieces	Other Pieces
Husband	82%	60%	86%	64%
Mother or mother-in-law	6	9	2	5
Friend	12	19	4	8
Decorator	4	2	3	3
Other relative	16	15	10	13
Other person	3	3	2	2
No one else	5	22	7	24
No answer	1	3	1	2

Federal Express (Canada)

Gordon H. G. McDougall
and Keith Dorken

Anita Kilgour, the Office Manager for Desktop Innovations (DI), was still upset as she mailed the letter to Federal Express (FedEx). The letter (shown in Exhibit 1) detailed the problems she had encountered in shipping two packages from Kitchener, Ontario to Simpsonville, South Carolina via FedEx. Only one of the two packages, each containing one-half of a display booth, had arrived for the trade show. The show was a disaster for the dealer who was at the trade show promoting DI's software product.

Anita knew the importance of this trade show to the firm. DI, a small software company located in Kitchener, produces the MainBoss Maintenance software package (software designed to control a company's maintenance activities), which it licenses to dealers that market the software to end users. In this case, the dealer, Heat Treating Services Unlimited, was going to market DI's software package to potential customers at the Greater Charlotte Plant and Engineering Maintenance Show. The dealer expected to receive around 100 potential sales leads based on DI's experience at similar trade shows. While Anita didn't know the number of leads or sales the dealer would have obtained, when she talked to the dealer to confirm that half of the booth was not going to arrive he said that he thought the show would be a "write-off."

Anita was very disappointed in the way that FedEx had handled the situation. FedEx was known as an innovative, reliable company that had won awards for its excellent service. It had a reputation for delivering "on-time, every time." (See Exhibit 2 for information on Federal Express.) Anita was aware that FedEx provided a delivery guarantee, having dealt with the company for a number of years. She checked the FedEx materials she had received when she set up DI's account and found the following statement under Money-Back Guarantees: "As always, we stand behind our services. FedEx offers two money-back guarantees for your shipments within Canada: if your shipment arrives even 60 seconds late, or if we can't tell you the precise status of your package within 30 minutes after you inquire, you're eligible for a full refund or credit. *Some restrictions apply. Call 1-800-Go-FedEx or see the current FedEx Worldwide Service Guide for details." (Exhibit 3 provides the guarantee conditions given in the Service Guide.)

How could they do this? she wondered. *And after I called FedEx to find out the best way to get the boxes to Simpsonville, allowed plenty of time to get the boxes there, and kept calling them when things went wrong, it still didn't work. I'll be really interested in seeing how they reply to my letter, if they do.*

EXHIBIT 1	Letter to Federal Express

October 16, 1998

To: Federal Express
Attn: Julie Curry
Executive Desk, Customer Service
1300 Central Parkway W., Suite 200
Mississauga, ON L5C 4G8

From: Anita Kilgour
Office Manager
Desktop Innovations
Re: Waybill 400-3947-4352

I am writing to complain about the service my company received in shipping two packages recently. Not only did FedEx lose one of the packages for a considerable length of time, they repeatedly failed to follow through on promises they made once the package was found. In particular, several FedEx employees said they would phone me to confirm various shipping details, but not one ever actually made a phone call as promised.

Desktop Innovations is a small company whose software packages are sold by dealers throughout Canada and the U.S. As part of our marketing efforts, we have put together a display booth that our dealers can set up at local trade shows to advertise our software. The display booth packs away into two boxes.

On Wednesday, October 7, I contacted FedEx about the best way to ship the two boxes from Kitchener, Ontario to Simpsonville, South Carolina. Simpsonville is the headquarters of one of our dealers: Heat Treating Services Unlimited. The dealer intended to set up the booth at a trade show in Charlotte, NC, on October 14–15.

EXHIBIT 1	Letter to Federal Express (continued)

We wanted the boxes to arrive in Simpsonville by Monday, October 12. This would give the dealer plenty of time to transport the boxes on to Charlotte. The FedEx representative said that International Economy would get the boxes there by Monday.

Unfortunately, only one of the boxes made it to Simpsonville on time. According to FedEx, the other lost its shipping bill while passing through Memphis. Because the box still had our company address on it, Memphis sent it back to Toronto as a first step in getting it back to us in Kitchener. However, even though the box arrived in Toronto on Friday, October 9, no one contacted us that it was there and no one tried to send it on the rest of the way to Kitchener.

In the afternoon of Tuesday, October 13, our dealer became concerned that he'd only received one box. When he called me, I phoned FedEx and asked them to trace the missing box. They said they would check and get back to me. They never called back.

I called again before going home from work. FedEx assured me they would call and leave a message on my voice mail, telling what was going on.

That night, I checked my office voice mail. Again, no phone call. Therefore, I called FedEx from my home. At this point, I was finally told that FedEx had been unable to track down the package. (The FedEx employee said, "We don't like to use the word *lost*.") However, the person I talked to said he would continue checking and would call first thing Wednesday morning to tell what was going on.

Of course, no one called Wednesday morning. Eventually, I phoned and was told someone would get back to me within an hour. No one did.

In the afternoon, I called again. Finally, someone had found what happened to the package: that it had been sitting in Toronto all this time. FedEx promised to ship it out ASAP...but by now, our dealer was at the trade show in Charlotte, not in Simpsonville. (And the first day of the trade show had been wasted.)

I arranged with FedEx to send the package to Charlotte rather than Simpsonville. FedEx's Charlotte office was supposed to call our dealer on his cellphone when the package came in. They also promised they would phone me to confirm that the package was on its way.

Naturally, I never got any phone call.

That night, I phoned FedEx again to see how things were going. It was important for the package to get to our dealer by 8:00 a.m. so that he would have time to set up before the trade show opened. Unfortunately, the FedEx staffer, Mike, still thought the package was supposed to go to Simpsonville. After a long conversation, I finally convinced them that it should go to Charlotte, and once again, I asked them to make sure they called our dealer and also called me to make sure things had worked properly.

No one called me. No one called our dealer. The package never showed up in Charlotte. Our dealer called the North Wendover office in Charlotte where the package should have been. Apparently, it had been shipped to the Simpsonville depot.

Since our dealer intended to leave Charlotte when the trade show was over, there was no point in delivering the package to FedEx's Charlotte office anymore. Therefore, I made one more phone call to get FedEx to deliver the package to our dealer's Simpsonville office. Somewhat to my surprise, the package eventually got there. It arrived late in the afternoon, today.

EXHIBIT 1	Letter to Federal Express (continued)

Needless to say, I was unhappy with FedEx's performance with all this. I spoke to a FedEx supervisor named Chris yesterday and asked him what FedEx intended to do to make amends. He immediately said we would not be charged for the shipping, but that hardly satisfied me—if we were invoiced, I would have refused to pay the bill. Chris said he would check with his superiors to see what else FedEx was willing to do; after all, our dealer had wasted two days and $600 booth fees at the Charlotte trade show, and I had accumulated more than three hours on the telephone trying to get things straightened out. (We also wasted $600 on the Charlotte trade show, paying for a booth that never got set up.) Chris promised to get back to me by 3 p.m. yesterday with an answer on what else FedEx might do to make it up to us…but of course, he never did.

Today, I received a basket of chocolates and other goodies from FedEx—amusing, but not what I'd call an apology.

I understand that foul-ups happen, especially with the quantity of packages that FedEx ships every day. However, I think FedEx itself should be worried by the consistent inability of its personnel to make a single one of the phone calls they promised. Even the supervisor named Chris would rather send an anonymous box of chocolates than actually talk to a customer. Perhaps your customer relations policies need an in-depth review.

Yours sincerely,

Anita Kilgour

EXHIBIT 2	Federal Express Canada–Selected Company Information

FedEx's success as the leader in the air express cargo transportation business is based on the philosophy that "when people are placed first they will provide the highest possible service, and the profits will follow."

The *people* priority acknowledges the importance of employee satisfaction and empowerment to create an environment where employees feel secure enough to take risks and become innovative in pursuing quality, service, and customer satisfaction.

Service refers to the consistent and clearly stated service quality goal of 100% customer satisfaction, 100% of the time.

A corporate *profit* should result, if the people and service goals have been met.

The people-first philosophy is implemented through a number of processes including: an annual employee satisfaction survey, promotion from within, an employee recognition and reward program, regular employee communication, pay for performance, an open door program, and a guaranteed fair treatment procedure.

FedEx has been the leader in the use of high technology to improve its services including:

- COSMOS—a computerized tracking system designed to determine the exact location of a package at all times.

- DADS—a computerized dispatch system which communicates with couriers in their vans via computer screens.

EXHIBIT 2	Federal Express Canada–Selected Company Information
	(continued)

- EXPRESSCLEAR—a customs clearing system which electronically transmits information to Customs so that processing can begin prior to the arrival of the actual packages.
- Call centre technology—approximately 250 customer service representatives work at three Canadian locations, responding to 33,000 calls per day. The representatives are accessible 24 hours per day, seven days per week.
- Initiated the 10:30 a.m. service commitment.
- Offered the first money-back guarantee on service commitment and is the only company to offer a money-back guarantee for the ability to track a package within thirty minutes.
- Is the first and only express transportation company to automate the entire process over the Internet.

Some facts about FedEx:

- FedEx employs more than 137,000 people worldwide and provides service to 212 countries.
- A North American radio network dispatches 25,000 couriers (nearly 1,500 in Canada), enabling fast response to customer requests and constant tracking of every shipment.
- FedEx Canada employs more than 3,500 employees in 60 facilities, who serve Canadian shipping needs from coast-to-coast, to the U.S. and internationally to 212 countries.
- FedEx achieves the most rigorous international standards for Quality Management and Assurance by earning ISO 9000 registration for its global operations.
- In 1990, FedEx became the first company in the service category to win the Malcolm Baldrige National Quality Award in the U.S.
- FedEx planes carry more than 2.9 million packages every night, weighing more than 2 million pounds.

Source: www.fedex.ca

EXHIBIT 3	Federal Express Money-Back Guarantee Policy

Money-Back Guarantee Policy*

We offer two Money-Back Guarantees, subject to the terms and conditions set out in this Guide. These Guarantees can be suspended or revoked without notice, at any time, and from time to time, in respect of all customers or any particular customer. These two Guarantees are:

(a) Service Failure

For U.S. and Canadian based payers, we will, at our option, and upon request, either refund or credit to the applicable invoice only your transportation charges, if we

EXHIBIT 3	Federal Express Money-Back Guarantee Policy (continued)

deliver your shipment 60 seconds or more after the applicable delivery commitment time ('service failure'). The following limitations apply:

1. Where Customs or other regulatory clearances are delayed, our delivery commitment time may be modified by adding one business day for each day (or portion thereof) that such clearances are delayed.

2. An exact delivery commitment time can be obtained only by telephoning Customer Service at 1-800-Go-FedEx, and supplying us with the following:
   - Commodity being shipped
   - Date of the shipment
   - Exact destination
   - Weight of Shipment

   Any transit time published in this Guide or elsewhere or quoted by Customer Service without the above noted information is only an estimate and is not a stated delivery commitment time.

3. If the sender or recipient specifies a Customs Broker other than FedEx (where this service is available), notification will usually be given to the broker by 12:00 noon for FedEx® International Priority shipments and 5:00 p.m. for FedEx International Economy® shipments on the first business day the shipment is available for Customs clearance in the destination country, and such notification constitutes timely delivery. If the actual shipment is released to the broker in bond, our responsibility terminates at the time we relinquish custody of the shipment to the broker. However, if we retain custody of the shipment and are responsible for the delivery of the shipment, following receipt of the appropriate Customs release paperwork from another Customs broker, our delivery commitment time is modified by adding one business day for each day (or portion thereof) that our receipt of the paperwork is delayed.

4. For invoiced shipments and for shipments sent using an automated device, we must receive your notification (in writing or by telephone) of a service failure within 30 days from the invoice date. You must furnish with your payment the invoice numbers to which your payment applies. If an invoice is not paid in full, the reason for each unpaid charge must be noted with its waybill or package tracking number.

5. For shipments that we do not invoice (paid by cash, cheque, money order or credit card), you must notify us (in writing or by telephone) of a service failure within 30 days from the date of shipment.

6. Notification of a service failure must include the account number, if any, the waybill or package tracking number, the date of shipment and complete recipient information.

7. A service failure will not be deemed to have occurred if within 30 days after you notify us we provide you with:
   i) Proof of timely delivery, consisting of the date and time of delivery and name of the person who signed for the shipment, or
   ii) Service exception information reflecting that the failure to timely deliver resulted from circumstances described under "Liabilities Not Assumed."

EXHIBIT 3	Federal Express Money-Back Guarantee Policy (continued)

We are not obligated to respond if your request is not received within the time limits stated above.

8. A service failure will not be deemed to have occurred if payment is not made in accordance with the terms set out in this Guide and the package was held until alternate payment arrangements were secured.

9. Only one refund or credit is permitted per package. In the case of multiple-package shipments, this Money-Back Guarantee will apply to every package in the shipment. If a service failure occurs for any package within the shipment, a refund or credit will be given only for the portion of the transportation charges applicable to that package.

10. A refund or credit will be given only if complete recipient information was provided at the time of shipment. Complete recipient information must be provided on either the waybill or through any FedEx automated device.

11. A refund or credit will not be given for shipments delayed due to incorrect addresses or to the unavailability or refusal of a person to accept delivery or sign for the package or due to any of the causes described under "Liabilities Not Assumed."

12. A refund or credit will not be given when we have been authorized to deliver a package without obtaining a signature, but we do not deliver such package without obtaining a signature.

13. This Money-Back Guarantee does not apply to requests for invoice adjustment based on overcharges (see "Billing") or shipments to P.O. Box addresses acceptable for delivery (see "Post Office Box Addresses").

14. This Money-Back Guarantee applies only to transportation charges paid by U.S.- and Canadian-based payers and does not apply to duties, taxes or any other charges.

15. A refund or credit will not be given to customers using FedEx automated shipping devices if incorrect package tracking numbers are applied to the subject package or shipment.

16. This Money-Back Guarantee applies only to shipments tendered using FedEx First Overnight™, FedEx®, Priority Overnight, FedEx International First® and FedEx® International Economy. Contact FedEx Customer Service at 1-800-Go-FedEx® for further information.

17. This Money-Back Guarantee does not apply to undeliverable or returned shipments or any shipment containing Dangerous Goods.

18. This Money-Back Guarantee does not apply to delays in delivery caused by adherence to FedEx policies regarding the payment of duties and taxes prior to Customs clearance or at delivery.

19. See "FedEx® International Broker Select" for additional restrictions on the Money-Back Guarantee applicable to such shipments.

20. Credits for transportation charges will be applied to the payer's account only, and refunds will be made payable to the payer only.

EXHIBIT 3	Federal Express Money-Back Guarantee Policy (continued)

Written requests for refunds or credits under this policy should be directed to:

When by mail: Federal Express Canada Ltd.
                P.O. Box 2700
                Streetsville Postal Station
                Mississauga, Ontario L5M 2L8

When by FedEx service: Federal Express Canada Ltd.
                         1270 Central Parkway West
                         Suite 200
                         Mississauga, Ontario L5C 4P4

(b) Package Status

At our option, we will either refund or credit transportation charges upon request, if we cannot report the status of your package within 30 minutes of inquiry (unless due to the fault of the customer). Package status is defined as the most recent electronically-scanned location of your package reflected in our COSMOS tracking system. In order to qualify for this Money-Back Guarantee due to untimely package status reporting, the following limitations apply:

1. You must telephone us within our business hours and make your request within 15 days after the date of shipment.

2. Written requests will not be accepted.

3. The response period under this Money-Back Guarantee is 30 minutes per package. Where more than one package status inquiry is made in a call, we will respond within 30 minutes of our receiving all package related information.

4. You must provide your account number, if any, the waybill or package tracking number, date of shipment, pieces and weight and the recipient's name, address and postal/zip code on the first call.

5. Only one refund or credit is permitted per package. In the case of multiple package shipments, this Money-Back Guarantee will apply to each package in the shipment, but a refund or credit is only available on those packages whose status is not timely reported.

6. This Money-Back Guarantee is only applicable to shipments within Canada or from Canada to the continental U.S. and does not apply to those delivery points outside FedEx direct service areas. Call 1-800-Go-FedEx® for further information on FedEx direct service and extended service areas.

7. This Money-Back Guarantee does not apply to requests made to FedEx via the Internet.

8. Credits for transportation charges will be applied to the payer's account only and refunds will be made payable to the payer only.

* Offer void where prohibited by law.

Source: FedEx WorldWide Service Guide, Book 9, August 15, 1998, 23-25.

City of Kentner

Charles B. Weinberg

Marco Porter, Chief Engineer of the Department of Water in Kentner, did not know how to react to the first rain in weeks in the drought-stricken Cascadia area. He did know, however, that he must develop and implement a politically acceptable plan to reduce citywide water consumption by 25 percent. It was the beginning of 2001 and close to the end of what was normally considered the "wet" season in the region.

He wondered whether a few days of rain would result in a decrease in water-conservation efforts. Marco realized that he could not continue to rely on the effect of the strong and extensive newspaper stories that had announced the launching of the initial water conservation campaign in January with headlines such as "Save Water or Else...Area Warned" and "Water Cut Target 10%."

THE DROUGHT

For the second year in a row, Cascadia had experienced record drought conditions, with rainfall less than 50 percent of normal and reservoir levels at record lows.

Shortly after the start of the year, most people realized that the unseasonably dry weather had the potential to change people's lifestyles, to cause industrial problems, and to threaten the existence of farms and ranches that depended upon irrigated water.

In the early months of the year, many magazines and television stations had reported extensively on the drought. People generally smiled at slogans like "Save Water—Shower with a Friend," while trivia buffs prospered with such gems as "The toilet accounts for 40 percent of all indoor household water usage—up to seven gallons a flush." However, the lack of rain has serious consequences. For example, utilities in the Pacific Northwest, which used hydroelectric energy as a source of power, would have to turn to more expensive sources. Some jurisdictions had imposed rolling blackouts. Forest rangers were worried about fire hazards; outdoors enthusiasts about the loss of fishing and boating opportunities; and homeowners about keeping lawns and gardens green. Many reservoirs had gone dry, and there was no chance of any change in that condition until the end of the year. No one had dared to consider the consequences of a third drought year.

PUBLIC OPINION IN CASCADIA

In March, the Cascadia Poll conducted a representative survey of 1,202 residents and published the results in newspapers throughout the region. Eighty-five percent of those surveyed believed the drought was either "extremely serious" or "somewhat serious." When asked which user class should be cut the most if mandatory rationing became necessary, respondents replied as follows:

User Class	Percentage Saying Cut This Group Most
Business and Industry	50
Households	33
Health and Safety	3
Agriculture	3
No Opinion	11

With regard to reduction of household water usage by 25 percent, only 10 percent of respondents said it would cause severe problems; however, 51 percent said a 50-percent cutback would cause severe problems. Finally, 93 percent claimed to be practising some form of water conservation, such as using less water for bathing (70%), watering lawns less (67%), and less frequent car washing (58%). Twenty-four percent claimed to have installed devices in their toilet tanks to reduce the amount of water used to flush, and 16 percent said they had installed water-flow restrictors to reduce the rate of water flow in their showers.

CITY AND REGION

Cascadia's average annual rainfall of 39 cm occurred mainly from October through March. It almost never rained in June, July, and August. In the past two years, the rainfall had been less than half of normal levels.

Kentner, a city of 55,000 people located about 35 kilometres south of the capital city of Calberta, was one of a number of cities that formed an extensive urban corridor along the length of the Cilbert River.

Kentner residents tended to be highly educated and had a median income level among the highest in the nation. They took an active interest in city affairs, and their city government was considered to be very well run. The *Kentner Times*, with a circulation of 50,000 in the surrounding area, reported extensively on the actions of the local city governments. Kentner fell within the circulation area of the *Calberta Chronicle*. The presence of a major university nearby, as well as other factors, had stimulated the development of a high-technology emphasis in many companies located in Kentner. The business community of Kentner had in the past been supportive of most community projects and had demonstrated an effective response to the initial water-conservation program. Civic groups had also been supportive of community conservation projects.

THE WATER SYSTEM IN KENTNER

The Kentner Department of Water (DW) was responsible for the planning, production, and marketing of the city's water supply.[1] Marco Porter was in charge of the operations of the DW. The DW's primary goal was to serve the populace with an adequate supply of drinking water for domestic, industrial, commercial, and public needs at reasonable rates. Although profit maximization was not a goal, the DW sought to provide revenue to Kentner's general fund by operating efficiently and earning a reasonable (5 to 8 percent) return on investment.

These broad goals had been effectively translated into measurable operating goals. The DW maintained water pressure within narrow tolerances. The quality of the potable (drinkable) water supplied was consistently monitored and checked against a preset quality standard. The customer service department had a goal of a 15-minute response time to a customer complaint. Currently a service crew arrived on the scene to investigate a complaint within 30 minutes of notification.

In addition, the DW provided such complementary services as technical advice on methods and new devices that could be employed by industrial and manufacturing customers to conserve water and consequently reduce costs. Marco and his staff had worked successfully with a number of local companies in developing efficient water usage programs well before the current crisis arose. In recent years, a number of local companies had achieved significant reductions in water consumption by recycling water used for cooling, by watering grounds at night when less evaporation took place, and by preventive maintenance programs.

Water Supply and Demand

The source of supply for Kentner was the Calberta Water Department (CWD) System, which served the city of Kentner and more than 30 communities in the area. The primary

---

[1.] The city of Kentner supplied electricity, gas, and water to all residents and commercial or industrial customers in the city. Usage and billing rates for each utility were separately itemized on the monthly bill sent to all residents. While online billing was an option, less than 2% of residents had opted for this format. However, 16% of residents paid their monthly bills through an automatic bill paying system.

source for the CWD were the Lake Dirckx and Lake Rena Reservoirs in Yenton National Park, nearly 200 kilometres away. Rain and snow melt in the Yenton area of the mountain range filled these reservoirs, and the water was conveyed to the area through a series of pipelines. The DW had a contract with the CWD that expired in 2015. If there is insufficient water in the CWD, the contract stated that water supplied to all users (including the city of Calberta) would be cut back by a uniform percentage of the previous year's usage. The total amount of water supplied by CWD to Kentner was metered, and monthly dollar sales were determined at a preset rate. Monthly sales figures (volume of water) for the most recent six-year period are given in Exhibit 1.

Because the city's population was stable, the demand for water in Kentner had been practically static for several years (Exhibit 1); no increase in demand was projected in the future. The DW categorized its customers by usage into the following segments: domestic, commercial, industrial, and public. The domestic consumers were further broken down into single-family and multiple-family (apartment and condominium-type) units. In the latter case, each family was not metered separately; instead, the complex as a whole was metered. Customer data are shown in Exhibits 2 and 4.

Pricing Policy

The pricing policy for water in Kentner was based on the following criteria:

1. An equitable allocation of revenues and cost for the various classes of customers;
2. To provide a reasonable return on investment;
3. To provide the minimum basic requirement of a family for water at the lowest possible price (this was termed a "lifeline rate"); and
4. To encourage conservation.

The level of prices was based primarily on the cost of the supply from CWD (which accounted for approximately 63 percent of total revenue). Other costs such as distribution, administration, and general expenses accounted for approximately 19 percent of revenues.

The scale of charges was approved by the City Council based on the DW's recommendation. The current scale of charges had been in effect since last July 1. Until that date, the scale of charges had been such that the marginal cost decreased with increased consumption. The new structure made the unit price greater as consumption increased, so that a user of more than 1,000 CCFs (1 CCF = one hundred cubic feet) per month would pay about 10 percent more per CCF above 1,000 than would a user of 50 CCFs per month.[2] In addition, a general price increase of 8 percent was made. Careful analysis had shown that demand for water was not materially affected by this pricing strategy. As shown in Exhibit 3, rates were similar to those in nearby cities.

The Water Shortage Problem

Despite the two years of record drought, it was only in mid-January when Marco heard on the radio that all area cities would need to cut water consumption by 10 percent. The need for reduced water usage immediately received extensive coverage in the local newspapers.

[2.] Water consumption is measured in terms of "units" of one hundred cubic feet. One unit = 1 CCF = 3000 litres.

The City's Water Conservation Program

Following the CWD's request of a voluntary curtailment of 10 percent in water consumption, the DW developed a conservation program aimed at all users, with special emphasis on domestic and industrial users. The thrust of the campaign was the conservation of water for the benefit of the community in general. After the Kentner City Council had adopted a resolution on water usage curtailment, all Kentner residents were sent a message from the Mayor, some informational materials (Exhibit 5), and two water-flow restrictors. A water-flow restrictor (a disc installed on the pipe leading to the shower head) reduced the flow of water by as much as half when showers were taken.

Marco felt that it was too early to assess the long-run effect that DW's campaign would have. However, because of the extraordinary publicity given to the water shortage problem by the media, the community was well aware of the problem; it had reacted by reducing consumption by 17 percent compared to 2000, since the emergence of the water shortage problem. The figures, in fact, were so satisfactory that there was a temptation to complacency. However, other resource crises (such as the fuel one of 1973) had shown the public's memory to be very short, and Marco feared that if the issues were no longer of interest to the media the public would very rapidly return to its previous levels of consumption. The current shortage was clearly not just a short-term problem. Because there was little expectation of significant amounts of additional rainfall before summer, the water shortage problem would probably last until the end of the year.

Marco knew that 70 percent more water usage occurred in the summer months, when people tended their gardens and watered their lawns and companies maintained the extensive landscaping around their factories, laboratories, and research centres (see Exhibit 4). Would those who conserved water when it was supposed to rain also conserve when it was not supposed to rain?

The Need for Further Conservation Efforts

Though there was awareness of a water shortage problem in the community, Marco was concerned that the nature of the problem might not have been fully understood. Thus, he wanted to develop a plan that would ensure that the public had the correct perception of the long-term nature of the problem and was provided with the information, motivation, and methodology they needed to help overcome the problem. Marco had a budget of $24,000 for a water conservation program. Nearly $14,000 had already been invested in the current campaign.

Marco had to devise and implement a second water conservation plan that would reinforce the impact of the initial conservation campaign and encourage greater conservation in the immediate future. Although some had suggested a "mandatory" water conservation program, allocations for different user classes would have to be made and decisions about how to treat unmetered apartment dwellers would be required. Typically, apartment buildings had one central water meter, so it was not possible to determine how much water each separate unit was using.

With regard to households, a mandatory limit on water consumption could be stated as a flat amount per person resident in the household or as a percentage reduction from usage in the same month of the previous year. The first approach was insensitive to variation in individual needs; the second approach would penalize those who had been efficient in previous years.

Past experience had suggested that a small price increase would have little effect, and even the doubling of the current water rates would only raise the average household bill to $16.00. It was very unlikely that the City Council would approve a policy banning the watering of lawns and, even if approved, the enforcement of such a ban would be exceedingly difficult.

As Marco sat pondering the problem and looking out his window at the rain, his telephone rang with the news that the Calberta Water Department had imposed a 25-percent mandatory reduction in water consumption throughout its service area. Marco realized he had a few weeks to prepare a water conservation plan for the City Council to discuss and, hopefully, adopt at its March 31 meeting. In presenting this plan, he knew that he not only would need to defend it against alternative proposals, but also indicate why he believed that his plan would work.

EXHIBIT 1	Water Supplied by CWD to DW (Million cubic feet/month)						
	1995	1996	1997	1998	1999	2000	Average
January	40	46	47	45	48	52	46
February	50	46	45	45	52	58	49
March	45	52	44	46	47	55	48
April	60	71	60	54	53	67	61
May	66	83	79	74	67	82	75
June	86	92	94	94	100	98	94
July	93	95	104	89	99	101	97
August	98	100	95	95	100	97	98
September	92	90	89	100	89	82	90
October	73	71	71	72	73	67	71
November	65	49	54	63	58	66	59
December	48	44	45	48	56	50	49
Average	68	70	69	69	70	73	70

EXHIBIT 2	Number of Customers and Annual Water Usage by User Class

Number of Customers Each Year

	1995	1996	1997	1998	1999	2000
Single-Family	14,083	14,150	14,178	14,146	14,251	14,268
Multi-Family	1,235	1,261	1,281	1,240	1,252	1,253
Commercial	1,321	1,332	1,425	1,490	1,496	1,513
Industrial	227	228	265	271	272	271
Public Facility	198	200	218	213	208	203
City	121	124	71	207	259	260
Total	17,185	17,295	17,438	17,567	17,738	17,768

Annual CCF per Customer

	1995	1996	1997	1998	1999	2000
Single-Family	224	236	225	209	210	204
Multi-Family	435	415	398	410	431	413
Commercial	709	768	744	662	890	855
Industrial	7,886	7,835	7,410	7,734	8,211	8,229
Public Facility	3,924	4,144	3,495	4,319	2,601	2,827
City	2,571	2,608	3,426	1,497	1,212	991
Total	436	452	444	443	448	455

EXHIBIT 3	Average Monthly Water Bill for Kentner and Other Nearby Cities

	Usage* (CCF)	Kentner ($)	City A ($)	City B ($)	City C ($)
Residential	18	8.00	7.66	9.31	7.71
Commercial	60	22.78	24.05	31.52	24.61
Industrial	630	224.58	238.70	296.74	241.65
Industrial Large (1)	2,500	889.33	940.50	1,167.69	950.65
Industrial Large (2)	5,000	1,784.78	1,761.00	2,338.20	1,827.40
Industrial Large (3)	10,000	3,567.28	3,329.70	4,661.25	3,496.20

* Average usage in Kentner for different user classes

EXHIBIT 4   Water Demand—Monthly and Quarterly Average (thousands of units—one unit = 1 CCF)

	Quarter I				Quarter II				Quarter III				Quarter IV			
	Jan	Feb	Mar	Tot.	Apr	May	June	Tot.	July	Aug	Sept	Tot.	Oct	Nov	Dec	Tot.
Industrial	146	170	163	479	168	183	196	537	213	216	197	626	201	177	156	534
Public Facility	42	45	45	132	50	66	84	200	86	85	85	256	68	55	44	167
City Departments	16	22	16	54	14	32	42	88	46	41	39	126	24	23	16	63
Domestic Single-Family	180	163	167	510	190	273	379	842	406	363	361	1130	243	194	176	613
Domestic Multi-Family	41	43	38	122	39	42	52	133	54	51	53	158	43	40	40	123
Commercial	77	88	83	248	75	90	110	275	123	120	110	353	93	79	71	243
Total	502	531	512	1545	536	686	863	2075	928	876	845	2649	672	568	503	1743

EXHIBIT 5   Water Conservation Tips

YOUR PERSONALIZED WATER SAVING PLAN

Use the chart below to determine where the water is used in your house each day and where you want to cut back.

Directions:

1. Locate in the "Water use" column all the ways you use water.
2. On the row next to each water use write the number of times per day you use water in that way.
3. Multiply the number of litres indicated for that water use by the number of times per day. Enter the answer in the "Litres per day" column.
4. After you finish filling in the "Litres per day" column, add up the total number of litres in that column.
5. The total litres per day can be used to devise your own water saving plan. If you wish to save 10% of the water you use, multiply the total by .10.
6. Now go back to the chart and figure out how you can save that number of litres. For example, a family of four took four showers per day. For their water saving plan they decided to insert a flow restrictor in their shower. The first three rows in the chart show how their entries for "Shower" would look.

(continued over)

EXHIBIT 5 | **Water Conservation Tips** (continued)

Water Saving Plan

Water use		Typical litres per use	No. of times per day	Litres per day	Water Saving Plan	
					No. of times per day	Litres per day
Example						
Shower	Normal, water running	100	4	400	4	272
	1 flow restrictor, water running	68				
	Wet down, soap up, rinse off	16				
Shower	Normal, water running	100				
	Flow restrictor, water running	68				
	Wet down, soap up, rinse off	16				
Bath	Full	144				
	Minimal water level	44				
Brushing Teeth	Tap running	40				
	Wet brush, rinse briefly	8				
Shaving	Tap running	80				
	Fill basin	4				
Dishwashing	Tap running	120				
	Wash & rinse in dish pan or sink	20				
Automatic Dishwasher	Full cycle	64				
	Short cycle	28				
Washing Hands	Tap running	8				
	Fill basin	4				
Toilet Flushing	Normal	20				
	Water saving toilet	12				
	Toilet with displacement bottles	16				

EXHIBIT 5 | Water Conservation Tips (continued)

Water Saving Plan (continued)

Water use	Typical litres per use	No. of times per day	Litres per day	Water Saving Plan	
				No. of times per day	Litres per day
Other					
Washing Machine	Full cycle, top water level 32* Short cycle, minimum water level 16*	No. of times per week			
		No. of times per week			
Outdoor Watering	Average hose (40 litres per minute)				

Water saving total _____

Note: To compare this with your utility bill, 3,000 litres are equal to one unit. Total litres per day _____

10% saving (total litres × .10) _____

Water saving goal _____

* The figures are the average per day for once a week use

Riverside Credit Union

Jeff Schulz and
Peggy Cunningham

Frank Timmerman, Vice-President of Marketing at Riverside Credit Union, sat at his desk with a smile on his face. After months of effort, he believed he now really had a handle on Riverside Credit Union's membership. He had been in charge of the initiative to segment the membership base to see if he could better understand how different members contributed to the profitability of the credit union. He also wanted to know which members he should concentrate on in terms of building their business to ensure future profitability. Having a better understanding of the various segment profiles, he believed, would also help his Credit Union better target appropriate financial products to members.

BACKGROUND

Riverside Credit Union is a well-established credit union with just over 100,000 retail members and a small but rapidly growing business membership of about 10,000 members. Credit unions are similar to banks in many respects, but they also have a number of key differences. Like banks, they offer many financial services—everything from savings and chequing accounts to investment advice. However, unlike banks, credit unions don't have customers—they have members. The members are the actual owners of the credit union. Furthermore, credit unions have a strong sense of their social responsibility in addition to their financial responsibility.

Riverside Credit Union, for example, describes itself as a democratic, ethical, and innovative provider of financial services to its members. It is committed to doing business not only in a way that strengthens its own long-term success but also in a manner that contributes to the social, economic, and environmental well-being of the community in which it operates.

Riverside Credit Union has been quite successful and has assets under administration of almost $2.5 billion. Much of its success is due to its excellent member service culture, the regular introduction of new competitive products, and an aggressive pricing policy that ensures members are always getting some of the best rates available. Riverside Credit Union also has a good distribution network with which to serve its members. It has 15 branches, 30 ATMs, PC banking, a call centre that is mostly dedicated to serving members, and an interactive voice-response phone banking system. It also has a number of mortgage development managers. During the past two years, the branch salesforce had been realigned to focus more on relationship selling. The salesforce has placed the greatest emphasis on members with high deposit balances.

Riverside Credit Union is located in a large urban area that has until recently been growing a little faster than the rest of the country. During the last year or so the economy has been slowing, resulting in much more competition among financial institutions. There is also more competition from category killers that are focusing on specific product areas like credit cards and mortgages. The Internet has facilitated this type of banking and that done by other "direct" financial institutions, which are aggressively competing for savings and investment accounts, with rates approaching term-deposit levels. Continuing pressure on margin has made it impossible for Riverside Credit Union to maintain its aggressive pricing policy, and as such it has seen some erosion of its core business.

Riverside Credit Union has long prided itself on having a strong product marketing group. Frank Timmerman was a member of this group. One of the tools that has been invaluable to the marketing group has been the member database information system (MDIS). This database captured all of the product information (except the off-balance mutual fund business). Frank knew that although there had been a lot of member analysis and research, most of it revolved around specific products. Little was known about the full value or nature of the relationships Riverside Credit Union had with its membership.

Thus, under Frank's leadership a new project was launched so that the marketing department could deepen its understanding of the membership. Frank thought it was critical that Riverside Credit Union be able to anticipate its members' needs and to build long-term relationships with the members. The information currently available in the database wasn't up to this task. Therefore, a detailed segmentation analysis was conducted of the entire retail membership. The marketing team hired an expert in segmentation to assist with the work. When the project started, no one knew exactly what the results would show.

SEGMENTATION APPROACH

Frank believed that getting this type of information was a pressing need given the growing competition in his marketplace. Since he had only a short time frame within which to complete the initial study, he decided to use only the data currently available in the MDIS for the analysis. Any external data he might want, or external research he might conduct later, could be added once he had a firmer understanding of the various member segments. Frank and the team felt that information like share of wallet would be too difficult to get for the entire membership, or would be too inaccurate to be useful.

Frank and the team decided there were three things they most needed to know about the membership: (1) profitability of the relationships, (2) behaviour of the members with regard to their usage of various Riverside Credit Union products and services, and (3) future potential. Details on each of these dimensions and the data that were used in the analysis are outlined below.

Profitability was examined by summing the margin, fee, and service charge revenue for each member and then subtracting the expenses. With the assistance of Accounting, the total cost for each transaction type was identified and then divided by the total number of transactions to generate a per-transaction cost. With input from Sales and Branch operations, setup and maintenance costs were also determined. Expenses were subtracted from revenues to calculate profitability for each member. Even though there were a few missing numbers, the team agreed that the calculation would represent the relative profitability of one member versus another. Profitability would be looked at by value and by decile to understand the dynamics of the membership.

Member behaviour, or the type of financial relationship the person had with Riverside Credit Union, was the next variable analyzed. To understand this, Riverside compiled all of the data it had for each member for the past year. These included transactional data, member age, their account information, information on what channel they used, length of their membership, and so on. A clustering technique was used to group members so that those who demonstrated similar "behaviour" were grouped together while keeping the groups as distinct as possible from the other groups.

To assess *potential,* predictive models were developed for the core products offered by Riverside Credit Union (RRSPs, mortgages, term deposits, loans, credit cards and lines of credit, etc.). These models were created using statistical techniques (such as regression). The models were formulated using data from members who had previously purchased the product. The model can then be used to predict future sales of that particular product. Riverside Credit Union had used predictive models successfully in the past to target product campaigns, and it was pretty comfortable with their use. Each member would be scored for each product. This information was then added to the analysis.

SEGMENTATION RESULTS

Profitability: Exhibit 1 summarizes the annual member profitability analysis.

Behaviour segments: Seven different member segments emerged from the analysis. They are described in Exhibit 2 in order of average profitability. Each segment profile also includes a description of average funds under administration (FUA) and average products per member.

Frank conducted some further analysis that quickly showed that although segments 6 and 7 had the lowest average profit and did cost Riverside Credit Union money to serve, the majority of the members that had negative profitability were in segment 4 (30 percent of segment 4 generated approximately 60 percent of the total negative profit). The segment 4 members did a lot of transactions across all channels, but they did not have high enough balances or revenue to offset the transaction costs.

Potential: All of the behaviour segments had some members who had higher predictive scores for some products. When the overall scores were combined to give an indication of relative potential, Frank was able to create an index for each segment. Under the indexing system, a score of 100 is average; anything over 100 means higher than average potential. Exhibit 3 outlines the segment indexes.

The segmentation analysis provided tremendous insight to the marketing department, not only about the current status of the membership but also about the future potential of the individual segments. With more knowledge about which members were profitable, they were able to develop member-focused strategies that were geared to either help Riverside Credit Union retain the member or to grow the relationship through targeted cross-selling programs. The marketing department used the information to help restructure their department. Frank was convinced it would help in the transition from being product-focused to being more member-focused.

EXHIBIT 1	Annual Member Profitability Analysis			
Profit Tier	No. of Members	Percentage	Cum %	Avg. Annual Profit
Top 10%	300	.3	.3	$9,000
10 to 20	1,000	1.0	1.3	$2,700
20 to 30	1,300	1.3	2.6	$2,077
30 to 40	1,900	1.9	4.5	$ 1,421
40 to 50	2,300	2.3	6.8	$ 1,174
50 to 60	3,000	3.0	9.8	$ 900
60 to 70	4.000	4.0	13.8	$ 675
70 to 80	6,000	6.0	19.8	$ 450
80 to 90	8,000	8.0	27.8	$ 338
90 to 100	35,000	35.0	62.8	$ 77
Zero Profit	19,200	19.2	82.0	$ 0
Negative Profit	18,000	18.0	100.0	($ 100)
Total	100,000			

| EXHIBIT 2 | Member Segments in Order of Average Profitability | | | |

Segment	No. of Members	Avg. Profit	Avg. FUA	Products/Member
1	12,000	$900	$150,000	4.5
Complex relationship, with multiple products, mortgage holders, with RRSPs, high lending, utilize all channels with high transaction levels.				
2	8,000	$600	$51,000	3.5
High balance non-RRSP savers, average transaction levels, traditional channel usage (phone, branch, ATM), slightly older, low lending.				
3	13,000	$310	$27,000	2.3
Older, average transactions, average balances, low lending, ATM and branch transactions.				
4	25,000	$225	$22,000	3.2
High lending, high transactions, all channels, similar to segment 1 except low mortgage usage, high credit-card penetration				
5	15,000	$135	$10,000	2.2
Savers (RRSP and other), average balances, low transactions, limited channels.				
6	7,000	$20	$3,100	.3
Younger, savers with lower balances and average transactions.				
7	23,000	$17	$1,100	1.1
Single-product accounts, inactive, low transactions, low balances.				

| EXHIBIT 3 | Segment Indexes | |

Segment	Potential Index	High Potential Products
1	125	Mortgage, RRSP, LOC, Credit Card
2	150	Terms, RRSP
3	140	RRSP, Term
4	200	RRSP, Mortgage, Credit Card, Loans
5	100	RRSP, Mortgage, Credit Card
6	55	Term
7	40	Low on Most, Some Credit Card

Irwin Sports Limited

Michael A. Guolla
and Grant Conrad

On June 6, 1996, Greg Anger, newly appointed Director of Marketing for Irwin Sports (IS), faced the task of creating the 1996–97 communications strategy for the company's two newest products, Ice and In-line Cover Ups, for the annual budget meeting to take place in three weeks.

Ice Cover Ups were goalie pad covers that provided a custom look and rejuvenated or extended the life of used pads. In-line Cover Ups were similar, but provided protection and sliding ability to ice hockey goalie pads when used on abrasive in-line hockey playing surfaces. One year ago, IS had licensed the products from three Ottawa-area university students in a royalty agreement. Consequently, IS could not launch the products until the trade shows held in February 1996; however, the licensors' prototypes were displayed at trade shows in the second half of 1995.

Sales to date had been slow despite the positive reaction received from trade buyers. IS obtained orders for Ice and In-line Cover Ups from one American sports retail chain for its five Canadian outlets in 1996–97. In-line Cover Ups were also sold in 48 independent stores throughout the United States. Price appeared to be an issue, as some trade members had expressed their concern. Canadian Sales Manager Don Jamieson said, "Everyone loves the idea, but no one will bite at this price. I think the magic retail price point is $99.99. At that price I could sell thousands." IS was pursuing a price skimming strategy, with Ice Cover Ups retailing at $195 and In-line Cover Ups retailing at $179. Greg wondered if he could keep these price points as he was putting together a communications strategy that he believed could achieve greater trade acceptance and stimulate consumer sales.

COMPANY BACKGROUND

Irwin Sports (IS) was a division of the Irwin Toy Corporation of Toronto. Irwin Toy marketed its own toy lines and was the Canadian distributor for other major brands. IS followed a similar strategy as it marketed and distributed many leading brands, including Cooper baseball equipment and inflatables (footballs, basketballs, etc.); the WinnWell line of ice hockey equipment; and the recently introduced brand of in-line hockey equipment called Redline by WinnWell.

WinnWell offered a complete line of ice hockey equipment except for skates, helmets, and goalie equipment. IS typically followed a niche strategy for this line based on high-volume sales of moderate-quality equipment to big accounts such as Wal-Mart and Zellers. While IS offered high-end versions for some products, this had not been a priority. Both Ice and In-line Cover Ups were marketed under the WinnWell brand as both products complemented one another.

IS distributed its products throughout Canada and the U.S. and also had representation in 35 other countries. Canadian distribution was handled by a sales manager, two salaried sales reps, and nine sales agencies. Approximately 1,200 Canadian retailers carried IS brands. The sales manager and salaried reps managed about 55 percent of these accounts, which belonged to major chains. The remaining independent accounts were managed by sales agencies that had specific geographic regions and typically employed one or two sales reps. U.S. distribution was handled by a sales manager and 14 sales agencies. Approximately 2,200 retailers carried IS products, but Cooper Baseball accounted for most of the sales. The sales manager was responsible for the major accounts (40%), while the agents handled the remaining accounts (60%) and employed about three reps each. Retailers and agents in both countries typically carried competing sporting goods lines and normally received a 50-percent margin or 5-percent commission, respectively, for low-volume, high-margin items like the Cover Ups. Communication between IS and all reps consisted of two yearly sales meetings, informal meetings at major trade shows, and weekly shipments of promotions and new-product information.

THE PRODUCT CONCEPT

Ice Cover Ups were goalie pad covers that conformed like a second skin to all makes of existing goalie pads. Composed of a lightweight, durable cordura nylon, Ice Cover Ups allowed goalies to match their pads with team colours to complete the professional look of their uniform (Exhibit 1). It also allowed goalies to rejuvenate or extend the life of older pads, which was an attractive option considering the high replacement cost. Ice Cover Ups could be attached and removed quickly, as the existing straps of the goalie pad could pass through the appropriate holes. Finally, the universal design accommodated the variances associated with different pad widths.

Ice Cover Ups were limited to medium and large sizes (e.g., fit 30" to 36" pads) and to red/white, blue/white, and black/white colour options. The size limitation restricted the market to goalies 14 years and up with sufficient height (e.g., 5'4") to require 30-inch pads. To minimize the number of stock-keeping units, IS planned to evaluate the need for a small size for shorter goal pads, and the possibility of more colour options or custom designs, during the first two years.

In-line Cover Ups were a spinoff from the similarly designed Ice Cover Ups. It allowed goalies to protect their leather pads used for ice hockey with a cover so that they could play in-line, ball, or street hockey. Despite the popularity of the sport, in-line leagues suffered from a lack of goalies due to the inherent awkwardness of the position and the excessive costs associated with being an in-line hockey goalie. The awkwardness of in-line goaltending was attributed to a goalie's weak lateral mobility due to the in-line skate design and limited sliding ability due to the friction between leather goal pads and the concrete or asphalt playing surfaces. In-line goalies potentially faced substantial costs from replacing their pads more often since the friction produced significant wear and tear. The Cover Ups had strategically placed hard plastic surfaces that gave goalies ice-like sliding ability and lateral movement while protecting goal pads from wear and tear. The increased sliding ability also decreased energy exerted during play, which subsequently decreased the inevitable rise in body temperature that is so problematic for heavily equipped goalies. In-line Cover Ups were offered in the same size and colour options as Ice Cover Ups.

ICE HOCKEY GOALIES MARKET

Ice hockey was the fastest-growing team sport in North America, and the number of minor hockey goalies was 80,376 in 1995 with 22-percent growth expected in 1996 (Jim Rennie's Sports Letter, May 1996). No exact numbers existed for the number of adult goalies; however, a conservative estimate by Hockey Canada suggested that the number approximated one-quarter of minor hockey participation for Canada and the U.S. Ice hockey's popularity appeared to be the result of the expansion of professional hockey in the U.S. and the subsequent increased television coverage. Participation was higher in Canada and the states that bordered Canada (Exhibit 2).

IS was impressed with the concept, prototypes, and market research that the licensors put together in their proposal. Greg felt that this information combined with his existing knowledge of the industry could be the basis for a solid plan. There were five groups of North American ice hockey goalies: sponsored goalies; competitive and noncompetitive minor hockey goalies; and competitive and noncompetitive adult-league goalies. Sponsored goalies were not a viable market for Cover Ups, but were important for establishing equipment-usage trends. Sponsored goalies were those who play in leagues where goalie pads are provided by the company that has attained the rights to supply the league or particular goalie (e.g., NHL, IHL, AHL). In recent years, the suppliers initiated a trend of custom-designed equipment that complemented the colour and design of team uniforms and reinforced the individual identity of the goalie. As a result, goalies at all levels—and sports fans in general—desired and expected a coordinated uniform. For example, Grant Fuhr was certain he would be traded when he began the 1994–95 season with the Buffalo Sabres, so he played with a pair of plain white pads since this was the only colour that would match his new team colours. During the 1995–96 season, interested fans and media in Ottawa wondered when goalie Damian Rhodes would find a pair of pads to match his new team colours after he had been traded to the Senators and had difficulty replacing the blue pads he wore when playing for the Toronto Maple Leafs.

Minor hockey players in Canada and the U.S. typically begin at age six and continue until ages 18 to 20. A distinction can be made between competitive and noncompetitive hockey. Competitive minor hockey includes the levels referred to in Canada as AAA, AA, and A. It requires a player to make the team and entails much greater expense with more games played over greater distances. Noncompetitive minor hockey includes B- and C-level leagues, where players simply sign up to play relatively fewer and more localized games. In general, a competitive goalie has professional or scholarship aspirations and exhibits greater dedication to the game. A higher level of competition also required higher quality equipment, and the competitive atmosphere surrounding these games made coordinated uniforms a priority.

Adult goalies range in age from 20 to 55 years. A competitive and noncompetitive differentiation also exists as leagues are organized to allow participants to play at their desired level. Differences are seen in the number of games played, quality of players, and the types of rules and restrictions in place. While adult-league games are generally played locally, competitive leagues schedule more games over greater distances, and allow body contact and slap shots.

A focus group was conducted to determine the viability of the goalie pad cover concept (Exhibit 3). The high number of pads worn in each member's career could be explained by the growth children experience. Thus, every fall a goalie would borrow a different pair of pads from an association or buy new or used pads as they outgrew their old ones. It was observed that minor hockey's team colours vary greatly from year to year and that finding a pair of pads to match each season's colours was difficult. Members estimated at which point they would have become interested in goalie-pad covers and listed characteristics such a product should require.

A survey of goalies was conducted at Ottawa-area tournaments that had both competitive and noncompetitive goalies between the ages of 7 and 17. At that time, the product had not been licensed and therefore the decision to limit sizes had not been made. Respondents came from Ontario, Quebec, and New York. The sample had 20 competitive minor hockey goalies and 20 parents; 20 noncompetitive minor hockey goalies and 20 parents; and 20 competitive and noncompetitive adult-league goalies. Response from noncompetitive minor goalies and their parents and noncompetitive adult goalies was weak, which limited the scope of the research.

One question asked the source of their pads, since this might indicate each group's willingness to purchase new equipment and their susceptibility to sponsored-goalie trends.

	New	Used	Borrowed
Competitive Minor Hockey Goalies:	79%	14%	7%
Noncompetitive Minor Hockey Goalies:	19%	29%	52%
Competitive Men's Hockey Goalies:	87%	13%	0%
Noncompetitive Men's Hockey Goalies:	72%	28%	0%

Competitive hockey respondents rated the importance of goalie pads on five attributes, since these purchase criteria were expected to be the same for goalie-pad covers.

	Competitive Minor Hockey Parents		Competitive Minor Hockey Goalies		Competitive Adult Hockey Goalies	
	Very important (%)	Important (%)	Very important (%)	Important (%)	Very important (%)	Important (%)
Price	18	73	0	25	35	21
Weight	73	9	75	8	47	27
Durability	64	9	25	25	53	24
Colours	18	36	58	33	18	37
Brand	18	27	5	25	42	27

IN-LINE HOCKEY GOALIES MARKET

The combined popularity of in-line skating and hockey made in-line hockey one of the greatest sports crazes ever to hit North America. This primarily American phenomenon also quickly doubled the participation of ice hockey. In California more in-line hockey players were registered than amateur baseball players in 1995. The growth and a lack of organized leagues compared to ice hockey paved the way for the emergence of the National In-line Hockey Association (NIHA), which promoted regional and continental championships as the governing body of the sport. Given this situation, market research was non-existent but market size and geographical distribution estimates were developed by surveying in-line associations and publications. In 1994, 183,000 goalies played in-line hockey in North America with an expected annual growth of 15 percent.

In-line hockey had the same five groups of goalies as ice hockey. In-line goalies also looked to sponsored goalies as role models, as in ice hockey. Many in-line equipment companies were established ice-hockey equipment companies whose sponsored goalies now promoted both ice and in-line equipment under the same brand name. Only one group of sponsored players existed to promote in-line equipment alone: the professional in-line hockey league, called Roller Hockey International (RHI), which had teams in 3 Canadian and 17 American cities.

Where sufficient organization of the sport had been achieved, minor in-line hockey had both the competitive and noncompetitive levels of play. While much participation was organized under NIHA, participation often still took the form of arranged games of pick-up hockey in parking lots or other suitably surfaced areas. This was primarily a phenomenon of non–ice hockey markets in the southern U.S. where people did not expect the level of organization of ice-hockey markets.

A number of factors made in-line hockey somewhat different from ice hockey. Participation was dominated by younger age groups, and adult players ranged from 20 to 30 years. This was reinforced by the youth-oriented images in the advertising of the equipment manufacturers. It was expected that the average age of participants would increase as the sport matured and the younger players joined adult leagues. Second, in-line goalies in strong ice hockey markets tended to be transplanted ice hockey goalies, owned or had access to relatively new goalie equipment, and were more knowledgeable about the position. In comparison, in-line goalies in weak or non-existent ice hockey markets knew relatively little about the position and used antiquated equipment. Third, in-line hockey had two full playing seasons. The primary season occurred in the summer months from May to August and ran throughout North America. The secondary season occurred during the winter months (e.g., November to February) in weak ice hockey markets like the southern U.S. states. Finally, in-line hockey equipment was lighter than ice hockey equipment due to its ventilation, and it offered less protection. This was necessary because of the warm climate of the in-line seasons, the lesser weight of the puck, and the fact that body contact was not a part of the sport. Aside from skates, very little in-line equipment was sold in strong ice hockey markets since players used their ice hockey equipment and were reluctant to buy two sets. In contrast, players in the trend-setting California region were known to pay huge premiums for in-line equipment. For example, players were known to spend twice as much for top-of-the-line in-line skates compared to Canadians.

COMPETITION

As a patent-pending product, Ice Cover Ups had no direct competition. However, the licensors provided IS with a summary of indirect competition that came from three goalie pad customizing options: new; used and painted; and one repair option.

Large and small goalie pad manufacturers had been offering an increased range of colour and design options to coincide with the options available to sponsored goalies. Typically, the colour options available were designed around the colours of NHL hockey teams. A wide range of colours was offered on customized and high-end pads, while a weaker selection was offered on low-end pads. The cost of new pads ranged from $800 to $1,300. An additional obstacle was that new pads required an extensive breaking-in process. It was quite some time before a goalie was comfortable or confident that saves could be made and that rebounds could be controlled.

Goalies could purchase used pads that were less expensive, at only $100 to $500. Used pads lacked the new pad look and were difficult to find in the desired colour. However, they did have the advantage of being previously broken in, although goalies always ran the risk of buying pads with diminished structural integrity. Used pads that were new enough to be found in a desired colour and still be intact fell in the high end of the price range.

Goal pads could be painted in the desired colours. This little-used option was expensive at $150 to $250, difficult to find, and could affect the integrity of the pads since the process required complete dismantling and reassembly. Repairing goal pads was a service provided by shoe repair establishments in ice hockey markets. The process involved gluing leather patches over worn areas; however, this was a temporary solution since the patches wore off and left pads looking old and tattered.

Competition for In-line Cover Ups was limited, since equipment options for goalie pads were restricted with such a new sport. These options included pads made for street hockey; new and used ice hockey pads; and pads made specifically for in-line hockey. Each of these options could be compared in terms of price, sliding ability, durability on abrasive playing surfaces, and the quality of the fit (e.g., attach securely and comfortably).

Street hockey pads ranged between $40 and $70 but provided poor performance in the areas of sliding, durability, and fit. New ice hockey goal pads provided superior fit, yet lacked in the areas of durability and sliding when used on abrasive surfaces. Because of the cost, usage of new pads appeared limited to RHI goalies, although some transplanted ice hockey goalies used their high-end goalie pads if they could not justify investing in another set. Used ice hockey pads purchased specifically for in-line hockey were an option for goalies who attempted to limit their investment. In-line hockey goalie pads, priced between $250 and $600, had a similar design and a comparable fit to ice hockey pads; however, the design did not permit the use of In-line Cover Ups. In addition, in-line hockey pads had a rubberized exterior that increased durability at the expense of sliding ability.

COMMUNICATIONS—JULY '95 TO JUNE '96

IS regularly attended the four major trade shows for the sporting goods industry: the Atlanta and Montreal shows in February, a Chicago show in July, and a Toronto show in October. Both products were presented at all four shows during the past year; however, the official launch did not occur until the two February trade shows because of the time required for final designs and production and because advance orders occurred at this time for the ice and primary in-line hockey seasons.

IS premiered the products at the Chicago show in July. This show was primarily for the in-line market, although many companies showed their ice hockey equipment since buyers were usually responsible for both sports. Only the licensors' prototypes were available, since the Cover Ups had been licensed for only two weeks. The in-line booth presented the new Redline products, while the much larger baseball booth presented the Cooper line and some ice hockey equipment. Both Ice and In-line Cover Ups were shown at the Redline booth since only the Redline product manager had sufficient product knowledge. In-line Cover Ups impressed the buyers, who recognized the unique benefits. In-line Cover Ups were subsequently featured in *In-line Magazine*, a consumer publication, several months after the show. Ice Cover Ups received some attention and interest from buyers for strong ice hockey regions, however they expressed concern regarding the price.

In September, IS also attended the NIHA North American Championships and Trade Show held in Las Vegas. It featured championship in-line games and booth space for exhibiting products to buyers and consumers. The championships drew teams from across North America, and the show was rapidly becoming a good forum for introducing new in-line products. In-line Cover Ups received substantial interest from buyers and consumers alike. The Toronto show in October was the smallest of the major shows and had both ice and in-line equipment. A spark of interest occurred for both products, but this was still tempered by concern over the price. IS distributed sell sheets and displayed the licensors' prototypes at both of these fall trade shows.

At the Atlanta and Montreal shows in February, IS promoted Ice and In-line Cover Ups as full-fledged members of the WinnWell line. IS put signage on two walls approximately 10 feet high and 12 feet wide that featured both text and enlarged photos of Ice and In-line Cover Ups. One wall showed factory prototypes of both versions, while the other wall prominently faced passersby to attract attention. Cover Ups were also colourfully featured with a full page in the 1996 WinnWell catalogue, which had WinnWell's complete ice hockey line and the Redline products for in-line hockey.

The trade expressed interest in the in-line version at the Atlanta show; however, IS was unable to secure any advance orders. In Montreal, IS rented substantial booth space and presented their full line of ice hockey equipment at the world's premier ice hockey trade show. The launch of the Ice and In-line Cover Ups coincided with the launch of Don Cherry's "Original Series" youth hockey equipment. Don Cherry, a former NHL coach and a regular commentator on CBC's *Hockey Night in Canada*, attended the show and spoke with buyers and signed autographs. As expected, the WinnWell booth proved to be the most popular as Don Cherry significantly outdrew celebrities at competing booths. IS obtained one order after the Montreal show. The Sports Authority, a large American sporting goods chain, ordered both versions to test in its five Canadian outlets.

For the launch, each rep was given one In-line Cover Up and one goalie pad to demonstrate the product to retail accounts. This proved useful since some retailers, particularly those in the southern U.S. states, carried no inventory of pads. Consumer promotion for WinnWell took the form of NHL player sponsorship. IS signed eight NHL players to wear its gloves (another product in the WinnWell line) for the 1995–96 season. Among these players were Rick Tocchet, Dale Hunter, Turner Stevenson, and Bill Lindsay.

COMMUNICATIONS DECISIONS FOR 1996-97

By June 1996, IS had also received orders from 48 independent retailers from across the U.S. in addition to the advance order from the Sports Authority. Greg was encouraged, because these were sales to consumers who ordered through a retailer after seeing the catalogue or talking to a rep. Greg hoped that similar results might happen for Ice Cover Ups. Despite this optimism, Greg was keenly aware of the potential price problem that kept arising at the trade shows. With these thoughts in mind Greg turned his attention to the communications plan, of which some would be the same. IS planned to attend the same four trade shows and seven new shows sponsored by regional buying groups and major retail chains. These new and smaller shows allowed individual outlet owners to evaluate competing product lines in a more casual environment. Further, the NHL player sponsorship agreements would continue to support the WinnWell name. With these in place, Greg had to determine how to spend the remaining $115,000 among these or any other options that came to mind.

- *Sports Authority Account:* Greg wondered if he should initiate any advertising or promotion with the Sports Authority account to stimulate sales. Since the Sports Authority had committed to stocking the products in Canada, Greg realized that this could be a way of ensuring future Canadian orders and possible U.S. penetration. Greg also understood that buyers from other chains would be watching, so any idea had to be effective and transferable to other accounts.

- *Print Advertising:* Greg considered print advertising. He wondered what creative message should be used and whether it would be effective in generating consumer interest. Further issues included what vehicles to select and the number of ads that should be placed (Exhibit 4).

- *Sponsorship:* Four sponsorship options were possible. First, amateur in-line leagues could be sponsored at an average cost of $3,000 each. This total included advertising on rink boards, $400 toward league jerseys, on which the WinnWell name would be seen, and four sets of In-line Cover Ups with a total manufacturing cost of $160. Greg considered leagues of 12 teams or greater to be the most viable, which could be found

only in larger urban centres. Second, Triple Crown Promotions In-line Tourneys operated in major North American cities. These were modelled after their famous 3-on-3
basketball events. IS could become an official sponsor at any event for $10,000. IS
would receive recognition as an official sponsor on signage and printed materials,
have logos placed on rink boards, and be allowed to supply product as tournament
prizes. Third, IS could return to the NIHA North American Championships and Trade
Show as an official sponsor, which would include its logo on rink boards and booth
space in the trade show area, for a total cost of $30,000. This event would be covered
by the Prime Sports Network. Fourth, IS could be an official sponsor at the "Taste of
Chicago" City Fair in July, for a total cost of $40,000. This event attracted 3 million
visitors and featured an in-line tournament with more than 100 northern U.S. teams.

| EXHIBIT 1 | Illustration of Cover Ups |

EXHIBIT 2	Distribution of North American Goalies		

Regions by Country	Ice Hockey	In-Line Hockey
Canada	**60.6%**	**1.6%**
Ontario	24.1%	
Prairies	14.3%	
Quebec	12.1%	
British Columbia	5.8%	
Maritimes	4.3%	
United States	**39.4%**	**98.4%**
Mid Atlantic (PA, RI, DE, CT, NY, MD)	12.6%	25.3%
East North Central (MN, WI, MI, IN, IL, OH)	10.7%	14.5%
New England (MA, VT, NH, ME)	5.1%	4.4%
Pacific (WS, OR, CA)	3.4%	29.9%
West North Central (ND, SD, ID, WY, MT, NB)	3.3%	7.1%
South Atlantic (GA, FL, NC, SC, VA, WV)	2.1%	9.5%
Mountain (CO, NV, UT)	1.3%	4.0%
West South Central (AZ, NM, TX, OK, KS)	.6%	2.2%
East South Central (MO, AR, LA, MS, AL, TN, KY)	.4%	1.5%

Source: Canadian Hockey Association, USA Hockey, Industry Canada, Jim Rennie's Sports Letter, and National In-line Hockey Association

EXHIBIT 3	Focus Group Results				

Name	Age	Levels Played	Years Played	Number of Pads Worn	Number of Uniform Colour Changes
Brent	22	A, AA, AAA Tier II Jr. A Major Jr. A Industrial League	10	8	16
Felix	22	C, B, A, AA Jr. B, Tier II Jr. A Industrial, Intramural	10	8	16
Mike	22	C, B Industrial	6	4	10
Chris	22	C, B, A, AA Jr. B, Tier II Jr. A Industrial	8	7	9

EXHIBIT 3	**Focus Group Results** (continued)

Level at which matching pad colour with uniforms would be desired

House League:2/4	Jr. B:		2/2
B:	3/4	Tier II Jr. A:	3/3
A:	2/3	Major Jr. A:custom pads provided	
AA:	3/3	Industrial:	1/4
AAA:	1/1	Intramural:	0/1

Characteristics required of a goalie pad cover

1. Cannot inhibit the play of the goalie
2. Cannot add any significant amount of weight to the pads
3. Must look as good as or better than a new pair of pads
4. Ease of attachment
5. Durability of the product
6. Effective protection for the pad underneath
7. Reasonably priced
8. Colour options

EXHIBIT 4	**Print Advertising Options**

Publications by Country	Circulation (Canada)	Circulation (U.S.)	Number of Issues per Year	B & W (Full Page)	Four-Colour (Full Page)
Canada					
Sports Business Magazine	6,748		5	$2,945	$4,110
United States					
Roller Hockey Magazine		18,700	9	$1,812	$2,212
Let's Play Hockey		9,342	29	$950	$1,350
Hockey Player		19,620	12	$1,055	$1,505
Sports Illustrated					
New England		186,440	52	$11,436	$16,910
Eastern U.S.		885,041	52	$41,617	$62,838
Mid-Western U.S.		772,198	52	$37,341	$56,380
Western U.S.		626,585	52	$31,631	$47,774
Southern U.S.		713,432	52	$34,989	$52,829

EXHIBIT 4	Print Advertising Options (continued)

Publications by Country	Circulation (Canada)	Circulation (U.S.)	Number of Issues per Year	B & W (Full Page)	Four-Colour (Full Page)
North America					
Inside Sports	16,675	662,819	12	$23,965	$35,765
The Hockey News	50,313	67,658	42	$3,635	$4,535
Hockey Digest	21,434	76,738	8	$1,000	$1,750
The Sporting News					
Eastern U.S. & Canada		167,762	52	$5,200	$6,435
Mid-Western U.S.		187,802	52	$6,240	$7,725
Southern U.S.		169,022	52	$5,825	$7,225
Western U.S.		111,421	52	$4,995	$5,150
Hockey Yearbook (Sept.)	9,000	95,000	1	$4,450	$5,260
In-line Magazine	4,552	69,091	9	$6,995	$7,995

Use the fraction of full page cost for other ad sizes (e.g., 1/2, 1/4). One percent discounts are offered for extra inserts (e.g., 2 times = 2%, 3 times = 3%). Add 10% for inside cover placement and 20% for back cover placement. Four-colour for Hockey Digest is available on covers only. Cost is average for three covers.

Artventure Children's Creative Art and Party Centre

Mark Haber and
Christopher A. Ross

In May 1999, Eileen Walfish and Tina Diamant, the owners and only employees of Artventure, were reviewing the results of their first year of operation. While they were satisfied with the results, they were concerned about the years ahead. They expected significant challenges because of increased operating expenditures, especially wages, increased competition, and the introduction of new programming such as a proposed summer camp for 1999. Their challenge was to develop a long-term strategic plan for Artventure that would ensure the continued growth and profitability of the business.

Artventure is a creative and educational centre. Through a wide variety of activities and specialized programs, it provides artistic and educational stimulation to children between the ages of 8 months and 12 years. Artventure is not a daycare centre. Artventure's mission is "to enhance the creativity and self-esteem of young children and pre-teens through various activities centring around the arts, as well as entertaining and coordinating children's birthday parties catering to every parent and child's needs." The owners aim to develop in children a love for the arts and sciences, in a pleasant, well-supervised environment. They also want to foster the child's intellectual growth, interpersonal and artistic skills, and self-esteem through a broad range of programs and activities. Artventure's services include photography, dance, animated music and cognitive games, as well as children's birthday parties. There are 100 party packages from which parents can choose.

BACKGROUND

Eileen and Tina had no previous business management experience, but both had training in early childhood education as well as practical experience working with children.

Eileen began working with children at the age of 12, at a day camp. She had experience putting on puppet shows and plays. She also organized activities for children between the ages of 2 and 8. In the summer of 1992, Eileen became the Program Director and Counsellor-in-Training, where she gained supervisory experience. Subsequently, she became involved in creating and teaching different activities such as swimming, dance, music, art, nature, and science for children 2 to 8 years old. In addition she had organized graduation ceremonies, birthday and other children's parties, and holiday shows, and had conducted private art workshops in clients' homes. Eileen has a D.E.C. in Literature and Arts from Marie-Victorin College[1] in Montreal, and a Bachelor's degree in Education and Religion from Concordia University. During her educational years, she had received good citizenship awards, good sportsmanship awards, and achievement awards in physical education and drama.

Klimentina (Tina) has a degree in Education from the University of Sarajevo. Prior to her arrival in Canada in 1993 she had been Director and Coordinator of a youth theatre in the field of puppetry, and was experienced in the design and creation of marionettes. She was also responsible for scenery and costume design for various plays in which she had acted. That experience brought her new positions in children's television, cartoon animation, and as a TV show host in Sarajevo.

In Canada, she maintained a strong interest in early childhood education and earned a D.E.C. in Education. She worked as an early childhood educator at a nursery, where she was responsible for planning, programming, and managing activities in creative art, dance, and shows. She also had experience coordinating special events for parents. In 1997 she became the art and jewellery specialist at a day camp, where she organized and conducted innovative and creative projects for children between the ages of 3 and 12.

In their past positions, the owners had developed strong relationships with clients—children as well as parents—which earned them an excellent reputation in the Jewish community in Côte-Saint-Luc, Hampstead, and Westmount.

THE CENTRE

Eileen and Tina believe that activity centres are needed to provide extended entertainment and education for children. The market, according to the owners of Artventure, needs centres that provide ongoing creative, innovative projects that challenge and enhance the child's creative talents and which also cater to the needs of parents. Since parents have little time to spend with their families, these centres can act as "added parents," providing education, creative stimulation, and fun during the hours when it is difficult for parents to provide supervision.

Artventure commenced operations on May 3, 1998, and is located at 6900 Decarie Square, a shopping centre in Montreal. At this location, parking is plentiful and free of charge. Decarie Square lies next to Highway 15, a major north–south highway running

---

1. In Quebec, a student makes the following progression through the educational system: kindergarten, primary, secondary, CEGEP and university. Marie-Victorin College is a CEGEP, and one normally attends for two years. CEGEP is an acronym for Collège d'enseignement général et professionnel.

through the city of Montreal (Exhibit 6, page 191). This location makes it very convenient to drop off and pick up children at the Centre. Artventure has 1,120 square feet of available space, which is more than enough to run its programs. Decarie Square, however, is not an upscale shopping centre. Much of the space is unoccupied and there is low customer traffic. While Artventure is nicely decorated, clearly indicating to mall traffic that it is a children's centre, one space next door is empty and the space on the other side is a clothing repair shop. Opposite to Artventure are a fruit shop and a home decoration store. Recently, some companies such as Aldo, Stokes, and Au Coton have established liquidation outlets at this shopping centre.

Eileen and Tina see Artventure as a provider of high-quality programs aimed at systematically developing the whole child. Artventure offers creative, stimulating, and entertaining activities such as original art activities, puppet shows, and drama plays for small children, enjoyable food and refreshments for children and parents, cognitive games, and animated music activities. Eileen and Tina believe that constant variation in activities allows for new and exciting experiences and that this variety is an effective method of capturing the attention of young children as they explore their creative spirits.

ARTVENTURE'S PROGRAMS

Artventure offers four programs:

- Program 1, Creative Junior Tots, is for children between the ages of 15 months and 4 years. This program is subdivided into two age categories and both run for a period of four weeks. Mom and Tot, offered on Tuesday and Thursday, includes art, music, live animals, drama, stories, and creative movement. Junior Tots, offered on Monday, Wednesday, and Friday, includes science, music, and dance. For both programs, peanut-free kosher snacks are served. Exhibit 1 shows the two categories, their times, and prices. These two programs generate approximately 30 percent of Artventure's annual revenue.

- Program 2, Photography Fun, is intended for children 4 years and over. This program involves taking and developing pictures. More specifically, this program allows the children to see the results of their creativity. Artventure believes that Photography Fun is a great way for children to discover themselves and develop self-esteem. The children are also able to show family and friends the pictures that they have taken. The cost for a seven-class session is $112.00.

- Program 3, Funky Dance, is for children 5 years old and over. This program introduces the participants to modern dance techniques and fosters body coordination. It also incorporates costumes and props such as wigs, thereby enhancing the creative element. Upon completion of the program, Artventure invites parents to watch a dance recital performed by the participants. The cost for a seven-class session is $95.00. Funky Dance and Photography together contribute 20 percent of Artventure's revenue.

- Program 4, Children's Birthday Parties, includes a creative and original atmosphere where children between the ages of 4 and 12 celebrate their birthday. Artventure offers theme parties or specialized parties. The theme parties focus, for example, on the child's favourite sports, TV shows, super heroes, or toys. Dramatic plays, puppet shows, treasure hunts, art activities, and many other cognitive activities capture the children's imagination while they participate in an original and zestful birthday party. The specialized parties focus on areas such as art, drama, jewellery, music, dance, photography, and video production.

Artventure provides juice, paper crafts and toys, specialized birthday cards, party surprises, art materials, decorations, animators, and coffee for the parents. Additionally, the parties have a unique style and emphasize an unlimited amount of fun. The parties last for two hours, from 4 p.m. to 6 p.m. from Monday to Friday and, by special appointment, any time during the day on weekends. The price is $200.00 for 20 children or fewer and $5.00 for each child thereafter. Artventure derives 50 percent of its revenue from birthday parties.

CUSTOMERS

Eileen and Tina feel that more young parents are seeking early educational development for infants and toddlers, thus creating a high demand for Parent and Tot programs. Furthermore, social interaction and a strong sense of the arts and culture for preschoolers and preteens make extracurricular activities a must during school hours and on weekends.

They also observed that parents increasingly hold their children's birthday parties outside of the home. In the last six years, the popularity of this concept has grown as more mothers continue to join the workforce. In addition, many parties have up to 40 guests, so that all classmates, relatives, and friends outside school can be invited. In sum, they feel that there is a strong demand for this service.

Artventure identifies their potential clientele as families with children aged 8 months to 12 years. These families are affluent. Many parents are university graduates and have careers in fields such as medicine, law, finance, and business ownership (e.g., jewellery, insurance, manufacturing, retail, import/export, and stockbrokerage). Although Artventure welcomes all religious, ethnic, and racial groups, the owners have built a strong reputation within the Jewish community and are trusted and known by many in that community. Ninety-five percent of the children attending Artventure are from Jewish families. The other 5 percent is made up of Italians, Greeks, and francophones. In fact, one of the owners' desires is to increase the number of children from other ethnic groups.

Eileen and Tina describe the parents as having a strong interest in recreational activities, a high regard for the arts—dance, drama, creative arts—and a strong belief in education that enhances self-esteem and the intellectual growth of their children. The parents also want attractive, clean, spacious, and safe environments with innovative programming where their children can have fun. They believe that parents appreciate the involvement of the owners in the day-to-day activities of the centre and the children. Price, available equipment, quality of the programming, and small classes are important considerations for parents. They look for style to keep up with other members of the community and the "latest trends." They are loyal to a service if it impresses them. The parents are also helpful and supportive, especially when they are more familiar with the business owners. They are potential promoters of the business when they are satisfied with the services offered.

Because of Eileen and Tina's experience and reputation in the Jewish community, this community was their major target. Until the 1970s, Montreal was the most important Jewish centre in Canada. Since the mid-1970s, however, a large percentage have moved to other areas in Canada, especially Ontario. By 1999, Toronto had replaced Montreal as the home of the largest Jewish community. There are, however, more than 100,000 members of the Jewish community in Montreal. In Montreal, 60 percent of Jewish children go to Jewish primary schools and 30 percent go to Jewish high schools. Artventure identified Côte-Saint-Luc, Hampstead, Town of Mount Royal, and Westmount as their principal markets. Exhibit 2 provides demographic data on these and neighbouring cities.

Eileen and Tina know that demand for their various offerings varies depending on the season. During the summer, for example, parents enroll their children in outdoor day camp programs. Therefore, afternoon art classes from June to August are quiet periods. Not all camps accept children under the age of 3, so Artventure is planning to design a day camp program for children between the ages of 2 and 5 years, while continuing to offer their Parents and Tots program for children between 15 months and 24 months. Many camps have half-day programs from 9 a.m. to noon for children between 3 and 5 years old, so the owners want to offer special art classes to this age group from 1 p.m. to 3 p.m. For birthday parties, June to August is slow since many families are on vacation, or hold pool parties, or choose to wait for the school year so they can invite classmates. October to May is the busiest time for parties.

Eileen and Tina interviewed 50 families in the Hampstead and Côte-Saint-Luc areas and found that they had spent an average of $600.00 or more on birthday parties for their children. Given the income levels of their target market, the owners believe that these families, even in a recession, would continue to use these centres, especially for parties, since parents would find it difficult to deny their children a birthday party.

COMPETITION

Eileen and Tina believe that the industry of children's recreation and party centres is in a period of growth. In 1992, there was only one private play and party centre that catered to families with children between the ages of 1 and 6 years in areas such as Hampstead, Côte-Saint-Luc, Westmount, Town of Mount Royal, Saint-Laurent, and even the West Island. In 1999, however, similar centres can be seen in many areas. For example, there is Kidnasium Gym & Party Centre in NDG; Neverland in the West Island; Crayons Art & Party Centre in Cavendish Mall; Artfolie in the Monkland area; and Adath Israel Kiddie Korner in Hampstead (Exhibit 6). Even the City of Westmount (at its Greene Avenue Centre) and Concordia University offer activities for children. Other centres, such as Bedrocks, Coconuts in the West Island, and Enfantastique Drop Off & Party Centre in Place Vertu and Carrefour Angrignon, which had sprung up to meet the demand, ceased operations in 1998.

Tina and Eileen identified three centres that they considered direct competitors:

(1) **Le Castelet,** an artistic awakening centre, is a preschool located about 3 to 4 kilometres from Artventure, on Sherbrooke St., one of the major arteries in Montreal. This centre is divided into three rooms, two of which are designated for artistic and intellectual usage. The third and larger room is used for dance and physical play. The centre is located directly across from a municipal park, which is easily accessible. The goal of Le Castelet is to provide an atmosphere of interaction that will prepare children for their entrance into primary education.

Le Castelet's programs centre on music, theatre, dance, and arts/crafts. Le Castelet designs these activities to encourage children to interact with other kids and to instill a sense of learning and openness. This Centre specializes in the artistic environment and tries to implant a taste for the arts. The courses are conducted mostly in French. The instructors can communicate in English, but there is greater emphasis on communicating in French. The hours of operation and prices are as follows:

Morning sessions: 8:30 a.m. to 12:00 p.m. at $16.75 per morning
Full-day sessions: 8:30 a.m. to 5:30 p.m. at $24.50 per day.
On a monthly basis the costs are as follows:
2 mornings/week = $134.00
3 mornings/week = $201.00
4 mornings/week = $268.00
5 mornings/week = $335.00

These programs follow the school calendar of the regular elementary schools. The year, therefore, is from September to June. There is also a summer day camp program that focuses more on outdoor activities like playing in the park. The price for the summer day camp is the same as the school-year program. The classes are divided into groups of eight per instructor. The age group for instruction is from 2 to 5 years old.

The school also has theme days every other week. These are used to teach the children about art, nature, and other subjects of interest. An example of a theme day would be Forest Day, whereby children learn about the different kinds of trees and animals in the forest. Parents supply all food, such as snacks and lunches. The school supplies fruit drinks. Birthday parties are celebrated for the children who attend Le Castelet; parents supply the cake.

(2) **Kidnasium** is a 6,000-square-foot facility that opened its doors approximately two years before Artventure. It enjoys fair success. The facility is divided into two parts: the indoor playground with a foam floor surface and playground equipment, and the gym. The goal of this centre is to provide children between the ages of 1 month and 6 years with noncompetitive programs in a group setting.

This centre is located at the corner of Somerled and Grand Blvd in NDG and offers four programs. These are as follows:

1. A gym program, which includes an instructor. The instructor teaches the children aerobic-type gym skills as well as tumbling and coordination. This program runs for fifteen 45-minute sessions at a cost of $225 per child, tax included. The maximum number of children per group is 12.

2. The dance program, "Tooney Loonz," runs for fifteen 45-minute sessions at a cost of $215 per child, tax included. Two reputable instructors provide children with animated performances such as guitars and "sing-alongs."

3. The open gym program does not include an instructor. The price is $6 per child, $10 for two children.

4. The last type of program is birthday parties. Playground parties for 20 children cost $225 each. For 30 children or more, the cost is $285. A gym party costs $300 for 20 children or fewer and $385 for more than 20 children. Both parties last for two

hours and include paper products, balloons, and fruit juice for the children; coffee for parents; and instructors for the gym activities.

Extra costs for the birthday party program, which can run up to an additional $400, include food for guests, cakes, loot bags, and entertainment such as music, clowns, and magicians. The location of this centre is not very central for the important market areas of Hampstead, Westmount, Town of Mount Royal, Côte-Saint-Luc, and the West Island or Saint-Laurent. Moreover, parents must also supervise their own children because of the high risk of injury in the gym area. The limited variety of programming for parties also forces parents to hire entertainment in order to please party-goers.

(3) **Crayons Art & Party Centre,** situated in Cavendish Mall, Côte-Saint-Luc, has been in existence for about 18 months. It is a drop-off centre; this means that there are few scheduled activities. Anyone, at any time, can walk into the centre and participate in the art class of the day. The centre serves children older than 3 years old. It also offers art programs to senior citizens. The fee for drop-off is $10.00 per hour per person. A special six-week program is available at a cost of $90.00. This program concentrates on only one area of art, such as painting, drawing, and so on. Crayons offers these programs at hours that do not coincide with regular school hours, so this program is geared more to adults and senior citizens. Thus Eileen and Tina believe that this centre is not a significant threat to Artventure. Crayons is strictly an Arts and Crafts Centre and does not offer any programs in the other areas of the arts. The centre offers birthday parties. These parties cost between $140 and $210, with a choice of a party in jewellery or pottery. All materials are included as well as juice, paper products, and coffee for parents. The variety of parties is limited and does not capture the attention of party-goers for the full two hours. This centre is also physically small—about 800 square feet —and it gets very crowded when there are many children. Exhibit 3 is a comparison of Artventure's birthday party offerings with two competitors.

In addition to the three competitors described so far, there are other potential competitors. Adath Israel Kiddie Korner, for example, offers morning classes for 2- to 5-year-olds. It also offers specialty activities such as ballet, creative movement, and computers. Furthermore, there is a Mom and Tots group with programs for kids 18 to 24 months from 9:00 a.m. to 10:45 a.m., and for kids 12 to 17 months from 11 a.m. to 12 p.m. This centre also offers "Music with Tooney Loonz" on Tuesday, Wednesday, and Friday. The City of Westmount at its Greene Avenue Centre offers children programs that include "Magical Fun" from 11:00 a.m. to 12:30 p.m., "Tumbling Tots Indoor Playground" from 9:30 a.m. to 11:30 a.m. for preschoolers, and "After School Home Away from Home" from 3:30 p.m. to 6:00 p.m. for kindergarten to 6 years. Concordia University's Department of Education offers "Children and Parents Learning Together" for 3- and 4-year-olds on Tuesday, Wednesday, and Thursday, from 9:00 a.m. to 11:30 a.m. Parents and teachers discuss child-rearing on Thursday mornings.

Babysitters are also an ongoing competitive threat to any centre. Many parents prefer dealing with people who they know and trust. Babysitters and domestics provide the service of "watching over" your children.

THE ENVIRONMENT

In spite of the growth in centres, the owners believe that the market is large enough for another centre to be successful. Their reasoning is that each centre focuses on different age groups and activities and they are situated in different locations. They estimate that some centres average $84,000 per year in birthday parties alone. They believe that in the Montreal region there is plenty of room for new players who cater to party-goers aged 6 to 12. The major centres do not offer services to this age group. They are also limited in their offering of different types of recreational activities other than art.

The owners of Artventure believe that as long as high-income families continue to cater to their children's desires and that mothers are in the workforce, party centres will have a strong and healthy place in the market. The industry is growing rapidly because of a new generation of parents who have healthy incomes yet no time or energy to be entertainers and creative specialists in their children's lives. These parents therefore seek outside assistance. With the increasing number of families where both parents are in the workforce, proper child care plays a critical role in the everyday lives of families. These trends, plus a genuine love of children, prompted the creation of Artventure.

Eileen and Tina are concerned, however, that at some point government regulations would make the business less appealing. For example, the government may enforce more rigorous safety requirements, or require that all centres carry high levels of insurance. They also feel that the ongoing political debate about the possible separation of Quebec from Canada makes conditions increasingly difficult for the business. They fear that many English-speaking families, Artventure's target market, will relocate outside of Quebec. Other possible administrative threats lie in the Quebec laws and regulations governing the use of language on all signs and mailings. Artventure may, in the future, face the prospect of bilingualization—both to comply with government regulations and to increase the pool of prospective clients.

PROMOTION AND STRATEGY

Artventure relies primarily on word of mouth and print advertising to generate awareness. Eileen and Tina believe that their attempts at advertising have been unsuccessful. In trying to increase growth in the number of clientele, Artventure advertised in a weekly newspaper, *The Suburban;* delivered at no cost to residents, the paper has a circulation of 101,000, with approximately 41,000 distributed to homes on the West Island. The remainder are distributed in the other English sectors of Greater Montreal. Artventure feels, however, that the cost is relatively high compared to the results obtained. A one-quarter-page advertisement costs $600. They also advertised in the weekly *Canadian Jewish News*. The circulation of the Montreal edition of this newspaper is 18,735 households, and 96 percent are paid subscriptions. A quarter-page ad costs $320 for a maximum of four insertions. Beginning in November 1998 they placed advertisements in each issue of *Montreal Families* at a cost of $400 per insertion. *Montreal Families,* like *The Suburban,* is distributed free of charge at pickup points every other month in both the West Island and the English-speaking sectors of Greater Montreal. Circulation for *Montreal Families* is 25,000. Finally, Artventure uses a mailing list of about 300 families.

mixed messages

Artventure's strategy is to provide top-quality creative programs and parties at a price that "will not burn a hole in parents' pockets." The activities they offer—drama, art, dance, and music—do not require expensive apparatus. Expensive apparatus do not necessarily capture a child's attention, Eileen and Tina believe. In addition to their advertising in *The Suburban*, Artventure also offers discounts of up to 15 percent on the price of its programs to those parents who register their children early or who bring a friend. The service component of their strategy is to develop strong relationships with parents, subcontractors, suppliers, and with the children who participate in the activities. They take into consideration the different schedules and needs of the different age groups and design programs to suit clients. Services are unique and not repetitive, and entertainment services are included in party packages. Exhibit 4 shows Artventure's income statement, and Exhibit 5 is a copy of the balance sheet. (In the first year of operation, Eileen and Tina did not take a salary from the business. Their 1999 salary was paid by an agency of the provincial government, in the context of a program designed to encourage small business and entrepreneurship.)

At this point Eileen and Tina have completed one year of operation and they are wondering whether they are on the right track. They had heard about the planned opening of Childzplay Party Centre in October, in their shopping centre. This venture, a 3,000-square-foot entertainment haven, "will be replete with all number of attractions for kids under 10 including in-line skating, floor hockey, dance, jewellery making, magic, cartooning, animals, slides, a magic store, an earth ball and a multitude of fun-filled activities. Childzplay will also be mommy-friendly with a cafe bistro where tired parents can sip on a cappuccino or nibble on a dessert while watching the kids explore the centre." They wondered about the possible effect on their business of this new arrival and what else they should be doing to ensure the long-run survival of their business. Should they, for example, take their activity centre to schools and cruise ships? What they did not want to do was to develop their centre into a computer games arcade. A computer games strategy was not part of their vision. They also believed that these games did not stimulate the creativity and self-esteem that they wanted to develop in children. However, they believed that they had a winning formula with their services, but they wondered whether they had a sustainable strategy.

EXHIBIT 1	Creative Junior Tots				
Age Category	Classes per Session	Duration of Classes	Classes per Week	Price per Session	Children per Group
15 to 24 months	8	9:30 a.m. to 11 a.m.	Tuesdays & Thursdays	$192.00	Min: 6 Max: 10
2 yrs to 4 yrs	12	9 a.m. to noon	Monday, Wednesday & Friday	$288.00	Min: 6 Max: 10

EXHIBIT 2	City Demographics				

	Côte-Saint-Luc	Hampstead	Westmount	Mtl-West	Mt-Royal
Pop 1991	30,126	7,219	20,239	5,180	18,212
1996	29,705	6,986	20,420	5,254	18,282
Total Male	13,280	3,310	9,200	2,565	8,610
0-4 years	640	225	435	210	475
5-9 years	710	205	520	220	570
10-14 years	710	220	590	235	615
Total Female	16,425	3,675	11,220	2,690	9,670
0-4 years	590	205	420	140	455
5-9 years	665	225	500	225	525
10-14 years	680	215	540	185	515
Mother Tongue					
English	15,205	4,615	12,035	3,655	5,305
French	3,300	835	4,065	465	7,215
Home Language					
English	20,265	5,520	14,245	4,370	7,190
French	2,920	735	3,745	330	7,400
Jewish Population	19,395	4,935	4,345	825	2,625
Undergraduate or Higher	6,190	2,520	8,850	1,715	6,640
Number of Families	8,075	1,930	5,235	1,455	5,005
Median Family Income	$51,099	$93,855	$101,525	$81,156	$90,983
Family Income					
< $10,000	380	85	160	30	120
$10K - 19,999	680	85	240	60	220
$20K - 29,999	990	70	250	100	275
$30K - 39,999	995	95	305	95	370
$40K - 49,999	905	145	255	80	310
$50K - 59,999	760	105	240	95	400
$60K - 69,999	540	130	280	140	335
$70K - 79,999	460	110	270	105	180
$80K - 89,999	490	95	320	95	265
$90K - 99,999	325	80	240	65	205
$100,000+	1,555	920	2,670	590	2,320

Source: Statistics Canada. Profiles of Census Divisions and Subdivisions. Ottawa: Industry Canada, 1999. 1996 Census of Canada. Catalogue No. 95-186-XPB

EXHIBIT 3	Birthday Party Grid			

Birthday Centre	Parties Offered	Services/Party Materials	Costs	Extra Costs
Artventure	Theme parties: Physical, cognitive and artistic activities. Parties in music, drama, jewellery, dance	Entertainment, specifically designed decorations, party animators, party favours, paper products, juice, coffee, birthday cards, balloons, birthday crowns	$200-$250	Food $40-$100
Crayons	Art and jewellery parties	Art materials, coffee, juice, paper products, monitors	$140-$210	Food, loot bags, entertainment Up to $400
Kidnasium	Gym and playground parties	Instructor, juice, paper products, balloons	$225-$385	Food, loot bags, entertainment Up to $400

EXHIBIT 4	Artventure Income Statement[1]

For the Year Ended April 30, 1999

Sales		$46,633
Less: Cost of Sales		$ 23,841
Gross Operating Profit		$ 22,792
Less: Sales Expenses		$ 5,014
Less: Rent		$ 17,592
Less: Administrative Expenses	$ 4,200.00	$26,806
Net Profit (Loss)		($ 4,014)

[1] In their first year of operation, Eileen and Tina were paid an "off-balance-sheet" salary by an agency of the provincial government. This subsidy was designed to promote entrepreneurship and small business in the province. This subsidy was available only for the first year of operation.

EXHIBIT 5	Artventure Balance Sheet as at April 30, 1999

ASSETS

Current Assets

1. Bank account	$ 5,000
2. Start-up expenses	$ 0
3. Deposit-rent	$ 2,800
4. Total current assets	$ 7,800

Fixed Assets

5. Incorporation	$ 610
6. Betterment	$ 4,000
7. Art equipment and accessories	$ 9,028
8. Office equipment	$ 1,265
9. Party equipment	$ 3,180
10. Computer equipment	$ 4,000
11. Less: Accumulated depreciation	($ 2,000)
Total Assets	$ 27,883

LIABILITIES

Current Liabilities

12. Accounts payable	$ 0
13. Current portion of long-term debt	$ 3,000

Long-term Liabilities

14. Long-term debt	$ 0
Total Liabilities	$ 3,000

Equity

15. Young promoters grant	$ 12,000
16. Capital investment	$ 16,897
17. Loss from operations	$ 4,014
Total Equity	$ 24,883
Total Liabilities and Equity	$ 27,883

EXHIBIT 6 | Map of Montreal

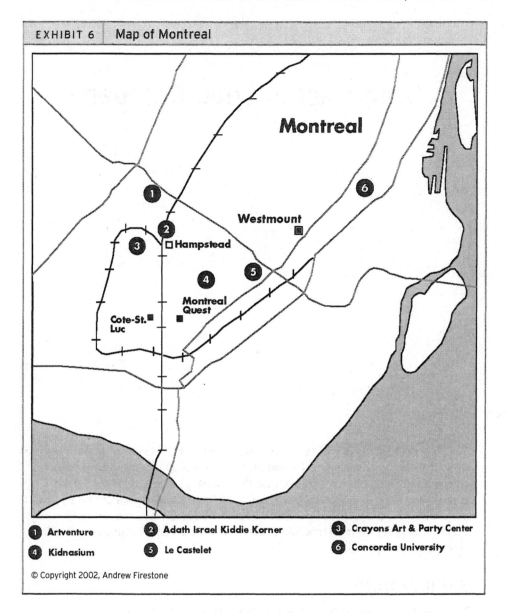

1 Artventure
4 Kidnasium
2 Adath Israel Kiddie Korner
5 Le Castelet
3 Crayons Art & Party Center
6 Concordia University

© Copyright 2002, Andrew Firestone

Green Acres Seed Company

Thomas F. Funk

Tom Simmons, Marketing Manager for Green Acres Seed Company, faced the problem of increasing the company's sales and profits in the highly competitive Ontario seed corn market. One option was to increase the company's share of the market for silage corn seed. Although this was a small market compared to the grain corn seed market, Tom believed the silage market offered good potential. This option would be a major strategic move for Green Acres, and Tom would have to build a strong case to gain top management's approval.

BACKGROUND

The Ontario seed corn industry was very competitive: seven companies competed for a total market estimated to be approximately $80 million per year. Pioneer, the leading company, was estimated to have more than 50 percent of the market. Novartis and Dekalb each had approximately 13 percent, while Green Acres' share was about 11 percent. Green Acres' management believed that Pioneer would continue to dominate the market for the foreseeable future and that the market shares of the smaller companies would change only as a result of mergers.

Farmers grow corn for two very distinct purposes: grain corn, in which only the ear or grain is harvested, and silage corn, which is harvested by cutting the entire plant. Grain corn is either stored on the farm in bins and subsequently fed to livestock, or sold after harvest to local grain elevators. Silage corn, on the other hand, is stored in silos and fed directly to livestock on the farm. Silage corn does not enter commercial markets. In the past, with the exception of lower-priced silage blends, seed companies had not sold separate silage varieties; the same varieties were used by farmers for both grain and silage corn.

At the present time in Ontario, slightly over two million acres of corn was harvested as grain corn compared with less than 600,000 acres harvested for silage. Over the past several years both the acreage of grain corn and the acreage of silage corn had experienced very low growth. It was not known whether this trend would continue. All the major seed companies concentrated their research and marketing efforts on grain corn because of the larger size of the market.

Two types of dealers distributed seed corn to customers; store dealers and farmer dealers. Store dealers were farm supply outlets that sold crop supplies such as fertilizer and agricultural chemicals. Many of these retailers wanted a complete line of crop supplies so they also carry seeds from one or two seed companies. Farmer dealers are farmers who supplemented their income by also selling seeds.

Green Acres had approximately 175 dealers of the total (500) in Ontario. Most of the dealers sold multiple brands of seeds. While approximately 20 percent of Green Acres dealers were large-volume outlets, most were relatively small and served a limited number of customers. Most Ontario farmers would be no further than 16 kilometres from a Green Acres dealer. Green Acres' sales force of seven people coordinated the selling activities of dealers. Dealers received a 10- to 15-percent commission (based on the selling price to farmers) on the seed they sold, depending on the volume.

The average price of seed corn to farmers was $90 per unit and ranged from $75 per unit to $125 per unit. Higher prices were charged for better-performing varieties, while lower prices were charged for poorer-performing or discontinued varieties. In general, varieties mainly used for silage sold at the low end of the price range ($75 to $80), while varieties mainly used as seed for grain corn sold at various prices within the entire range. Each unit of seed planted approximately three acres. For all the companies, including Green Acres, direct production costs for seed averaged 55 percent of the average selling price to dealers, leaving a contribution margin of roughly 45 percent to cover all fixed costs and profits.

SILAGE PRODUCTION

Farmers who were in the beef or dairy business often found it advantageous to raise silage corn for feeding to their livestock. In many cases, they would raise both grain and silage corn on their farms. Generally, they would follow the same management and cultural practices for each crop, including using the same seed varieties. A very common attitude among farmers and seed companies was that if a variety was good for grain production, it was also good for silage production. As a result, farmers often spent considerable time selecting a grain corn variety and then used the same variety for their silage corn.

The performance of a grain corn variety is relatively simple to assess. Basically, farmers are concerned with yield, normally measured in bushels or tons per acre. After harvesting the crop, a farmer simply measures the amount of grain sold or put into a bin to determine yield. Measuring the performance of silage varieties is not as straightforward. As in the case of grain corn, many farmers estimate yield by observing how full the silo is after harvest. Although this gives a measure of volume, it does not measure protein or energy, the two factors important in subsequent feeding. These can be measured only by taking samples of the silage to a laboratory for feed analysis. Relatively few farmers take the time to have this sort of analysis carried out. Instead, they fall back on the guideline stated earlier that a good grain corn variety is also a good silage corn variety.

For many years the Ontario Ministry of Agriculture, Food and Rural Affairs had operated a variety-testing program in which they scientifically measured corn variety yields and published the information for farmers to use in making purchase decisions. At the present time, the only measures of performance assessed in this program were related to grain corn production. Several scientists, as well as some farmers, were advocating the incorporation of silage performance measure in this program, but to date this had not been done. The yield information generated through this program was published in a booklet and circulated to most corn growers in Ontario. It was widely used by farmers in making variety selection decisions.

SILAGE STRATEGY

Tom Simmons felt that Pioneer's current dominance of the total seed corn market would make it very difficult for Green Acres to increase its market share if the company continued to concentrate on seed for grain production. He reasoned that it might be much easier to gain share by targeting the silage producer with hybrids having high silage performance attributes, and therefore avoiding direct competition with the market leader. Several reasons seemed to support this strategy:

- No market leader existed in the silage market.
- A silage strategy would allow Green Acres to differentiate itself from competition.
- Recent field data indicated that some Green Acres varieties had better silage performance characteristics than competitors' varieties.

There appeared to be a substantial product-use overlap in the sense that many farmers grew both grain and silage corn. As a result, the silage strategy might allow the company to gain new customers initially by selling them silage varieties and then later trying to sell them Green Acres' grain varieties. Such a "back door" approach would avoid head-to-head competition with Pioneer, Novartis, and Dekalb in attempting to get new customers. While Tom felt he would pick up some new grain customers with the silage strategy, the primary goal was to sell more silage seed.

The primary measure of silage performance the company decided to use was harvestable energy, or TDN (total digestible nutrients). Crop scientists at many universities supported this approach. Their research had proven that grain yield was not the most suitable measure of silage performance because it had been consistently found that the highest yielding varieties often have lower levels of energy.

The research department at Green Acres had been developing and testing silage varieties for some time. The company had six varieties that produced a significantly higher level of TDN than most competitive varieties tested. Two varieties in particular yielded more than 8,000 pounds of TDN per acre compared with the best Pioneer silage variety, which yielded only about 7,800 pounds of TDN per acre. The selling price for any of the six varieties that Green Acres had developed would reflect the level of TDN. That is, the higher the level of TDN the higher the price.

Under the so-called "silage strategy," the company would attempt to maintain current sales in the grain corn segment, while directing growth efforts at the silage segment. Implementation of the strategy would require additional resources for promotion, field-testing, and program coordination. Tom estimated that he would need an additional $150,000 per year for promotion and one full-time person to coordinate the strategy at approximately $75,000 per year. Field-testing expenses were hard to estimate, but probably would be in the neighbourhood of $100,000.

MARKET RESEARCH

To provide information to help decide whether to pursue the silage strategy, Tom commissioned a market research study of silage growers in Ontario. The study involved interviewing a random sample of 400 farmers from all areas of the province. The sample was geographically balanced to ensure that the major silage producing regions were represented in the proper proportion. All interviews were conducted on the telephone.

The basic purpose of the marketing research was to assess the viability of the silage seed strategy. In addition, the research was designed to provide information to further develop the strategy if it was determined to be sound. Specific objectives of the research were to:

- Determine the size of the corn silage seed market in terms of number of buyers and number of acres.
- Determine the decision-making process used by farmers in buying silage seed.
- Determine basic attitudes farmers have about corn silage seed.
- Determine possible segments that exist in the corn silage seed market.

The major findings of the study are shown below.

- Current market shares for grain corn and silage corn seed were estimated to be:

	Grain Corn	Silage Corn
Pioneer	53%	54%
Novartis	13%	13%
Dekalb	14%	12%
Green Acres	12%	11%
All others	8%	10%

- Approximately 70% of the farmers growing silage corn in any year also grow grain corn in the same year.
- The total number of Ontario farmers growing silage corn is 11,800. The average farmer grows 49 acres of silage.

- Farmers tend to make their decision concerning which varieties to plant in the fall and early winter months. Actual orders are placed with seed dealers in the early winter.
- High yield of feed per acre is the most important reason cited by farmers for feeding corn silage. Other reasons given were source of energy and source of protein.
- Most farmers indicated that they planned to grow the same amount of silage corn in the future as at the present time. A small percentage said they planned to grow less silage corn in the future compared to the present time.
- Approximately 35% of all silage growers change seed varieties from one year to the next. Beef producers are more likely to switch than dairy producers. Many farmers who switch varieties stay with products produced by the same company.
- More than 60% of farmers who grow both grain corn and silage reported using the same varieties for both.
- Approximately one-third of all silage growers reported having their silage analyzed for its feeding value. More dairy farmers than beef farmers have this type of analysis done. Almost all farmers who have feed analysis done use the information to balance rations. Less than 5% use the results to aid in silage variety selection.
- The information sources used by farmers in selecting a silage variety together with the percentage of farmers rating each as either useful or very useful are shown below:

	Percentage Rating Source as Useful
Own experience	93%
Other farmers	92%
Seed company information	84%
OMAFRA trial results	84%
Seed dealers	82%
Silage test plots	80%
OMAFRA extension	74%
Farm magazine ads	66%
Television ads	25%
Radio ads	24%

- Farmers hold a variety of attitudes concerning silage seed. Some of these attitudes, and the percentage of farmers agreeing with each, are shown below:

	Percentage Agreeing with Each Statement
When I plant my corn I know which fields will be harvested for silage	83%
The energy of corn silage comes mainly from the grain	81%
I think I could do a better job evaluating my silage corn	78%
If there were more silage testing, I would use it to choose my silage variety	76%

	Percentage Agreeing with Each Statement
I would use performance information on silage varieties if it were available	65%
Different varieties have different levels of protein	59%
There is quite a bit of difference among varieties in the energy they produce	54%
The best grain variety makes the best silage variety	50%
Total tonnage per acre is the only reliable method to evaluate silage varieties	45%
Currently no seed company has reliable silage performance information	40%
A tall corn variety usually makes the best silage variety	39%
Most lower price varieties perform as well for silage as higher price varieties	34%

The study also generated some interesting results in terms of market segmentation. Based on cluster analysis of the results, four segments emerged. These segments were named performance, potential performance, dual purpose, and price. The distinguishing characteristics of each segment are outlined below.

- The **performance** segment consists of those farmers who are concerned with performance characteristics of silage varieties. This concern has been demonstrated by the fact that these farmers carefully evaluate silage variety performance by using performance evaluation methods such as setting up silage test plots, using feed analysis to evaluate varieties, and/or weighing off loads of silage varieties to accurately determine yield.

- The **potential performance** segment consists of those farmers who do not currently use performance evaluation methods for selecting silage varieties, but have favourable attitudes toward using this type of information in the future.

- The **dual purpose** segment consists of those farmers who grow both grain corn and silage and consistently use the same variety for both.

- The **price** segment consists of those farmers who consistently purchase lower-priced varieties for silage compared to grain corn.

Exhibit 1 shows a detailed profile of the four segments in terms of demographics, buying behaviour, and attitudes.

With this information, Tom began considering his recommendation. Tom was particularly intrigued by the segmentation analysis and felt that the viability of the silage strategy would be based on the extent to which he used a general versus a targeted marketing campaign. Should he pursue a different strategy per segment? How many varieties of silage should he offer? At a minimum, he was considering two varieties at different price levels. What price should he charge for the varieties? As well, he wondered what implication the segmentation results would have for his marketing strategy, in particular what communications/advertising strategy would be appropriate. As he considered these issues, Tom realized that the marketing research results and segmentation analysis would be of considerable assistance in preparing his plan.

EXHIBIT 1	Silage Segment Profiles			

	Performance	Potential Performance	Dual Purpose	Price
Demographics				
Age	Youngest	Middle age	Oldest	Middle age
Farm size	Larger than average	Average	Smaller than average	Smaller than average
Silage acres	Larger than average	Slightly less than average	Average	Slightly less than average
Grain acres	Larger than average	Average	Smaller than average	Smaller than average
Size of dairy operation	Above average	Average	Smaller than average	Smaller than average
Size of beef operation	Large	Average	Medium	Small
Buying Behaviour				
Green Acres share	15%	10%	5%	25%
Brand loyalty	Lowest level	Low level	Highest level	Average
Timing of purchase	Latest	Early	Earliest	Early
Source of information	Government testing	Government testing	Farm magazines	Seed dealers
Measure of performance	Performance indicators	Visual estimates of volume	Visual estimates of volume	Visual estimates of volume
Attitudes				
There are differences among hybrids in protein and energy	Strong agreement	Agreement	Neutral	Neutral
If there were more testing for silage varieties, I would use it to choose varieties	Strong agreement	Agreement	Neutral	Neutral
The best grain variety makes the best silage variety	Neutral	Neutral	Strong agreement	Agreement
When I plant my corn, I know which will be harvested for silage	Agreement	Strong agreement	Neutral	Strong disagreement
Segment Size				
Percentage of all silage growers	10%	50%	20%	20%
Average silage acres	72	46	43	46

Lieber Light

Charles B. Weinberg

Alice Howell, President of the Lieber Light Division of Fraser Co., leaned forward at her desk in her bright, sunlit office and said, "In brief, our two options are either to price at a level that just covers our costs or to risk losing market leadership to those upstart Canadians at Vancouver Light. Are there no other options?" Tamara Chu, Lieber's marketing manager, and Sam Carney, the production manager, had no immediate reply.

Lieber Light, based in Seattle, Washington, had been the area's leading manufacturer of plastic moulded skylights for use in houses and offices for almost 15 years. However, two years earlier Vancouver Light, whose main plant was located in Vancouver, British Columbia, 240 kilometres to the north of Seattle, had opened a sales office in the city and sought to gain business by pricing aggressively. Vancouver Light began by offering skylights at 20 percent below Lieber's price for large orders. Now, Vancouver Light had just announced a further price cut of 10 percent.

COMPANY BACKGROUND

The primary business of Fraser Co., which had recently celebrated its 50th anniversary, was the supply of metal and plastic fabricated parts for its well-known Seattle neighbour, Boeing Aircraft. Until the 1960s Boeing had accounted for more than 80 percent of the company's volume, but Lieber then decided to diversify in order to protect itself against the boom-and-bust cycle that seemed to characterize the aircraft industry. Even now, Boeing still accounted for nearly half of Lieber's $50 million[1] in annual sales.

Lieber Light had been established to apply Fraser's plastic moulding skills in the construction industry. Its first products, which still accounted for nearly 30 percent of sales, included plastic garage doors, plastic gutters, and plastic covers for outdoor lights, all of which had proved to be popular among Seattle home builders. In 1968 Lieber began production of what was to be its most successful product, skylights for homes and offices. Skylights now accounted for 70 percent of Lieber's sales.

THE SKYLIGHT MARKET

Although skylights varied greatly in size, a typical one measured 1 m x 1 m and was installed in the ceiling of a kitchen, bathroom, or living room. It was made primarily of moulded plastic with an aluminum frame. Skylights were usually installed by home builders upon initial construction of a home or by professional contractors as part of a remodelling job. Because of the need to cut through the roof to install a skylight and to then seal the joint between the roof and skylight so that water would not leak through, only the most talented "do-it-yourselfer" would tackle this job on his or her own. At present, 70 percent of the market was in home and office buildings, 25 percent in professional remodelling, and 5 percent in the do-it-yourself market.

Skylights had become very popular. Homeowners found the natural light they brought to a room attractive and perceived skylights to be energy conserving. Although opinion was divided on whether the heat loss from a skylight was more than the light gained, the general perception was quite favourable. Home builders found that featuring a skylight in a kitchen or other room would be an important plus in attracting buyers and often included at least one skylight as a standard feature. Condominium builders found that their customers liked the openness that a skylight seemed to provide. Skylights were also a popular feature of the second homes that many people owned on Washington's lakes or in ski areas throughout the area.

In Lieber Light's primary market area of Washington, Oregon, Idaho, and Montana, sales of skylights had levelled off in recent years at about 45,000 units per year. Although Lieber would occasionally sell a large order to California home builders, such sales were made only to fill slack in the plant and, after including the cost of transportation, were break-even propositions at best. No sales were made to Canada.

Four home builders accounted for half the sales of skylights in the Pacific Northwest region of the United States. Another five mid-sized builders bought an average of 1,000 units each, and the remaining sales were split among more than 100 independent builders and remodellers. Some repackaged the product under their own brand name, and many purchased only a few dozen or fewer.

Lieber would ship directly only to builders who ordered at least 500 units per year, although it would subdivide the order into sections of one gross (144) for shipping. Most builders and remodellers bought their skylights from building supply dealers, hardware stores, and lumberyards. Lieber sold and shipped directly to these dealers, who typically

---

[1.] All prices and costs are in U.S. dollars.

marked up the product by 50 percent. Lieber's average factory price was $200 when Vancouver Light first entered the market two years ago.

Lieber maintained a salesforce of three people, who contacted builders, remodellers, and retail outlets. The salesforce was responsible for Lieber's complete line of products, which generally went through the same channels of distribution. The cost of maintaining the salesforce, including necessary selling support and travel expense, was $90,000 annually.

Until the advent of Vancouver Light, there had been no significant local competition for Lieber. Several California manufacturers had small shares of the market, but Lieber had held a 70-percent market share until two years ago.

VANCOUVER LIGHT'S ENTRY

Vancouver Light was founded in the early 1970s by Jennifer McLaren, an engineer, Carl Garner, an architect, and several business associates in order to manufacture skylights. They believed there was a growing demand for skylights. Their assessment proved correct, and because there was no ready source of supply available in western Canada their business was successful.

Two years ago the Canadian company had announced the opening of a sales office in Seattle. Jennifer McLaren came to this office two days a week and devoted her attention to selling skylights to only the large-volume builders. Vancouver Light announced a price 20 percent below Lieber's with a minimum order size of 1,000 units, to be shipped all at one time. It quickly gained all the business of one large builder, True Homes, a Canadian-owned company. In the previous year that builder had ordered 6,000 skylights from Lieber.

A year later, one of Lieber's sales representatives was told by the purchasing manager of Chieftain Homes, a Seattle-based builder that had installed 7,000 skylights the previous year, that Chieftain would switch to Vancouver Light for most of its skylights unless Lieber were prepared to match Vancouver's price. Lieber then matched that price for orders above 2,500 units, guessing that smaller customers would value highly the local service that Lieber could provide. Chieftain then ordered 40 percent of its needs from Vancouver Light. During the same time, two mid-sized builders switched all their business to Vancouver Light as well, taking advantage of Vancouver Light's lower prices. Before Vancouver's latest price cut had been reported, Tamara Chu, Lieber's marketing manager, projected that Vancouver Light would sell about 11,000 units this year, compared to the 21,000 that Lieber was now selling.

Lieber had asked its lawyers to investigate whether Vancouver Light's sales could be halted on charges of export dumping; that is, selling below cost in a foreign market, but a quick investigation revealed that Vancouver Light's specialized production facility provided a 25-percent savings on variable cost, although a third of that was lost due to the additional costs involved in importing and transporting the skylights across the border from Canada to the United States.

THE IMMEDIATE CRISIS

Alice Howell and her two colleagues had reviewed the situation carefully. Sam Carney, the production manager, had presented the cost accounting data, which showed a total unit cost of $135 for Lieber's most popular skylight. Vancouver Light, he said, was selling a similar model at $144. The cost of $135 included $15 in manufacturing overheads directly attributable to skylights, but not the cost of the salesforce or the salaries, benefits, and overheads associated with the three executives in the room. General overheads, including the salesforce and executives, amounted to $390,000 per year at present for Lieber as a whole.

Tamara Chu was becoming quite heated about Vancouver Light by this time. "Let's cut the price a further 10 percent to $130 and drive those Canadians right out of the market! That Jennifer McLaren started with those big builders and now she's after the whole market. We'll show her what competition really is!"

But Sam was shocked: "You mean we'll drive her *and us* out of business at the same time! We'll both lose money on every unit we sell. What has our salesforce been doing all these years if not building customer loyalty for our product?"

"We may lose most of our sales to the big builders," cut in Alice Howell, "but surely most customers wouldn't be willing to rely on shipments from Canada. Maybe we should let Vancouver Light have the customers who want to buy on the basis of price. We can then make a tidy profit from customers who value service, need immediate supply, and have dealt with our company for years."

Seagate Software

John D. Claxton and
Geraldo Lopez

In July 2000, Peter Harborow, Project Manager eBusiness for Vancouver-based Seagate Software, reflected on the eBusiness Web Site Impact Task Group Preliminary Report that he had just received (Appendix A). Peter's department faced a steady stream of requests for new Internet services from other parts of the company. While he and his group could usually make a reasonable estimate of the cost of each new eBusiness service, the benefits were extremely difficult to evaluate.

To date, eBusiness project priorities had been based on intuitive estimates of the likely benefits of the proposed projects. It was clear to Peter that a more formalized method was needed if his department's resources were to be used to their best advantage. As a start, a month earlier he had set up the Web Site Impact Task Group to begin a formal evaluation of Web site impact. This approach was triggered by his view that the first step was to develop ways to think about metrics for judging impact, both qualitative and quantitative. While he had read articles about the assessment of Web site return on investment (ROI), he had found the suggestions to be overly simplistic. The purpose of the new Task Group was to evaluate the business value of Seagate Web site activities, and the preliminary report was now completed.

COMPANY HISTORY

Since its inception, when it was known as Crystal Services, Seagate Software was involved in the rapidly growing business intelligence industry. In 1985 the company introduced Crystal Reports, the first Windows-based report writer, to the market. A key turning point for the company occurred in 1992, when Microsoft bundled Crystal Reports with Microsoft Basic, thereby introducing more than a million Visual Basic developers to the benefits of the Crystal reporting technology. This initial partnership solidified Crystal Reports as the industry standard for reporting. By 1994 Crystal Services had become a world leader in business intelligence; that same year it was acquired by Seagate Technology, and Seagate Software was born.

Since its initial success with Crystal Reports the company had added new products, expanded distribution channels, and experienced a rapid increase in sales revenue. For the year ending June 30, 2000, the company had revenues of US$126.5 million and employed 1,100 people (informationweek.com, August 3, 2001).[1]

SEAGATE'S CUSTOMERS AND PRODUCT LINE

Seagate Software has customers in more than 75 countries. These customers included organizations such as Charles Schwab, Nike, Deutsche Bank, Boeing, NASA, American Airlines, FedEx, Aetna, and Pepsi-Cola. In addition, Seagate Software has established strategic relationships with such industry leaders as Hyperion, IBM, Informix, Lotus Corporation, Microsoft, PeopleSoft, and SAP.

Seagate Software envisioned a future in which virtually every corporate desktop would have business intelligence tools. Thus, it had focused its efforts on creating Web-enabled products that were easily deployed at reasonable cost, and that used the familiar Internet-browser interface. Seagate's view was supported by forecasts by the Gartner Group, a leading business technology and market research firm, which expected the business intelligence market to exceed US$6 billion within three years.

While Seagate was actively involved in various training and consulting services, its core business was a set of software products designed to facilitate the reporting, analysis, and dissemination of information. These products are described below.

Crystal Reports (CR) is a software tool that enables people to access and analyze information gathered from a variety of corporate databases. For example, information on sales by product and customer could be analyzed by region, by customer size, by product group, by time period, and so on. The user is able to use CR to determine sales in a broad category, and then drill down to subcategories, display results graphically, and print reports as needed.

Seagate Info extends the benefits of CR by facilitating the secure distribution of reports and information to a broad set of users with diverse needs and skills. British Petroleum, a leading petrochemical firm, uses Info to make financial data accessible to more than 1,000 users, with reports viewed from Info's client/server desktop or over the intranet using a Web browser.

Seagate Analysis is a desktop tool that helps individuals access and analyze information from virtually any database. Using a data cube approach the analyst uses a worksheet-style view of the data to navigate, drill through, and chart data of interest.

---

[1] Since the case was written, there has been a change in the ownership structure and in 2001 the company name was changed to Crystal Decisions. Portions of the case were revised in September 2001 by the editors to reflect current Web site (www.crystaldecisions.com) information.

Seagate Holos provides a development environment for IT professionals. Holos is used to build scalable applications that use a variety of data mining and forecasting tools and that are adapted to suit specific company needs.

SALES CHANNELS

Seagate used four main sales channels, which are described below. The direct sales and channel sales groups each accounted for between 30 and 40 percent of revenues. OEM sales and the eStore accounted for about 15 percent each. In addition, support services generated something less than 5 percent of total revenues.

Direct Sales

A salesforce of approximately 100 people sold Seagate Software products to business customers. These sales were usually to larger firms with internal IT professionals. These sales representatives were located in more than a dozen offices around the world.

Channel Sales

Seagate software products were also marketed through distributors and value-added resellers. For example, major implementation firms such as KPMG and PricewaterhouseCoopers frequently developed systems for customers using Seagate software as components of the system.

OEM Sales

Seagate Software made OEM (original equipment manufacturer) agreements to bundle and integrate Seagate Software reporting and analysis tools into the products of other software developers. The current success of Seagate products was attributed largely to a history of strategic alliances with OEM vendors such as Microsoft.

eStore Sales

Seagate Software also sold products and consulting, training, and technical support services through its online store Web site.

EBUSINESS ACTIVITIES AND EVALUATION

Peter Harborow and the eBusiness department had developed the Seagate Web site with the following eight functions:

- Marketing communications
- Demo downloads
- Contact requests
- Software sales
- Job posting and résumé collection
- Technical support

- Product registrations
- Seminar registrations

The first four of these functions were most directly related to the sales process, and were of interest for preliminary analysis by the eBusiness Web Site Impact Task Group. See Exhibit 1 for a summary site map and Exhibit 2 for an example Web page.

To evaluate the contribution of the eBusiness activities, and to guide judgments about future eBusiness expenditures, Peter Harborow established a task group to provide preliminary thinking and analysis. In his initial meeting with the group they discussed the need to evaluate both quantitative and qualitative Web site impacts. The discussion of quantitative metrics centred on return on investment (ROI), where profits could be compared to the resources invested. On the other hand, assessment of some of the more intangible benefits would require a more qualitative tool. For example, Web site components that generate sales could be linked to profitability and ROI. However, components that might be argued as increasing goodwill would certainly be more difficult to assess. The task group decided to call the qualitative metric value-added support (VAS). This metric, similar to ROI, would need to compare benefits to costs. However, since it would apply to more intangible factors, the results would be a more subjective rating, from *very high* to *very low*. The purpose of attempting VAS analysis would be to provide insights that would help compare and contrast the qualitative and quantitative impacts of Web site activities.

The eBusiness Web Site Impact Task Group Preliminary Report began by defining the software sales cycle as a process that starts with the target market and ends with repeat customers. The task force recognized that the Web site could impact this process at several stages, such as awareness generation and relationship building. On the other hand, other

---

EXHIBIT 1	Summary Site Map: seagatesoftware.com

Home Page

Products
- Seagate Crystal Reports
- Seagate Info
- Seagate Holos
- Seagate Analysis
- Analytical Applications
- Euro Compliance

Services
- Consulting
- Training
- Certified Partner Program
- Support Packages

Support
- Fix a Problem
- Learning
- Support Services
- Communicate

Partners
- Strategic Partners
- Partner Programs
- Training Partners
- Consulting Partners
- Partner Listings
- Distributor Partners
- Reseller Partners
- Partner Extranet

About Us
- Our Company
- Success Stories
- Events
- Press
- Reviews & Awards
- Jobs

Contact
- Offices Worldwide
- Sales & General Inquiries
- Technical Support
- Feedback

Seagate activities, such as sales calls, could have overlapping impacts. The preliminary report examined a number of metrics for analyzing Web site impacts, and presented the analysis of four months of data concerning leads and the movement of leads to converts.

The preliminary report covered a lot of ground, but as the report itself concluded, "We are clearly some distance from having a clear assessment of Web site impact on ROI. We recommend a meeting to identify further steps that are likely to have maximum benefit." As Peter prepared to call a meeting for the following week, he wondered to himself, Where do we go from here?

EXHIBIT 2	Example Web Page—www.seagatesoftware.com

Appendix A

eBusiness Web Site Impact Task Group Preliminary Report

SCOPE

As discussed in our task group planning meeting, the Seagate Software Web site has impact in four areas: [1] marketing & sales, [2] attracting new hires, [3] technical support, and [4] product & seminar registrations. The purpose of this preliminary report is to focus on the first of these, marketing & sales.

This report is divided into the following sections:

- 1.0 Impact Overview
- 2.0 Software Sales Cycle
- 3.0 Web site Impact: Data & Metrics
- 4.0 Preliminary Analysis
- 5.0 Additional Analysis
- 6.0 Preliminary Conclusions

1.0 IMPACT OVERVIEW

The Web site has the potential to impact overall profitability by either increasing revenues or reducing costs, with either happening in a variety of ways.

Marketing & Sales

- The Web may facilitate contact with new customers.
- The cost per contact may be lower than other means.
- Providing information downloads may be cheaper than printing.
- Visitors to the site may be subsequent customers.
- Customers buying online can have direct revenue impact.

Human Resources

- Online job posting may provide a broader set of applicants.
- Online résumé administration may be less costly than alternatives.

Technical Support

- Online self-serve help may be more efficient than alternatives.
- 24 by 7 self-serve may increase customer satisfaction.

Product & Seminar Registrations

• Online registrations may be more effective and efficient.

As this listing implies, assessing the broad set of potential Web site impacts would require the collection of a very broad set of data, and hence the reason that this preliminary report will focus on only the marketing & sales issues.

2.0 SOFTWARE SALES CYCLE

The framework that we used to evaluate marketing & sales impacts is shown in Figure 1. The significance of this framework is that it emphasizes that sales happen as a result of a process that customers follow starting from first gaining an awareness of a software product through to the purchase and the potential for repeat purchases. Given this cycle it is important to make two observations:

• The Web site can have impact at several points in the cycle.

• The Web site is not the only factor that might impact purchase.

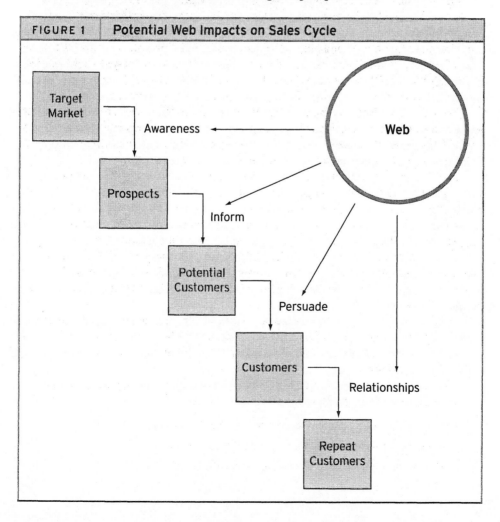

| FIGURE 1 | Potential Web Impacts on Sales Cycle |

Several Points of Impact. The implication here is to recognize that the goal of the Web site might be to increase awareness, or generate leads, or generate sales. Depending on the goal(s) the metric(s) of success would clearly differ.

Web Site Not Only Factor. The implication here is the need to avoid simplistic assumptions about what drives sales. In other words, the site might be doing a good job of generating leads, but the sales reps may not be doing a good job of follow-up. In which case judging Web impact based on sales results would be misleading.

3.0 WEB SITE IMPACT: DATA & METRICS

The sales cycle framework suggests the following types of data and metrics are needed to assess the various Web impacts.

Awareness. One rather crude metric for awareness building would be total Web site HITS. However, since the site receives thousands of visits per month, and since these visits vary from accidental to final software purchases, it seems unlikely that aggregate hits would be a useful metric for awareness (or anything else). It might in the future be useful to select of sample hits and attempt to categorize the nature of each visit.

Inform. Our goal at this stage in the sales cycle is to develop a metric that indicates the number of customers that look promising. In other words, we are looking for a metric that provides an indication of number of "sales leads." As a first cut, we decided that the LEADS metric would be the sum of the site visitors that [1] requested further contact [CONTACTS], or [2] requested a demo download [DOWNLOADS]. Each of these data sets contains the name, company, address, and e-mail of the customer contact.

Persuade. Three metrics were used for this phase of the sales cycle. The first was CONVERTS, the number of customers that had been LEADS and subsequently purchased software. The second was conversion ratio, the proportion of customers that moved from LEADS to CONVERTS, and third was average revenue per convert.

Note 1: A related issue that we had to address prior to the calculation of these metrics was to identify the length of the purchase cycle. In other words, it would not be useful to calculate conversion ratios based on data obtained for a period as short as a week, since our experience is that customers take as much as six months to decide to purchase. For the analysis shown later in this report we examined data based on a four-month time frame.

Note 2: It was not uncommon for the LEADS data to include several individuals from one firm. These individuals were sometimes at the same address and sometimes not. A CONVERT was defined as a match between LEAD and Sale in terms of the company name and location.

Relationships. To date we have made only limited attempts to assess relationship building. As will be seen later, a detailed analysis of a sample of the "contact request" data indicated that almost half of these customer requests dealt with issues that related to ongoing customer relationships.

Other Possible Metrics. A review of a variety of publications suggested the following additional metrics that might be considered in the future.

- Sales to Web costs ratio vs. sales to advertising costs ratio
- Marketing collateral costs vs. number of demo downloads
- Estimates of tech support savings associated with online self-help

- Comparison of mailed vs. downloaded demo costs
- Life Time Value (LTV) estimates by customer

4.0 PRELIMINARY ANALYSIS

The preliminary analysis focused on LEADS and CONVERTS. This analysis should be viewed with the following observations in mind:

- The data analyzed covered four months, July 1 through October 31.
- The sales data were for the U.S. and Canada only.
- The sales data include the company's direct sales and online sales only.

TABLE 1	Leads & Converts		
Source of LEAD	DOWNLOADS	CONTACTS	TOTAL
Number of LEADS	24,582	2,549	27,131
CONVERTS (Those with Subsequent Sales)	1,686	500	2,186
Sales Conversion Ratio	6.9%	19.6%	8.1%
Total sales to CONVERTS	$7,781,046	$4,033,689	$11,814,735
Sales per CONVERT	$4,615	$8,067	$5,405

As indicated in Table 1, the total number of LEADS during this period was 27,131. Approximately 8% of these subsequently purchased software. The total revenue from this group was $12 million, for an average of $5,405 per CONVERT.

5.0 ADDITIONAL ANALYSIS–DOWNLOADS & CONTACTS OVERLAP

Identification of CONVERTS indicated that a number of the customers had used both demo download and contact request functions. In other words, as indicated in Table 2 the number of CONVERTS identified from DOWNLOADS was 1,686 and the number identified from CONTACTS was 500. This suggests a total of 2,186 CONVERTS. However, since 308 customers used both, the actual number of CONVERTS during the four-month period was 1,878.

TABLE 2	Downloads & Contacts Overlap	
Number of CONVERTS	Original Analysis	Overlap Removed
DOWNLOADS	1,686	1,378
CONTACTS	500	192
Both		308
Total	2,186	1,878

TABLE 3	Content of Contacts Sample		
CONTACTS Sample of 766 Requests			
Request Category		**Number**	**Percent**
INFORM	1. Collecting information	254	33%
PERSUADE	2. Close to purchasing	79	10%
RELATE	3. Technical support	159	
	4. Training issues	14	
	5. Information on upgrades	133	
	6. Customer satisfaction/dissatisfaction	34	
	7. Miscellaneous customer requests	20	
	TOTAL Relationships requests	360	47%
OTHER	8. Channel participant requests	47	6%
	9. Garbage	129	17%
Total requests categorized		869	113%
Multiple requests (more than one per customer)		103	13%
Total CONTACTS sample		766	100%

Note 1: The categorization of the CONTACTS data required considerable judgment. The method that we used involved each request being categorized by a pair of task group members. After an initial practice period the raters agreed on 90% of the requests, with 10% requiring further discussion.

Note 2: The motivation for evaluating the requests was to work towards a method of identifying requests that have high payoff potential, and then focusing sales efforts where they are most likely to have high impact. At this point we had not developed a method for setting these priorities, but believe that such a method is possible.

Detailed Analysis of CONTACTS Sample. As was expected a cursory assessment of the contents of the contact requests indicated a wide range of customer interests. To better understand the nature of these requests, content analysis was done on a sample of 766 of these requests. Based on a preliminary assessment it was determined that these requests were of nine general types:

- Collecting information
- Close to purchasing
- Technical support
- Training issues
- Information on upgrades
- Customer satisfaction/dissatisfaction
- Miscellaneous customer requests
- Channel participant requests
- Garbage

Relating these to the Sales Cycle model, the purpose of responding to Category 1 is to "Inform," responding to Category 2 is to "Persuade," and the purpose of responding to Categories 3 through 7 is to build "Relationships." Categories 8 and 9 were not directly related to the customer sales cycle. Table 3 provides a summary of the sample evaluated, and indicates that 33% of the requests were from new customers seeking information, 10% were from new customers close to purchase, 47% were requests from current customers, 6% were from channel partners, and 17% were viewed as garbage.

6.0 PRELIMINARY CONCLUSIONS

The work to date on Web site impact has focused on marketing and sales issues. In particular we have made initial attempts to identify Web site impacts on what we have referred to as the software sales cycle. Our preliminary work has identified some of the difficulties associated with developing easily applied metrics of Web site success. For example, the CONTACTS data required considerable analysis before clear evidence of impact could be assessed.

Assessing Web Site ROI. Although we have spent considerable time identifying and evaluating relevant data, we are clearly some distance from having a clear assessment of Web site impact on ROI. There appear to be several possible "next steps." We recommend a meeting to identify steps that are likely to have maximum benefit.

Tanunda Winery

Gordon H. G. McDougall
and Larry Lockshin

George Steen, Marketing Manager for the Tanunda Winery, had just been given an interesting assignment—to evaluate the feasibility of launching a major export drive. The Tanunda Winery, an Australian producer of quality table wines, had experienced strong growth in Australia but had achieved only marginal success in international markets. At a strategy meeting held in early 2000, the senior management group, which included George, decided that a significant growth opportunity existed in export markets. George agreed to prepare a feasibility study for the next strategy meeting.

As George sat in his office, Bruce Clark, the general manager, came in and they began to discuss the assignment. George said, "There will never be a better opportunity for us to get into foreign markets in a big way. The Australian wine industry report has forecast a very positive environment in several export markets and we produce great wines." Bruce replied, "I agree, it's a good opportunity for growth. My major concern is whether we're capable of doing it and making a profit. The competition is fierce on a worldwide basis and the old-world countries, particularly France, Italy, and Spain, are experts at producing large volumes of value-priced, well-recognized wines. Also, new-world countries like the U.S., Chile, and South Africa are focusing on export markets. Even though many Australian wines are world-class, the old-world countries still have much greater recognition in the key international markets. I know our wines are as good as and in many instances better than comparable European wines, but outside of the United Kingdom consumers don't know that. Many countries have barely heard of Australia in any context, although that should change with the Olympic Games in Sydney this year." "That's true," George agreed, "but we only need a small share of any one of a number of markets to sell a large volume of wine. I think it's a matter of selecting two or three markets and going after them." Bruce responded, "You are probably right but I'm more cautious. I'll be very interested in hearing what you recommend. Our future growth may depend on your report."

THE COMPANY

The Tanunda Winery, one of the leading mid-sized wineries in Australia, was located in the Barossa Valley of South Australia. It was started in 1976 by a young Australian-trained winemaker, Colin MacIntosh. By 1985, the Tanunda Winery was producing a range of white and red wines that were rapidly gaining acceptance in the marketplace. In that year, the firm won two awards for its red wines at one of Australia's major wine shows. Since then, the firm had captured numerous awards every year at national and regional wine shows for both its red and white wines. By 1990, the company had established a solid reputation in Australia as a consistent producer of high-quality premium table wines.

The company was also known for its marketing skills. George, who joined the company in 1988, instituted various marketing initiatives including a series of labels that were regarded by many industry analysts as exceptional in terms of communicating the quality of the wines and standing out among the many competitive brands. As well, George established a distribution system that resulted in the prominent display of the company's products in many retail outlets in Australia. Finally, many of the advertising campaigns prepared for the Tanunda Winery were judged as innovative and contributed to the recognition and acceptance of the company's brands. In summary, the Tanunda Winery was considered an excellent producer and marketer of wines within Australia.

These efforts had resulted in rapid growth for the company. Between 1995 and 1999 sales increased from $33,200,000 to $49,400,000 and profits before tax from $4,800,000 to $5,700,000 (Exhibit 1). Although profits were increasing, the rate of increase was declining, as were average returns as measured by profits as a percentage of sales (Exhibit 1). One way for the winery to increase profits would be to use its fixed assets, mainly processing equipment, more efficiently by producing and selling more wine.

With respect to export activity, up to now Tanunda Winery could best be described as a passive exporter. While George had made one overseas trip in the past two years (the trip covered stops in the U.S., Canada, and the United Kingdom) to drum up some business with wine importers, no explicit export strategy had been established. In fact, the company's export sales had been generated by wine importers who had approached the Tanunda Winery. The interest of those wine importers (primarily from the United Kingdom) in Tanunda Winery products was due to the increasing recognition by many knowledgeable buyers of the quality of Australian and the company's wines. On various occasions wine experts from the United Kingdom visited Australia and sampled numerous wines. On their return to England, many wrote glowing reports on the quality of these wines, including the Tanunda Winery's products. Moreover, in the past three years George had entered some of the company's wines in a number of international wine shows in Europe and the wines had won six awards, usually for being one of the top three in a particular category.

In 1999, the company exported 31,000 cases of wine valued at $2,800,000, an increase of 35 percent in volume and 59 percent in dollar value, compared to 1995 (Exhibit 1). In fact, 1999 was the first year the company received the same average price for its wine in both the domestic and export markets.

While company executives were pleased with the overall performance of the company, they were concerned about two general trends. Domestically, wine sales in total in Australia had grown only marginally and the bottled table wine market, in which Tanunda Winery competed, had shown erratic sales patterns (Exhibit 2). Internationally, Australian wine exports had grown dramatically; between 1997 and 1999 the value of export sales had increased by 79 percent (Exhibit 2). These trends led company managers to consider aggressively entering export markets.

THE AUSTRALIAN WINE INDUSTRY

In many ways, the Australian wine industry is similar to other world wine markets. The first requirement for producing good wines is to have the appropriate climate and soil conditions. Many regions of Australia have these conditions and produce wine grapes including such classics as Cabernet Sauvignon, Merlot, Shiraz, and Pinot Noir for red wines, and Chardonnay, Riesling, and Sauvignon Blanc for white wines. Most medium and large sized wineries in Australia make a complete range of wines, each with their own individuality. The Tanunda Winery makes six different white wines with two brands, Tanunda Chardonnay and Tanunda Riesling, making up more than 80 percent of the company's white wine sales. The company produced five different red wines and, again, two brands, Tanunda Cabernet Sauvignon and Tanunda Shiraz, accounted for the majority of the sales. Dry red wines accounted for 65 percent of total company sales.

A second requirement for producing good wines is to have a skilled winemaker. Colin MacIntosh had quickly established a reputation throughout Australia for producing high-quality wines on a consistent basis. He was renowned for his ability to purchase the finest grapes (the company did not own any vineyards but instead purchased its grapes using long-term contracts from among the more than 4,000 grape growers in Australia) and to use the latest technology in producing many award-winning wines.

The third requirement is the ability to market the company's wines. Few, if any, product categories offered the consumer as wide a choice of varieties and brands as the wine category. For example, one of the large wholesalers of beer, wine, and spirits in Australia listed 577 brands of bottled table wines, including 256 red wines and 273 white wines. Most of these listed wines would be supplied by the 30 medium to large wineries in Australia. The ten largest companies in Australia sell approximately 80 percent of all wine in Australia, and most distribute their own wine domestically. While approximately 1,000 companies produced wine, more than 900 were small firms and relied on cellar-door sales (i.e., sales at the winery) and distributors.

Retail liquor outlets would not carry the complete range of wines offered by a wholesaler, but a typical outlet would handle at least 100 different brands of red and white bottled table wines. This large selection meant that marketing was critical in getting a brand known and recognized by consumers. While wine connoisseurs understood the differences among the varieties and brands of wine, these consumers constituted a small percentage of the wine-buying public. A second group, who knew a reasonable amount about wines and could identify the major and some minor brands, tended to purchase the majority of the bottled table wines.

In terms of quantity, the largest volume of table wine in Australia was sold in soft packs (two- or four-litre casks) to consumers who were relatively price sensitive. Retail liquor outlets in Australia could advertise and offer beer, wine, and spirits at any price. A consumer could purchase a four-litre soft pack of average quality Riesling for $9.99 on sale with a regular price of $12.00, or a 750-mL bottle of slightly higher quality Riesling for $6.99 on sale with a regular price of $9.00. As shown in Exhibit 2, soft packs of table wine constituted about 59 percent of total table wine sales, while bottled table wines constituted about 41 percent of total table wine sales by volume.

On a broader scale, the volume of wine consumption in Australia was relatively stable. This could be attributed to a variety of reasons including changing tastes, an aging population, and increased prices. However, the table wine market, which constituted 83 percent of all wine sales, was experiencing moderate growth. Within the table wine market, there were significant shifts in both the type of wine sold (red versus white) and sales by package type (bottled versus soft pack). White wine had experienced no growth, while red wine had experienced significant growth. Bottled wine sales were growing while soft pack sales were declining (Exhibit 2).

Another significant change in the market was the dramatic increase in mergers and acquisitions in the early 1990s. Some of Tanunda Winery's main competitors, such as Wolf Blass and Leasingham, were now part of large conglomerate wineries. The four largest conglomerates, Southcorp, BRL Hardy, Orlando-Wyndham, and Mildara Blass, were each made up of many smaller companies, which had become labels within a major portfolio. These large companies dominated the retail trade both within Australia and in the Australian export sector. The mid-sized companies, such as Tanunda Winery, were increasingly fighting for a smaller part of the market. Tanunda Winery did differentiate itself from some of the mid-sized companies by its focus on a relatively small range of high-quality wines, rather than trying to compete at both low and high price points.

Against this backdrop, the Tanunda Winery competed in the bottled table wine markets—its target market the relatively sophisticated wine drinker who was somewhat knowledgeable about wines and was likely to drink wine with his or her evening meal two or more times a week. Within this target market the Tanunda Winery competed with virtually all the wineries in Australia, as this was the most profitable segment.

In summary, the domestic Australian wine sector was currently in a period of overall low growth in volume, while exports were growing rapidly. Also, although a few very large companies dominated the industry, approximately 1,000 companies competed for market share, resulting in a wide variety of consumer choice and considerable fragmentation. Finally, the wine market could be described as somewhat volatile as changes in consumer taste and packaging led to shifts in the type of wine sold. Now most of the wine sold was table wine, and while most of that was white table wine sold in soft packs, bottled wine was increasing at the expense of soft packs (Exhibit 2).

THE WORLD WINE INDUSTRY

On a worldwide basis, the wine market was dominated by the European Union (EU) and, within the EU, by three countries: France, Italy, and Spain (Exhibit 3). The EU and the three mentioned countries had, and would continue to have, an important influence on the world wine industry because they are the historical and cultural centres of world viticulture. Collectively, the old-world countries produced more quality wine than any other area of the world and they provided a source for learning of traditional cultivation and production techniques and wine styles.

The EU vineyards accounted for approximately 31 percent of the total area of the world under vines, 40 percent of the world's grapes, and 58 percent of the world's production of wines. In 1997, France, Italy, and Spain accounted for 53 percent of the world's production but only 37 percent of the world's consumption (Exhibit 3). These three countries produced 5.5 billion litres more than they consumed, most of which was destined for the export market. In recent years the production of wine by EU nations had declined (Exhibit 3). However, a surplus of wine was still produced within the EU, and the countries collectively exported approximately four billion litres of wine annually. This was about 70 percent of the total wine exported in the world. To put the size of the exports of the EU in perspective, on an annual basis Italy exported approximately two and a half times as much wine as Australia produced. In many wine importing countries, France and Italy were synonymous with wine. This was especially true in Asia and in traditional European countries like Germany, where the new world had yet to establish a strong prestige factor for their wines.

While the old-world countries dominated the overall world wine market, "new world" countries like the U.S., Australia, and Chile were having a substantial impact. In particular, U.S. wineries were rapidly gaining a share of the overall export market; export volume in 1998 was 272 million litres, with a total value of US$537 million (equivalent to AUS$852.4 million). This compared to Australia's export sales in 1998 of 1,958 million litres at a value of AUS$883 million. In many markets, including the UK, Canada, and Japan, Australian wineries were often competing with U.S. firms. The U.S. had many of the same advantages as Australia—highly technical grape growers and winemakers with good access to capital and experienced brand marketers. Estimates were for U.S. exports to increase by about 20 percent for the next few years.

Chile was another major competitor for Australian wine exports. Chile had an ideal climate, a long history of grape and wine production, and relatively low growing costs. Chile had also been a major recipient of U.S. investment in their wine industry as a low-cost producer of quality table wines. Chile had also seen some major investments by Spanish wine firms. Even Australian firms, such as BRL Hardy, had joint ventures in Chile. However, Chile's viticulture still had technical improvements to make and the producers were relatively inexperienced in branded wine marketing. Chile had nearly doubled wine production from 1990 to 1998 and, in 1998, exported 229.8 million litres of wine, or 43.6 percent of total production. Most of that wine went to Europe and the U.S. About 35 percent of their exports were in bulk, with only 65 percent in bottled wines, but plans were to increase bottled exports.

AUSTRALIAN WINE EXPORTS

Australia has experienced a remarkable growth in exports in the past few years; between 1997 and 1999 export sales by volume increased by 49 percent (Exhibit 2). Even more remarkable was the increase in value/litre from $3.85 to $4.63, which resulted in an overall increase of 79 percent in dollar sales. In the same period, exports as a percentage of total wine sales (domestic and export) increased from 32 to 40 percent (Exhibit 2). This dramatic growth in volume and value was attributed to a variety of reasons including increased awareness of the health benefits of wine (particularly red—see Exhibit 4), greater levels of consumer sophistication, strong global economic growth, and more promotion and advertising spending on wine. One factor in this success was the more favourable exchange rate, as the Australian dollar had fallen against many foreign currencies in the past few years. Predictions for the Australian dollar through 2002 were that it would stay in a band centred around about US$.70. The other factors in the success of Australian exports were the strong branded wine marketing and co-operation among the wine companies in promotional efforts.

Australia's old-world competitors relied on prestige and thousands of small wine growers to market their wine. In developed countries wine was increasingly sold through chain supermarkets and specialty shops. For example, in the UK (Australia's major export market), the five major supermarket chains accounted for more than 65 percent of wine sales. These huge chains demanded sophisticated logistics and consistent quality. They used major promotions and pricing to attract consumers and focused on selling high-quality BOBs (buyers own brands, e.g., Sainsbury Australian Chardonnay), which Australian wineries could readily offer. Intense competition within Australia had engendered a strong brand-based marketing culture with high-quality, reasonably priced brands. The larger wine companies produced BOBs for major UK chains, while using that production as leverage to gain shelf space for their more profitable major brands. The Australian marketers were skilled in negotiating major promotions that could run to 100,000 or more cases.

All of this was done under the guidance of the Australian Wine Export Council (AWEC), which was funded by the industry's self-imposed export levy. AWEC tested and tasted every Australian wine applying for an export licence in order to make sure only quality wine was exported. AWEC had offices in the UK and the U.S., and recently opened offices in Germany, Scandinavia, Canada, and Japan. AWEC did little promotion itself, but acted as a clearinghouse for organizing Australian participation in major wine events: it organized tastings for the press and visits to Australia by major wine writers; developed tastings at major consumer events; provided advice on export and import regulations; and helped smaller wineries find proper representation in export markets. Australian wineries could often be found pouring both their own and their Australian competitors' wines at tastings around the world; thus, they competed and co-operated in gaining recognition.

The United Kingdom was the major market, by volume, for Australian wine, accounting for 49 percent of total export sales, followed by the United States (22%), New Zealand (6%), Canada (5%), and Germany (2%) (Exhibit 5). By country the price per litre ranged from a high of $6.59 (Singapore) to a low of $2.97 (New Zealand), with an average of $4.63. These prices reflect older markets buying mainly bulk and cask wine, and newer markets buying more high-value bottled wine. All markets were showing increasing prices per litre, reflecting Australia's focus on branded bottled wine exports. By region, North America and Asia (Northeast and Southeast) were attractive markets in terms of average price/litre (Exhibit 5). The overall Asian market had been increasing even with the Asian financial downturn of 1998 (a drop in Southeast Asia sales was more than compensated for by an increase in sales to Japan).

In total, more than 400 Australian wineries exported wine with the top four wine companies accounting for more than 70 percent of all export revenue. The two largest Australian wineries, Southcorp and BRL Hardy, had sales of $660,000,000 and $463,000,000 respectively and profits of $137,000,000 and $61,000,000 respectively. These two wineries had grown rapidly in the 1990s, primarily due to merger and acquisition strategies. Both were very successful in export markets. Southcorp was Australia's largest wine exporter and had international offices in the UK/Europe, North America, Singapore, and New Zealand. BRL Hardy exported to more than 60 countries and also had offices in the UK/Europe, North America, and New Zealand. Both companies recently opened offices in Canada. These two wineries, plus the Orlando-Wyndham Group and Mildara Blass, accounted for about 70 percent of all export sales from Australia. In fact, just ten of the nearly 1,000 wineries held 84 percent of the total domestic production, and 6 percent of the brands on the Australian market accounted for more than 75 percent of sales.

Smaller wineries also were having export success, though not in the huge volumes of the major wine producers. As Australian exports grew in a country, so did the awareness of Australian wine. Since wine is a category with a huge array of choices, consumers often would try new and different wines. This behaviour resulted in most export buyers also sourcing a range of smaller Australian wines to complement their major brands. Not all wineries could be successful in this niche: they had to provide excellent quality; professional presentations; good logistics; and be willing to develop promotional deals.

THE EXPORT DECISION

In preparing the report, George first considered the possible countries where the Tanunda Winery could achieve significant sales. Based on a preliminary screening, he decided to limit his investigation to the four countries that he felt offered a good potential for the company's products: the United Kingdom, the United States, Canada, and Japan. He then prepared a "fact sheet" on each market.

United Kingdom

The UK is by far Australia's largest and most important wine market. The total market is over 800 million litres in size, and Australia holds an overall share of 11 percent in the total market and has a share of about 25 percent in the £4–£5 (AUS$10.00–$12.50) sector. In the past year, the UK represented 45 percent of all Australia's wine exports, a value of AUS$489 million. Australia's sales have grown by over 12 percent annually for the past few years.

The retail structure of the UK market is highly concentrated; about 65 percent of all wines are sold through the five major grocery chains. The majority of these wines are under £5.00 (AUS$12.50). The grocery market is mainly served by the major wineries' brands and some of them bottle BOBs for the chains as well. Typically, small and medium sized wineries do not have the volume or the promotional budgets to maintain a strong presence in this sector.

Since about 65 percent of all wine sales are in major grocery chains, the rest of Australian wineries are competing for the 35 percent of wines sold in specialty stores. Two specialty chains had the majority of non-grocery wine sales. This structure benefits the larger of the medium-sized wineries, because they can serve this market, and the specialty chains are looking for wines to differentiate themselves from the grocery stores. The Barossa region was well known as a premium wine region and it was seen as an advantage to be able to sell Barossa-sourced wines, something the larger Australian wine companies rarely did.

The UK is a very open market. There are no barriers to sales across the regions and cities. Pricing is important, but volume discounts and other trade deals are expected from larger wineries. Small wineries with "scarce" wines can usually avoid these discounts. The Australian Wine Bureau continues to build the reputation and awareness for Australian wines by running various promotions throughout the year. To participate in these promotions, a winery needs to join the UK Group (run by the Bureau), which costs about AUS$10,000, and then they must provide wine and personnel for the various promotions. The Bureau is also very useful in helping decide on the parameters for locating and retaining a good agent.

As always, distribution is key for this market. Exporters must first choose a marketing strategy and then locate an agent servicing the proper outlets. Most wineries appoint an importer/distributor for the whole country after considering their marketing strategy. Promotion is done through tastings and often by discounting lower-priced brands. Higher-priced wines should consider tastings, through AWEC, and public relations. Wine writers are influential, and major newspapers in the cities usually have a weekly wine column. Because the UK market is very competitive, extensive advertising, point-of-purchase displays, and price specials are often used at the retail level to promote individual brands.

United States

The U.S. is Australia's second largest wine market, with exports of 39 million litres of wine worth AUS$231 million (value/litre of $5.92) in the past year. The U.S. appears to be a solid market for premium wines. Australia has risen from an almost negligible player ten years ago to having more than 6 percent of wine imports, about 1.6 percent of the overall market. The U.S. market is growing slowly, about 3 percent per year, and total consumption in 1999 was slightly over 2,000 million litres.

There are two key issues in understanding the U.S. market. The first is that, although the overall market is large, domestic wines account for almost 85 percent of table wine sales. This leaves a relatively small import market for Australia to compete in. The second is that the structure of the U.S. market is very complex. It is legally a three-tier system—producer, distributor, and retailer—with laws restricting ownership to only one tier. Through the Bureau of Alcohol, Tobacco, and Firearms the federal government collects taxes, reviews labels, and sets all regulations. Additionally, each state may levy differential amounts of taxes and require a separate label approval. A licensed distributor must be appointed for each state in which an importer sells wine. This usually entails separate label approvals and licence fees.

There are no truly national distributors or national retail chains. Regulations differ by state; in some states wine can be sold in grocery stores and in others only in special shops, while in a few states wine is sold only through state-owned stores. The best way to approach the U.S. market is to consider which region or area holds the most promise and to focus at first on this region or area. This will reduce the number of licences and transactions.

For Australian wines, the East Coast of the U.S. is the best starting point. California and the western states drink more local wines and fewer imported wines, while the opposite is true for New York and other major cities in the East. The top metropolitan markets for imported wine are, in order, New York City, Chicago, Boston-Lawrence-Lowell-Brockton, Washington, D.C., and Los Angeles.

The total adult U.S. population is 143 million, but only 16 million are regular wine drinkers (at least once a week) and they account for 88 percent of all wine sales. It is a fairly narrow audience to reach and convince to try premium Australian wine. There are about 26 million marginal consumers who drink wine once a month, and about 58 million who drink alcohol but do not drink wine. There are 43 million non-drinkers in the U.S. Females are the majority in the regular and marginal drinkers (over 60%), and males are the majority in the non-wine drinkers.

The Australian Wine Export Council has had an office in the United States since 1995. The staff can help organize the choice of an importer and/or agent as well as promotions for individual and groups of Australian wine companies.

The U.S. is a very discount-oriented market. Prices are usually quoted in U.S. dollars and discounts are offered for volume purchases. Larger wineries also are expected to give promotional allowances. These must be registered several months in advance of the activity. A wine that has a full retail price of $12.00 would usually be offered for sale somewhere between $9.00 and $10.99. Markups over received (laid in) cost are typically about 100 percent to the retailer and then are marked up an additional 33 percent before discounting.

The lowest price points for bottled wine in the U.S. are under $3 per 750-mL bottle. This represents almost 48 percent of all bottled wine, although this part of the market is shrinking. "Popular" premium wines sell for $3–$7 per bottle and represent about 38 percent of the market. The biggest growth areas are in the "super premium" ($7–$14) and "ultra premium" (above $14) ranges, although these currently represent only 14 percent of sales.

The distribution channels in the U.S. are quite complex. When a new wine is to be imported to the market, a company has several choices of how to distribute. Small companies often appoint an importer to cover the whole country. This importer would have salespeople in key markets working with local distributors. Another way a small to medium sized company can gain distribution is to appoint an importer for only one region who works with local distributors. Other importers can then be appointed for different regions as the brands grow.

Promoting wine in the U.S. can be very expensive due to the cost of media and the many regions. Public relations is the tool most often used. Newspaper wine columns appear in the largest wine markets, and some newspapers in the medium markets use syndicated columns. Magazines like *Wine Spectator* are very influential.

Canada

Exports to Canada, Australia's fourth largest wine market, have been growing at more than 10 percent per year for the last five years. Sales in the past year were 8 million litres valued at AUS$44 million. The value increased almost 30 percent over the previous year, while volume increased only 11 percent.

Domestic wine production accounts for about 30 percent of sales. France is the biggest exporter with 24 percent of sales, followed by Italy with 15 percent, the U.S. with 10 percent, and Australia with 5 percent.

The Canadian liquor market is highly regulated at the provincial level (ten provinces). In all provinces except Alberta, Liquor Boards operated by the provincial governments are the sole importers and retailers of liquor. Hotels and restaurants can sell to guests, but they must obtain wine through the Liquor Boards.

The major drawback to the Canadian market is the difficulty in getting a general listing in a province. Australian wines compete against all other wine-producing countries for listings. Up to 2,000 listing requests are received by the boards each year, and a provincial selection committee might list 25 to 50 new wines. Chances of acceptance are improved by a personal visit to present the listing application. Price (within a given quality range) appeared to be the dominant criterion in getting accepted on the list. Wineries improved their chances not only by filling out the required forms, but also by making a case for why their product should be carried. Awards, promotional budgets, and advertising results from other markets can be used to make a case for listing. In total there are more than 4,000 import wines listed by the ten provinces, as well as more than 2,500 domestic wines.

Once a listing is gained, each province has slightly different rules about how much wine can be imported and stored. The Liquor Boards sell a relatively small range of "general" lower-priced wines, with a quota assigned to each brand. If the brand does not meet the quota, it is taken off the official list. "Specialty" wines are brought in with lower quotas or are done by trial with no long-term agreement to reorder. It is critical to promote a wine during the trial period to ensure that sales targets are achieved to maintain the listing. A separate marketing program is necessary for each province in which the wine gains a listing.

Most Australian wine producers who export to Canada use agents to perform the marketing function. The agents work on a commission basis (usually 10 percent of the landed cost in Canada), and their prime role is to obtain product exposure. This can be done by convincing restaurants and hotels to include the product on wine lists, by conducting tastings, and by obtaining good press for the product. Agents are valuable because the need for "below the line" activity (e.g., personal selling) is considerable in Canada. The larger Australian producers, like Southcorp and BRL Hardy, have offices and staff in Canada.

More than 80 percent of the 30 million Canadians live in four provinces. The largest province is Ontario, with 35 percent of the wine by volume and over 11 million people. Quebec is next in size (7 million), followed by British Columbia (4 million), then Alberta (3 million). Many Australian exporters focus on just a few of the top markets, either provinces or cities (e.g., Toronto—3 million, Montreal—2 million, Vancouver—over 1 million), especially if they are selling wines priced at over $10 per bottle.

The Australian Wine Export Council (AWEC) maintains an office in Toronto, Canada's largest city. The office can help with the paperwork necessary to get samples into the various Liquor Boards and with the other regulations. The office coordinates tastings in major cities and runs a series of promotional events throughout the year.

Japan

Japan is a promising market for Australian wines. Even when the economy was in recession, Australian wine sales effectively doubled in the two-year period 1997–1999. In 1999, Australia had sales of 4.5 million litres worth $24.8 million ($5.47/litre), about 2 percent of the Japanese wine market. Per capita consumption is low, at 1.5 litres per head, and is conservatively forecast to grow to 2.9 litres in the next few years.

Japan is the only export market where the U.S. has a greater share than Australia. This has been fostered by close economic and cultural ties over the past decade. The U.S. and France are the major competitors for higher-priced premium wines.

The structure of the wine market in Japan is quite unique. People have small homes and do little entertaining there. Most wine is consumed in wine bars and restaurants. Until recently, wine was available only in Western-style restaurants and typically represented the ethnic style (i.e., Italian wine in Italian restaurants). There are several Australian restaurants and wine bars in Japan, and more Japanese restaurants are now carrying wines.

The distribution structure has been very complex, with up to four or five levels from importer to consumer. Recent reforms have seen a major reduction in these levels. Now many supermarkets and department stores import directly from overseas producers. A large difference from other markets is that traditional wine and liquor agents are not specialists. Major importing companies have very diverse merchandise, ranging from machinery to electronics to wine. This is disconcerting to wine exporters used to dealing with specialist importers, but seems to work well in the Japanese market.

The population of Japan is approximately 128 million people and stable. Japan has a small, very active wine-consuming minority. Alcohol in general is widely used, and beer and sake are the main drinks. Until recently these drinks and the associated behaviour was linked to Japanese men going to bars and clubs each night after work.

The two main consumers of wine in Japan are wine-knowledgeable men, typically middle-aged and upper income, and younger women. Japan has numerous wine bars, and recent statistics showed that more than 10,000 people were enrolled in wine appreciation courses (including an Australian wine appreciation club with more than 1,000 members). Most of the people in the courses and clubs are younger women, who prefer not to follow the male "model" of drinking beer and spirits in clubs.

Japanese culture imbues its citizens with a demand for quality. All aspects of a product from its reputation to its packaging must exude high quality. In this sense, premium wines are a good match for this market. The majority of wine consumers are very knowledgeable and should be relatively easy to convince of the merits of premium wines. Though it will take time to gain a reputation, the Japanese market is an excellent prospect for premium wines.

There are over 131,000 licensed liquor outlets, so having a strong agency presence is necessary. Like other complex markets, it is important to gain the services of an agency with access to the distribution and retail channels best matched to the style of wine being sold. For the most part, Australian wines will need to access specialty shops, department stores, and a range of restaurants and clubs.

Pricing in Japan is not a major consideration. The reform of the distribution channels has reduced the average price of wine available for sale and increased the volume. Wines are now available at prices around AUS$6.00 and this has opened the door to a wider range of potential wine consumers. To gain sales of higher priced wines, a positive reputation for the country, the region, and the winery is necessary. The major pricing problem is the exchange rate. Australian currency has gained about 75 percent in value (as has the U.S. dollar) during the recent Japanese recession. This has constrained wine price increases.

PRELIMINARY COST DATA

With respect to the costs of production, George had read a recent newspaper article on the costs of wine and was surprised at how close those costs were to those of the Tanunda Winery. As shown in Exhibit 6, the production cost for a 750-mL bottle of good quality premium wine was $5.01. By the time the consumer purchased it, the price was $17.73. While the cost of grapes for some of the other varieties of wines could be less, most of the price of a bottle of wine ($12.72 per the example) was made up of margins and taxes.

George prepared some preliminary calculations on the average costs of getting a case of wine to each of the four markets and what it might sell for at retail (Exhibit 7). The estimated retail price after taxes ranged from $19.67 in the UK to $23.12 in Canada.

George also worked out some preliminary estimates of what it would cost to actively enter the export market. In terms of personnel, the cost of an export sales manager was about $60,000, and if the manager made six overseas trips a year this expense would be about $100,000. One or two sales clerks might be required at a cost of $30,000 each. Preparation of custom requirements, including documentation, obtaining label approvals, and sending samples, could cost up to $30,000. Promotion costs were difficult to estimate, but they could exceed $100,000 for expenditures on wine tastings and shows for both the public and the trade, advertising expenditures for consumers and the trade, and public relations.

Although the Tanunda Winery had not aggressively pursued the export market, George was quick to capitalize on any export opportunity that was presented. For example, if a British importer expressed interest in any of the company's products, George or a member of the marketing group would provide free samples, information on the wines, details of any awards won, and product availability. If an importer placed an order, George ensured that the order was shipped as quickly as possible with proper documentation. As George once joked to a colleague, "We may not go after the export business, but if anybody comes to us, we'll offer better service and support than any other winery in Australia."

THE DECISION

Having gathered the preliminary data, George began thinking about the report. He was not certain what he should recommend. On the one hand, export sales were growing with little effort and expense on the company's part. Possibly with a little more effort, sales could be increased without going "full speed ahead" into exporting. On the other hand, the tenuous nature of the company's relationship with its exporters and importers suggested that some action should be taken. Also, the time appeared to be right for a more aggressive assault on the export market.

George knew that the senior management group was expecting a report that contained specific recommendations, including whether the Tanunda Winery should aggressively enter the export market, and, if so, how many markets to enter. The group would also expect to receive details of the proposed strategy George would pursue for the next three years in the export area. With these thoughts in mind, George began writing the report.

EXHIBIT 1	Tanunda Winery: Selected Company Statistics (1995-1999)

	1995	1996	1997	1998	1999
1. Profit & Loss (in $000,000)					
Sales	33.2	37.3	42.0	45.9	49.4
Cost of goods sold	21.4	24.2	27.5	30.3	32.9
Gross margin	11.8	13.1	14.5	15.6	16.5
Marketing expenses	5.0	5.7	6.6	7.3	7.8
Net margin	6.8	7.4	7.9	8.3	8.7
Administration and overheads	2.0	2.3	2.6	2.8	3.0
Profit before tax	4.8	5.1	5.3	5.5	5.7
2. Sales by volume					
(000 litres)[1]	3,500	3,850	4,250	4,600	4,900
(000 cases)	389	428	472	511	545
3. Average selling price per case ($)	85.38	87.10	88.90	89.82	90.64
4. Export statistics					
Export sales (000 litres)	212	219	230	255	280
Export sales (000 cases)	23	24	26	28	31
Average selling price/case ($)	76.40	78.97	82.73	86.02	90.26
Export sales ($000)[2]	1,760	1,895	2,150	2,410	2,800

[1] One case equals 9 litres (12 bottles containing 750 mL).

[2] It was estimated that additional marketing expenses and administrative and overheads amounted to 4% for export sales.

EXHIBIT 2	Australian Wine Market: Selected Statistics (1997-1999) (000,000L)		
	1997	**1998**	**1999**
DOMESTIC L			
Total wine sales	336.6	338.8	348.3
Table	268.8	278.4	287.4
Fortified[1]	25.6	24.6	23.9
Sparkling[2]	32.6	31.1	32.6
All other[3]	9.6	4.7	4.4
Table wine sales			
White	185.0	189.5	188.3
Red	83.7	88.5	99.1
All other[4]	.1	.4	–
Table wine sales			
Soft pack/white	126.5	125.3	117.9
Soft pack/red	41.6	41.3	44.7
Bottled/white	56.2	59.4	63.3
Bottled/red	41.1	46.7	53.7
All other[5]	3.4	5.7	7.8
EXPORTS			
Sales L	154.9	193.7	230.5
Sales ($000,000)	596.2	812.7	1,068.3
Export val/L $	3.85	4.20	4.63
TOTAL SALES DOMESTIC AND EXPORTS L	488.5	532.5	579.5
IMPORTS L	13.6	25.6	N/A

[1] Includes sherry and dessert wines
[2] Includes Champagne and carbonated wines
[3] Includes flavoured and vermouth
[4] Includes rosé
[5] Includes rosé and other sizes

EXHIBIT 3	World Wine Industry: Selected Data

	Per Capita Consumption		Production[1]		Consumption[1]		Exports[1]	
	1980	1997	1996	1997	1996	1997	1995	1996
Top Ten								
France	91	60	57,047	53,612	34,795	34,941	11,396	12,937
Italy	80	58	58,772	50,847	34,693	33,820	15,832	13,415
Spain	60	37	31,000	33,887	14,459	14,528	6,260	6,729
United States	10	7	17,442	20,223	19,191	19,835	1,329	1,615
Argentina	76	39	12,681	13,500	13,365	13,505	2,148	1,215
South Africa	9	9	8,739	8,702	4,022	4,022	1,295	1,200
Germany	25	23	8,642	8,495	18,580	18,580	2,302	2,465
Romania	29	25	7,663	6,688	7,260	5,889	305	454
Australia	17	19	6,734	6,174	3,297	3,472	1,141	2,340
Portugal	70	53	9,711	5,727	7,360	5,889	1,553	1,947
Selected Others								
United Kingdom	12	14	27	13	6,811	8,157	109	215
Ireland	3	5	–	–	205	289	6	6
Netherlands	12	14	–	–	2,058	2,102	89	124
Canada	8	7	333	345	2,106	2,101	13	12
New Zealand	11	11	573	550	356	388	79	111
Singapore	N/A	N/A	–	–	N/A	N/A	N/A	N/A
Japan	1	2	675	675	1,718	2,121	3	3
World Total			268,535	259,645	220,172	222,568	55,720	55,730

[1] Hectolitres (1 hectolitre = 100 litres)

EXHIBIT 4	Australian Wine Exports by Product Type (Volume and Value) (1998-99)

	Volume[1]		Value[2]		Value/Litre ($)	
	1998	1999	1998	1999	1998	1999
Bottled red	74.2	94.0	400.1	555.5	5.39	5.91
Bottled white	74.1	89.1	321.8	403.3	4.34	4.53
Total bottled table wine	148.3	183.1	721.9	958.8	4.87	5.24
All other wine[3]	45.4	47.4	90.8	109.5	2.00	2.31
Total	193.7	230.5	812.7	1,068.3	4.19	4.63

[1] 000,000L

[2] 000,000$AUS

[3] Includes cask, flagon, and bulk (red and white) and fermented sparkling and other.

EXHIBIT 5	Australian Exports by Region and Country (Volume and Value) (1998-99)

	Volume[1]		Value[2]		Value/Litre ($)	
	1998	1999	1998	1999	1998	1999
European Union	113.1	140.0	464.6	615.6	4.10	4.40
United Kingdom	92.5	112.4	382.0	489.0	4.13	4.35
Ireland	4.6	6.0	23.2	33.3	5.04	5.50
Germany	3.6	5.7	15.1	26.1	4.19	4.54
Netherlands	2.9	5.3	12.3	26.2	4.24	4.98
All other	9.5	10.6	32.0	41.0	3.36	3.87
North America	39.1	48.3	213.9	283.0	5.47	5.87
United States	31.5	39.1	174.9	231.3	5.55	5.92
Canada	7.7	9.2	39.0	51.7	5.06	5.63
Oceania	24.1	23.1	58.2	69.1	2.41	2.99
New Zealand	22.4	21.0	52.2	62.2	2.33	2.97
All other	1.7	2.1	6.0	6.9	3.53	3.29
South East Asia	5.6	6.2	32.4	37.2	5.78	5.97
Singapore	1.3	1.8	8.3	11.6	6.94	6.59
All other	4.3	4.4	24.1	25.6	5.60	5.82
North East Asia	6.4	5.2	32.0	27.3	5.00	5.26
Japan	5.7	4.5	28.9	24.8	5.07	5.47
All other	.7	.7	3.1	2.5	4.42	3.57
All other	7.5	7.7	32.0	36.1	4.26	4.68
World	195.8	230.5	833.1	1,068.3	4.25	4.63

[1] 000,000L
[2] 000,000$AUS

EXHIBIT 6	Typical Cost Structure for a Bottle/Case of Wine

	Per Bottle	Per Case
Product[1]	$2.17	
Packaging	1.49	
Bottling	1.35	
Total production cost	5.01	60.14
Manufacturer margin (50%)	2.51	
Price to wholesaler	7.52	90.21
Wholesaler margin (25%)	1.88	
Wholesaler price	9.40	112.76
Retail margin (33%)[2]	3.10	
Retail price before tax	12.50	149.98
Taxes[3]	5.23	
Retail price after tax	17.73	212.82

[1] Based on grape costs for premium fruit at a price of approximately $1,600 per ton. One ton will produce about 700 bottles of 750-mL wine. A case contains 12 bottles (9 L).

[2] Retail margins can be as high as 50% in some markets.

[3] Includes a GST of 10% plus an added Wine Equalization Tax to maintain revenues of 29% added after the retailer purchases the wine.

EXHIBIT 7	Estimated Retail Price of a Case of Tanunda Wine in the Four Markets

	United Kingdom	United States	Canada	Japan
Tanunda Winery price per case	$90.24	$90.24	$90.24	$90.24
Transportation to destination[1]	1.64	2.04	2.04	1.39
Landed costs	91.88	92.28	92.28	91.63
Import duties and excise tax[2]	$9.00	7%	54.8%	21.3%
Landed cost with duties/taxes	100.88	98.74	142.85	111.15
Importer/agent margin[3]	30%	30%	10%	20%
Importer price	131.14	128.36	157.13	133.38
Wholesale margin[4]	20%	33%	NA	35%
Wholesale price	157.37	170.72	NA	180.06
Retail margin[5]	50%	33%	70%	35%
Other taxes[6]	NA	5%	14%	5%
Retail price	236.06	238.41	289.12	255.23
Bottle price (750 mL) in $AUS	19.67	19.87	24.09	21.27
Bottle price in local currency[7]	£7.89	13.11	23.12	1488.85
On-shelf retail price[8]	£7.50	$11.99	$23.12	¥1489

Assumptions:

[1] It costs $244 to ship a container from the Barossa Valley to Port Adelaide. On average a container holds 1,000 cases. One case contains 9 L or 12 bottles (750 mL). Port Adelaide to UK is $1,400 per container; to U.S. or Canada is approximately $1,800; to Japan is $1,150.

[2] Duties and Excise taxes by country.

[3] Importer margin in UK ranges from 25% to 40% of landed cost (assume 30% for estimation purposes); in U.S. range is 25% to 40% (assume 30%); in Canada agents average 10%; in Japan 20%.

[4] Wholesale margins in U.S. range from 20% to 40% (assume 33%). Most wine in the UK goes directly to the retailer; in Canada the wholesaler and retailer are both province-owned; in Japan the wholesale margin ranges between 20% and 50% (assume 35%).

[5] Retail margins in UK are about 50%; in U.S. from 30% to 40% (assume 33%), but prices are often discounted in the store; in Canada range from 55% to 123% of landed cost (assume 70%); in Japan about 35%.

[6] Some markets levy a sales tax or equivalent on the retail bottle price.

[7] Currency conversion rates: UK 0.40; U.S. 0.66; Canada 0.96; Japan 70.0.

[8] Estimated retail price after discounts.

J.M.'s Signature Restaurant

*Lisa Callaghan and
Gordon H. G. McDougall*

Joshua Mathew had just finished reviewing his accountant's evaluation of his plan to open a new high-class restaurant, J.M.'s Signature Restaurant, in the entertainment district in Toronto. He was troubled to see that his accountant considered his goals to be overly optimistic. Joshua, an experienced restaurant owner, had the idea for the new restaurant when he learned that a restaurant had recently failed in a location directly across from the Cedarcroft Centre, one of Toronto's largest and best known theatres. He liked the downtown location, and the landlord was offering a very attractive lease. While the area was heavily populated with restaurants, Joshua believed the opportunity was too good to pass up—a great location with a low lease rate. He knew he would have to move quickly to obtain the space.

Based on his previous success in the restaurant business, Joshua had set a goal of $4 million in revenue for J.M.'s Signature Restaurant's first year of operations. However, he knew he should carefully review his plan in light of his accountant's comments to determine if he should move forward as well as to determine the most appropriate marketing plan to ensure J.M.'s Signature Restaurant's success.

RESTAURANT INDUSTRY

The total Canadian restaurant industry was estimated at $38 billion in annual sales, with growth in the 2- to 4-percent range in recent years. The growth could be attributed, in part, to a shift in consumption patterns, with more of the household food dollar being spent in the fast-food segment. It was estimated that 15 percent of all personal expenditures were spent on food and 34.6 percent of every dollar spent on food was spent in restaurants. The industry was highly competitive, with more than 63,000 restaurants offering consumers everything from fast food to fine dining where the bill could exceed $100 per person. The majority, 65 percent, of restaurants were independently owned and operated. Of these, approximately 5 percent failed in 2000. Industry data revealed an interesting phenomenon: new independent restaurants had a higher failure rate, 18 percent, in their first year of operation.

Overall, the restaurant industry catered to virtually every taste and consumer, from ethnic to fast food; from chains to independents; from low to high price; and from middle of the road to trendy. As well, the industry could be broadly delineated into two different markets, full service and partial service, and was often further categorized by bill size per person. Selected financial information on full-service restaurants in Canada is provided in Exhibit 1.

J.M.'s Signature Restaurant would be competing in the full service/higher bill size per person segment. In this highly competitive segment, traditional areas of competitive advantage including food quality and service were rapidly becoming a strategic necessity. Today, high-class restaurants often sought a competitive advantage through alternative means such as décor. It was not unusual for restaurants with an average bill over $50 per person to spend more than $4,500 on décor per seat. Reputation was another key factor; a strong positive reputation was an intangible asset that could translate into real value, especially in an industry that was heavily influenced by hot trends and fickle customers. As well, 70 percent of annual restaurant sales were from repeat customers.

TORONTO AND THE ENTERTAINMENT DISTRICT

Toronto, with a city population of approximately 1 million residents, was Canada's largest urban centre. Approximately 5.2 million people resided within a one-hour drive of the downtown core, and 22 million tourists visited Toronto each year. Selected demographic and income-based statistics for Toronto are provided in Exhibit 2.

Toronto's entertainment district was located in downtown Toronto, bordered by Queen Street to the north, Lakeshore Boulevard to the south, Spadina Avenue to the west, and Jarvis Street to the east. This district partially overlapped with, and extended slightly south of, the Toronto downtown business district. Major entertainment centres in the theatre district included the Cedarcroft Centre, a 3,200-seat house for ballet, opera, concerts, and musicals; the SkyDome, home of Toronto's professional baseball and football teams; the Air Canada Centre, home of Toronto's professional hockey and basketball teams; the historic Elgin & Winter Garden theatre; the Pantages theatre, best known as the home of Andrew Lloyd Webber's "The Phantom of the Opera"; Roy Thomson Hall, home of the Toronto Symphony Orchestra; and the Royal Alexandra Theatre. This downtown area, which included the financial district, supported the largest business workforce in Canada, with thousands of individuals commuting from surrounding communities to work in the downtown core. It was well populated with hotels and amenities. Approximately 12,000 first-class hotel rooms were within walking distance of the theatre district.

Within this district there were more than 100 restaurants, each offering a different dining experience. One critic commented about the district that there were "so many restaurants, bars and shops that on some streets they are stacked on top of each other." The recent economic prosperity of the late 1990s and early 2000s was causing new restaurants to "spring up like mushrooms after rain." There were approximately 71 prominently advertised restaurants in downtown Toronto that fell within a similar price range to J.M.'s Signature Restaurant. Of these restaurants, 12 showcased a European or French atmosphere. Specifically in the theatre district, 29 restaurants with average bills per person greater than $41 were being advertised on the Internet in Toronto restaurant guide Web sites. More than 55 percent of these restaurants had average bills per person greater than $50.

One key to being successful in this segment was style. A popular food critic for a Toronto paper commented that a restaurant with great food and no style (or the wrong style for the moment) will flunk out faster than you can say "Pass the crème brûlée." It could be perilous to ignore the latest fashions and trends. One of J.M.'s Signature Restaurant's main competitors would be Reds—a bistro located in the First Canadian Place in the heart of Toronto's financial district. Its ultra-cool bistro brand had become the darling of the young downtown business crowd since it opened in October 2000. Even though some critics found the food itself to be unappealing, the restaurant was always packed—except on Saturday nights, when the financial district became deserted.

JOSHUA MATHEW

As a child, Joshua loved food and its preparation. In high school he had even written a restaurant column for a local paper. After completing a degree in commerce, Joshua went on to pursue a career in hotel management. However, when the opportunity arose he opened his own European-influenced restaurant in 1987. Unfortunately, the critics were not kind, and the restaurant lost money before ultimately closing in 1990. However, in 1997, Joshua went on to open a second restaurant, Karma, located in the heart of the Toronto downtown business community. Unlike its predecessor, Karma was an instant success and acclaimed as a trendy restaurant in the business market. Joshua's reputation as a restaurateur grew dramatically with Karma, and not only his restaurant but also his name was well known in the business sector. Despite its short hours (Monday to Friday, 11:30–2:30 and 5–10), the low building lease rate, convenient location, and check size ranging from $27 to $70 per person translated into $7 million annual revenue in its most recent year of operation and a net income rate between 12 and 20 percent over the recent past. Joshua had since opened another successful restaurant called Lynx (see Appendix A for descriptions of the two restaurants, both of which had won critical awards). He was confident that he could repeat this success with J.M.'s Signature Restaurant and make it the trendy place to dine in the theatre district.

THE PLAN FOR J.M.'S SIGNATURE RESTAURANT

A key strategy in Joshua's business plan included taking over the lease of the failed Cape Cod Club, located across from the Cedarcroft Centre. The Cape Cod Club was run by a previously successful restaurateur and well known chef, but the Toronto crowd never warmed to its wood-panelled New England atmosphere. In hindsight, many critics blamed both the atmosphere and the location for its dismal performance. One such critic commented "the theatre district is a terrible location, where dining is only an afterthought and never the main event." Joshua was negotiating to take over the lease and pay the base rent at $22 a square foot per year. Given the revenue forecast, Joshua viewed this lease rate as a bargain.

Joshua envisioned renovating the interior to portray a décor that was "French bistro with London cool." He felt that a spacious décor was necessary to generate the right feel and was considering incorporating more open space (the plan was for 96 seats plus a 40 seat bar) and using a well trained staff of 71 to cultivate a feeling of preppy informality. He envisioned the maître d' sporting a James Bond–style tuxedo to let people know that J.M.'s Signature Restaurant was about show business. Joshua was focused on attracting business clientele who would see J.M.'s Signature Restaurant as a place where "love affairs, business deals, and friendships begin." Every two weeks, the chef would create a special signature dish meant to demonstrate the quality of the dining experience and to provide a reason for coming back. As a special service, customers could choose to have the recipes e-mailed to them—to remind them of the meal, or, for the adventurous, to allow them to try this at home (see Appendix B). The award-winning chef Joshua had hired was enthusiastic about this concept, and they agreed to a restaurant with a traditional European selection (Exhibit 3). They believed that diners wanted fantastic yet predictable food in a great atmosphere. The chef suggested they should strive to be the "corporate cafeteria to the six-figure lunching crowd."

Lunch was anticipated to be a busy time, but the signature menu should attract evening business as well. Joshua also envisioned Sunday brunch as a highlight of the seven-days-a-week operation. The average bill during the dinner hours was forecast to be $55 per person.

MARKETING

To reach his goal of quickly making J.M.'s Signature Restaurant a hot and trendy place, Joshua considered various marketing tools including mailing 2,000 postcards to a client base that had frequented his other restaurants and inviting newspapers and magazines to view the development of the restaurant. In Joshua's mind, any media coverage would be good coverage, as long as it was free. Additionally, the use of the Internet as a marketing tool for restaurants was growing in popularity, and Joshua wondered about its applicability for J.M.'s Signature Restaurant.

Joshua knew that the average full-service restaurant spent approximately 5 percent of revenue on advertising and promotion. Of this, 70 percent was directed toward advertising, while the remaining budget was generally allocated to promotions. Given the average full-service restaurant revenue of $610,000 (Exhibit 1), a reasonable marketing budget for an average restaurant would be estimated at approximately $30,000. J.M.'s Signature Restaurant's would probably be considerably higher. Joshua had researched the costs of advertising across different media in Toronto (Exhibit 4). Knowing that his reputation would draw an initial crowd, Joshua wondered how much his advertising budget should be.

THE ACCOUNTANT'S COMMENTS

Joshua had asked his accountant, Sheila Bruyn, to review his concept. Sheila focused on industry averages and the plan that Joshua had proposed. First, she based her revenue projections on an average of one turn for lunch and for dinner ("turns" in the restaurant business were defined as the number of customers per seat per meal period—breakfast, lunch, or dinner—or per day). She recognized that the bar would also contribute to the total revenue figures and accounted for it in her revenue calculations (Exhibit 5). Second, cost of goods sold (the food costs) averaged 35 percent. Third, the restaurant industry was very labour-intensive. Generally salaries consumed 30 percent of revenue, and the average annual sales per full-time employee were around $50,000. She noted that Joshua planned to have a staff of 71 and based her salary expense on those numbers. Mismanagement of this key area could spell disaster for a restaurant. After estimating the remaining expenses, she calculated a net profit of $28,400.

Sheila was very concerned that the 5,800-square-foot restaurant would have only 96 seats (excluding the 40-seat bar), which would require a high seat turnover at an average of $20 per meal at lunch and $55 per meal at dinner to generate $4 million in annual sales. She noted that the average square feet per seat for full-service restaurants was 28.1 (Exhibit 1). In summary, Joshua would need to outperform the industry by a considerable margin to achieve the target revenue of $4 million. Joshua had estimated startup costs at $750,000, which covered redecorating, some salaries, initial rent, insurance, and permits.

THE DECISION

The accountant's comments and estimates troubled Joshua. Sheila was concerned that the proposed business plan would be insufficient to generate targeted revenues, even if capacity were met. Had his previous success made him overly optimistic? Was he overstaffed? How much advertising did he really need? Should he decide to move forward? If so, what marketing plan would ensure the required instant success?

EXHIBIT 1	Selected Financial Information–Full-Service Restaurants
Average annual revenue	$610,000
Average pretax net income	6.4%
Average sales per square foot	$498
Average annual sales per seat	$14,000
Average square feet per seat	28.1
Seat turnover*	.9

*On average, on a per day basis, there are .9 customers per seat.

Source: Various sources

EXHIBIT 2	Toronto: Selected Statistics

City of Toronto (excludes East York, North York, Etobicoke, Scarborough and York)

Population:	993,700
Income:	45% above the national average
Working population:	612,238
	Spend 10.7% of household expenditures on food.
Business mosaic:	10.8% of all businesses are "eat, drink and be merry," 3.2% are commerce and 2% are large investment and service companies. Mid sized business services = 11%

Financial mosaic:	Platinum card elite:	4% of households
	Gold card boomers:	3%
	Prosperous planners:	4%
	Middle class and mature:	10%
	Still getting established:	30%

Metro Toronto

Population:	5,016,400
Income:	17% above national average (3rd highest per capita income for cities in Canada with populations greater than 100,000)
Working population:	2,444,025

Source: Statistics Canada

EXHIBIT 3	Sample Menu from J.M.'s Signature Restaurant

Appetizers

2 dozen steamed mussels	$9.25
(with frites)	$16.25
Grilled sea scallops	$14.75
Fish soup	$9
Vegetable pistou soup	$7

Main Course

Rare entrecôte steak with wild mushrooms and escargot butter	$26
Loin of Provimi veal with prune stuffing, gratin dauphinoise of melted goat cheese with thyme-coated potatoes	$26

Dessert

Plateau de fromage du chariot (cheese platter)	$12
Assiette du citron	$10.25
lemon pot de crème, lemon tart, and lemon sour ice	
Lemon grass infused Concord grape soup	$9
Earl Grey tea	$3

EXHIBIT 4	Various Advertising Costs in Toronto

Newspapers

Toronto Star

    Saturday delivery,

    Circulation in Ontario 693,038

    General advertising, 1/6th of a page $5,830

Globe and Mail

    Saturday delivery,

    Circulation in Ontario 299,329

    Travel, Special Interest and Technology section, 1/6th of a page $4,670

    News and Report on Business section, 1/6th of a page $7,450

Magazines

Toronto Life

    12 issues per year
    Circulation in Ontario 100,000

Advertisements per year	1	3	6	9	12
½ page colour*	$7,710	$7,520	$7,325	$7,135	$6,940
Full page colour	$11,185	$10,905	$10,625	$10,345	$10,065

Food & Drink

    6 issues per year
    Circulation in Ontario 520,800

# of ads per year	1	2	3	4	5	6
½ page colour*	$8,311	$7,896	$7,502	$7,130	$6,773	$6,437
Full page colour	$13,309	$12,642	$12,012	$11,414	$10,841	$10,301

* costs per advertisement

Radio*

CHFI

    Breakfast   5 am–10 am

    Midday   10 am–3 pm

    Drive   3 pm–8 pm

    Evening   8 pm–1 am

    Overnight   1 am–5 am

EXHIBIT 4	Various Advertising Costs in Toronto (continued)				

	1	2	3	4	5
Breakfast					
60 sec**	$1,270	$890	$740	$660	$600
30 sec	$635	$530	$460	$410	$375
Midday					
60 sec	$1250	$865	$720	$645	$585
30 sec	$325	$520	$450	$400	$365
Drive					
60 sec	$1,010	$690	$575	$515	$470
30 sec	$505	$420	$365	$325	$295
Evening					
60 sec	$290	$205	$170	$150	$135
30 sec	$145	$120	$105	$95	$85
Overnight					
60 sec	$400	$80	$70	$60	$55
30 sec	$70	$60	$40	$35	$30

* Reaches 22% of population weekly. On average people are tuned in for 11.4 hours/week, which is the most of any Toronto radio station surveyed.

** Costs are per advertisement. Discount given for higher repetitions.

Internet

Banner Ad: $30 per thousand impressions (monthly rate). An impression is the number of times an advertisement is located on a comprehensive Web site. The ad will appear in locations appropriate for the target market.

Minimum number of impressions: 400 / month

Maximum number of impressions: 200,000 / month

Average Toronto Life impressions (equivalent to circulation) are 3 million a month.

Brochures

Corporate program	$5,100
100 corporate locations in Toronto	
35,000 brochures, colour, 4"x 9"	

Hotel program	$8,430
185 Toronto hotels	
70,000 brochures, colour, 4" × 9"	

EXHIBIT 5	Accountant's Assessment

Revenue[1]	$2,772,000
Cost of goods sold[2]	970,200
Gross margin	1,801,800
Expenses	
Salaries and benefits[3]	1,170,000
Occupancy costs[4]	207,000
Direct operating expenses[5]	155,200
General and administrative[6]	102,600
Marketing[7]	138,600
Total expenses	$ 1,773,400
Net profit[8]	28,400

[1] Assume average lunch bill of $20; 96 seats, 350 days open, 1 turn (each seat generates one customer at lunch). Total lunch sales equals $672,000. Dinner same at bill of $55 ($55 × 96 × 350 × 1). Total dinner sales equals $1,848,000. Assume bar generates $18/seat/day × 350 days equals $18 × 40 seats × 350 days equals $252,000. Total equals $2,772,000.

[2] Industry average is 35% of sales.

[3] 71 total staff. Assume 60 staff @ $8.00 per hour × 34 hours/week × 50 weeks. Total equals $840,000. Assume 11 staff × $30,000/year equals $330,000. Total equals $1,170,000.

[4] $22/square foot × 5,500 square feet equals $127,000. Property taxes and insurance equals $80,000. Total equals $207,000.

[5] Direct operating expenses include paper supplies, cleaning supplies, linens, tableware and kitchen utensils. Industry average is 5.6% of sales equals $155,200.

[6] General and administrative includes office supplies, postage and telephone, data processing, commissions on credit card charge collection fees, and other related expenses. Industry average is 3.7% of sales equals $102,600.

[7] Marketing expenses include advertising and promotions. Industry average is 5% of sales equals $138,600.

[8] Net profit before taxes. Total startup costs are $750,000.

Appendix A

Joshua Mathew Restaurants

KARMA

Karma still seems to be everyone's favourite. Many of our critics simply want more diners to discover the superlative job the chef is doing at creating memorable dishes. One dish cited among many was "an artistic course of scallops, perfectly cooked, with a spinach wrap in a light polenta with tomato coulis and parsley oil." Others saluted the "astounding fish soup" and the "truly remarkable rack of lamb." The silky service of the wait staff is a true delight. Great food, superb staff, and views from a top floor building help explain the restaurant's success with busy lunchtime patrons and more leisurely diners.

LYNX

Lynx neatly merged two recent Toronto dining trends: the born-again embrace of all things French, and the shift to a more evolved style of bistro dining. The kitchen is anchored by Andre Miller, a cook of enormous discipline. "Order the soup—Miller's are always delicious, especially his new stringing lobster bisque," said one critic.

One veteran observer called it a "lovely big open space with the kitchen as view. Great food, and a menu that surprised several of our critics—one of whom announced that Miller "has made a clear shift from the modern Italian cooking that made his name" to a "broader card that is more French than Italian."

Appendix B

J.M.'s Signature Dishes

J.M.'S DUCK

1 duck, giblets removed
1 onion, peeled and cut in half
4 sprigs parsley
4 sprigs fresh thyme
2 stalks celery, cut into 3-inch-long pieces
2 teaspoons ground ginger
½ cup of sugar
½ cup soy sauce
1 teaspoon salt
½ cup sherry or Madeira
1 small bunch of watercress, trimmed and washed

1. The day before, stuff the duck with onion, celery, parsley, and thyme. Place the duck breast side up in a large soup pot with enough water to half cover it. Add the ginger and bring to a boil. Cover and reduce the heat so that it simmers gently for an hour.

2. After one hour, turn the duck over. Add the sugar, soy sauce, and salt. Continue simmering for another hour. Turn duck once again and simmer until tender and almost falling apart, about another hour. Turn off the heat and, when cool enough, remove duck from pot and place in a roasting pan. Cover and refrigerate until the next day.

3. Pour the broth into a container and use for soup or sauces.

4. Before serving, bring duck to room temperature in roasting pan. Preheat oven to 350 degrees. Add the sherry or Madeira and 1 cup of the duck broth to the roasting pan and place in the oven. Roast uncovered for 30 to 45 minutes, basting occasionally with the juices from the pan. The duck is done when it is heated through and the skin is crisp and chestnut brown.

5. Transfer the duck to a serving platter and garnish with watercress.

Result: Dinner for 4.

PAELLA SUPREME

6 chicken thighs or half breasts of chicken
3 ounces prosciutto, cut into ¼-inch dice
2 tablespoons extra-virgin olive oil
1 ounce chorizo, cut into ¼-inch dice
1 medium Spanish onion, finely chopped
1 clove garlic, lightly crushed
1 bay leaf
1 tablespoon chopped fresh thyme
1 tablespoon saffron threads soaked overnight in 2 cups chicken stock
1 cup uncooked long-grain rice, rinsed until water runs clear and drained
1 jalapeno pepper, seeded and minced
1 medium red bell pepper, finely chopped
1 medium beefsteak tomato, blanched, peeled, seeded and coarsely chopped
3 oz fresh shelled English peas, blanched in salted water and rinsed until cold
24 mussels steamed until shells open
2 cups diced cooked lobster or peeled cooked prawns
8 oz scallops lightly cooked in a little butter
1 or 2 pinches cayenne pepper
Salt and freshly ground white pepper to taste

1. Preheat the oven to 350 degrees. Sauté the chicken and prosciutto in oil in a casserole over medium heat for 5 minutes, until lightly brown. Add the chorizo and sauté 3 minutes more.

2. Add the onions and garlic, cover and cook until the onions are soft. Stir in the rice and jalapeno and cook for 3 minutes.

3. Add the broth with saffron and tomato and bring to a boil. Stir in the saffron. Cover and bake for 15 minutes, until the rice is al dente.

4. Stir in the peas and seafood.

5. Bake for 15 minutes, basting with oil every 5 minutes.

Result: Dinner for 6.

Part 3   Strategic Marketing

case twenty-three

Becel Margarine

Phil Connell and
Peggy Cunningham

On December 15, 1999, Ross Hugessen, Brand Manager at Unilever Canada, reflected on the last several months of managing Becel Margarine, one of the company's most important brands. Becel had just been awarded a CASSIE* for advertising effectiveness, and it appeared as though Becel would end the year with a record market share in the $450-million margarine/butter category. It seemed as though things had never been better for the business. Ross knew, however, that as soon as he returned from Christmas break he would be faced with some important issues regarding the brand's future.

For some time, Becel had been a very strong player in the market, having grown substantially in its relatively short history. But while Becel was still growing, the growth trend was below that of prior years—and well below what senior management had come to expect. Positioned as the "best margarine for your heart's health," Becel had a compelling point of differentiation that seemed to be one of the key reasons the brand had done so well. However, this positioning had been attracting several new competitors at a price point considerably below the premium price Becel had built its business on. In addition, the margarine category had some very tight regulations (for example, margarine in Quebec had to be white, not butter coloured, and no dairy ingredients could be added), which limited the potential for margarine brands like Becel to come forward with much innovation.

The CASSIE awards are given biannually to recognize significant achievements by Canadian advertisers.

Ross had to evaluate the brand from all angles to determine the best strategic plan to deliver both the short- and long-term significant growth that was expected by Unilever. Even though the brand had met with a record share, the rate of growth had fallen below what was expected for 1999. Becel had been built by targeting older, educated, and affluent adults, but Ross began to question the ability to attract any higher proportion of this target market. Furthermore, although the Becel communication strategy had been very success-ful, it didn't seem to be driving the rates of growth it had initially, even though advertising had been clearly proven to drive sales. The advertising campaign had been running for many years and had been developed by his boss. Ross knew he would be challenged to keep the level of advertising spending on his brand if the returns were less than before, especially as other brands in the company were vying for the budget.

He wondered if the brand team could determine a convincing strategy that would shape the future success of Becel margarine and maintain its share leadership and growth momentum.

UNILEVER CANADA

Unilever Canada, a division of the international Unilever group, is headed by two parent companies, Unilever NV and Unilever PLC, headquartered in Rotterdam and London, respectively. Unilever was formed in 1930 when the British soapmaker Lever Brothers merged with the Dutch company Margarine Unie. This allowed both companies to benefit from many raw materials and resources that they had in common. Today, Unilever is one of the world's largest consumer products companies.

In 1999, Becel Margarine fell under the Foods division, Lipton. In addition to having a category-leading position in the margarine market with more than eight brands, each of which was managed separately, Lipton also sold products in the tea, soup, packaged side dish, and pasta sauce markets. Unilever's other major division was Home Care and Personal Products, marketing such products as Dove, Sunlight Detergent, Salon Selectives, and Degree. The Personal Products brands often took priority for marketing budgets due to the competitive nature of their markets.

BECEL MARGARINE

A History of the Becel Brand

Becel Margarine was launched in 1978 as a premium-priced product, positioned as the heart-healthy margarine choice. Lipton's intention at the time was to create a brand that helped consumers meet their needs for heart health, as had been the position in Europe for 20 years prior to the Canadian introduction. Becel entered the market using very direct communication about the health advantages of the product.

Over the years, as Becel began to gain some success with its positioning, it increasingly attracted competitive attention. Nabisco, with its Fleischmann's brand, was most threat-ened, since it was the leader in the health segment of the market. Kraft also responded as it realized that the health-segment growth was taking share away from mainstream brands like Parkay. Also, the Dairy Bureau (butter) increased its marketing and advertising sup-port; the target market for Becel and butter seemed to be the same. Furthermore, private-label brands launched their own products using "me-too" positioning strategies at significantly reduced prices.

Despite the uniqueness of the positioning, Becel struggled for many years. By 1991 the brand had managed to establish only an 8.1-percent share of the market, and had very limited growth at only 1 to 2 percent per year. Furthermore, as a result of new legislative guidelines, many of the direct, rational messages about Becel's heart health benefits could no longer be used. By 1991, Lipton knew it had to take the brand in a new direction or risk discontinuing the brand.

The company considered several options for growing the Becel brand. Lipton considered a price decrease, to increase volume; however, health brands in other categories typically had large price premiums that successfully delivered strong profits and communicated a price/quality relationship. The company also thought about repositioning the product—maybe not enough Canadians were concerned with heart health. Finally, Lipton considered dramatic increases in advertising support for Becel, but getting approval for heavy investment in a brand with poor volume was not really an option. Management decided that the only viable alternative was to try to grow the brand through a new breakthrough communication strategy without any change in expenditure. Any advertising budget would have to support the margarine, as well as the newly launched line of cooking oil and spoonable dressings.

In 1991, Lipton was able to devise a strategy that would eventually make Becel the leading brand of margarine in Canada. They decided to develop a communication strategy that would revolve around the notion of "living a life that is young at heart." This strategy allowed Lipton to communicate a simple message that became the emotional benefit of consuming Becel.

Becel's "Young at Heart" advertising campaign depicted the benefits of being young at heart through consumers' hope and optimism as expressed in the tagline "Becel takes your health to heart." The ads featured active, fit, outgoing seniors enjoying life to the fullest while enjoying a heart-healthy diet—which included the consumption of Becel. Seniors were used to create an association between Becel and living life to the fullest at a time in life that is often associated with health deterioration. The TV campaign, featuring the famous Jimmy Durante song "Young at Heart," focused on the emotional benefits of Becel, while a comprehensive print campaign delivered the rational heart-health messages (see Exhibit 1 for sample Becel print ads). This communication strategy provided consumers with a powerful reason to believe in the product. Becel was ready to embrace mass consumption.

In addition, Becel started to educate consumers and health professionals about the dietary benefits of margarine through the Becel Heart Health Information Bureau. The Becel Heart Health Information Bureau sought to disseminate key brand messages based on sound scientific principles, while maintaining its objectivity and credibility. With increased marketing spending directed to health professionals, Becel built a solid reputation as a leader in heart health and nutrition education.

In 1998, Becel continued to develop the communication strategy even further and launched an interactive Web site (www.becelcanada.com). The Web site was an extension of the Becel Heart Health Information Bureau and provided information on meal planning, cooking recipes, the basics of heart health, and, of course, product information on the Becel lineup. In addition, there was a portion of the site dedicated exclusively to health-care professionals.

Becel Today
Brand Performance

As a result of the comprehensive Becel communication strategy, the brand went from being a small player to being the market leader within a relatively short time frame. In 1992, when the "Young at Heart" campaign was launched, Becel had a 17.7-percent dollar share of the market. By early 1997, the dollar share had increased to 28.4 percent. Sustained growth and impressive market share results had been achieved while Becel had commanded the highest price premium of any brand in its category. This price premium helped to provide a justification for advertising spending (see Exhibits 2A/B for a full analysis of the market share data and Exhibit 3 for a profit/loss statement; Exhibit 4 shows media costs).

Brand Awareness, Trial, and Loyalty

The success of this communication and positioning strategy was even further realized in the consumers' awareness of Becel in the market. Brand awareness of Becel increased substantially from 1992 onward. In addition to consumer brand awareness, the number of consumers in the market who had tried Becel had also increased substantially. Even more impressive was that Becel had the highest consumer loyalty of any brand in the category, at 50 percent—this in a category where brand switching was very high (see Exhibit 5 for a full analysis).

Given that brand awareness was so high, it is not surprising that consumers also had a very good understanding of Becel's position in the marketplace. It was very clear that Becel's heart health message was getting through; substantial portions of the market believed that Becel was the heart health expert. Overall, there was no question that Lipton had developed a successful strategy for a strong product.

The Spreads Category
Competitive Environment

By 1999 the health segment of the margarine market had become very competitive, with many brands attracted by the success of Becel and consumer interest in healthy products. Even with the health segment growing, Becel's most formidable competitor was butter. Butter had just over 50 percent of the market in Canada, and Ross knew that for Becel to grow it had to make further inroads with butter consumers. The Dairy Bureau (which markets butter on behalf of Canadian dairy farmers) was very aggressive with positioning butter on its primary benefit of taste and naturalness. The campaign highlighted the "naturalness" of dairy over the perceived "processed food" reputation of margarine. The butter industry led the category in advertising spending with over a 50-percent share of voice, with about $7 million in spending every year in television and print. Further, Parmalat, a large producer of butter, had recently begun to promote its Lactantia margarine brand of products. Using a positioning that leveraged the association with butter—"the makers of great tasting butter now bring you great tasting margarine"—Parmalat had only a small portion of the margarine market share, but it was increasing off a smaller base at a rate faster than Becel. Ross could not ignore the potential threat posed by this brand.

Finally, there were two other brands that were growing that Ross knew he had to keep an eye on. Canola Harvest was a product that had a small share of the national market, with its strongest market being in western Canada. This product was positioned as the margarine with the best taste and best health because it contains canola oil. Retailers liked the product because it seemed to offer many of the same benefits of Becel but at a much cheaper price. The other product was Olivina, which was positioned using a "Mediterranean diet" association. This product had secured only about 0.6 percent of the national market, but was showing strong growth. Ross knew that health professionals were starting to favour recommending olive oil over margarine. Ross also knew about the growing interest in olive oil, since Unilever had recently bought the Bertolli brand. This caused Ross to wonder if he had the right range of products (Exhibit 6).

Examining the Marketing Mix

Targeting the Market

The demographics of the margarine and butter category are quite diverse, although they do identify some interesting trends in the consumers that Becel and its competitors attract. Specifically, there is an interesting dichotomy between the types of consumers who purchase margarine versus those who purchase butter. A substantial portion of the volume of margarine purchased is by people with large families, particularly ones with four or five members, and who tend to have lower than average incomes (Exhibit 7).

Conversely, the total volume of butter consumed was disproportionately weighted toward families without children and families with older children. Furthermore, a large portion of butter consumers tended to be over 55 years of age, and the most affluent buyers. The target market for Becel tended to be very close to that of butter. However, most households bought both margarine and butter. Ross knew that the reasons people bought butter were quite different from the reasons they bought a health margarine.

These data made Ross's job more difficult. The demographics showed that Becel had been doing exactly what it was intended to do, serving the needs of those pursuing heart-healthy lifestyles. In addition, they had secured very high customer loyalty. Those who purchased Becel satisfied almost half of their margarine volume requirements with Becel. Most brands did not have remotely close to this degree of loyalty. Yet the rate of growth for Becel was beginning to slow down. Ross wondered why.

He had a look at some market data that showed what consumers tend to look for when purchasing margarine (Exhibit 8). The data showed that individuals who purchase margarine exclusively on the basis of taste seemed to account for the lowest volume of margarine purchased. Those who purchase exclusively on the basis of health or price reasons accounted for almost the same percentage of volume of margarine sold. However, this was really just scratching the surface. For the most part, consumers purchase products for a variety of reasons, and margarine is no exception. Thus, the data further showed what percentage of margarine consumption was based on the interaction among taste, health, and price. Apparently individuals considering all three attributes purchased the largest percentage volume of margarine. Looking at these data, Ross realized that he would have to consider the complex interaction of taste, health, and price in deciding his go-forward recommendation.

Pricing Considerations

Becel's price has remained relatively consistent over time, but since its inception Becel has been priced at a premium to other margarines to reflect the premium quality formulation (see Exhibit 9 for pricing information).

Interestingly, though, all margarines are priced lower than butter. Butter was the highest-priced spread in the category and had the ability to demand a premium price because of its strong heritage and loyal user base. Butter had always been the gold standard for taste and best for baking. Margarine had always been considered a cheaper alternative to butter and so the largest share of the margarine market was held by more price-driven brands. In fact, in consumer surveys, price/value was the biggest reason for buying margarine over butter. The pricing strategy was an important area Ross had to give more consideration to if he wanted to grow volume.

Channel Considerations

The channels of distribution for packaged goods are quite broad: grocery stores (Loblaws, Sobeys), convenience stores (Becker's), discount super stores (Wal-Mart, Zellers) and club stores (Costco) are just a few examples of where packaged goods are sold. However, the dominant force in these channels is the grocery channel. Throughout Canada in the last decade, the grocery industry has seen intense consolidation and increased growth of private-label products. In 1999, the consolidation became even greater as Canada's biggest grocery chain, Loblaws, acquired Quebec's Provigo chain. Historically, Quebec had been the biggest market for butter and the weakest market for Becel.

THE FUTURE OF BECEL

Ross glanced out his office window as he considered the various strategies that Becel could follow. Becel was an important business and any strategy taken also got lots of attention from the European head office. In fact, the Europeans were strongly considering using the Canadian advertising idea, which his boss was very proud of. Ross needed to carefully review what he saw to be some of his major alternatives before proceeding with a decision that would reinvigorate the expected growth for Becel.

Ross began to prepare his recommendation on the long-term vision for Becel, which was due within a month. As he considered a number of options, he got a call from his new advertising agency telling him about some new butter print advertising that was challenging the health benefits of the product. The ad actually made a specific reference to the ingredients for Becel, paralleling butter as "Nothing but Good Stuff."

Note: Becel, Lipton, Sunlight, Salon Selectives, Dove, Degree, and Fleischmann's are all trademarks of Unilever Canada.

EXHIBIT 1	Sample Becel Print Ads

MARION IRVINE IS ON THE RIGHT PATH.

Making the choice to pursue a heart healthy lifestyle is important. Staying on that path is equally important.

Perhaps that's why so many choose Becel. It's low in saturated fat and non-hydrogenated (and therefore contains virtually no trans fat). No wonder more doctors and dietitians recommend Becel than any other margarine.

And to help you on the path to heart health, Becel is proud to support and make available the Heart and Stroke Foundation's booklet: "Heart Healthy Eating On the Go."

becel *takes your health to heart.*

Please write to us for your free copy:
Becel Heart Health Information Bureau
PO Box 12073, Saint John, NB, E2L 5E7
www.becelcanada.com

EXHIBIT 1	Sample Becel Print Ads (continued)

THE BEST PART

ABOUT BEING OVER 70

IS STEALING THE GOLD

FROM AN UPSTART

58-YEAR-OLD.

The Canada Senior Games are what being young at heart is all about. That's why Becel is a major partner. For 20 years, we've educated Canadians about the rewards of choosing a balanced diet as part of a heart healthy lifestyle. And for many, that choice includes Becel. So here's to all the athletes – and everyone else who is young at heart.

BECEL IS A PROUD SPONSOR OF THE 1998 CANADA SENIOR GAMES.

Becel takes your health to heart.

| EXHIBIT 2A | Market Share Data Analysis: Margarine |

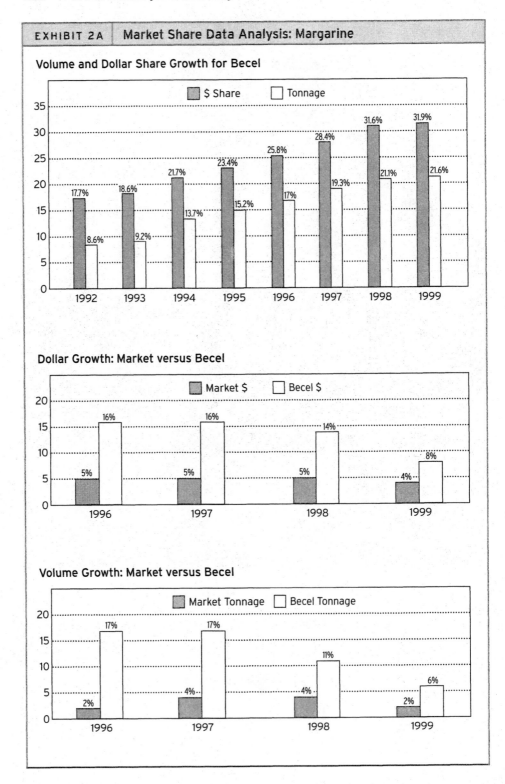

EXHIBIT 2B	Market Share Data Analysis: Margarine

Total Margarine/Butter Market 1999
Spreads Market
$450m   +2%

Total Margarine/Butter Market 1999
Tonnage   +2%

Competitive Brand Shares–
Margarine 1999
$222m   +3%

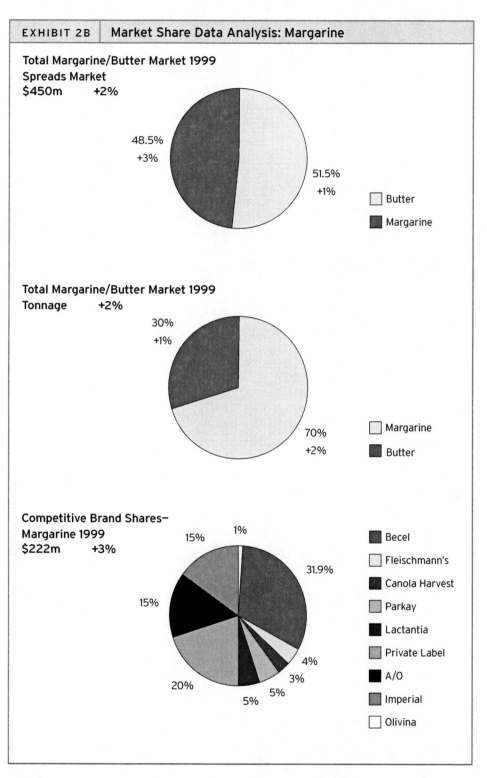

EXHIBIT 3	Becel Profit/Loss Statement	

	Actual 98 (000s)	Actual 99 (000s)
Standard Cases	1,537	1,562
Gross Sales	55,629	58,746
Total Costs	36,567	39,947
Gross Profit	19,062	18,799
Market Expenditure	5,200	3,800
Advertising	3,200	1,800
Promotion	2,000	2,000
Profit before Indirects	13,862	14,999

EXHIBIT 4	Media and Advertising Cost Estimates	

Primetime Television Commercial Rates (30 seconds)[1]

Network	Number of Stations	Basic Average Cost
Regional Television		
Atlantic TV Network	1	$90
ATV	4	$650
CBC		
Atlantic	5	$1,000
Central/Quebec	15	$6,000
Western	12	$2,500
Pacific	6	$1,000
Global	1	$7,000
MITV	2	$500
BBS Ontario	8	$5,000

Cost of Production: one commercial $300

Newspaper Advertising[2]

Newspaper	Cost of Advertisement	Cost per 1,000 People Reached (CPM)
Toronto Star	$11,340	$2,438
Globe and Mail	$16,938	$5,314
Toronto Sun	$5,463	$2,366

Cost of Production: one ad $25

[1] "Estimated Cost of Network Commercials" *Media Digest* 1999–2000 ed., p. 22.

[2] Tuckwell, Keith J., *Canadian Advertising in Action*, 5th ed., (Prentice Hall: Scarborough, 2000), p. 332.

EXHIBIT 5 | **Brand Awareness, Trial, and Loyalty**

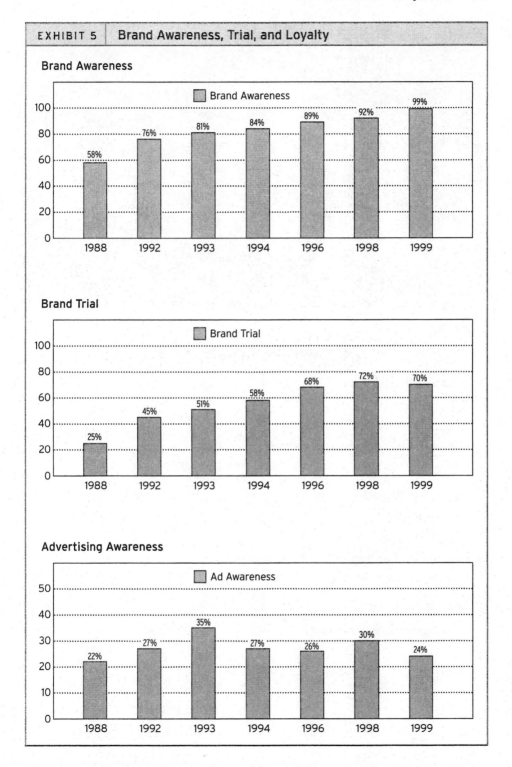

Brand Awareness

Brand Trial

Advertising Awareness

| EXHIBIT 6 | Becel's Lineup of Products, 1999 |

| EXHIBIT 7 | Consumer Household Profiles |

Margarine Households

- 4+ members
- head of household 45+
- strongest in lower income households
- families/empty nesters and childless couples (<$70,000)

Butter Households

- 3+ members
- head of household 45+
- strongest in high income households (+$70,000)
- strongest with empty nesters

Becel Households

- strongest with empty nesters
- 65+
- affluent with high income

Source: Nielsen Homescan

EXHIBIT 8	Margarine Buyer Considerations

**Taste vs Health vs Price
Homescan–National**

	Buyers (projected)	% Buyers	Eq Vol	% Volume
Taste or Health or Price	9,776	100.0	239,253	100.0
Excellent Health	1,644	16.8	27,646	11.6
Excellent Taste	1,333	13.6	21,118	8.8
Excellent Price	1,359	13.9	28,765	12.0
Health and Taste	1,176	12.0	27,842	11.6
Health and Price	711	7.3	17,925	7.5
Price and Taste	1,766	18.1	52,685	22.0
Taste and Health and Price	1,786	18.3	63,271	26.4

**Taste vs Health vs Price
1999–Buyer Interaction–100%
Total Margarine**

Exclusive Health

Exclusive Price

16.8   7.3   13.9

18.3

12.0   18.1

Interaction
Butter/Margarine Usage
70%

13.6

Exclusive Taste

EXHIBIT 9	Spreads Category Pricing Information

Product	Average Retail Price per Lb.
General Butter	$3.08
General Margarine	$1.45
Health Margarines	$2.09
Taste Margarines	$1.51
Price Margarines	$0.98
Becel	$2.10

Camar Automotive Hoist

Gordon H. G. McDougall

In September 2000, Mark Camar, President of Camar Automotive Hoist (CAH), had just finished reading a feasibility report on entering the European market in 2001. CAH manufactured surface automotive hoists, a product used by garages, service stations, and other repair shops to lift cars for servicing (Exhibit 1). The report, prepared by CAH's marketing manager, Pierre Gagnon, outlined the opportunities in the European Union and the entry options available.

Mark was not sure if CAH was ready for this move. While the company had been successful in expanding sales into the U.S. market, he wondered if this success could be repeated in Europe. He thought that, with more effort, sales could be increased in the U.S. On the other hand, there were some positive aspects to the European idea. He began reviewing the information in preparation for the meeting the following day with Pierre.

CAMAR AUTOMOTIVE HOIST

Mark, a design engineer, had worked for eight years for the Canadian subsidiary of a U.S. automotive hoist manufacturer. During those years, he had spent considerable time designing an above-ground (or surface) automotive hoist. Although he was very enthusiastic about the unique aspects of the hoist, including a scissor lift and wheel alignment pads, senior management expressed no interest in the idea. In 1990, Mark left the company to start his own business with the express purpose of designing and manufacturing the hoist. He left with the good wishes of his previous employer, who had no objections to Mark's plans to start a new business.

Over the next three years, Mark obtained financing from a venture capital firm, opened a plant in Lachine, Quebec, and began manufacturing and marketing the hoist, called the Camar Lift (Exhibit 1).

From the beginning, Mark had taken considerable pride in the development and marketing of the Camar Lift. The original design included a scissor lift and a safety locking mechanism that allowed the hoist to be raised to any level and locked in place. As well, the scissor lift offered easy access for the mechanic to work on the raised vehicle. Because the hoist was fully hydraulic and had no chains or pulleys, it required little maintenance. Another key feature was the alignment turn plates that were an integral part of the lift. The turn plates meant that mechanics could accurately and easily perform wheel alignment jobs. Because it was a surface lift, it could be installed in a garage in less than a day.

Mark continually made improvements to the product, including adding more safety features. In fact, the Camar Lift was considered a leader in automotive lift safety. Safety was an important factor in the automotive hoist market. Although hoists seldom malfunctioned, when they did it often resulted in a serious accident.

The Camar Lift developed a reputation in the industry as the "Cadillac" of hoists; the unit was judged by many as superior to competitive offerings because of its design, the quality of the workmanship, the safety features, the ease of installation, and the five-year warranty. Mark held four patents on the Camar Lift including the lifting mechanism on the scissor design and the safety locking mechanism. A number of versions of the product were designed that made the Camar Lift suitable (depending on the model) for a variety of tasks, including rustproofing, muffler repairs, and general mechanical repairs.

In 1991, CAH sold 23 hoists and had sales of $172,500. During the early years the majority of sales were to independent service stations and garages specializing in wheel alignment in the Quebec and Ontario market. Most of the units were sold by Pierre, who was hired in 1992 to handle the marketing side of the operation. In 1994, Pierre began using distributors to sell the hoist to a wider geographic market in Canada. In 1996, he signed an agreement with a large automotive wholesaler to represent CAH in the U.S. market. By 1999, the company had sold 1,054 hoists and had sales of $9,708,000 (Exhibit 2). In 1999, about 60 percent of sales were to the U.S. with the remaining 40 percent to the Canadian market.

INDUSTRY

Approximately 49,000 hoists were sold each year in North America. Hoists were typically purchased by any automotive outlet that serviced or repaired cars, including new-car dealers, used-car dealers, specialty shops (e.g., muffler repair, transmission repair, wheel alignment), chains (e.g., Firestone, Goodyear, Canadian Tire), and independent garages. It was estimated that new-car dealers purchased 30 percent of all units sold in a given year. In general, the specialty shops focused on one type of repair, such as mufflers or rust proofing, while "non-specialty" outlets handled a variety of repairs. While there was some crossover, in general CAH competed in the specialty shop segment and, in particular, those shops that dealt with wheel alignment. This included chains such as Firestone and Canadian Tire as well as new-car dealers (e.g., Ford) that devote a certain percentage of their lifts to the wheel alignment business and independent garages that specialized in wheel alignment.

The purpose of a hoist was to lift an automobile into a position where a mechanic or service person could easily work on the car. Because different repairs required different positions, a wide variety of hoists had been developed to meet specific needs. For example, a muffler repair shop required a hoist where the mechanic could gain easy access to the underside of the car. Similarly, a wheel alignment job required a hoist that offered a level platform where the wheels could be adjusted as well, providing easy access for the mechanic. Pierre estimated that 85 percent of CAH's sales were to the wheel alignment market in service centres like Firestone, Goodyear, and Canadian Tire and independent garages that specialized in wheel alignment. About 15 percent of sales were made to customers who used the hoist for general mechanical repairs.

Firms purchasing hoists were part of an industry called the *automobile aftermarket*. This industry was involved in supplying parts and service for new and used cars and was worth more than $54 billion at retail in 1999 while servicing the approximately 14 million cars on the road in Canada. The industry was large and diverse; there were more than 4,000 new-car dealers in Canada, more than 400 Canadian Tire stores, more than 100 stores in each of the Firestone and Goodyear chains, and more than 220 stores in the Rust Check chain.

The purchase of an automotive hoist was often an important decision for the service station owner or dealer. Because the price of hoists ranged from $3,000 to $15,000, it was a capital expense for most businesses.

For the owner/operator of a new service centre or car dealership, the decision involved determining what type of hoist was required and then what brand would best suit the company. Most new service centres or car dealerships had multiple bays for servicing cars. In these cases, the decision would involve what types of hoists were required (for example, in-ground, surface). Often more than one type of hoist was purchased, depending on the service centre/dealership needs.

Experienced garage owners seeking a replacement hoist (the typical hoist had a useful life of 10 to 13 years) would usually determine what products were available and then make a decision. If the garage owners were also mechanics, they would probably be aware of two or three types of hoists but not very knowledgeable about the brands or products currently available. Garage owners or dealers who were not mechanics probably knew very little about hoists. The owners of car or service dealerships often bought the product that was recommended and/or approved by the parent company.

COMPETITION

Sixteen companies competed in the automotive lift market in North America: four Canadian and 12 U.S. firms. With the advent of the Free Trade Agreement in 1989, the duties on hoists between the two countries were phased out over a 10-year period; by 1999 exports and imports of hoists were duty-free. For Mark, the import duties had never played a part in any decisions—the fluctuating exchange rates between the two countries had a far greater impact on selling prices. In the past three years the Canadian dollar had fluctuated between $.65 and $.70 versus the U.S. dollar (e.g., CDN$1.00 buys US$.65) and forecast rates were expected to stay within this range.

A wide variety of hoists were manufactured in the industry. The two basic types of hoists were in-ground and surface. As the names imply, in-ground hoists required a pit to be dug "in-ground," where the piston that raised the hoist was installed. In-ground hoists were either single post or multiple post, were permanent, and obviously could not be moved. In-ground lifts constituted approximately 21 percent of total lift sales in 1999 (Exhibit 3). Surface lifts were installed on a flat surface, usually concrete. Surface lifts came in two basic types, post lift hoists and scissor hoists. Surface lifts, compared to in-ground lifts, were easier to install and could be moved if necessary. Surface lifts constituted 79 percent of total lift sales in 1999. Within each type of hoist (e.g., post lift surface hoists), there were numerous variations in terms of size, shape, and lifting capacity.

The industry was dominated by two large U.S. firms, AHV Lifts and Berne Manufacturing, who together held approximately 60 percent of the market share. AHV Lifts, the largest firm with approximately 40 percent of the market and annual sales of about $60 million, offered a complete line of hoists (that is, in-ground, surface) but focused primarily on the in-ground market and the two-post surface market. AHV Lifts was the only company that had its own direct salesforce; all other companies used (1) only wholesalers or (2) a combination of wholesalers and company salesforce. AHV Lifts offered standard hoists with few extra features and competed primarily on price. Berne Manufacturing, with a market share of approximately 20 percent, also competed in the in-ground and two-post surface markets. It used a combination of wholesalers and company salespeople and, like AHV Lifts, competed primarily on price.

Most of the remaining firms in the industry were companies that operated in a regional market (e.g., California, British Columbia) and/or that offered a limited product line (e.g., four-post surface hoist).

CAH had two competitors that manufactured scissor lifts. AHV Lift marketed a scissor hoist that had a different lifting mechanism and did not include the safety locking features of the Camar Lift. On average, the AHV scissor lift was sold for about 20 percent less than the Camar Lift. The second competitor, Mete Lift, was a small regional company with sales in California and Oregon. It had a design that was very similar to the Camar Lift but lacked some of its safety features. The Mete Lift, regarded as a well-manufactured product, sold for about 5 percent less than the Camar Lift.

MARKETING STRATEGY

As of early 2000, CAH had developed a reputation for a quality product backed by good service in the hoist lift market, primarily in the wheel alignment segment.

The distribution system employed by CAH reflected the need to engage in extensive personal selling. Three types of distributors were used: a company salesforce, Canadian distributors, and a U.S. automotive wholesaler. The company salesforce consisted of four salespeople and Pierre. Their main task was to service large "direct" accounts. The initial step was to get the Camar Lift approved by large chains and manufacturers, and then, having received the approval, to sell to individual dealers or operators. For example, if General Motors approved the hoist, then CAH could sell it to individual General Motors dealers. CAH sold directly to the individual dealers of a number of large accounts including General Motors, Ford, Chrysler, Petro-Canada, Firestone, and Goodyear. CAH had been successful in obtaining manufacturer approval from the big three automobile manufacturers in both

Canada and the U.S. As well, CAH had also received approval from service companies such as Canadian Tire and Goodyear. To date, CAH had not been rejected by any major account; however, in some cases, the approval process had taken more than four years.

In total, the company salesforce generated about 25 percent of the unit sales each year. Sales to the large "direct" accounts in the United States went through CAH's U.S. wholesaler.

The Canadian distributors sold, installed, and serviced units across Canada. These distributors handled the Camar Lift and carried a line of noncompetitive automotive equipment products (for example, engine diagnostic equipment, wheel balancing equipment) and noncompetitive lifts. These distributors focused on the smaller chains and the independent service stations and garages.

The U.S. wholesaler sold a complete product line to service stations as well as manufacturing some equipment. The Camar Lift was one of five different types of lifts that the wholesaler sold. Although the wholesaler provided CAH with extensive distribution in the United States, the Camar Lift was a minor product within the wholesaler's total line. While Pierre did not have any actual figures, he thought that the Camar Lift probably accounted for less than 20 percent of the total lift sales of the U.S. wholesaler.

Both Mark and Pierre felt that the U.S. market had unrealized potential. With a population of 264 million people and more than 146 million registered vehicles, the U.S. market was almost 10 times the size of the Canadian market (population of 30 million, approximately 14 million vehicles). Pierre noted that the six New England states (population over 13 million); the three largest mid-Atlantic states (population over 38 million), and the three largest mid-Eastern states (population over 32 million) were all within a day's drive of the factory in Lachine. Mark and Pierre had considered setting up a sales office in New York to service these states, but they were concerned that the U.S. wholesaler would not be willing to relinquish any of its territory. They had also considered working more closely with the wholesaler to encourage it to "push" the Camar Lift. It appeared that the wholesaler's major objective was to sell a hoist, not necessarily the Camar Lift.

CAH distributed a catalogue-type package with products, uses, prices, and other required information for both distributors and users. In addition, CAH advertised in trade publications (for example, *AutoInc.*), and Pierre travelled to trade shows in Canada and the U.S. to promote the Camar Lift.

In 1999, Camar Lifts sold for an average retail price of $10,990 and CAH received, on average, $9,210 for each unit sold. This average reflected the mix of sales through the three distribution channels: (1) direct (where CAH received 100% of the selling price), (2) Canadian distributors (where CAH received 80% of the selling price) and (3) the U.S. wholesaler (where CAH received 78% of the selling price).

Both Mark and Pierre believed that the company's success to date was based on a strategy of offering a superior product that was primarily targeted to the needs of specific customers. The strategy stressed continual product improvements, quality workmanship, and service. Personal selling was a key aspect of the strategy; salespeople could show customers the benefits of the Camar Lift over competing products.

THE EUROPEAN MARKET

Against this background, Mark had been thinking of ways to continue the rapid growth of the company. One possibility that kept coming up was the promise and potential of the

European market. The fact that Europe became a single market in 1993 suggested that it was an opportunity that should at least be explored. With this in mind, Mark asked Pierre to prepare a report on the possibility of CAH entering the European market. The highlights of Pierre's report follow.

History of the European Union

The European Union (EU) had its basis formed from the 1957 "Treaty of Rome," in which five countries decided it would be in their best interests to form an internal market. These countries were France, Spain, Italy, West Germany, and Luxembourg. By 1990, the EU consisted of 15 countries (the additional ten were Austria, Belgium, Denmark, Finland, Greece, Ireland, the Netherlands, Portugal, Sweden, and the United Kingdom) with a population of more than 376 million people. Virtually all barriers (physical, technical, and fiscal) in the European Community were scheduled to be removed for companies located within the EU. This allowed the free movement of goods, persons, services, and capital.

In the last 15 years many North American and Japanese firms had established themselves in the EU. The reasoning for this was twofold. First, these companies regarded the community as an opportunity to increase global market share and profits. The market was attractive because of its sheer size and lack of internal barriers. Second, there was continuing concern that companies not established within the EU would have difficulty exporting to the EU due to changing standards and tariffs. To date, this concern has not materialized.

Market Potential

The key indicator of the potential market for the Camar Lift hoist was the number of passenger cars and commercial vehicles in use in a particular country. Four countries in Europe had more than 20 million vehicles in use, with Germany having the largest domestic fleet of 44 million vehicles followed in order by Italy, France, and the United Kingdom (Exhibit 4). The number of vehicles was an important indicator, since the more vehicles in use meant a greater number of service and repair facilities that needed vehicle hoists—potentially the Camar Lift.

An indicator of the future vehicle repair and service market was the number of new-vehicle registrations. The registration of new vehicles was important as this maintained the number of vehicles in use by replacing cars that had been retired. Again, Germany had the most new cars registered in 1997 and was followed in order by France, the United Kingdom, and Italy.

Based primarily on the fact that a large domestic market was important for initial growth, the selection of a European country should be limited to the "Big Four" industrialized nations: Germany, France, the United Kingdom, or Italy. In an international survey companies from North America and Europe ranked European countries on a scale of 1 to 100 on market potential and investment-site potential. The results showed that Germany was favoured for both market potential and investment site opportunities, while France, the United Kingdom, and Spain placed second, third, and fourth respectively. Italy did not place in the top four in either market or investment-site potential. However, Italy had a large number of vehicles in use, had the fourth largest population in Europe, and was an acknowledged leader in car technology and production.

Little information was available on the competition within Europe. There was, as yet, no dominant manufacturer as was the case in North America. At this time, there was one firm in Germany that manufactured a scissor-type lift. The firm sold most of its units within the German market. The only other available information was that 22 firms in Italy manufactured vehicle lifts.

Investment Options

Pierre felt that CAH had three options for expansion into the European market: licensing, joint venture, or direct investment. The licensing option was a real possibility, as a French firm had expressed an interest in manufacturing the Camar Lift.

In June 2000, Pierre had attended a trade show in Detroit to promote the Camar Lift. At the show he met Phillipe Beaupre, the marketing manager for Bar Maisse, a French manufacturer of wheel alignment equipment. The firm, located in Chelles, France, sold a range of wheel alignment equipment throughout Europe. The best-selling product was an electronic modular aligner that enabled a mechanic to use a sophisticated computer system to align the wheels of a car. Phillipe was seeking a North American distributor for the modular aligner and other products manufactured by Bar Maisse.

At the show, Pierre and Phillipe had a casual conversation where both explained what their respective companies manufactured; they exchanged company brochures and business cards, and both went on to other exhibits. The next day, Phillipe sought out Pierre and asked if he might be interested in having Bar Maisse manufacture and market the Camar Lift in Europe. Phillipe felt the lift would complement Bar Maisse's product line and the licensing would be of mutual benefit to both parties. They agreed to pursue the idea. Upon his return to Lachine, Pierre told Mark about these discussions and they agreed to explore this possibility.

Pierre called a number of colleagues in the industry and asked them what they knew about Bar Maisse. About half had not heard of the company but those who had commented favourably on the quality of its products. One colleague, with European experience, knew the company well and said that Bar Maisse's management had integrity and would make a good partner. In July, Pierre sent a letter to Phillipe stating that CAH was interested in further discussions; he enclosed various company brochures including price lists and technical information on the Camar Lift. In late August, Phillipe responded, stating that Bar Maisse would like to enter a three-year licensing agreement with CAH to manufacture the Camar Lift in Europe. In exchange for the manufacturing rights, Bar Maisse was prepared to pay a royalty rate of 5 percent of gross sales. Pierre had not yet responded to this proposal.

A second possibility was a joint venture. Pierre had wondered if it might not be better for CAH to offer a counter proposal to Bar Maisse for a joint venture. He had not worked out any details, but Pierre felt that CAH would learn more about the European market and probably make more money if they were an active partner in Europe. Pierre's idea was a 50–50 proposal where the two parties shared the investment and the profits. He envisaged a situation where Bar Maisse would manufacture the Camar Lift in its plant with technical assistance from CAH. Pierre also thought that CAH could get involved in the marketing of the lift through the Bar Maisse distribution system. Further, he thought that the Camar Lift, with proper marketing, could gain a reasonable share of the European market. If that happened Pierre felt that CAH was likely to make greater returns with a joint venture.

The third option was direct investment, where CAH would establish a manufacturing facility and set up a management group to market the lift. Pierre had contacted a business acquaintance who had recently been involved in manufacturing fabricated steel sheds in Germany. On the basis of discussions with his acquaintance, he estimated the costs involved in setting up a plant in Europe at (1) $250,000 for capital equipment (welding machines, cranes, other equipment); (2) $200,000 in incremental costs to set the plant up; and (3) carrying costs to cover $1,000,000 in inventory and accounts receivable. While the actual costs of renting a building for the factory would depend on the site location, he estimated that annual building rent including heat, light, and insurance would be about $80,000. Pierre recognized that these estimates were guidelines, but he felt that the estimates were probably within 20 percent of actual costs.

THE DECISION

As Mark considered the contents of the report, a number of thoughts crossed his mind. He began making notes concerning the European possibility and the future of the company:

- If CAH decided to enter Europe, Pierre would be the obvious choice to head up the "direct investment" option or the "joint venture" option. Mark felt that Pierre had been instrumental in the success of the company to date.

- While CAH had the financial resources to go ahead with the direct investment option, the joint venture would spread the risk (and the returns) over the two companies.

- CAH had built its reputation on designing and manufacturing a quality product. Regardless of the option, Mark wanted the firm's reputation to be maintained.

- Either the licensing agreement or the joint venture appeared to build on the two companies' strengths; Bar Maisse had knowledge of the market, and CAH had the product. What troubled Mark was whether this apparent synergy would work or whether Bar Maisse would seek to control the operation.

- It was difficult to estimate sales under any of the options. With the first two (licensing and joint venture), it would depend on the effort and expertise of Bar Maisse; with the third, it would depend on Pierre.

- CAH's sales in the U.S. market could be increased if the U.S. wholesaler would "push" the Camar Lift. Alternatively, the establishment of a sales office in New York to cover the eastern states could also increase sales.

As Mark reflected on the situation he knew he should probably get additional information—but it wasn't obvious exactly what information would help him make a yes or no decision. He knew one thing for sure—he was going to keep this company on a fast growth track, and at tomorrow's meeting he and Pierre would decide how to do it.

EXHIBIT 1	Examples of Automotive Hoists

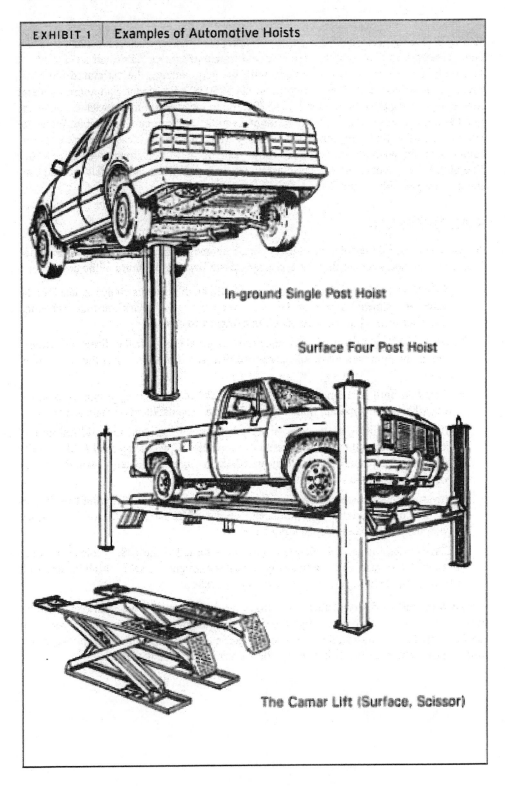

In-ground Single Post Hoist

Surface Four Post Hoist

The Camar Lift (Surface, Scissor)

EXHIBIT 2	Camar Automotive Hoist–Selected Financial Statistics (1997-1999)		
	1997	1998	1999
Sales	$6,218,000	$7,454,000	$9,708,000
Cost of Sales	4,540,000	5,541,000	6,990,000
Contribution	1,678,000	1,913,000	2,718,000
Marketing Expenses*	507,000	510,000	530,000
Administrative Expenses	810,000	820,000	840,000
Earnings Before Tax	361,000	583,000	1,348,000
Units Sold	723	847	1,054

Source: Company records

* Marketing expenses in 1999 included advertising ($70,000), four salespeople ($240,000), marketing manager, and three sales support staff ($220,000).

EXHIBIT 3	North American Automotive Lift Unit Sales, by Type (1997-1999)		
	1997	1998	1999
In-ground			
Single post	5,885	5,772	5,518
Multiple post	4,812	6,625	5,075
Surface			
Two-post	27,019	28,757	28,923
Four-post	3,862	3,162	3,745
Scissor	2,170	2,258	2,316
Other	4,486	3,613	3,695
Total	48,234	50,187	49,272

Source: Company records

EXHIBIT 4	Number of Vehicles (1997) and Population (000s)

Country	Vehicles in Use (000s)		New Vehicle Registrations (000s)	Population (000s)
	Passenger	Small Commercial		
Germany	41,400	2,800	3,500	82,100
France	28,000	4,900	2,200	59,000
Italy	33,200	2,700	1,800	56,700
United Kingdom	23,500	4,000	2,200	59,100
Spain	15,300	2,800	1,000	39,200

Lion Nathan China

Delwyn N. Clark

In April 1999, Paul Lockey, Chief Financial Officer of the New Zealand–based international brewing company Lion Nathan Limited (LN), was quite concerned as he prepared his mid-year report for the Board. Responsible for corporate strategy and finance, Paul realized that higher losses from LN's China operations were going to wipe out the company's profits from elsewhere. How long would the Board allow these losses to continue? When would the China operations break even? Competition was intensifying in the Chinese beer market, particularly at the higher-margin premium end, where LN had been successful in following its strategy of building strong brands. With overcapacity in the beer industry, consolidation was underway. Was LN's new deal to brew and market Beck's premium beer under licence going to provide the leverage needed to survive the shakeout?

Building on its market strength was one strategy. However, LN also possessed a new brewery in Suzhou Industrial Park that had excess capacity. This state of the art facility provided LN with a distinct cost advantage compared to other companies. Paul wondered whether LN should attempt to become a contract brewer for the many other international breweries that were eagerly eyeing the China market.

COMPANY HISTORY

In 1999 Lion Nathan Limited (LN) was an international brewer with divisions in New Zealand (population 3.8 million), Australia (population 19 million) and China (population 1,259 million). With a portfolio of more than 50 brands, the company owned and operated ten breweries in these three countries. To achieve greater international scale, LN also exported beer to 50 countries and licensed three brewers in Europe to produce and distribute Steinlager and Castlemaine XXXX. Through its 45-percent Japanese equity partner, Kirin Brewing Company, LN was part of the fourth-largest brewing group in the world.

In 1993, with limited growth in its home New Zealand and Australian markets, LN decided to enter the world's largest consumer market: China. According to Kerin Roberts, LN's Chief Operating Officer (COO), "China represented the single best opportunity for a number of reasons including size of market, growth potential, low barriers to entry and no established big guy in there." Two years and 40 brewery evaluations later, LN entered this market in April 1995 with a 60-percent joint venture in the Taihushui Brewery in Wuxi. Wuxi was one of the wealthiest cities in the heart of the Yangtze River Delta, China's fastest growing beer market (Exhibit 1). Buoyed by success, LN increased its shareholding in this brewery to 80 percent in 1996 and made a major commitment to build a brand-new $178-million brewery 30 kilometres away in the Suzhou Industrial Park. Construction of this 200-million-litre world-class brewery was completed $35.5 million under budget and two months ahead of schedule with "good planning, great people, combined with co-operation and teamwork." Commercial production began in February 1998, and the premium brand Steinlager was launched in September. In April 1999 LN announced a licensing agreement with German brewer Brauerei Beck to brew and market Beck's international premium beer. The addition of a high-margin brand to its portfolio enabled LN to use excess brewing capacity at Suzhou and to extend its market reach beyond the Yangtze River Delta.

Gordon Cairns, the CEO, described LN's charter as "profitable growth." Speaking at the company's annual meeting, Gordon said:

> There are five reasons that differentiate us as a stock. Firstly, we are virtually a pure beer company. Secondly, everywhere we compete we are investing to build brands. Thirdly, we believe beer is a regional business, with few truly global brands…. Fourthly, a key success factor is for us to be the lowest cost producer, everywhere we compete. And finally, we are measured, managed and motivated by shareholder value, where what we do should earn greater than the cost of capital.

Financial data for LN from 1994 to 1998 are provided in Exhibits 2A and 2B. For the six months to February 1999, LN's profit was $83 million ($0.3 million more than the February 1998 profit figure) with strong results in the Australian business (7.8% EBIT increase). With difficult market conditions in China and prices under pressure, a $20.4-million EBIT loss was reported (compared with a $17.1-million loss in February 1998).

THE BREWING INDUSTRY IN NEW ZEALAND

Historically, the New Zealand brewing industry was highly concentrated. In 1999, this industry was effectively a duopoly, with the two major competitors, LN and DB Breweries, controlling about 97 percent of the beer market. Microbreweries accounted for a very small percentage of the market. The two major players displayed a number of similarities. Both operated primarily on a national scale: DB had about 43 percent of the New Zealand market, LN some 54 percent. Both companies had brewing capacities of around 200 million litres per year. Both companies were vertically integrated and enjoyed substantial ownership in companies that supply their raw materials and wholesale distribution outlets. As both companies battled for leadership and control of a declining market, price competition was eroding profitability. Emerging developments in this industry included maturity of the beer market, proliferation of brands, and growth of brands.

THE BREWING INDUSTRY IN AUSTRALIA

In Australia, Carlton and United Breweries (CUB, with a 52% market share) and LN (46%) were the two major players. LN's acquisitions over the years led to a portfolio of local brands and provided the basis for its regional strategy and market leadership in Western Australia, South Australia, and Queensland. CUB worked to develop a national brand identity with several key brands including Foster's Lager, Victoria Bitter, Foster's Light Ice, and Carlton Gold. By 1999, as in New Zealand, demand growth was limited, per capita beer consumption was declining, and rising raw material costs were constraining profitability.

THE BREWING INDUSTRY IN CHINA

In 1998 there were more than 600 brewers in the highly fragmented Chinese brewing industry, producing 17.8 million tonnes of beer (1 tonne = 1,000 litres). The sheer size of this beer market, serving a population of 1.3 billion people, coupled with the growth potential due to increasing per capita consumption, attracted many international brewers to China. However, growth rates had decreased dramatically from over 20 percent per year in the 1980s to 12.5 percent on average between 1992 and 1997; growth near 6 percent was projected from 1998 to 2001. Beer consumption had risen to average 14 litres per capita in 1998, but this was still low compared with average consumption of 30–40 litres in the Asian region, 87 litres in New Zealand, and 95 litres in Australia. However, this aggregate level of analysis was of limited value in China as there were quite different patterns of consumption throughout the vast country, particularly between urban and rural communities. For example, per capita beer consumption was 21 litres in the affluent, urbanized Yangtze River Delta (YRD) region, and closer to 29 litres within the leading city of Shanghai. (In 1998, Lion Nathan had achieved an 8.3-percent share of the YRD market.) Each region in China was considered a different market. Provincial government requirements and limited transportation infrastructure for efficient distribution acted as specific constraints for multi-region or national participation.

The major segments in the China beer market were linked to the quality and price of the beer. Exhibit 3 shows the key segments with market size estimates. Sales for each segment in the Yangtze River Delta and Shanghai are shown in Exhibit 4. There were only 80 breweries in the country with capacity over 50 million litres; 18 of these had over 100 million litres capacity. The 10 largest domestic brewing groups accounted for less than 20 percent of the total market. Exhibit 5 shows some of the major international brewers operating in China in 1998 with their origin, type of investment, production capacity, and beer brands. Profiles of the major competitors are provided in Exhibit 6. Sales by major brands in the YRD are shown in Exhibit 8.

The low end of the China beer market, the largest segment, was served by several hundred small, state-owned, domestic brewers. Many of these breweries suffered from problems of quality, were unable to achieve efficient operations, had insufficient capital for any improvements, and were unable to return a profit. This segment was of little interest to LN and other international firms.

Brewers in the mainstream segment provided a higher quality beer at a slightly higher price (average 2.5 RMB, NZ$0.53, CDN$0.44). With higher margins, but major executional challenges in sales and distribution, the mainstream segment attracted some of the more adventurous international brewers including Asia Pacific Breweries with Reeb (i.e., beer spelled backward), Carlsberg with Karhu, Lion Nathan with Taihushui and Rheineck, and Suntory from the Japanese brewer Suntory.

The premium segment was most attractive for international brewers because of the higher margins and the long-term potential in the China market. Most of the brewers were involved with joint ventures or licensing contracts for domestic brewing with local partners (Exhibit 5). By 1999, with overcapacity intensifying competition and economic growth declining, several of these foreign brewers were cutting back their involvement, putting breweries up for sale (e.g., Foster's) and reconsidering their future options in China (e.g., San Miguel). The imported premium segment was a niche segment for the most expensive beer brands. Rather than taking advantage of lower-cost production within China, Heineken's premium beer was imported and therefore incurred higher transportation and production costs but also realized a substantially higher selling price.

Mainstream beer was generally purchased in small quantities (one or two bottles) from a nearby street stall and carried to a home in a multistorey apartment block. A typical stall might carry fewer than a dozen bottles of beer of various brands, some cans of soft drink, chewing gum, washing powder and other household items, sweets, and a shelf within a shelf containing packets of cigarettes and cheap lighters. Lion Nathan China sources estimated that there were 350,000–400,000 retailers of beer in the Yangtze River Delta region. Thirty local breweries operated in this region servicing the population of 70 million via 200–300 distributors and 6,000–8,000 wholesalers.

Premium beer was primarily consumed in restaurants, bars, and hotels. Status was a major influence on consumption in this segment. As a senior marketing executive explained, "As face is extremely important in China, you will drink internationally famous high quality beer when entertaining clients or staff at restaurants."

The beer market was volatile. New brands skyrocketed from obscurity to dominance within a few months with strong advertising, sales promotion, distribution and support. However, with numerous competing brands and limited brand loyalty, leading brands could also disappear just as quickly. Developing brand equity was therefore a key challenge for competitors in this industry.

LION NATHAN CHINA (LNC)

LN's research identified the Yangtze River Delta (YRD) as the best region for its entry to China. According to one executive:

> With a population of 70 million, the Delta is an area of relative wealth, high growth, and above-average beer consumption. It has a rapidly developing infrastructure including new highways along key corridors, express rail services, and a supply and service industry base suitable for foreign ventures.

LN's entry strategy was to take a small, measured step into an existing brewery with an upgrade path, learn, and then build on the experience. The Taihushui Brewery at Wuxi was a profitable joint venture with a good plant and astute management. LN's $50-million investment was used to double capacity to 120 million litres. The expansion program was successful, sales and profits grew, and LN increased its ownership in this joint venture to 80 percent.

LN's second step into China was a bold commitment to build a large world-class brewery in nearby Suzhou. Located within a 70-square-kilometre special development zone, Suzhou Industrial Park (SIP), established by the Chinese and Singaporean governments in 1994, enabled LN to create a privileged asset. Wholly foreign ownership, which was highly restricted for breweries elsewhere in China, was a unique advantage that SIP offered for early investors. Capacity at Suzhou was also expandable as the plant design allowed for a mirror operation to be built on the same site. In 1998, LNC used one-third of the new plant's capacity (60,000 tonnes), which allowed for 100-percent volume growth in 1999.

Efficient transportation links were available from Suzhou to Shanghai and other key YRD cities. SIP provided utilities such as water, power, and telecommunications for industrial and residential usage. Other key support services for investors included a one-stop service for company incorporation and construction permits, local customs clearances, and warehousing and distribution. This infrastructure and SIP's services were important for LN's "green field" project. The company also saved $50 million on import duties for plant and equipment; this duty-free policy ceased in 1997. A turn-key approach, driven by performance-based contracts and international sourcing of materials, enabled LN to complete the "single best facility in China" in just 16 months.

STRATEGY

The vision of Lion Nathan China was "to become the leading brewer in the YRD by 2000 and the market leader in the Shanghai-Nanjing corridor." LNC's five-point strategy involved (1) leading the mainstream beer segment market within the Shanghai-Nanjing corridor of the Yangtze River Delta, (2) developing a differentiated brand portfolio including premium and mainstream brands, (3) selling premium beer outside the YRD, (4) outexecuting the competition, and (5) leading industry consolidation.

Reflecting on LNC's strategic position in February 1999, after 18 months as Managing Director for China, Jim O'Mahony said:

> We are focusing on five key cities in the Shanghai to Nanjing corridor, south of the Yangtze River. We are number 1 or number 2 in three of those cities already [in mainstream beer]...but Shanghai is going to be a real battle.
>
> We have four brands now in our portfolio: Taihushui, meaning "water of lake Tai," is a high-quality mainstream beer for blue-collar workers; Rheineck, launched in 1997, with a foreign name and packaging linked to Germany, is positioned as a more outgoing mainstream beer for blue- and white-collar markets; Carbine is a dark, niche beer positioned at restaurants, so it's a beer with food. Then we have Steinlager, launched in September 1998, positioned as a trendy premium beer in a curvy bottle for sale in night venues and upmarket restaurants. The gap in our portfolio is a premium beer in the status segment occupied at the moment by Budweiser, Beck's, Tiger, San Miguel, and Carlsberg. Our objective is to forge an alliance with another international player to get access to a major premium brand. We are just about ready to make an announcement. Then we'll have done the portfolio work.

> We've been constrained in terms of moving outside the Delta because of lack of a premium brand that can actually do it for us.... Apart from 3 million kiwis [New Zealanders], nobody's ever heard of Steinlager. But when we announce the deal with the international alliance partner, as it is already a brand that's got presence throughout China, we'll have an immediate volume that we can piggyback Steinlager onto.

Adopting a regional strategy in the Yangtze Delta not only was consistent with the company's expertise in its home markets, but it also aligned closely with an understanding of the economic drivers in brewing. Paul Lockey explained that LNC was "a small player in global terms, but we are the biggest where we are." He believed the company was "well positioned with the lowest cost position and among the largest capacity." However, continued growth was not without its problems, as Paul elaborated:

> Sustaining growth at 70 percent [as in 1998] is quite extraordinary. A lot of that growth has come from entering new cities. You have to recognize that there are only so many cities you can enter. At that point you have to compete more aggressively in the cities you are already in. There are some dynamics about just how far you can go. In the mainstream market, for instance, you can only ship the beer about 300 kilometres before the freight costs just kill profits. Whereas in the premium market it is a little bit different. The product is heavy relative to its value, unlike shampoo or microchips. So worldwide this tends to be a business where local production is a dominant factor.

LION NATHAN CHINA: SALES AND DISTRIBUTION

Producing large volumes of top-quality beer to match local tastes was comparatively straightforward for LNC and other international brewers entering the China market. However, developing sales and distribution networks within this environment was significantly more challenging and complex than experienced elsewhere. LNC developed different systems for its two major market segments: (1) selling mainstream brands for off-premise consumption through "mom and pop" stores and supermarkets, and (2) selling premium brands for consumption on-premise in restaurants, cafes, hotels, and bars.

LNC's off-premise system involved selling mainstream brands from five warehouses to 400 wholesalers, who then sold the beer to 70,000 retailers. Sales teams were established for the five YRD target cities with account managers assigned to each wholesaler and merchandising managers providing the supporting merchandise (e.g., posters, price boards, shelf displays) for the retailers (to create consumer demand).

> The primary wholesaler is a man with a truck and a storage shed amid an enclave of houses down a track. He distributes the beer to the next-tier wholesaler, who stacks up a bike or rickshaws with heavy loads for distribution to small open-fronted shops (kiosks).
>
> Most people in China go to the store next door and they buy whatever they need to buy for that day or that half-day. They go to the wet [fresh] markets and buy what they need to buy in the wet market, the fruit market or whatever. Until that changes we're not going to see much of a change in the distribution infrastructure in China. The people are going to buy very small quantities, frequently, and from the closest place to where they live as possible. They will walk 100 metres. The normal quantity of beer purchased is one or two bottles at a time.

Shanghai, a city of 13 million people in 6,340 square kilometres, was projected to be the leading consumer market in the 21st century. LNC had 41,000 retail outlets systematically mapped and allocated to sales teams. Albert Chu, General Manager for Mainstream

Beer Sales, had 160 permanent sales staff for Shanghai. Albert outlined his ideas on this challenge as follows:

> I was National Sales Director for Johnson & Johnson before joining LNC. I learned that increasing the proportion of stores stocking a product to 85 percent is needed to provide significant benefits from scale and market share.... I am very keen to push the Rheineck brand to that level of coverage.

PREMIUM BRANDS

The on-premise system for selling premium brands involved the use of distributors to sell beer to wholesalers, as well as making some direct sales to large retail accounts. Selection of distributors and wholesalers was critical for success, as Jim O'Mahony explained:

> There is always a big fight annually to get the best distributors and the best wholesalers. We have a system of annual contracts that run January through December. There is an annual rebate for hitting volume targets. We are in the middle of negotiating the 1999 contracts right now [February 2]. It is a competitive process. Distributors and wholesalers have catchment areas; they have loyal retailers, and then there are floating retailers. So capturing the best distributors and wholesalers is critical. After that it's brand strength and how much support you are prepared to put into it.

prob

Higher margins for premium beer extended the distribution zones for these brands. Furthermore, improved inter-city transportation infrastructure made it easier to supply beer to a broader region. Marketing Beck's, a top-tier premium brand, with LNC's other brands was expected to significantly improve LNC's access to retail outlets within the YRD, and to springboard distribution well beyond the delta; Beck's was already sold in over 40 cities along the coast, from Shenyang to Guangzhou. Distribution systems were generally a table stake in most developed markets, but in China mastering logistical difficulties would be advantageous.

LION NATHAN CHINA: MARKETING

Like Procter & Gamble, LN had a portfolio of brands, rather than a single brand based on its corporate name. This provided flexibility to select and adapt beer brands for Chinese markets. As Jim O'Mahony noted, "Unlike Budweiser or Carlsberg or Foster's, we don't have to push a particular brand." Launching a new brand, even in just one region of China, was extremely costly. CEO Gordon Cairns reported at the annual general meeting that 37 cents of every dollar earned in China was being invested in building brands.

MAINSTREAM BRANDS

In the mainstream segment, Taihushui, which was acquired with the Wuxi brewery, was upgraded and relaunched in 1996 as a high-quality local beer for everyday drinking, with comfort and affiliation messages. According to Steve Mason, Chief Marketing Officer (CMO), these messages were designed to convey a sense of closeness and belonging—"because it is from around here, you should feel comfortable drinking it." Taihushui was a market leader in Wuxi and Suzhou and had the second-highest market share in Changzhou. Although a very strong performer, this brand was geographically locked.

Rheineck, which was from the New Zealand portfolio, was adapted and launched very successfully in 1997 as a pan-delta brand positioned as a beer "you drink with friends." LNC targeted a younger profile of more upwardly mobile consumers, with images of good times with good friends. Rheineck was an affordable foreign lager beer, brewed locally. As the market share figures in Exhibit 8 show, Rheineck rocketed into second or third place in key YRD cities in 1998. Building on experience with Taihushui, LNC achieved significant volume growth within 12 months in Nanjing (17,000) and Shanghai (22,000).

Rapid turnover in popularity of beers was particularly obvious in the premium segment, where many major international competitors battled for on-premise market share; positioning of these international brands was generally based on status. Steve Mason outlined LNC's promotional strategies for each premium brand as follows:

> We launched Steinlager as a progressive premium beer for the "new generation" in Shanghai in September 1998. To differentiate this beer and position it as trendy, we used a curved green bottle, labelled it as an "international award winner" and offered it in upmarket western-style bars, hotels, and restaurants. We also had a dark-coloured niche beer, Carbine, which was sold in restaurants positioned as "a beer with food."

The addition of Beck's beer to the portfolio of premium brands that LNC brewed and marketed was expected to provide significant leverage in the future. Although Beck's volume and market share in the key YRD cities had declined significantly from 1997, the brand was still ranked number-two behind Budweiser in four of these cities, and was number one in Changzhou.

PROMOTION

Significant investments were involved to promote brands and obtain access to retail outlets. Image building activities such as advertising, signage, event sponsorship, or merchandising to build brand equity were categorized as "above-the-line" expenditures. There were also "below-the-line" expenses for transactional deals with the trade, which were standard practice to gain access in China. With overcapacity in the on-premise segment, the costs to compete were increasing, as Jim O'Mahony explained:

> A restaurant will typically stock two or three premium beers. They know that there are seven or eight producers of premium beer out there. It becomes an auction for which beers will be stocked. It comes down to who pays the most money. So, therefore, the costs to compete have risen. You know whether it's a listing fee, or whether it's promotional support, whether it's paying for new signage, redecoration of the restaurant, whatever it happens to be.... The other thing that has happened is the costs of TV advertising have risen as a result of demand. Again, when you've got seven or eight players looking for the same spot on TV, then you have to pay more for it.

REVENUES

In 1998, sales revenue for LNC increased 91 percent to $56.2 million on volume growth of 73 percent; this result was impressive in a beer market growing at less than 5 percent. According to one senior executive:

We're playing in the premier league now. We've got to realize that it's a big game. We've got to act like a big player, not like a small amateur player. And that takes courage. Our loss of NZ$ 30-million is nothing [compared] to the likes of Budweiser and the other big players. Margins are very low and it's very competitive. Pricing is very hard to maintain. So all these things are stacked against us in the short term. But that could turn in two years with a few exits, income growth, the economy turning around... then we could be doing very well.

The faster we grow, the more we lose. In the broadest sense, the faster we grow, the more chance we have of winning, but in the short-term the more we would lose. We can improve our financial performance by slowing down.

As margins for premium beer were 50 percent higher than mainstream beer, increasing the proportion of premium beer LNC sold was a top priority. Brewing Beck's beer under licence in Suzhou would also help to use brewing capacity and accelerate break-even. Using its low-cost state of the art facility, LNC could look to become a source of brewing capacity for other international beer companies with strong brand names. Geographic expansion to new cities offered volume and sales growth, but there were major setup costs involved in establishing a salesforce in a new city. As Jim O'Mahony indicated, "every time you open a sales office you could be looking at $1 million loss in year one." This would typically be followed by achieving break-even in year two and making a profit in year three. Another dynamic factor influencing profitability was the stage of brands in their life cycle; new brands required significantly more investment than older brands.

THE FUTURE

In 1998, LNC had achieved record growth in volume and sales in this difficult market. Yet CFO Paul Lockey recognized that the challenges in China were far from over. How was LNC going to ensure success in this volatile market? While many alternatives were available, at least two stood out. One was to increase market share and volume of LNC brands in the YRD market. The other was to find ways to use its excess brewing capacity by forming production alliances with other strong marketers. Paul had prepared some estimates of costs and growth potential for these alternatives (Exhibits 7, 9, and 10). With mounting losses, LNC management knew that other breweries faced strong pressures on sustainability. However, unlike others, LNC had such limited growth prospects in its home markets that leaving China would be a dangerous move.

| EXHIBIT 1 | China: Yangtze River Delta Region |

| EXHIBIT 2A | Financial Results (millions of NZ dollars) |

	Revenues	Earnings Before Interest & Tax (EBIT)	Net Earnings
1998	$1,806	$346	$136
1997	1,744	333	127
1996	1,757	378	156
1995	1,772	382	214
1994	1,674	379	204

Note 1: Taxes averaged NZ$84 million = 1996–98, but only NZ$5 million in 1994–95.

Note 2: In 1999, NZ$1 = US$0.563 = CDN$0.837 (CDN$1 = US$0.673).

EXHIBIT 2B	Financial Results by Geographical Segment for 1998

	New Zealand	Australia	China	Total
Sales	25.3%	71.6%	3.1%	NZ$ 1806
Assets	22.2%	68.2%	9.6%	NZ$ 3878
EBIT	25.0%	83.7%	-8.7%	NZ$ 346

EXHIBIT 3	China Beer Market Segments

	Retail Price Points[1] (RMB)	China 1998 (Tonnes)	China 2001 (Tonnes)	Examples
Imported Premium[2]	10.0	40,000	50,000	Heineken[3]
Premium	5.0–6.0	722,000	920,000	Beck's/ Budweiser/ Carlsberg
Mainstream	2.0–3.50	2,100,000	2,800,000	Reeb/Rheineck
Low-End	Under 2.0[4]	14,900,000	14,500,000	Guangming
		17,762,000	18,270,000	

[1] Off-premise retail price points in Chinese renminbi (RMB).

[2] With 0.2% market share, the category was usually included with other Premium beer.

[3] Retails for 12.50 RMB.

[4] Most are priced close to 1.0 RMB.

EXHIBIT 4	Yangtze River Delta 1998 Beer Sales by Segment (all figures in tonnes)

	Premium	Mainstream	Low-End	Total
Shanghai	70,000	230,000	120,000	420,000
Suzhou	15,000	50,000	40,000	105,000
Wuxi	11,000	54,000	27,000	92,000
Nanjing	26,000	70,000	18,000	114,000
Changzhou	4,000	36,000	30,000	70,000
	126,000	440,000	235,000	801,000

EXHIBIT 5	Major Brewers and Representative Brands in China, 1998

Brewers	Origin	Investment Type[1]	Capacity[2,3]	Premium	BRANDS Mainstream	Low-End
Anheuser-Busch	USA	JV in Wuhan	250	Budweiser		
		5% in Tsingtao				
Asia Pacific	Singapore	JV in Shanghai	200	Tiger	Reeb	
	Holland	imported		Heineken		
		JV in Hainan	200	Heritage		
		JV in Fuzhou	100			
Asahi	Japan	JV in Hangzhou	600	Asahi		
Beck's	Germany	JV in Fujian	150	Beck's		
Carlsberg	Denmark	JV in Shanghai	180	Carlsberg	Karhu	
Changzhou	Local					Guangyulan
Foster's	Australian	JV in Shanghai	120	Foster's		Guangming
				Haoshun		Pujing
						Shanghai
Lion Nathan	NZ	WFO in Suzhou	200	Steinlager	Rheineck	
		JV in Wuxi	120	Carbine	Taihushui	
Kirin	Japan	JV in Shenyang	120	Kirin		
Miller	USA	JV in Beijing	200	Miller		
Pabst Blue Ribbon	USA	JV in Guangdong	350		Pabst	
San Miguel	Philippines	JV in Baoding	600	San Miguel		
South African	South Africa	5 breweries	950			Snowflake
Suntory	Japan	JV in Shanghai	200		Suntory	
Tsingtao[4]	Qingdao	5 breweries	800		Tsingtao	

Notes:

[1] International ownership varies for these joint venture partnerships

[2] Capacity is in Million litres

[3] Capacity utilisation is generally low

[4] Largest local brewery in China

JV–Joint Venture

WFO–Wholly Foreign Owned

Source: Lion Nathan China

EXHIBIT 6	Key Players in the China Beer Industry

Anheuser-Busch

The world's largest brewer selling its premium Budweiser brand in 60 countries was aiming for 20% of the world's market share. Anheuser-Busch entered the China market with a joint venture (80%) in Wuhan (on the Yangtze River for transportation access) in 1994; 1,160 km by road, to Shanghai. Establishing a small stake in Tsingtao, China's largest domestic producer and exporter of beer, provided local connections for Anheuser-Busch and a status partner for Tsingtao. Budweiser was the leading premium beer brand with 30% of the China market in 1998. Anheuser-Busch invested heavily in marketing to build brand equity; it also used its dominant international brand and resources to establish deals for access to on-premise retailers. By raising the costs to compete, Anheuser-Busch reduced the ability of most competitors to obtain profits from the premium beer segment in China, which lead to industry rationalization.

Asahi

Founded in 1889, 90% of the Japanese Asahi Breweries' sales were from its flagship brand, Asahi Super Dry, which was marketed in over 30 countries. In 1998, Asahi was a major player in the premium segment (estimated at 7% share of the China market) with very large-scale capacity (600 million litres). The company had joint ventures in Beijing, Quanzhou, and Hangzhou. Asahi was investing heavily in television and media to develop its premium brand; however, its foreign image positioning was not as distinct as the American or European premium brands.

Beck's

The company had a strong international focus. The Beck's brand was differentiated with a distinctive shaped bottle and positioned as a top-quality, world-class premium beer. The company had strict quality guidelines for raw materials and the brewing process, to achieve its unique quality and flavour. In China, Beck's beer was sold in over 40 cities, primarily located along the coast from Shenyang to Guangzhou.

Kirin

Kirin, the fourth-largest brewing group in the world, attempted initially to enter the Chinese market through a licensing arrangement, but then formed a joint venture with a local brewer at Zhuhai in Guangdong province. Kirin's premium beer was positioned as a high quality beer, targeting Japanese expatriate consumers. Kirin's beer was also produced under licence at Shenyang, in northern China, by South African Breweries. Kirin, with a 45-percent equity stake in Lion Nathan, was planning to have some beer brewed under contract at Lion Nathan's brewery in Suzhou.

South African Breweries

South African Breweries had 16 brands providing 98% of the domestic beer market in South Africa. The company's entry strategy in China involved buying into a local brewery with a joint venture agreement, then upgrading the operations and brands, rationalizing costs and building distribution infrastructure. This approach was replicated five times in the northern region of China.

EXHIBIT 6	Key Players in the China Beer Industry (continued)

Tsingtao

China's largest domestic brewer, Tsingtao was founded in 1903 by British and German businessmen and taken over by the Qingdao Municipal People's Government in 1949. Tsingtao provided nearly 3% of the total Chinese beer production in 1998. In addition, Tsingtao exported beer to over 30 countries. The company responded to intensifying competition from foreign brewers by increasing its production capacity and revamping its sales and distribution network. Tsingtao beer was the best selling domestic brand, sold at a premium to other domestic beer because of its popularity and reputation for award-winning quality taste.

EXHIBIT 7	Lion Nathan China: Financial Data

Volumes

1000 litres = 1 tonne

100 litres = 1 hectolitre

LNC's Ex-Brewery Gate Prices (in standard 640-mL bottles)

Taihushui	RMB1.90
Rheineck	RMB2.08
Carbine	RMB4.00
Steinlager	RMB5.70 (700mL)

Employee Remuneration in China

Average brewery worker	RMB2,000–15,000
Seasonal contact workers (for peak periods)	RMB800–1000 per month
Good sales staff	RMB24,000 per annum
Good managers	Over RMB100,000 per annum
Skilled local senior managers	Package over RMB500,000 per annum
Corporate executives (LN)	Up to 60% of pay package depends on individual and company performance

Exchange Rates

NZ$1 (1999)

U.S.	$0.563
China	RMB 4.67
Canada	$0.837

EXHIBIT 8 | Yangtze River Delta Key Cities: Market Size for Key Brands, 1996–1998 (all figures in tonnes)

Shanghai

Premium	1996	1997	1998	Mainstream	1996	1997	1998	Low end	1996	1997	1998
(total)	420000		70000	(total)			230000	(total)			120000
Budweiser	11000	16000	15000	Reeb	133152	88154	70182	Guangming	37000	40000	49000
Beck's	18600	18800	10836	Suntory	58000	43030	50000	Shanghai	31840	31331	30000
Carlsberg	2800	2900	2800	Rheineck	0	10407	22000	Swan	17017	14115	14000
Tiger	2335	2961	3903	Tsingtao	26000	24200	25000				

Suzhou

Premium	1996	1997	1998	Mainstream	1996	1997	1998	Low end	1996	1997	1998
(total)	105000		15000	(total)			50000	(total)			40000
Budweiser	3360	6200	1000	Taihushui	10000	16050	14664	Zhangjiagang	30000	27696	8000
Beck's	4200	4100	800	Rheineck	0	1700	10345	White Swan	15000	12602	6000
Carlsberg	840	550	200	Reeb	1500	2200	5000	Bawang	6000	4020	5000
Tiger	60	160	100	Tsingtao	200	300	600				

Wuxi

Premium	1996	1997	1998	Mainstream	1996	1997	1998	Low end	1996	1997	1998
(total)	92000		11000	(total)			54000	(total)			27000
Budweiser	1500	2200	2900	Taihushui	27000	29384	30000	Zhangjiagang	15000	13800	12000
Beck's	3300	3000	2000	Shanjuan	10000	10916	10000	Fuli	6000	5850	4000
Carlsberg	500	450	234	Rheineck	0	3550	2934				
				Tsingtao	400	500	700				

Nanjing

Premium	1996	1997	1998	Mainstream	1996	1997	1998	Low end	1996	1997	1998
(total)	114000		26000	(total)			70000	(total)			18000
Budweiser	4300	6000	11500	Jinling	33070	33613	27000	Shenquan	10000	9500	9000
Beck's	3500	2500	1000	Yali	11860	38175	25000	Tiandao	4000	4500	5000
Carlsberg	1200	800	400	Rheineck	0	1700	17000	Tianjin	3000	3500	4000
				Tsingtao	2900	2950	3000				

Changzhou

Premium	1996	1997	1998	Mainstream	1996	1997	1998	Low end	1996	1997	1998
(total)	70000		4000	(total)			36000	(total)			30000
Budweiser	800	1200	1000	Guangyulan	32622	26214	20000	Tianmuhu	11100	26214	27000
Beck's	1500	1400	1400	Linkman	2896	2959	10000	Zhangjiagang	2400	2300	2400
Carlsberg	230	250	200	Taihushui	3200	3800	3939				
				Rheineck	0	40	1659				

EXHIBIT 9	Projected Sales Assuming 10% Growth Rate of Existing Brands and New Premium Brands (in tonnes)

(Management Estimates)

	1998	1999	2000*
Mainstream			
Taihushui	48,600	53,460	58,800
Rheineck	54,000	59,400	65,430
Premium			
Carbine	5,000	5,500	6,050
Steinlager	0	10,000	12,000
Beck's	17,000	18,700	20,500

* If Lion Nathan were to do contract brewing for other premium brands, it was estimated that up to two contracts could be obtained in 2000, one for 10,000 tonnes and another for 5,000 tonnes.

EXHIBIT 10	Pro-Forma Income Statement (with current strategy)

	Estimates	Best Case	Worst Case
Sales	100%	100	100
Cost of Goods Sold	(40-60%)	40	60
Gross Margin	60-40%	60	40
Less			
Freight & Warehousing	(10-15%)	10	15
Marketing	(30-100%)	30	100
Admin & Other Overheads	(10-40%)	10	40
Profit or (LOSS)		10%	(115%)

[handwritten notes:] male assumption on worst case — when changing strategy go for high margin beers so make money

Ahrens Farm Supply

Thomas F. Funk

On a cool, rainy day in late November 2001, Len Dow, owner of Ahrens Farm Supply, was sitting in his office looking over the past season's records. He felt he had brought the fertilizer outlet a long way since he had purchased it in February 2000. Volume, which had declined to 7,000 tons in 1999 due to poor management, increased to 8,400 tons in 2000 and to 10,000 tons in 2001 (Exhibit 1). Total sales for 2001 had reached $2,400,000 and profit margins, which were also lower in 1999, had returned to their normal 6-percent level in 2001 due to Len's management skills (Exhibit 2). In spite of all this, Len was not completely satisfied; he wanted to increase the volume and profitability of the outlet, but was not sure what direction he should take.

THE COMPANY

Ahrens Farm Supply is located in Hanton, a town centrally located in a major corn and potato-producing area of Ontario. Ahrens does most of its business within an 8-kilometre radius of Hanton (60%); however, it does have some sales and distribution extending 32 kilometres from its plant (35%), and a small wholesale market over 160 kilometres away in northern Ontario (5%). At the present time Ahrens is involved only in the sale of fertilizers and related services. Dry bulk blends and bagged blends make up the majority of Ahrens' fertilizer volume (9,000 tons), with 28-percent liquid nitrogen making up a much smaller portion (1,000 tons). Potato and vegetable farmers purchase almost 60 percent of Ahrens' production, corn and cereal farmers account for 33 percent, and sod farmers purchase the remaining 7 percent (Exhibit 3). Ahrens' dry fertilizer plant has a peak-season capacity of approximately 10,000 tons under ideal conditions.

Ahrens sells a custom application service for bulk fertilizers and rents application equipment to farmers who wish to apply their own fertilizer. Since Len purchased the company he cut the full-time staff from seven to five including himself. One of his newest employees was a young agricultural university graduate who spent most of his time in a sales capacity calling on present and potential customers in the area. Len also spends some of his time making farm calls.

Of Ahrens' 85 local customers in 2001, five were merchant dealers who resell to farmers. These five dealers accounted for 2,000 tons of Ahrens' business and ranged in volume from 100 to 1,000 tons each. For the most part these dealers were located on the fringes of Ahrens' 32-kilometre trading area. Of the remaining 80 local customers, Len's records showed that 70 were within 8 kilometres of the Hanton plant and ten were at a greater distance. Almost all of these customers were large customers who purchased more than 50 tons of fertilizer a year from Ahrens.

Ahrens sold ten tons of micronutrients in 2000 and more than 100 tons in 2001. Micronutrients are basic elements that a plant requires in relatively small amounts, compared to the larger amounts of nitrogen, phosphorus, and potassium found in most regular, blended fertilizers. Micronutrients have been proven by university and industry research in the U.S. to improve the quality and yield of crops. Commercial trials carried out in Ontario have indicated similar positive results.

THE MARKET AND COMPETITION

The total market for fertilizers in Ahrens' trading area has been stable at approximately 50,000 tons for the past several years. This was not expected to change significantly in the future, although some shifts in types used were possible. Within eight kilometres of Hanton there were four major fertilizer outlets competing with Ahrens for approximately 25,000 tons of fertilizer business, and within 32 kilometres there were an additional three fertilizer outlets competing for the remaining 25,000 tons. There were approximately 550 farmers within an 8 km radius of Hanton.

Although the market for fertilizer was very competitive, Len felt that he had been able to better his competition by offering excellent service, remaining open extended hours, offering advice and timely delivery to his customers, and knowing how to deal with the large farmer. Len quickly came to realize that farmers placed service ahead of price when deciding where to buy fertilizer as long as the price was close to that of competitive outlets. Len felt that by offering a superior service, he had nurtured a high level of dealer loyalty in his customers that resulted in a lower turnover relative to his competition.

GROWTH OPPORTUNITIES

Although the business had been doing well, Len realized that growth was essential to future success. He had given this matter considerable thought and was able to identify several avenues of growth. Now his problem was to evaluate each and arrive at a plan for 2002 and beyond.

Liquid Nitrogen

Len had been considering getting into 28-percent liquid nitrogen in a bigger way. He estimated that the total current market in his 32 km trading area was 4,000 tons, of which he sold 1,000 tons to three corn farmers. This type of fertilizer was of interest mainly to the larger corn farmer because it can be mixed with herbicides for combined application and because of its ease of handling.

Although its price per ton was less than the price per ton for dry fertilizers, it was comparable in terms of price per unit of actual nitrogen. This was because it usually was less concentrated than other forms of nitrogen, such as dry urea, which contained 45-percent nitrogen compared to the 28-percent concentration in the liquid form.

Liquid nitrogen was very corrosive, which meant that the farmer must also purchase a stainless steel sprayer costing about $2,000. This relatively high initial capital outlay restricted use to fairly large farmers. Of the 400 corn farmers in Ahrens' trading area, approximately 200 had sufficient acreage to be possible 28-percent liquid nitrogen users. Len estimated that about 20 farmers were using 28-percent liquid nitrogen in 2001. Price was the major purchase criterion since the product was a commodity and little service was involved. Most of the volume of 28-percent liquid nitrogen was sold in December for delivery in the spring. Prices and margins for Ahrens' fertilizers are provided in Exhibit 4.

Ahrens' current holding capacity is 10,000 gallons, or 50 tons. If output is increased, additional storage and nurse tanks would have to be purchased, as well as another pumping system. A pumping system costs $4,000; storage tanks cost $.15 per gallon; and a 1,400-gallon nurse tank costs $1,000. Len estimated that one additional pumping system, one more 10,000-gallon storage tank, and two more nurse tanks would provide sufficient capacity for large increases in sales. No matter what Len decided to do, he wanted to stay ahead of his competition by at least two years. Because he believed that 28-percent liquid nitrogen could be a big thing in the future, he was excited about this possibility. He had seen a new type of potato planter that required only liquid fertilizer. If this type of planter became popular, the potential for liquid fertilizer would increase dramatically. Despite these positive feelings about this market, Len was concerned about the relatively low liquid nitrogen margins and the slow growth of this market in the past.

Micronutrients

Another opportunity was to try to significantly expand micronutrient sales. Ahrens was a dealer for the Taylor Chemical Company, which produced and sold a complete line of micronutrients. Included in their line were manganese, zinc, iron, copper, molybdenum, boron, calcium, and sulphur. These materials were sold separately or in various combinations designed to treat specific crops. An example of the latter was the company's vegetable mix, which contained magnesium, sulphur, copper, iron, manganese, and zinc in fixed proportions. The individual materials and mixes were sold in two ways: in a dry form for mixing by the dealer with other fertilizer products, and in liquid form for spray application by the farmer on the foliage of the growing crop. Although foliar (i.e., leaf) application was more bother for the farmer and might result in some leaf burning, some farmers preferred it because they could postpone micronutrient application until visible signs of deficiencies occurred. Also, there was some research that indicated that micronutrients could be most effective if absorbed through the leaves at the peak growth period of the plant. Despite the apparent advantages of foliar application, Len had not sold any micronutrients in this form during his first two years in this business. He believed that liquid micronutrients, if properly applied, offered the most value to his customers, yet he noticed a great deal of reluctance and skepticism on the part of even the most progressive farmers in his area to try this product form.

Sales of the dry, mixed micronutrients had grown considerably over the past year and it appeared that the products offered real value to customers. One of Len's customers applied micronutrients to half of a large potato field and treated the other half as he normally did. The treated field yielded 327 hundredweight, whereas the untreated portion yielded only 304 hundredweight. This 23-hundredweight gain resulted in a $111.55 higher revenue per acre when computed at the $4.84 per hundredweight price to the farmer. Unfortunately, the University of Guelph, which farmers looked to for technical information, was not promoting or even recommending the use of micronutrients (see Appendix A). The university's soil-testing service, which analyzed soil samples for most Ontario farmers and made fertilizer use recommendations, did not even include an analysis for micronutrients. The competition did not want to get involved in this business unless there was a very high demand and they started to lose their other fertilizer business.

Of the 100 tons sold in 2001, 75 went to six large potato farmers representing 3,500 acres, 10 tons went to vegetable farmers, and 15 tons went to corn farmers (Exhibit 5).

Len had been receiving excellent service and advice from the company distributing the micronutrients. He felt that the farmers using them were accepting the use of micronutrients, and that sales should rise in the future. Len chuckled to himself as he recalled the day two very large potato farmers, who were brothers, were sitting in his office and the subject of micronutrients came up. One of the brothers, Jack, asked the Taylor sales rep if he thought they should be using micronutrients. The sales rep related all of the advantages of using micronutrients to them, whereupon Jack turned to his brother and asked, "Well, what do you think?" His brother replied, "Yes, I think we should be using them." With that, Len landed a micronutrients order worth several thousand dollars.

Len was convinced that micronutrients had potential in his area. His major concern was how he could convince farmers to spend an additional $10 to $15 per acre on a product for which there was no objective basis for determining need.

Northern Ontario

Len was also considering expanding sales in northern Ontario. Currently, he had three dealers selling bagged fertilizer for him in Sault Ste. Marie, New Liskeard, and Kenora. Ahrens' current volume was approximately 500 tons of bagged fertilizer only. Several Co-op outlets had most of the market in this area. Prices were very competitive, and there appeared to be strong dealer loyalty to the Co-ops. There were many small farms in the region with 75 to 100 acres of workable land per farm. The crop types in the area were mixed grain, barley, hay, and a few hundred acres of potatoes near Sudbury. On the average, farmers in northern Ontario who used fertilizer purchased 2 to 3 tons of bagged fertilizer per year and did their purchasing in the winter months. Because the retail price of fertilizer in northern Ontario was similar to that around Hanton, the margin to Ahrens was reduced by about $17 a ton, the sum of the $12 dealer commission and the $5 freight cost. The lower margin was offset to some extent by lower personal selling costs, since dealers were used. Although the growing season was only two to three weeks behind that of Hanton, because most sales in the area occurred in the winter months, Ahrens' ability to service the Hanton area in the spring was not affected by what they did in northern Ontario.

In addition to the lower margins earned on sales in northern Ontario, Len was also concerned about possible credit problems, particularly because the cost of collection could run very high due to the distance involved. On the more positive side, Len was quite optimistic about the long-run potential growth of this market. He felt that the total industry potential in this market was 50,000 to 60,000 tons of dry fertilizer, of which 10 to 20 percent had been developed at the present time.

Agricultural Chemicals

So far, Ahrens' product line consisted only of fertilizers. However, Len observed that all of his competitors carried insecticides, herbicides, and fungicides as well. Although he had always believed that concentrating on one line was the way to go, lately he wondered if he should be getting into the agricultural chemical business. By doing this, he would be able to better meet the needs of some customers who prefer to purchase all their products from the same supplier. It could also be a way to attract new customers that could be sold fertilizer as well as agricultural chemicals. In the past, Len sized up his customers as not wanting to buy everything from one dealer, so he was satisfied to receive all of their fertilizer business and to leave the other lines to the other dealers. Increasingly he wondered if this assessment were correct.

Agricultural chemicals were very competitively priced, leaving small margins in the neighbourhood of 5–10 percent for the dealer. The setup costs for carrying chemicals would be approximately $20,000 for warehouse upgrading. No other direct costs would be attributable to the chemical line, but Len knew that servicing the line would take valuable time away from servicing and selling the fertilizer line, which could possibly result in lower sales and profits. Len estimated that the average farmer in his trading area spent $3,000 to $5,000 per year on agricultural chemicals.

Dry Fertilizers

An alternative Len found particularly attractive was to expand dry fertilizer sales in his local trading area. Although he had a substantial share of this market, he felt he could pick up additional business through aggressive marketing. He was especially interested in this alternative because no matter what he did his present plant, which was more than 20 years old, would have to be upgraded. As part of his strategy to do this, he was thinking about adding another person to his staff who would act as a second salesperson and develop and offer a comprehensive crop management service to interested farmers. He was also considering the possibility of developing a local advertising program aimed at creating more awareness and interest among farmers outside his immediate 8 km concentrated area. The total cost of the new sales specialist would be about $35,000 per year, and the local advertising would cost about $10,000 per year. Since he was near capacity now, expanding fertilizer sales would require an addition to his plant that would cost approximately $60,000.

THE DECISION

Len knew he would have to make a decision soon if he were to make changes for 2002. Although he had identified what he thought were several good opportunities for future growth, he knew he could not pursue all of them right away and, therefore, he would have to establish some priorities. To help in this assessment, he recently wrote away to the University of Guelph and received a publication entitled "Farmer Purchasing and Use of Fertilizers in Ontario." (Appendix B provides a summary of the study.) With this new information, plus his own sizeup of the situation, Len began the process of planning for 2002 and beyond.

EXHIBIT 1	Ahrens Fertilizer Sales	
Year	Tons Liquid and Dry Fertilizers	Tons Micronutrients
1997	11,000	–
1998	11,000	–
1999	7,000	–
2000	8,400	10
2001	10,000	100

EXHIBIT 2	Ahrens Farm Supply Profit and Loss (2001)				
	Liquid Nitrogen	Dry Fertilizer	Micronutrients	Total	%
Sales	$154,000	$2,232,000	70,000	$2,456,000	100
Cost of Sales	134,750	1,830,240	59,500	2,024,490	82
Gross Margin	19,250	401,760	10,500	431,510	18
Fixed Expenses	20,000	260,000	5,000	285,000	12
Net Income	(750)	141,760	4,500	146,510	6

EXHIBIT 3	Ahrens Fertilizer Sales by Farm Type, 2001	
Farm Type	Percentage of Dry Fertilizer Sales	Percentages of Acres Served
Potato and vegetable	60	35
Corn and cereals	33	60
Sod	7	5

EXHIBIT 4	Fertilizer Prices and Margins

	Dry Fertilizers		28% Liquid Nitrogen				Micronutrients	
	$/ton	%	Winter $/ton	%	Spring $/ton	%	$/ton	%
Average selling price	248	100	138	100	170	100	700	100
Cost of sales	203	82	131	95	136	80	595	85
Gross margin	45	18	7	5	34	20	105	15
Estimated fixed costs	$260,000			$20,000			$5,000	

EXHIBIT 5	Micronutrient Sales by Crop, 2001

Crop	Tons Sold	Acres	Application Rate	Cost/Acre
Potatoes	75	3,500	50 pounds per acre	$15.90
Corn	15	1,300	25 pounds per acre	$ 8.00
Vegetables	10	400	50 pounds per acre	$15.90

Appendix A

No Substitutes for Rotation

This past year there has been a lot of interest in Perth and Huron counties about micronutrients. There are numerous plots about this year with different formulations and mixes and ways of application, both on corn and beans. We are sure there will be a lot of discussion this winter about the subject.

Some things are becoming evident about micronutrients, at least we think they are. The first is that you cannot expect dramatic yield increases with individual nutrients on small areas.

Secondly, none of the micronutrient sales staff has been able to explain to us the problem of over applying micronutrients. They suggest if you put too much potash you may tie up magnesium. If you put on too much phosphate, you will need to put on more zinc and magnesium. We believe, without variable soils, in some fields you can put on too much zinc and magnesium.

Finally, these micronutrients seem to be the most attractive to farmers with poor crop rotations. Some of your neighbours have gone to poor crop rotations and their yields have dropped. (You know the ones that think Pioneer corn followed by Cargill corn is crop rotation.) Now they are searching for something to pull their yield back to former highs. Micronutrients appear to be the answer.

What puzzles us is why some of you are willing to spend large sums of money on products you are not sure will work: shotgun micronutrients. We both know what the problem is. You have to get more crops into the rotation, especially perennial forages. I suppose the bottom line is when you hear your neighbour talking about all the micronutrients he is using, that's just a polite way for him to tell you he has a terrible crop rotation.

Source: This article was written by a soils and crops specialist with the Ontario Ministry of Agriculture and Food. The article appeared in an issue of "Cash Crop Farming," a publication widely read by Ontario farmers.

Appendix B

Results of Fertilizer Marketing Research Study

1. Only 7 percent of total crop acreage in southern Ontario is not fertilized at the present time. This acreage is almost entirely in soybeans, pasture, and forages.

2. The average fertilizer application rate for southern Ontario farmers is 384 pounds per acre. Most farmers use soil test recommendations from the University of Guelph to determine the application rate. There is some tendency for farmers to apply more fertilizer than recommended by their soil tests.

3. The major types of fertilizer used by southern Ontario farmers are dry bulk blends and liquid nitrogen. Of lesser importance are dry bagged fertilizers, anhydrous ammonia, and liquid mixes (N-P-K). Liquid nitrogen fertilizers are almost exclusively used by very large farmers.

4. Most farmers find the quality and availability of fertilizers to be very good.

5. In southern Ontario as a whole, a relatively small percentage of farmers purchase a large percentage of the fertilizer products sold. The breakdown is as follows:

	% of Farmers	% of Purchases
Under 25 tons	30%	10%
26-50 tons	35%	25%
51-100 tons	20%	20%
Over 100 tons	15%	45%

6. Over 70 percent of all dry fertilizers are sold to farmers in April and May. This figure is somewhat lower (50 percent) for liquid nitrogen.

7. Thirty percent of Ontario farmers use dealer custom application services, while 75 percent apply the fertilizer themselves using rented dealer application equipment. There is some tendency for larger farmers to be more inclined to want custom application services.

8. In the course of a year, farmers discuss their fertilizer program with a number of parties to get information and advice on various aspects of fertilizer use and dealer selection. The influence groups most widely consulted are the local fertilizer dealer, other farmers, and family members. In addition to these influence groups some farmers consult fertilizer company representatives, agricultural extension officials, and university scientists. In the case of company representatives and university scientists, proportionately larger farmers visit these people than smaller farmers.

9. Farmers also obtain fertilizer information from soil test results, various government publications, company-sponsored farmer meetings, dealer demonstration plots, and company and dealer displays at farm shows and fairs.

10. Over 60 percent of all farmers contact more than one fertilizer dealer before making a purchase. Larger farmers have a tendency to contact more dealers than smaller farmers.

11. Over 50 percent of all farmers reported receiving an on-farm call by a fertilizer dealer in the last year. Larger farmers reported receiving more dealer calls than smaller farmers.

12. In addition to fertilizers, southern Ontario farmers purchase, on the average, more than three other products from their fertilizer supplier. Of these, the most common are herbicides, insecticides, general farm supplies, and seeds. Large farmers are more likely to purchase herbicides and insecticides from their fertilizer supplier than are small farmers.

13. Six dealer services were identified as being essential to all but a very small proportion of farmers: application equipment, which is available when needed and in good repair; custom application services; custom fertilizer blending; fertilizer information through a well-informed staff, brochures, newsletters, and farmer meetings; soil testing; and demonstrations.

14. Other dealer services that were reported as being important to smaller groups of farmers were crop management assistance, help in securing expert assistance with problems, and custom herbicide application.

15. Dealer location, price, and availability of product when needed are the major factors farmers consider when selecting a fertilizer dealer. In general, dealer location and availability of product when needed are more important to smaller farmers, while price is more important to larger farmers.

16. Over 45 percent of all farmers purchase fertilizer from their nearest dealer. On the average, farmers purchase from dealers located less than 8 km from their farms.

17. Thirty percent of all farmers purchase from more than one dealer. Larger farmers have a greater tendency to spread their purchases over more dealers than do small farmers.

18. Analysis of dealer switching showed that one-third of the farmers made no dealer changes in the past five years, one-third made only one change, and the remaining one-third made two or more changes. Those farmers making several dealer changes are the larger, younger farmers.

Danier Leather

Hamid Noori

In late July 2000, Jeffrey Wortsman, President and CEO of Danier Leather, was flying back from Hong Kong and reflecting on the future of the company. Three months ago he had officially stated:

> In terms of our future growth plans, we remain firmly committed to both investing in the Danier brand equity and creating shareholder value. Our growth initiatives include expanding our existing product lines, introducing new product lines and increasing our market share and brand recognition worldwide. Our balance sheet strength provides us with the flexibility and confidence necessary to fund our continuing expansion plans and take further advantage of the buying opportunities for leather and finished garments.

Expansion of the brand and retailing activity was a major concern if the 20-percent annual sales and profit growths he had set as objectives for the company over the next few years were to be reached. Jeffrey was considering four options: more aggressive expansion of Danier's online venture (www.danier.com), further penetration of the Canadian market, further expansion into the U.S. market, and expansion into Europe where he felt there was a relatively untapped market for value-oriented fashion leather.

Since 1994, Jeffrey had focused on growth, pursuing two strategies simultaneously. He had diversified the company's retail channels, stores, and power centres; and

Alternatives

expanded geographically across Canada and recently to the U.S. This strategy had been successful, and sales had grown from $69.7 million in 1997 to $109 million in 1999 to projected sales of $143 million in fiscal 2000.

Two years earlier, Jeffrey saw the Internet as a new growth opportunity and had championed the online store development. The company had opened its online shopping site in December 1999. Although he was very encouraged by the results and would continue to invest in e-commerce initiatives, the online shopping option raised many issues. Some were strategic in nature, such as differentiating the company and its product offering online or increasing traffic to the site, and others were more operational, as in the case of delivery or returns—but all hinged on making the best of this new opportunity. He felt the company's key success factors had brought Danier to where it was today:

> Our main key success factor is our prices. We are very competitive in our market. Then come service, design and quality, very close to each other. Finally, I would say our manufacturing flexibility and time to market are strong assets.

However, he was uncertain as to how these positioned Danier for e-tailing both domestically and internationally, especially in Europe. He felt the company had an advantage over pure e-players ("dot-coms") such as Amazon.com and CDNow.com, because of its bricks-and-mortar structure that could be leveraged to create synergies. But how could this best be done?

COMPANY HISTORY

Founded in 1970 in Toronto by Mr. Wortsman, Jeffrey's father, the company began as a manufacturer of custom leather clothes for racecar drivers, a wholesaler for large department stores, and a contract belt and wallet manufacturer for retailers. Left unexpectedly with a large returned order in 1973, the company opened its first Leather Attic store to sell the returned goods. As this retailing was successful, Mr. Wortsman discontinued the wholesale operation and became an integrated manufacturer/retailer. The advertising slogan was "We make it, We make it well worth it." At that time, the company produced about ten styles and strived to offer value to customers. By 1981 there were 19 Leather Attic stores located in malls in Ontario and Manitoba.

In 1981, the company opened a high-fashion clothing store in the Toronto Eaton Centre, one of Canada's premier shopping malls. The store operated under the name Danier to convey a sense of European flair and carried many high-fashion clothing brands. Realizing there was a market for fashion leather, the company expanded its product line. The Danier label was created for more fashionable, higher-quality leather and suede clothing, and Danier boutiques were installed in a few select Leather Attic stores.

In 1986, Mr. Wortsman's son, Jeffrey, joined him as Vice-President. After studying economics, Jeffrey had obtained a law degree and an M.B.A. and worked in the brokerage industry. Encouraged by the success of the boutiques, Mr. Wortsman and Jeffrey opened the first Danier Leather store carrying mostly Danier Label merchandise, and launched an ambitious and aggressive advertising campaign. Sales, which had been about $17 million a year, reached $40 million in three years. By 1990, the 33 Leather Attic stores had been revamped to the new image and the name changed to Danier Leather.

In 1994, Jeffrey was appointed President and CEO. The company went public in 1998 and 5,740,000 subordinate voting shares were offered on the Toronto Stock Exchange under the name Danier Leather Inc., at a price of $11.25 a share. Jeffrey retained 17 percent of the subordinate voting shares and enough multiple voting shares to retain 67 percent of the total number of votes.

In 1997, the company opened a very small wholesale outlet in London, UK, to test the European market. The company wanted to evaluate the differences in taste and style in Europe. Results were positive, but securing a high-traffic retail location in London would have cost the company $1 million, which was too expensive at the time. Management also believed the time required to run such an operation was prohibitive. As a result, this operation was closed a year later.

THE INDUSTRY

The Canadian market for apparel had had very little growth in recent years; between 1992 and 1997 the total market increased from $8.3 billion to $9 billion. Canadian manufacturers were losing market share to imports; the domestic market share fell from 55 percent in 1992 to 47 percent in 1997.

In 2000, the leather apparel sector, a specialty segment of the apparel industry, was a fragmented mature industry undergoing consolidations. "Mom and pop" operations were being driven out of business. This sector, like the rest of the industry, was seasonal in nature and was affected by fashion trends. The leather apparel market, which could be increased by offering new products, was estimated at $450 million at retail with growth of about 5 percent annually.

In Europe, similar trends were taking place, leading analysts to believe that a handful of pan-European apparel chains that focused on their own brand line and that were vertically integrated would dominate the market.

In 2000, retailing in North America and Europe was carried out through the traditional channels of store and catalogue and, increasingly, through the Internet (Exhibit 1).

THE COMPETITION

Danier was the world's second largest leather retailer, behind the U.S.-based company Wilsons The Leather Experts, which had stores in the U.S., Canada, and the UK. Wilsons had 18 percent of the U.S. market, and Danier had 30 to 35 percent of the Canadian market. In Canada, Danier also competed with smaller leather retailers such as the Leather Ranch and Boutique of Leather. In the U.S., leather was primarily retailed by department stores, and Danier competed with stores such as Macy's and Bloomingdale's. As there were no Canadian retailers directly comparable to Danier, the company benchmarked itself against specialty apparel retailers, as well as branded retailers in both Canada and the U.S. (Exhibit 2).

DANIER LEATHER 2000

Danier was a vertically integrated designer, manufacturer, and retailer of high-quality, high-fashion leather and suede clothing and accessories for men and women. It endeavoured to be a market leader with a fashion/value image. It retailed its merchandise under its own brand name, Danier, in 75 Danier Leather locations in Canada and the U.S. and through its newly opened online retail site (www.danier.com). Danier had established itself as a brand retailer that marketed its product on the strength of the brand name rather than a specific product offering (Exhibit 4). It offered an extensive selection of leather and suede apparel and accessories and had 1,285 active stock-keeping units (SKUs). Danier's customers were mainly value-oriented, fashion-conscious men and women between 25 and 54, with middle to upper household incomes. The Danier Couture product line attracted higher-end consumers. Exhibits 3 and 5 display a breakdown of the company's revenue per product line and the annual financial statements. Danier has been a profitable company for 26 consecutive years.

The Organization

Danier employed 1,000 people in retail, 200 people in manufacturing, and 70 people at its headquarters. The senior management team was composed of the Chief Operating Officer (COO), the Chief Financial Officer (CFO), the Chief Information Officer (CIO), the Chief Merchandising Officer (CMO), and the Vice-President E-Commerce, who all reported directly to the Chief Executive Officer (see Exhibit 6). Jeffrey regularly involved senior management in decision making and trusted their judgment. The seven-member Board of Directors, including the CEO, played a very active part in running the company. All board members had strong business backgrounds and Jeffrey felt confident he could consult them for advice.

Geographic Expansion

The company had first expanded across Canada, establishing stores in 50 shopping malls and opening 24 power centres, which were positioned as factory outlets (Exhibit 7). In 1998, with such a wide Canadian coverage, management decided to expand to the U.S. An extensive market study carried out in order to choose the best location indicated the following:

- Although geographically close, retail preferences in southern Ontario and Michigan differed widely. What worked well in Windsor might not necessarily do as well across the river in Detroit, Michigan.
- The East Coast of the U.S. was culturally very similar to southern Ontario. It was more European than the rest of the U.S.
- The East Coast had a high population density.
- To be successful in the U.S. a company needed a product that was unique and better than what was already there.
- Price and value were not key success factors, as many U.S. retailers excelled in these factors.
- Many Canadian retailers, including Future Shop and Canadian Tire, had entered the U.S. market and failed.

As a result, in July 1998, the first U.S. store was opened in a newly renovated mall on Long Island. After one year, Danier was doing better than the average retailer in the mall. In spring 2000, a second store was opened in a large mall in the same area.

By opening stores in the same area, Danier was pursuing a "cluster strategy" in the U.S. This allowed them to have more effective advertising, decrease transportation costs, and build a strong brand image in an area before expanding to another region. The U.S. stores received their merchandise from headquarters in Canada.

Product

Danier carried four main product lines:

- Danier Style: Outerwear, sportswear, and evening wear manufactured from high-quality lamb leather, calf suede, and cow hide, and pigskin leather and suede.
- Danier Couture: Sophisticated, high-end garments inspired by couture fashion trends and produced from European lambskin leather and suede.
- Danier Coordinates: Wool sweaters and casual cotton or nylon shirts designed and manufactured under the Danier label to complement the Danier garments.
- Danier Accessories: Quality, fashionable leather purses, belts, wallets, portfolios, gloves, and day-timers.

All four lines had three key attributes: modern contemporary styling, high-quality fabrication, and unmatched value.

[handwritten margin note: Problem - ever changers - need flexibility]

Danier products reflected current fashion styles. The company's design team based at the Toronto headquarters designed all products. Team members travelled regularly to New York, Paris, and Milan, where they attended trade shows to monitor international fashion trends. They also subscribed to numerous design and fashion magazines. Following fashion in fabrics, cotton, wool, and silk, they interpreted the styles for leather and suede apparel. Styles were adapted to Canadian and even provincial preferences within Canada, as these could vary widely. Danier worked with a U.S.-based fashion consulting firm that provided forecasts of styles, fabrics, colours, and silhouettes; 70 percent of the collection was black, which was the most popular colour for leather apparel and accessories.

At the beginning of each season, a collection was manufactured for each product line. The company produced 300 to 500 apparel styles and 130 to 150 accessory styles per season. Danier also developed, test marketed, and introduced new designs throughout the year. This was made feasible by the vertically integrated structure of the company. The design expertise and the possibility to produce small quantities in-house, in as little as three days if required, allowed Danier to continually introduce, test, and decide very quickly if new items should be produced on a larger scale.

Production

Danier operated two manufacturing facilities in Canada: a 130,000-square-foot wholly owned plant (used for manufacturing, alterations, warehousing and distribution) at its headquarters and a 19,500-square-foot leased manufacturing and warehousing plant at a nearby location.

[handwritten margin note: low cost prod.]

While all design was done at headquarters, only one-third of production was domestic. The more fashionable and trendy garments were produced at the company's two plants, but subcontractors located primarily in China, Indonesia, and Korea produced the more classic styles. This allowed Danier to be more price competitive in the latter category. Danier had recently opened an office in Korea and employed on-site inspectors to check garments before they were shipped to its headquarters.

Supplies

An important factor for success in this industry was the sufficient procurement of good quality, competitively priced skins. Two major factors affected the quality of skins: poor shearing, which could mark a skin, and climate changes, which could cause stretch marks on a skin as the animal's weight changed with weather conditions. Possible uses for a skin depended on the time of year the animal had been killed, its age, and the country where the animal had been raised. Some of the best skins came from New Zealand, Great Britain, Italy, Spain, and South Africa.

Danier had established strong long-term relationships with suppliers. This, together with the large volumes purchased by the company, helped Danier obtain high-quality skins at competitive prices. Furthermore, as Danier operated all year, it could plan its purchases strategically to take full advantage of market opportunities. Colour selection was finalized only weeks before an order was to be shipped, making inventory management easier.

Skins used by the company were a byproduct of the food industry, and the company had not faced regulatory issues or environmental lobbies.

Distribution Channels

The company retailed all its products under its own label, Danier. Danier Leather was distributed through its own Danier Leather retail outlets, including shopping mall stores, street-front stores, and power centres, as well as through its newly opened online site.

Danier usually leased its stores for a five to ten-year period, which gave the company flexibility in its location strategy. Before deciding to open a new shopping mall store, management needed to be assured the new store would generate at least $800,000 in sales a year in Canada or US$1 million in the U.S. This was found to be the minimum required for a store to create value for the company. Initial costs of opening a mall store in Canada ranged from $200,000 to $250,000 for renovations, working capital of approximately $100,000, and inventory of approximately $200,000. Opening costs for a U.S. mall store were equivalent to a Canadian mall store but in U.S. dollars.

In 1994, Danier had started opening "Power Centres" in suburban areas of major cities. Getting prime location in a mall or finding new malls had become extremely difficult. To get a good site in a mall, landlords would often put pressure on a company to accept a poor site in another mall. Faced with such pressures, management had first opened three power centres, in Toronto, Vancouver, and Winnipeg.

Power centres were much larger than stores, and rents and associated costs were lower (Exhibit 8). Power centre prices were the same as store prices for current season items, leading to higher profit margins. However, power centres offered customers a greater selection of merchandise. They carried the four product lines, one-of-a-kind samples, seconds, and previous season collections at a reduced price. Initial cost of opening a power centre in Canada ranged from $350,000 to $450,000 for renovations, net working capital of approximately $200,000, and inventory of approximately $500,000.

At first, management was concerned about the possible damage power centres could cause the Danier brand. This concern, however, quickly dissipated as sales rose from $70 million to $109 million. In 2000, Danier had 24 power centres across Canada that showcased the Danier brand. They represented 50 percent of total sales. The top centre had annual revenues of about $6 million, and several others reached $4 million—compared to $1 to $2 million for a typical shopping mall or street-front store (Exhibit 8).

Marketing and Advertising

In-Store Marketing and Merchandising

Danier used three strategies to market its brand through stores:

- Compelling, similar front-window presentations, in-store displays of merchandise, and placements of posters and signage throughout all stores.
- New models introduced throughout the year, providing new selections to expand the customer base and entice customers to come back regularly.
- A specifically chosen merchandise mix adapted to local markets with regard to taste and price.

External Marketing and Advertising

Danier spent about 6 percent of revenues on marketing and advertising. An eight-person team was responsible for all aspects of marketing and advertising except photography and printing, which were outsourced. Management believed that carrying this function internally helped them portray a consistent image, react quickly to market changes, and control costs. With all advertising, the goal was to ensure that the advertising approach was tailored to reflect the lifestyle of the Danier customer—defined as sophisticated, urban, and fashion focused. Three of the main marketing tools were:

- *Print Advertising*: High-quality print advertisements and mini-catalogue inserts in 20 leading daily newspapers for a total circulation of about 2.3 million, at the time a new collection was introduced, or a store was opened, or for the holiday season or sales.
- *Direct Mail*: The company has a database of 650,000 customers that it uses for direct mail, such as promotional coupons or postcards based on each customer's purchasing history. Many stores have the data necessary to better service their customers' needs.
- *Danier Credit Card*: In 1997 Danier introduced the Danier Account Card. This provided the customer with the opportunity to pay over a longer period of time, and provided Danier with valuable information about its customers. About 10,000 customers had an account card. The Danier Account Card was administered by National Retail Credit Services. The same organization also collected credit card accounts.

Online Shopping Site

Danier displayed its collection through its Web site, which was a fully operational online shopping site.

Management closely monitored the effectiveness of its marketing campaigns. Return on marketing investments was calculated for any activity by comparing expenditure and incremental sales to historical sales during a previous comparable period. Management also tracked shoppers entering the stores and conversion rates of potential to actual customers, by store and region, during the period a campaign was running. These data were then used to help develop future advertising campaigns.

Information System

Danier had installed an enterprise-wide fashion-based relationship system, STS, which was a retail, merchandising, finance, and point-of-sale system. It used a relational database, Sybase, to analyze the data obtained from the STS system. This allowed the company to monitor daily sales information by location and product. The stock distribution was based on weekly inventory balances obtained from the STS system. The system could also recommend transfers of merchandise between stores.

In-store traffic was monitored by a traffic counting system, which allowed management at headquarters to track customers entering and exiting stores and purchases being made in 15-minute increments. This, linked to product purchase information, provided management with a tool to measure sales staff performance and schedule store staffing.

New manufacturing software, ISD (Intelligence Standard Data), was currently being implemented. This system replaced a previous system and would monitor output rate, costing, timing, overtime, merchandise planning, and direct sourcing. ISD was not linked to the STS system or to the company's suppliers. The only extranet in place had been set up to enable the transmission of some data files to National Retail Credit Services for administration of credit card accounts.

As the information system was not integrated, information provided by the three systems described above was input into the company's PC/Mac network for use by management.

The State of E-Commerce

At a time when electronic commerce was growing very fast and threatening the way business was traditionally done, the fastest growing segment was B2B (business-to-business), where cost savings and speed were the main attractions. It represented 80 percent of online transactions in the U.S. and amounted to US$160 billion in 1999. The B2C (business-to-consumer) sector was also increasing. In 1999 the online retail business in Canada and the U.S. represented 1 percent of total retail sales, CDN$1.7 billion and US$20 billion, respectively.[1] This was expected to grow to represent 5 percent of retail sales in a few years. Some studies suggested that the growth in online retail sales would cause the annual growth rate of offline (traditional retail) sales to drop from 5 to 3 percent per year. The extent to which the "social" component of shopping would limit the growth of e-tailing was still unknown. Consumers were still strongly attached to traditional shopping, but many changes had occurred in the last 50 years, from corner shops to large out-of-town superstores. Low-touch merchandise, such as books, CDs, and tickets, were more easily purchased online than high-touch merchandise, such as clothing or food.

The story of e-tailing was reminiscent of the beginnings of catalogue shopping. More than 100 years ago, the new channel had offered shoppers similar advantages; shopping from home, a large selection, and competitive prices. The success of catalogue shopping worldwide in the clothes and food sectors, such as Quelle, L.L. Bean, and Omaha Steaks,

---

[1] In July 2000, CDN$1 equaled US$0.65.

suggested, therefore, that the Internet might also become successful in that area. In the apparel industry more companies were using this new channel to either maintain or expand their current customer base. In 1999 apparel sales online amounted to US$1.6 billion in the U.S. Sites such as www.fashionmall.com offered shoppers leading-edge labels and technology, including the first virtual-reality change rooms. They claimed to offer "a totally new lifestyle proposition, which is going to revolutionize the way we shop."

As technology evolved, e-commerce opportunities were expected to increase. Faster broadband Internet connections, more secure payment systems (such as E-Money), and information privacy would make shopping on the Internet more attractive. To date, one of the major effects of the Internet had been to allow customers to do quick price comparisons.

don't compete on price

It had become obvious that doing business over the Internet was not as simple as it had first appeared. A strong supply chain was required and new players needed to invest time and money to develop an appropriate supportive logistics and distribution system.

The economics of traditional retailing were also changing. New factors, such as Web site loading speed, ease of Web site navigation, and product delivery within 24 hours of ordering were replacing key success factors (e.g., location and product variety) for traditional retail stores. Furthermore customers expected services similar to those offered in a bricks-and-mortar shop, from credit card payment to product and service warranties and returned goods policies.

Designing the right Web site to maximize what could be called "economies of attention" was a new concept that replaced store layout. Furthermore, a customer had to be attracted to the site and enticed to stay and return. Two primary factors that influenced customers in that regard were trust and quality of information. Companies such as Amazon.com had spent astronomical amounts in site advertising. Customer acquisition costs were assessed to be US$42 per customer for many companies, compared with between US$5 and US$22 for multi-channel retailers.

As a result, whereas dot-coms had built their entire operations based on the Internet, bricks-and-mortar companies were seeing this as a "disruptive technology," which they found difficult to adopt for several reasons:

probs w online

- Fear of cannibalization of existing offline sales
- Distribution systems poorly adapted to new demands
- Customer information systems ineffective in providing the information required for Internet marketing (customer relationship management software packages now provided integration of back-office operations to online store operations, but were very costly and time-consuming to implement)
- Losses incurred when launching an e-tailing site reflected negatively on the firm's earnings and therefore on its share price

Although 90 percent of commercial Web sites were U.S.-based, e-tailing was also already well established in other parts of the world. According to the Boston Consulting Group, online retail sales in Europe had reached US$3.9 billion in 1999, and might reach US$9 billion in 2000. The cost of telephone calls was the main factor slowing growth in Europe, as these were estimated to be twice the average North American costs.

As a comparison, recent Internet usage across a number of countries showed the importance and absolute size of the U.S. market. In a typical month, 88 million U.S. consumers (of a total population of 277 million), either from home or work, used the Internet. Similar figures for Canada were 13 million usage (population 30 million); for the UK were 13 million usage (population 59 million); for Germany were 12 million usage (population 83 million); and for France were 8 million usage (population 70 million).

Two of the European markets that Danier thought offered potential for either online or retail sales were Germany and the UK (Exhibit 9). Rough estimates for establishing a European Web site that would be the host for both Germany and the UK were $100,000 for the initial setup and annual servicing of $100,000. Estimates for two staff who would be full-time integrators for Germany and the UK were $60,000 each. The other option would be to continue with the existing site and begin advertising the site in both countries to attract more customers. For all purchases, the consumer would pay for shipping.

Many American players had thought it would be easy to become global retailers through the Internet but had revised their position and returned to the domestic market. Regulatory issues in areas such as advertising, information content, product guarantee, and taxation had proved to create barriers to entry. The Value Added Tax (VAT) applied to goods in Europe could be as high as 25 percent in some countries. Other concerns, such as controversy about privacy or data protection and local competition, also worried some potential entrants.

DANIER ONLINE SHOPPING SITE

Management had started discussing the possibility of doing business over the Internet in 1996. They established their first Web site in 1997, outsourcing the development to a local Internet developer. The site offered product pictures, information about store locations, phone numbers, and e-mail contacts. However, because of a mistake, all customers on the distribution list became the target of spam. Danier admitted and apologized for its mistake and damage was judged to be minimal; for example, a Vancouver paper reported the incident merely as "Company learns from mistake."

Gradually the site had become more interactive, and headquarters received 20 to 30 e-mails a day. These were mostly store-related enquiries or complaints. One person dealt with the questions and redirected the complaints. Everyone received an answer.

In the summer of 1999, management decided to open an online store for the Christmas season. After looking at several contenders, IBM was selected to supply the technology and service, and both parties agreed on a product that met Danier's needs and a price that fit Danier's budget. IBM ran, housed, supported, and upgraded the entire site. Any upgrade was first staged in-house and then uploaded. Danier paid a monthly hardware fee as well as a maintenance fee. Videotaping, the chatline, and over-hour phone calls were outsourced to other companies.

At this stage the company made several strategic choices. As Philip Cutter, CIO, stated:

> We realized I should not run the e-commerce, it is not a technical job. It is more a catalogue and electronic store job. But we did not want to set up an entire duplicate structure and end up with two organization charts. So we decided to find a V.P. E-Commerce with very specific marketing skills. He/she would be responsible for e-commerce decisions and I would look at the ramification of his/her decisions from the technology perspective. We would work as a team.

Kevin Strachan was recruited as V.P. E-Commerce in September 1999. He had extensive experience in catalogue and direct marketing as well as home shopping. He reported directly to the CEO and was supported by the current infrastructure.

After opening the site in December 1999, the company had encountered a few problems, mainly due to on-site response time. However, by April 2000 results were very encouraging. The majority of online customers were new to Danier, 65 percent were from the U.S., and the average online transaction was $300. In the first seven months of operation, the sales volume had reached that of a small store and www.danier.com had attracted customers from throughout the U.S. as well as international customers from Ireland, Scotland, Sweden, the Netherlands, Japan, Taiwan, Singapore, and Australia.

Orders were delivered within 24 hours even though the order processing activities were not automated and were not done in real time. When an order came in, it was printed, the credit card information was verified, the product availability was checked, the credit card payment was validated to minimize the risk of fraud, the product was retrieved from the warehouse or head office store, and the purchase was processed as a normal transaction. UPS or FedEx then shipped the product.

Suede and leather samplers were prepared and sent to customers upon request, so they could see and feel the quality of the leather before purchasing a garment. Several test Internet kiosks had been set up in some stores, allowing customers to familiarize themselves with the online shopping concept, making it easier for them to shop in the store and giving them the opportunity to access the whole collection, as some items might not be in that store. The company had recently won a Fusion award for the way it had integrated the Internet and their bricks-and-mortar facilities.

A number of the executives at Danier felt that with the international reach and appeal of the Internet, and Danier's unique product offering, e-commerce had the potential over the next several years to become larger than the current Canadian base. The Internet was a new channel of distribution with international reach. However, other executives were more cautious, noting that it had been difficult for many apparel stores to achieve substantial sales on the Internet because of consumer reluctance to purchase clothing, particularly fashion clothing, from a Web site. Because clothing was a "high-touch" product, many consumers preferred to purchase it at a physical store.

Philip Cutter, CIO, felt the initiative had been a success:

> First, everyone in the company has been great in supporting the e-business initiative and that has come from the CEO. Everyone believes in it. Second, Kevin and I working together is key.

As to future directions, Kevin commented on some of the issues he faced:

> There are some very basic issues, such as spelling and terminology differences between Canada and the U.S., or the best number of items on a page. Then there are more complicated marketing issues, such as conveying an aspirational lifestyle picture. At the moment we have static product pictures. We are testing video and audio possibilities. Today "behind the scene" shows you a short model filming video clip. We would like the online site to be similar to home shopping through interactive TV for every product in the store. In the store, a salesperson deals with one customer at a time. We are prepared to do the same thing online.

As Jeffrey reflected on the growth targets for Danier he considered the four options again: more aggressive expansion of Danier's online venture, further penetration of the Canadian market, further expansion into the U.S. market, and Europe. He wondered what it would take to aggressively launch www.danier.com in Europe. Should Danier instead focus more on the U.S. market for online expansion? Or was the time right to create a physical presence in Europe in either the UK or Germany? The German market was very open to catalogue selling. Could an electronic catalogue capture that market? In the UK, online sales were expected to reach US$3 billion in 2000 and continue to increase in the foreseeable future. Could Danier enter that market? Danier was strong in Canada and could continue to build on that strength, but good locations were increasingly becoming difficult to find. The absolute size of the U.S. market was compelling. Before flying to Hong Kong, Jeffrey had asked senior management to think about these issues and any other viable possibilities for growth. They would meet tomorrow to begin planning the strategy to achieve the growth targets.

EXHIBIT 1	1999 U.S. Apparel Sales by Channel	

Channel	US$ ($M)	%
Store	162,976	88.6
Catalogue	17,226	9.4
Online/Internet	1,125	0.6
Not Reported	2,535	1.4
Total Apparel	183,859	100.0

Source: Retail Apparel Sales Statistics and Trends; http://retailindustry.about.com

EXHIBIT 2	Financial Synopsis of Major Apparel Retailers in Canada and the U.S.

Canadian Companies	1999 Sales (CDN$ M)	1999 Net Income (CDN$ M)	1999 EBITDA Margin	1999 P/E Ratio
Dylex	1,085.8	9.7	2.7%	9.3×
Reitmans	490.2	16.6	7.0%	10.6×
Suzy Shier	345.7	6.8	4.5%	8.9×
Mark's Work Warehouse	313.1	7.7	9.2%	6.3×
San Francisco	215.9	4.9	8.8%	17.9×
Chateau Stores	165.9	5.2	8.9%	7.9×
Shirmax Fashions	139.6	1.7	5.2%	11.5×
Danier Leather	126.2	8.6	14.8%	4.7×

(continued opposite)

EXHIBIT 2	Financial Synopsis of Major Apparel Retailers in Canada and the U.S. (continued)

	U.S. Companies			
	GAP		Wilsons	
	Fiscal 1999	Fiscal 1998	Fiscal 1999	Fiscal 1998
Income Statement				
Revenue	11,635	9,054	543	459
COGS	6,775	5.318	347	308
SG&A	3,043	2,403	136	113
Net Income	1,127	824	30	18
Balance Sheet				
Cash	450	565	125	116
Net Receivables	0	0	7.54	6.3
Inventories	1,462	1,056	79	85
Current Assets	2,197	1,871	221	204
Total Assets	5,188	3,963	272.5	248.8
Short-Term Debt	169	91	0	0
Current Liabilities	1,753	1,553	93.9	77.5
Long-Term Debt	785	496	43.9	70
Total Liabilities	2,955	2,390	141.4	150.6
Total Equity	2,233	1,573	131.2	98.2

EXHIBIT 3	Danier Revenue Distribution per Product Category, Fiscal 2000

Women's Outerwear	33%
Men's Outerwear	29%
Women's Sportswear	26%
Women's Accessories	5%
Men's Sportswear	3%
Men's Accessories	2%
Kid's Accessories	2%
Kid's Outerwear	0%*

*Less than 1%

| EXHIBIT 4 | A Typical Danier Online, Offline Ad |

EXHIBIT 5A	Danier Financial Statement

Consolidated Balance Sheets ($M)

	June 24, 2000	June 26, 1999	June 27, 1998
ASSETS			
Current Assets			
Cash and short-term deposits	775	1,628	6,753
Accounts receivable	762	369	591
Inventories	35,124	22,659	19,784
Prepaid expenses	197	242	185
	36,858	24,898	27,313
Other Assets			
Capital assets	20,631	14,810	5,429
Goodwill	355	369	383
Deferred income taxes	1,163	1,578	2,247
	59,007	41,655	35,372
LIABILITIES			
Current Liabilities			
Bank overdraft	–	–	–
Accounts payable and accrued liabilities	13,208	6,336	5,867
Income taxes payable	3,251	1,473	1,546
Current portion of long-term debt	270	247	226
	16,729	8,056	7,639
Long-term debt	833	740	988
	17,562	8,796	8,627
SHAREHOLDER'S EQUITY			
Share capital	24,236	25,204	25,204
Retained earnings (deficit)	17,209	7,655	1,541
	41,445	32,859	26,745
	59,007	41,655	35,372

Consolidated Statements of Earnings ($M)

	June 24, 2000	June 26, 1999	June 27, 1998
Revenue	143,011	108,977	88,663
Cost of sales	69,865	56,313	45,731
Gross profit	73,146	52,664	42,932
Selling, general and administrative expenses	54,051	41,740	34,085
Other expenses	–	–	27
Earnings before interest and income taxes	19,095	10,924	8,847
Interest expense (income)	33	(48)	1,234
Earnings before income taxes	19,062	10,972	7,613
Provision for income taxes	8,352	4,858	3,197
Net earnings for the year	10,716	6,114	4,416

EXHIBIT 5B	Danier Financial Statement (continued)

Consolidated Statement of Change in Financial Position ($M)

	June 24, 2000	June 26, 1999	June 27, 1998
Cash flows from operating activities:			
Net earnings for the year	10,710	6,114	4,416
Items not affecting cash:			
Amortization	3,461	2,298	2,358
Loss or disposal of capital assets	227	28	16
Deferred income taxes	186	80	(297)
	14,584	8,520	6,493
Change in operating assets and liabilities:			
Accounts receivable	(343)	222	(373)
Inventories	(12,465)	(2,875)	(7,665)
Prepaid expenses	45	(57)	180
Accounts payable and accrued liabilities	6,872	469	2,730
Income taxes payable	1,778	(73)	555
Net cash provided by operating activities	10,421	6,206	1,920
Cash flows from financing activities:			
Share capital issuance proceeds	–	–	67,950
Share capital issuance costs	–	–	(5,803)
Stock dividend, redemption and cancellation of share capital	–	–	(41,321)
Subordinate voting shares purchases	(2,006)	–	–
Repayment of term loan	–	–	(5,000)
Repayment of subordinate debt	–	–	(9,299)
Deferred income taxes related to IPO	474	589	487
Obligations under capital leases	(274)	(227)	1,214
Net cash provided by financing activities	(1,779)	362	8,228
Cash flows from investing activities:			
Acquisition of capital assets	(9,495)	(11,693)	(2,553)
Net cash used for investing activities	(9,495)	(11,693)	(2,553)
Net cash inflow (outflow)	(853)	(5,125)	7,595
Cash and short-term deposits (bank overdraft), beginning of year	1,628	6,753	(842)
Cash and short-term deposits, end of year	775	1,628	6,753

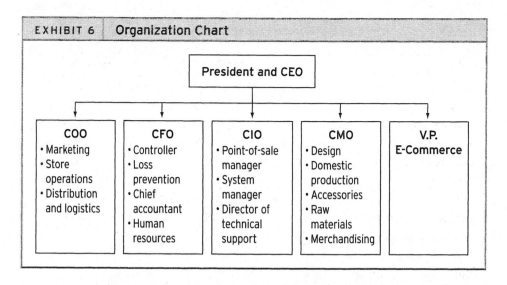

EXHIBIT 6   Organization Chart

President and CEO

COO	CFO	CIO	CMO	V.P. E-Commerce
• Marketing • Store operations • Distribution and logistics	• Controller • Loss prevention • Chief accountant • Human resources	• Point-of-sale manager • System manager • Director of technical support	• Design • Domestic production • Accessories • Raw materials • Merchandising	

EXHIBIT 7   Store and Power Centre Geographic Distribution

Province	Mall Stores			Power Centres		
	2000	1999	1998	2000	1999	1998
Ontario	22	24	23	15	12	6
Quebec	8	7	6	0	0	0
Maritimes	2	2	2	2	2	1
Manitoba	2	2	2	1	1	1
Alberta	5	4	6	4	4	2
B.C.	10	8	7	2	2	1
U.S.	2	1	0	0	0	0
Total	51	48	46	24	21	11

EXHIBIT 8	Average Store Revenues and Costs	
	Stores in Malls	Power Centres
Number of stores	51	24
Total sales	$75.1 million	$67.9 million
Sales per store*	$1.4 million	$3.2 million
Average size (sq.ft.)	1,600	6,600
Sales per sq.ft.	456	916
Rent/sq.ft.	$50	$17
Rent paid	Higher of rent or 6% of sales	Rent
Occupancy costs/sq.ft.	$35	$8
Rent & occupancy (% of sales)	10	5
Wages (% of sales)	11	10
Other direct store costs (% of sales)	2	3

* Sales per store in malls varied from a low of less than $800,000 to a high of over $2,000,000 and in power centres from a low of less than $2,500,000 to a high of over $6,000,000.

EXHIBIT 9	Comparison between UK and German Markets	

	GERMANY	UNITED KINGDOM
Total Population	82 million	58 million
Market Size	US$17 billion	US$35.8 billion
Market Growth	4.5% decrease from 1997–1999. Projected growth of 2–5% for the next 5 years.	20% growth in the past 5 years. Largest attributing factor: increased sales in women's wear.
Barriers to Entry/ Market Accessibility	• Population & commerce is geographically decentralized; business must be capable of serving a country-wide customer base. • Culture, style & fashion preferences reflect traditional European tastes (differ from Danier's current North American line).	• Packaging, labelling, shipping and safety requirements are ambiguous. • Distribution channels are more complex.
Foreign Retailer Concentration	• 65-75% of apparel in Germany is supplied by imports (Asia, North Africa, Italy, and U.S.).	• $6.6 billion in imports (Hong Kong, India, China, and Italy) have kept penetration and retail expansion to a minimum, focus primarily on local markets.
Consumer Characteristics	• Reluctant to accept many American styles (prefer traditional European look). • Introduction of Casual Fridays in many German offices has prompted sales in quality casual sportswear.	• U.S. styles & brands welcomed by female consumers – American styles on television programs (*Friends*) & worn by celebrities (Posh Spice). • Casual & functional way of dressing is refreshing compared to traditional European styles. • 15-17% of women in workforce wear image and brand-based apparel.
Competition	• Grupo Zara – 9% market share. • Hennes & Mauritz – 4.5% market share.	• Marks & Spencer – 15% market share (market leader). • Arcadia, Burberry, House of Fraser, and NEXT. • Explosion of U.S. designer flagship stores (Polo, Tommy Hilfiger, Calvin Klein, Gant, Ralph Lauren).
Consumer Purchase Criteria	• High quality – ranked most important by 46% of apparel consumers. • Brand name – ranked 2nd (28% of consumers). • Price – ranked 3rd (21% of consumers).	• Design – ranked most important by 35% of apparel consumers. • Style – ranked 2nd (26% of consumers). • Features – ranked 3rd (20% of consumers). • Service – ranked 4th (20% of consumers). • Value-added elements – ranked 5th (9% of consumers).

GoodLife Fitness Clubs

Gordon H. G. McDougall

These retention rates are poor. I need to do a better job of keeping members, thought Krista Swain, Manager of the GoodLife Fitness Club in Kitchener, Ontario, as she reviewed her retention rates for the 1999–2000 fiscal year.

As she was analyzing the report, Jane Riddell, Chief Operating Officer, entered her office. Krista looked up and said, "Hi, Jane. I've just been looking over the retention rates for the clubs. I'm not happy with my numbers."

"Neither is head office," Jane replied, "and that's why I'm here today. You run one of our best clubs, and yet your retention rates are around 60 percent, the average for the 40 GoodLife Clubs. We lose 40 percent of our members each year. By improving your club's retention rates from 60 to 65 percent, based on last year's figures gross revenues would increase by over $35,000. You are one of our top performers and you should be leading the way."

"I agree," said Krista. "We have to figure out how to keep the members enthused and show that the club offers them value."

"That's what I wanted to hear," replied Jane. "As a first step, let's both think about this and meet again next week with some ideas. Then I'd like you to prepare a retention plan that will be the model for all the clubs."

THE FITNESS MARKET

In a national study, the Canadian Fitness and Research Institute found that most Canadians believed that physical activity was beneficial in preventing heart disease or other chronic conditions, in reducing stress, and in maintaining the ability to perform everyday tasks with aging. However, physical inactivity remained pervasive in Canada, with 63 percent of adults aged 18 and older still considered insufficiently active for optimal health benefits in 1998.[1]

The study also revealed that for a variety of reasons most Canadians tended to talk positively about the importance of physical activity but didn't "walk the talk." The most popular physical recreation activities were walking (86% of Canadians had participated at least once in this activity within the past 12 months), gardening (75%), swimming (57%), bicycling (55%), and home exercise (50%). Exercise class/aerobics was ranked 13th (21%), with significantly more women (33%) than men (9%) participating.

While the overall physical activity of Canadians was relatively low, the fitness market was growing at approximately 6 percent a year. The growth was due to demographic changes (baby boomers were increasingly interested in maintaining a good level of physical fitness), marketing (increasing numbers of health/fitness clubs extolling the benefits of fitness through their programs), and individuals selecting fitness clubs over other physical activities as their choice for exercise.

Industry estimates were that about 10 percent of the Canadian population belonged to a health club. However, there was considerable "churning" (the percentage of members lost in a month or year), as many Canadians had good intentions and joined a club only to leave at the end of their membership for a variety of reasons. Industry research revealed the following major reasons for leaving: decline in interest, took too much time, too hard, and didn't like the club. It was estimated that on an annual basis the average health/fitness club in Canada lost between 36 and 45 percent of its members.

Another reason for the high average churn rates was that many clubs, referred to as "factories," did not take a professional approach in managing their operations. Typically, a sports personality (e.g., a retired hockey player) would own these "factories" and offer low initial memberships to get people into the club. These clubs had few trained instructors, frequent equipment breakdowns, and poor facilities maintenance. These clubs often failed within a year or two, leaving customers with a valid membership and no facility.

GOODLIFE

The Philosophy and Goals

In March 1979, David Patchell-Evans established GoodLife as a sole proprietorship. "Patch," as he was called, saw an opportunity—Canadian fitness clubs were largely cash- and sales-oriented with little emphasis on scientific fitness or member retention. By May 2000, Patch had built this privately owned fitness company to more than 40 clubs (10 were franchises, the rest were company-owned) in Ontario and Quebec. GoodLife had the largest group of fitness clubs in Canada, with more than 70,000 members. (Appendix 1 provides more details on the philosophy and growth of the GoodLife Clubs. Exhibit 1 shows a GoodLife brochure.)

---

[1] Canadian Fitness and Research Institute, 1998 Canadian Physical Activity Monitor

From the beginning, the company's goal was to provide the best in equipment, facilities, and service, with a well-trained staff. The goal was based on high-quality service with education and training, superior cleanliness, and programs that made the individual a member for life based on their "needs and goals." Underlying the plan to grow to 100 clubs by 2004 was the GoodLife motto: Measurable Constant Improvement—for the company, its staff, and its members.

Head Office

The head office was located at the Galleria Mall Fitness Club in London, Ontario. Head office personnel numbered approximately 40, led by Patch, Chief Operating Officer Jane Riddell, and National Director of Fitness Maureen Hagen. Head office's main role was to provide leadership and support for the franchisees and company-owned clubs. Among the group's major activities were determining the advertising strategy, designing new fitness programs, ensuring that all clubs maintained quality standards, providing training programs for staff, and keeping all club managers abreast of the latest trends and issues in the fitness industry.

One of Jane Riddell's responsibilities was the design and management of GoodLife University, where each month 50 to 60 new associates went through a one-week program. The training included an orientation to GoodLife (basic knowledge of GoodLife and its philosophy), personal training (skills required to assist members as a personal trainer), and computer program training. When club managers hired the associates, they typically spent their first few weeks "learning the ropes" at the club and then attended the University program. Jane led some of the training sessions and evaluation of the participants, some of whom failed and left GoodLife.

Jane was generally pleased with the calibre of the participants. She rated about 70 percent of them as good to great and 30 percent as poor. In the past, the GoodLife clubs had focused on hiring physical education and kinesiology graduates. However, as the economy improved in the late 1990s these graduates chose other job opportunities, requiring GoodLife to broaden its hiring criteria. Now GoodLife hired individuals with the right attitude (i.e., customer focused). However, the attitude of some new employees was that this was not a real job or a career. Rather, it was a fun place to be for a while, a cool, easy job until they got a real job. Jane felt that this was part of the issue of employee retention at GoodLife. In the past two years employee turnover had increased, and last year 600 employees (out of a total of 1,400) had left GoodLife. Jane estimated that most of the employee retention problem was GoodLife's fault—they either hired the wrong people, or didn't do enough to keep the right ones.

Advertising spending, at 6 percent of revenues, used a "call to action" versus a "branding" approach. The call to action used variations on "$99 for 99 days," "one month free," "no initiation fee," "save now," and so on (Exhibit 2).

The company allocated advertising expenditures by season: winter 40 percent, summer 25 percent, and October to December 35 percent—which reflected the general interest level of people in joining a fitness club. Each month headquarters evaluated each club on sales targets: the new members obtained through internal marketing (e.g., referrals, Yellow Pages), external marketing (e.g., newspaper, flyers, radio, television), and walk-ins (i.e., potential member walks into the club and asks about memberships). This information, along with conference calls with the regions, set the regional advertising allocation.

GoodLife's commitment to club members, staff, and community resulted in numerous awards and achievements. GoodLife was the first to bring many innovations to the fitness industry including the Fit Fix training concept and the PUNCH program. GoodLife raised more than $500,000 annually for various charities and supported a wide range of community activities.

The GoodLife Staff

GoodLife's size (more than 1,400 associates) and rapid growth provided many opportunities for advancement. The career path at GoodLife could take an associate to any number of areas: group exercise classes, personal training, sales, administration, management, accounting, and even to owning one of the clubs.

Compensation consisted of a base salary plus club sales commissions and bonuses. The club sales commissions were based on the number of memberships sold per week against a target. Depending on the type of membership sold and/or specialty programs sold, the associate could receive a commission on sales ranging from 5 to 15 percent. Bonuses were based on weekly targets set for the individual club. Depending on the hours and shifts worked by the staff, if the goals were met the staff member could earn a bonus of $15 or $25 per week. As well, there was an employee referral bonus: any current staff member who referred an individual for employment with GoodLife could receive a bonus of $100 or $200 for individuals hired on a part-time or full-time basis. Finally, there were incentive programs for good ideas—the rewards, called Patch Bucks, could be redeemed for fitness conferences.

GoodLife offered company awards on a monthly and yearly basis. On a monthly basis, awards were given to (a) group exercise coordinator (gift and plaque), (b) manager of the month ($200 and plaque), (c) associate ($100 and plaque), (d) sales manager ($200 and plaque), (e) sales associate ($100 and plaque), (f) personal training associate ($100 and plaque), and (g) customer service representative ($100 and plaque). On a yearly basis, awards were given to (a) manager (free fitness conference, valued at $2,500), (b) group exercise instructor, and (c) group exercise coordinator.

GOODLIFE KITCHENER

The New Location

In September 1998, the Kitchener GoodLife Club re-opened on the second floor of an indoor mall in downtown Kitchener, Ontario. Prior to that it was located two blocks away in a relatively small (12,000 square feet) and poorly designed facility. The new facility was larger (30,000 square feet), had an open concept design, and an extensive range of equipment and programs. Over the next 18 months membership increased dramatically under Krista Swain's guidance. As of May 2000, the club had 3,500 members, an increase of 2,300 over the original 1,200 members who moved from the old club.

Krista, a 1995 graduate in kinesiology and physical education from Wilfrid Laurier University in Waterloo, Ontario, worked for GoodLife as a fitness instructor while she was attending the university. After graduation, she joined the Waterloo GoodLife Club as a service trainer. In addition, she handled corporate sales for the GoodLife Women Only Club in Kitchener. Within ten months she was appointed manager of the Kitchener

GoodLife Club and was actively involved in the transition from the old to the new location. When asked how she had rapidly advanced to club manager, she said:

> I have a passion for fitness and I'm committed to the company. I'm convinced that the GoodLife values, mission, and philosophy are right; and I truly feel that we are helping people at GoodLife. I like working with people. My role is to be a coach and mentor, and I lead by example. I think the staff understand my goals and respect me because I respect them. Sometimes I can't believe what the staff are willing to do to help the club and the members. But I'll also say, if you are not a top performer, you won't fit in at GoodLife.

In early 2000, the Kitchener club was signing up more than 230 new members per month (Exhibit 3). At the same time, the club was losing about 100 members per month, for a net gain of about 130 members. On an annual basis, the club was losing 40 percent of its members. Overall, the rapid growth in membership had a very positive impact on revenues, which increased by more than 60 percent between June 1999 and March 2000 (Exhibit 4).

The Associates

The Kitchener club's 40 associates (10 full-time, 30 part-time) worked in four groups: sales, customer service, personal training, and service.

- The four sales associates (all full-time) were responsible for getting new members.
- Customer service employees, who were primarily part-time, worked the front desk.
- Personal trainers worked with individual club members on fitness programs.
- Service employees introduced new members to the club and its philosophy through a series of programs on fitness and equipment use.

All employees were involved in selling. Although the sales associates were dedicated to selling new memberships, the personal trainers spent time encouraging members to sign up for personal training. The customer-service employees would sell tanning programs and other services to members. Typically, each group or individual had sales targets and earned bonuses and commissions based on meeting those targets.

Most of the employees earned a base salary of $8.00 per hour, plus bonuses if they achieved the weekly targets. As an example, a sales associate might have a target of eight new members per week. If the target were achieved or exceeded, the associate could earn $1,250 or more every two weeks. Customer-service staff could earn up to $25 per week if they met targets that included phoning members to remind them of upcoming events, encouraging them to use the club, and selling various club products and services such as tanning. Personal trainers could make up to $27.00 per hour for personal training in addition to their base pay of $8.00 per hour. The more members the trainer signed up, the more hours he/she spent in personal training.

Through these incentive programs GoodLife encouraged its staff, particularly the sales associates, to be entrepreneurial. As Krista often said, "The staff have to make things happen; they can't wait for them to happen. Both GoodLife and the staff do better when they make things happen."

As noted, GoodLife had formal training programs for new employees. In addition, Krista spent time with the new employees teaching them the technical side of the job and establishing the norms and culture of the club. By emphasizing what was important to her, Krista hoped they would understand the importance of excellent customer service. "If I can show the new employees what's important to me, and get them to trust me, they come on board and are part of the team. For example, we hold weekly staff meetings where we discuss a number of issues, including how to improve the club. People don't miss the meetings. Every once in a while, a new associate decides not to come to the meetings. The team lets him or her know that's not acceptable. Those people either become part of the team or decide to leave GoodLife."

Employee turnover at the Kitchener GoodLife Club was slightly better than the average across all the GoodLife clubs. In the past year, Krista had a turnover of about 35 percent, with the rate for full-time slightly lower than for part-time. Part-time turnover was higher, in part, because many of the part-time employees were students who left to go to university or left after completing their degree programs.

Like Jane Riddell, Krista was concerned about employee turnover, but she wasn't sure what actions could improve the situation. She had noticed that some new employees were surprised at the amount of selling involved in their positions. She also felt that some employees were not satisfied with the base salary of $8.00 per hour.

Typically, when an employee left, Krista needed to hire a new associate relatively quickly. She would place an ad in the local paper, *The Record*; get some applications; conduct interviews; and hire the individual she felt was most suited for the position. With full-time employees, Krista was not always happy with the pool of applicants she interviewed; but there was always the pressure of filling the job, which had to be balanced against the quality of the applicants. With the economy improving and a low local unemployment rate, it was sometimes difficult to attract high-quality applicants.

The Members

Most new members joined the club through referrals. When an individual asked about joining the club, a sales associate would show them the club, discuss the benefits of membership, and explain the GoodLife philosophy. Assuming the individual decided to join, the sales associate would ask if he or she had any friends who might be interested in joining the club; if so, they would receive a free membership for one week. Typically, the associate tried to get five referrals. The associate would then contact these people, offer the free one-week membership, and set up a meeting with them if they accepted. The cycle was repeated with each new member. On average, the sales associates converted between one and two of the five contacts to new members. Referrals generated between 60 and 80 percent of all new members.

The price for a new membership varied depending on the promotion option. The two main options were (1) a $199 initiation fee with the first six months free and $40 per four weeks after that, or (2) the initiation fee was waived and the member paid $40 per four weeks. Payments were on a biweekly basis through an automatic payment plan that the member signed. The new member also paid a total of $54 for the membership card ($15) and a processing fee ($39). A new member could also decide to join for a three-month period for $180. Members could also decide to pay once a year and not use the automatic payment plan.

When an individual joined the club, an associate from the service group would take the new member through three programs as an introduction to the club and the GoodLife approach to a healthy lifestyle. The three programs were (1) Fit Fix 1, an introduction to strength training, (2) Cardio, basic information about cardiovascular training principles, and (3) Fit Fix 2, adding exercises to your program. Any new member could also have a fitness assessment (resting heart rate, body fat measurements, etc.). After six weeks, the new member could also have a second fitness assessment to track his/her progress.

The club offered a wide range of cardio equipment, weights, and personal training programs. Members could participate in more than 20 aerobics programs each week, from Steps'n'Abs to Circuit Training to Newbody to PUNCH. On average, 12 members were participating in each program. Typically, members had been going to these programs for years, and few new members joined any program. The club attempted to address this issue with new members by having a "new members only" aerobics class. On average, the club would get 50 new members to sign up for the program, then 15 would show up for the first class, and it would be down to six people when the class ended in 12 weeks.

This issue reflected a broader problem common to most of the GoodLife Clubs, often referred to as the "20-20-60 phenomenon." Twenty percent of the club members were hardcore fitness and health people; these members came three or more times a week, were serious about their training, and would tolerate a lot (e.g., uneven service) as long as it didn't interfere with their training. The second 20 percent were the new members. They were enthusiastic, wanted to get fit, and over time they either became committed or not. The largest group, the remaining 60 percent, were those members who came on an irregular basis. The club staff didn't know their names, these members often were not sure about how the equipment worked or what they should be doing, and they often wouldn't ask for help. Even when they stopped coming, this group kept their membership for a period until they decided to cancel. When one came to cancel, an associate tried to get her/him to stay, usually with little success.

Krista and other associates at GoodLife believed that getting members to feel that they were part of the GoodLife Club was important in retaining them. Krista believed that many of the 60 percent probably never felt they were part of the club as they didn't know many or any of the other members or the staff. Krista remembered that while many of the 1,200 members from the old club liked the new facility (open, spacious, more equipment, etc.) they felt that the club was more impersonal. In particular, as the membership grew, the "original" members felt less at home. Krista estimated that within a year about 50 percent of these members had left the club.

The advertising for GoodLife consisted of an ad in the Yellow Pages and ads in a local free weekly newspaper, the *Pennysaver*. Local businesses were targeted with brochures offering specials. Krista felt that most of the new members came from the referral program and the *Pennysaver* ads (Exhibit 2). As she said, "The Pennysaver ads get the phones ringing."

While Krista believed that overall the members were satisfied with the club, she felt there was always room for improvement. For example, members sent her about 14 written complaints or concerns every week through the suggestion box (where members could offer comments). Each week, the front-office staff received about a dozen verbal complaints. Most complaints or concerns dealt with equipment problems (e.g., equipment not working properly) and a few dealt with staff (e.g., a particular staff member was not friendly). Krista dealt with the complaints as they arose.

Competition

In the Kitchener-Waterloo area (Kitchener and Waterloo are twin cities) there were about 15 fitness/exercise clubs serving a population base of 450,000 people. The Kitchener GoodLife Club had four major competitors:

- The two YMCAs in Kitchener-Waterloo offered aerobic programs and had workout areas. The Ys had a good reputation as friendly, family-oriented clubs. The annual membership fee ranged from $400 to $650 depending on the type of membership and the services requested (e.g., towel service, locker, etc.).

- The International Family Fitness Centre was also located in downtown Kitchener, within three blocks of the GoodLife Club. It offered equivalent facilities to the GoodLife Club, was of a similar size, and had more than 40 programs a week. Its membership rates were very similar to those of GoodLife.

- Popeye's Gym previously had a reputation as a male-oriented facility where body builders worked out. However, the image was slowly changing to a men's and women's fitness club that offered aerobic programs and a variety of weight and training machines. It was located approximately 3 kilometres from downtown Kitchener and was open 24 hours a day. The membership fees were approximately $350 per year.

CUSTOMER RETENTION

As Krista prepared for the meeting with Jane, she knew that improved customer retention rates were possible but was uncertain as to what actions would be most effective. She identified three major areas that she could address: employee turnover, a new bonus system, and swipe-card technology.

Employee turnover, at more than 40 percent, created a lack of stability at the club. Every time a new employee started, he/she didn't know any members, then over time would learn the members' names (often those who visited frequently). If the employee left, so did the knowledge. Krista had always felt that members would have a greater sense of "belonging" to the club if the front-desk staff could greet them by name. Although many of the front-desk staff knew some of the members by name (most of these members were the hard-core regulars who came frequently), most of the front-desk staff were part-time associates or had recently joined GoodLife; therefore, they knew relatively few members by name. Further, because most of the "60 percent" group came infrequently, few staff knew their names.

Krista had two ideas for reducing employee turnover—both based on increasing wages. Increasing the hourly base rate from $8.00 to $9.00 for most employees (excluding managers and sales associates) would add about $4,000 per month to wage costs. The problem was that although she knew employee turnover would decline, she didn't know by how much, nor did she know the effect on retention rates. A second option was to focus only on the front-desk employees who greeted members. Increasing their rate to $9.00 would increase monthly wage costs by about $1,000. She preferred this option because the front-desk associates greeted all the members as they entered and swiped their card. With the increase in their wages, Krista would ensure that the front-desk staff knew that an important part of their job was to greet members by name.

Next, Krista considered introducing a bonus plan for increasing customer retention. Virtually all the targets and bonuses at GoodLife focused on increasing sales, reflecting, in part, Patch's aggressive growth targets. Although she didn't have a specific plan in mind, Krista felt that an allocation of at least $1,000 to bonuses for increased retention was feasible. Her initial idea was that for every percentage increase in retention rates per month (e.g., from 60% to 61%), staff would receive $200 in bonuses. Where Krista was uncertain was how the target should be set—on an individual or group basis. The front-desk staff had the most contact with members, but potentially all the employees could be involved. What was important to Krista was that the associates would have a goal and a bonus attached to customer retention. She knew that this plan would get the associates to focus more of their efforts on customer retention.

Krista felt that better use of the swipe-card information could improve retention. Members swiped their membership card when they visited the club. A valid card allowed a member to go through a turnstile; a non-valid card (because it had expired) did not release the turnstile. Krista knew that other information (e.g., number of member visits, etc.) was available, but no one at the club or head office had developed a software program to track member visits. Krista contacted two software companies, one of which offered a membership management program that would provide interface with swipe scanners and provide reports on members' frequency of visits, along with a host of other member information. The cost ranged from $3,500 for a licence for five sites up to $8,500 for unlimited site use.

One of the targets for the front-desk associates was to make "motivation" calls to members each week. Associates would call a specified number of members to reach their target. The associates would begin anywhere on the member list (a binder at the front desk) and begin calling members to encourage them to use the facilities or inform them of special events. After the call, the associate would record the date called and his or her name next to the member's name. Ideally, all members were called once every six weeks, but this didn't always happen.

With the new software system, reports could identify members who had not visited the club for a particular period. Staff could then contact members who had not visited for a specific time period (e.g., three weeks, four weeks, etc.). Krista felt that this would substantially improve the existing approach and would improve member retention rates.

Krista knew that there were other available approaches or tactics to improve retention rates. In particular, any activities that built a greater sense of "community" would increase interaction between members and a sense of "belonging." But it was difficult to find the time to figure it out. Managing a club with 3,500 members kept her very busy making sure everything was running smoothly, and she spent most of her time "doing," not "planning."

A week later, Jane met Krista in her office. Jane started the conversation. "Let me review the situation. As I mentioned last week, if we could improve your club's retention rates from 60 to 65 percent, based on last year's numbers, gross revenues would increase by over $35,000. In this business most of the costs tend to be fixed, probably about 60 percent of revenues, so most of the revenue would be profits. If we could do that for all the clubs, it would be great for business and I think we would have more satisfied members. And—just to put this in perspective—on average we have about 2,000 members per club."

Jane continued, "In the past year, the story has been about the same for most of our clubs. For every 100 new members signed up each month, we have about 40 people who don't renew or cancel their membership. We spend a lot on marketing to get them in the door. Then we spend time with them setting up an exercise or training program. They are enthusiastic to begin with, then they stop coming to classes or to exercise. Then they cancel or don't renew when their membership comes up. When they cancel, we ask them why they are leaving. The most common reasons are that they don't have enough time or they can't fit it in to their schedule. I think that about 30 percent of the time they have a good reason for leaving, such as they are moving out of town. I think that 70 percent of the time we could have done something to keep them with the club.

"From a head office point of view, we have had a number of debates about the amount of advertising we do, which is about 6 percent of revenues. That's a lot of money, and sometimes we think that we should be spending more of that in staff training. Another question is, what type of training would be most effective?

"Let me mention one other issue we are concerned about," Jane continued. "We don't use the swipe card to collect data. We need to do more with that."

"That was one of my thoughts," Krista replied. She then told Jane about the software program's capabilities and costs.

"Very interesting," replied Jane. "That's certainly something to consider." Krista then presented her other ideas to Jane. As she finished, Krista said, "I think my cost estimates wouldn't be too far out of line for our average club."

Then Krista added, "Sometimes I think that maybe we should focus more on service than sales. As an example, my front-desk staff have sales targets and other assignments as well as greeting members. Also, there are few opportunities for the staff to walk around and just talk to our members and see how they are doing. That's why I suggested a bonus plan based on increasing retention rates. We have very aggressive growth targets for each club and plan to add a lot more clubs. As an organization, we are really getting stretched. Most of our time is spent on growth, not service."

"Yes, but the strategy has worked well so far," Jane replied. "I'm not sure if we could justify adding more staff to focus on service; we would need to see a payback. But it's another interesting idea."

Krista and Jane continued their discussion and decided that Krista would prepare a customer retention plan for the Kitchener GoodLife Club with the goal of increasing retention rates by 5 percentage points or more within six months. "I want to at least get the average retention up to 65 percent," Jane said. "As I mentioned last week, we'll use this plan as the model for all the clubs."

As Jane left she said, "Krista, I have every confidence in you. I'm going to send an assistant manager from the other Kitchener club down here to help you run the club while you work on the plan. I look forward to positive results."

After Jane left, Krista sat down and began thinking about the approaches she could take to increase retention rates. She had always liked a challenge, and knew that she would do her best to meet this one.

EXHIBIT 1	GoodLife Brochure

Winner of the Business Achievement Award from the Chamber of Commerce

GoodLife
FITNESS CLUBS

- Named Canada's Top Fitness Club
- Transferable membership good at almost 50 clubs in Ontario & Quebec
- The best fitness equipment
- Great facilities
- Professionally trained, friendly staff
- Winner of the White Glove Award for cleanliness
- Competitive prices
- A club for beginners and experts
- Guaranteed results

Voted Best Club For Service in Canada   Get a GoodLife

EXHIBIT 2	Exhibit of GoodLife Ad

EXHIBIT 3	Kitchener GoodLife Club–Membership by Month

Month	Members lost during month	Members gained during month	Net members gained during month	Members (at end of month)	Retention rate per year (%)	Loss rate per month (%)
March '99	–	–	–	1900	–	–
April '99	58[1]	163	105	2005	63.5[2]	3.0
May '99	61	158	97	2102	64.0	3.0
June '99	73	156	83	2185	59.4	3.4
July '99	75	155	80	2263	60.9	3.3
August '99	68	150	82	2341	65.2	2.9
September '99	70	168	98	2423	64.8	2.9
October '99	108	196	88	2521	48.5	4.3
November '99	91	220	129	2609	57.9	3.5
December '99	90	223	133	2738	60.1	3.3
January '00	103	244	141	2871	56.4	3.6
February '00	99	238	139	3012	60.1	3.3
March '00	113	234	121	3151	56.4	3.6
Annual Average					59.8[3]	3.4

[1] At the beginning of April, the club had 1,900 members. The monthly loss rate for April is 3.0% (based on a yearly retention rate for April of 63.5% which is a yearly loss rate of 36.5%). The club lost 1,900 × .03 = 58 members in April.

[2] 63.5% of the members as of April '98 were still members as of April '99; 36.5% were no longer members.

[3] The average retention rate for the year shown is 59.8%; average loss rate per month is 3.4% (1−.598 = .402/12).

Source: GoodLife Fitness Clubs

EXHIBIT 4	Kitchener GoodLife Club–Selected Revenues and Expenses			
	June 30 '99 Month	June 30 '99 YTD (12 months)	March 31 '00 Month	March 31 '00 YTD (9 months)
Revenues	(%)	(%)	(%)	(%)
Membership	89.9	88.2	86.9	83.3
Services[1]	9.3	10.2	11.9	15.5
Other	1.8	1.6	1.2	1.2
Total Revenues	100.0	100.0	100.0	100.0
Expenses				
Sales wages and commissions[2]	10.5	12.1	8.3	8.9
Service wages and commissions[3]	9.0	7.1	5.3	12.3
Service and other[4]	19.4	28.6	20.4	17.1
Total Direct Expenses	38.9	47.8	34.0	38.3
Manager controlled[5]	9.2	15.6	4.8	10.4
Administrative[6]	31.8	31.1	26.3	32.6
Total Expenses[7]	79.9	94.4	65.0	81.3
Members	2,200		3,200	
Total Revenue ($)	120,000	1,004,000	195,000	1,177,000

[1] Includes personal training, specialty programs, tanning and pro shop

[2] Related to new membership sales

[3] Includes personal training and member services

[4] Includes service staff wages and expenses

[5] Includes utilities, supplies and services

[6] Includes advertising, administrative management, rent, realty taxes, equipment leasing

[7] Not included are depreciation, amortization, interest, and taxes

Source: GoodLife Fitness Clubs

Appendix 1

David Patchell-Evans may not be a natural athlete, but he's a confirmed fitness fanatic. He works and dreams physical fitness. Even his vacations are spent pursuing extreme sports such as mountain climbing or skiing. But that wasn't always the case. In his first year at university, a motorcycle accident paralyzed the right side of his body. Following extensive rehabilitation, Patchell-Evans was determined to return to full physical fitness. He took up rowing and eventually became a five-time Canadian rowing champion and a member of the 1980 Canadian Olympic team.

Those experiences taught Patchell-Evans the role health and fitness play in creating a satisfying life and fostered a life long commitment to sell the idea to others. In 1979 he bought a workout club in London, Ontario and began implementing his vision: to provide customers with an affordable club offering state-of-the-art equipment and, more importantly, knowledgeable staff eager to teach them how to get the most from it. "The opportunity in the marketplace," he says, "was to provide service."

In an industry notorious for dubious claims and fly-by-night operators, GoodLife Fitness Clubs has built its business on highly trained staff, innovative programming and reinvesting in its facilities. In 20 years, it has become Canada's largest health club chain, with 42 clubs, 100,000 members and 1998 sales of $40 million. In an industry that's adding new clubs and members at 9% a year, GoodLife is growing at almost three times that rate. By 2004 Patchell-Evans' goal is to have 100 facilities.

To reach the goal Patchell-Evans will rely on the same philosophies on which the chain was founded: providing health, fitness and self-esteem so that people feel better about themselves. It's part of the strategy to raise the bar of service excellence and bring a new professionalism to an industry where clubs were traditionally run by sports jocks with little business training. The GoodLife philosophy of ensuring consistently high standards in every club goes a long way to building brand loyalty among the members. "When people work out, they want to know that the shower will be clean, the equipment is going to work, and the staff know what they are talking about."

That philosophy has served GoodLife well as the chain expanded, opening new clubs and buying others that were doing poorly in strong locations. "One of the ways we grew in the early days was to take over clubs that really nobody else wanted to touch," Says Jane Riddell, GoodLife's Vice-President and Director of Franchising. "A classic example is our club at the corner of Queen and Yonge Street in downtown Toronto. When we took over the club, the membership was languishing around 100, and the facility was losing $60,000 a month. The club needed refurbishment and new equipment, but it had huge potential, with its high profile location in a dense work population." GoodLife invested $400,000 and the facility is one of the firm's most financially successful clubs with a membership of 3,000.

One fitness expert says; "GoodLife developed a niche underneath the well-established clubs. Patchell-Evans runs a professional organization and he has a well-honed management style that includes business and financial acumen. The old style clubs were run by squash players or golfers." One example was the innovative client billing system. While most fitness clubs demanded an up-front annual fee, Patchell-Evans debited monthly membership fees ranging from $30 to $50. Members like the system because it eliminates the needs for large up-front payments and it stabilizes cash flow for GoodLife, which is attractive to lenders and investors.

The key to any fitness club's success is attracting and keeping members. At GoodLife it starts with the staff. Some 75% of its 1,200 employees hold kinesiology or physical education degrees. In addition to competitive salaries, staff benefit from ongoing training—GoodLife's annual education and training budget exceeds $2.4 million—and recognition for individual achievement, such as a weekly top performer's list. "Good staff retention leads to good membership retention," says Jane Riddell. "Members don't have a relationship with a treadmill or a whirlpool. They have a relationship with the staff." That commitment to human resources gives GoodLife an edge, says the industry expert. "GoodLife has good equipment, but they also have a very proactive staff with an attitude that says they want to help you out. The club's employee training program is probably more extensive than any other in the industry. It's difficult for an independent operator to compete with this."

In 1998 GoodLife was recognized for its mandate to provide leading edge programs. The U.S.-based International Dance Exercise Association named the club's fitness director, Maureen Hagen, Program Director of the Year for her creative programming and leadership abilities. Hagen's innovations include Newbody, a low-impact, cardiovascular conditioning class designed for both fit and "underactive" participants.

Programming and services are also tailored to fit the demographics of each club. Some 70% of members are women, reflecting the club's focus on aerobics programs, to which women tend to gravitate. To ensure that women enjoy a high comfort level, GoodLife designated more than a dozen clubs for women only, where they are provided with such services as daycare, tanning facilities, and individual change rooms. GoodLife was one of the first clubs to develop the trend to women-only sections and clubs. As an example, GoodLife recently spent $500,000 upgrading the facility and equipment of a women's club in Cambridge, Ontario.

This formula to exceed customers' expectations is the foundation for GoodLife's aggressive growth plans for the future. Two trends will help the growth; industry consolidation, where GoodLife has achieved a critical mass, and an expanding market, where the number of people who will work out in clubs will increase substantially because the baby boomers want to stay in shape.

A challenge for Patchell-Evans is finding staff to keep pace with growth. "There was a time," he says, "when we had a bigger pool of people waiting for the next manager's job." To that end he says GoodLife will focus on giving staff the skills and knowledge they need to get to a higher level within the firm. "Staying on the cutting edge of the industry is a challenge, but it's also a passion for me," says Patchell-Evans. "Running a business is like a sport—you're driven to go fast, go hard, and find the ways you can do it better."

Excerpts from Louise Dearden, "Muscle Mania," *Profit*, May 1999, 46–49.

Fletcher Motors Ltd.

Christopher H. Lovelock

Viewed from Queen's Avenue, the Fletcher Motors dealership presented a festive sight. Strings of triangular pennants in red and white fluttered gaily in the late afternoon breeze. Rows of new-model cars gleamed and winked in the sunlight. Geraniums graced the flowerbeds outside the showroom entrance. A huge rotating sign at the corner of Queen's Avenue and Highway 23 sported the Ford logo and identified the business as Fletcher Motors Ltd. Banners below urged "Let's Make a Deal!"

Inside the handsome, high-ceilinged showroom, three new-model Fords were on display—a dark-blue minivan, a red convertible, and a metallic blue SUV. Each vehicle was polished to a high sheen. Two groups of customers were chatting with salespeople, and a young couple sat in the driver's seat of the SUV studying the controls.

Upstairs in the comfortably furnished general manager's office, Gail Fletcher finished running another spreadsheet analysis on her personal computer. She felt tired and depressed. Her father, David Fletcher, had died four weeks earlier at the age of 56 of a sudden heart attack. As executor of his estate, the bank had asked her to temporarily assume the position of general manager of the dealership. The only visible changes that she had made to her father's office were installing the computer and printer, but she had been very busy analyzing the current position of the business.

Gail did not like the look of the numbers on the printout. Fletcher Motors' (FM) financial situation had been deteriorating for 18 months, and it had been running in the red for the first half of the current year. Sales of new cars had declined, reflecting higher unemployment and a turndown in the provincial economy. Margins had been squeezed by promotions and other efforts to move new cars off the lot. Industry forecasts of future sales were discouraging, and so were her own financial projections for FM's sales department. Service revenues, which were below average for a dealership of this size, had also declined, although the service department still made a small surplus.

Had she made a mistake last week, Gail wondered, in turning down George Playter's offer to buy the business? It was true that the price offered had been substantially below the offer from George that her father had rejected two years earlier, but the business had been more profitable then.

THE FLETCHER FAMILY

David Fletcher had purchased a small Ford dealership in 1971, renamed it Fletcher Motors Ltd., and built it up to become one of the best known in the metropolitan area. Six years later, he borrowed heavily to purchase the current site at a major suburban intersection, in an area of the city with many new housing developments.

There had been a dealership on the site, but the buildings were 30 years old. David had retained the service and repair bays, but torn down the showroom in front of them and replaced it with an attractive modern facility, which was substantially larger than the old one.

Everybody had seemed to know David Fletcher. He had been a consummate showman and entrepreneur, appearing in his own radio and television commercials and active in community affairs. His approach to car sales had emphasized promotions, discounts, and deals in order to maintain volume. He was never happier than when making a sale.

Gail Fletcher, aged 28, was the eldest of David and Judith Fletcher's three daughters. After obtaining a Bachelor's degree in economics, she had gone on to take an M.B.A. degree and had then embarked on a career in health-care management. She was married to Dr. Fransico Forlippa, a surgeon at St. Michael's Hospital. Her 20-year-old sisters, twins Angela and Marilyn, were in their second year at university and lived with their mother.

While at university, Gail had worked part-time in her father's business on secretarial and bookkeeping tasks, and also as a service writer in the service department; she was quite familiar with the operations of the dealership. At business school, she had decided on a career in health-care management. After graduation, she had worked as the executive assistant to the president of St. Michael's, a large teaching hospital. Two years later, she joined Heritage Hospitals, a large multi-hospital facility that also provided long-term care, as assistant director of marketing—a position she had now held for almost three years. Her responsibilities included designing new services, handling complaints, doing market research, and introducing an innovative daycare program for hospital employees and neighbourhood residents.

Gail's employer had given her a six-week leave of absence to put her father's affairs in order. She doubted that she could extend that leave much beyond the two weeks still remaining. Neither she nor other family members were interested in making a career of running the dealership. However, she was prepared to take time out from her health-care career to work on a turnaround if that seemed a viable proposition. She had been successful in her present job and believed it would not be difficult to find another health management position in the future.

THE DEALERSHIP

Like other car dealerships, FM operated both sales and service departments, often referred to in the trade as "front end" and "back end," respectively. However, FM did not have a body shop for repairing damaged bodywork. Both new and used vehicles were sold, since a high proportion of new-car and van purchases involved trading in the purchaser's existing vehicle. FM would also buy low-mileage used Ford cars at auction for resale. Purchasers who decided that they could not afford a new car would often buy a "pre-owned" vehicle instead, while shoppers who came in looking for a used car could sometimes be persuaded to buy a new one.

The front end of the dealership employed a sales manager, seven salespeople, an office manager, and a secretary. One of the salespeople had given notice and would be leaving at the end of the following week. The service department, when fully staffed, consisted of a service manager, a parts supervisor, nine mechanics, and two service writers. The Fletcher twins often worked part-time as service writers, filling in at busy periods, when one of the other writers was sick or on vacation, or when—as currently—there was an unfilled vacancy. The job entailed scheduling appointments for repairs and maintenance, writing up each work order, calling customers with repair estimates, and assisting customers when they returned to pick up the cars and pay for the work that had been done.

Gail knew from her own experience as a service writer that it could be a stressful job. Few people liked to be without their car, even for a day. When a car broke down or there were problems, the owner was often nervous about how long it would take to get it fixed and, if the warranty had expired, how much the labour and parts would cost. Customers could be quite unforgiving when a problem was not fixed completely on the first attempt and they had to return their vehicle for further work.

Major mechanical failures were usually not difficult to repair, although the parts replacement costs might be expensive. It was often the "little" things like water leaks and wiring problems that were the hardest to diagnose and correct, and it might be necessary for the customer to return two or three times before such a problem was resolved. In these situations, parts and materials costs were relatively low, but labour costs mounted up quickly, being charged out at $75 an hour. Customers could often be quite abusive, yelling at service writers over the phone or arguing with service writers, mechanics, and the service manager in person.

Turnover in the service writer job was high, which was one reason why Gail—and, more recently, her sisters—had often been pressed into service by their father to "hold the fort," as he described it. More than once she had seen an exasperated service writer snap back at a complaining customer or hang up on one who was being abusive over the telephone. Angela and Marilyn were currently taking turns covering the vacant position, but there were times when both of them had classes and the dealership had only one service writer on duty.

By national standards, FM was a medium-sized dealership, selling around 1,100 cars a year, equally divided between new and used vehicles. In the most recent year, its revenues totalled $23.1 million from new and used car sales and $2.51 million from service (including parts)—down from $26.5 million and $3.12 million, respectively, in the previous year. Although the unit value of car sales was high, the margins were quite low. The reverse was true for service. Industry guidelines suggested that the contribution margin (known as the departmental selling gross) from car sales should be about 5.5 percent of sales revenues, and from service around 25 percent of revenues. In a typical dealership, 60 percent of the selling gross came from sales and 40 percent from service. The selling gross was then applied to fixed expenses, such as administrative salaries, rent or mortgage payments, and utilities.

For the most recent 12 months at FM, Gail had determined that the selling gross figures were 4.6 percent and 24 percent, respectively, both of them lower than in the previous year and insufficient to cover the dealership's fixed expenses. Her father had made no mention of financial difficulties, and she had been shocked to learn from the bank that FM had been two months behind in mortgage payments on the property. Further analysis showed that accounts payable had also risen sharply in the previous six months. Fortunately, the dealership held a large insurance policy on David's life, and the proceeds had been more than sufficient to bring mortgage payments up to date and pay down all overdue accounts.

The opportunities for expanding new-car sales did not appear promising, given the state of the economy. However, recent promotional incentives had reduced the inventory to manageable levels. From discussion with James Gable, FM's sales manager, Gail had concluded that costs could be reduced by not replacing the departing sales rep, maintaining inventory at somewhat lower levels, and trying to make more efficient use of advertising and promotion. Although James did not have David Fletcher's exuberant personality, he had been FM's leading sales rep before being promoted and had shown strong managerial capabilities in his current position.

As she reviewed the figures for the service department, Gail wondered what potential might exist for improving its sales volume and selling gross. Her father had never been very interested in the parts and service business, seeing it simply as a necessary adjunct of the dealership. "Customers always seem to be miserable back there," he had once remarked to her. "But here in the front end, everybody's happy when someone buys a new car." The service facility was not easily visible from the main highway, being hidden behind the showroom. The building was old and greasy, although the equipment was modern and well maintained.

Customers were required to bring cars in for servicing before 8:30 a.m. After parking their cars, customers entered the service building by a side door and waited their turn to see the service writers, who occupied a cramped room with peeling paint and an interior window overlooking the service bays. Customers stood while work orders for their cars were written up by hand on large sheets. Ringing telephones frequently interrupted the process. Filing cabinets containing customer records and other documents lined the far wall of the room.

If the work were of a routine nature, such as an oil change or tune-up, customers were given an estimate immediately. For more complex jobs, they would be called with an estimate later in the morning once the car had been examined. Customers were required to pick up their cars by 6:00 p.m. on the day the work was completed. On several occasions Gail had urged her father to computerize the service work order process, but he had never acted on her suggestions.

The service manager, Marshall Heyer, who was in his early fifties, had held the position since FM had opened at its current location. The Fletcher family considered him to be technically skilled, and he managed the mechanics effectively. However, his manner with customers could be gruff and argumentative.

CUSTOMER SURVEY RESULTS

Another set of data that Gail had studied carefully were the results of the customer satisfaction surveys that were mailed to the dealership monthly by a research firm retained by Ford Canada.

Purchasers of all new Ford cars were sent a questionnaire by mail within 30 days of making the purchase and asked to use a five-point scale to rate their satisfaction with the dealership sales department, vehicle preparation, and the characteristics of the vehicle itself. The questionnaire asked how likely the purchaser would be to recommend the dealership, the salesperson, and the manufacturer to someone else. Other questions asked if the customers had been introduced to the dealer's service department and been given explanations on what to do if their car needed service. Finally, there were some classification questions relating to customer demographics.

In the 30-day survey of new purchasers, Fletcher Motors achieved better than average ratings on most dimensions. One finding that puzzled Gail was that almost 90 percent of respondents answered "yes" when asked if someone from Fletcher had explained what to do if they needed service, but less than a third said that they had been introduced to someone in the service department. She resolved to ask James Gable about this discrepancy.

A second survey was sent to the new-car purchasers nine months after they had bought their cars. This questionnaire began by asking about satisfaction with the vehicle and then asked customers if they had taken their vehicle to the selling dealer for service of any kind. If so, respondents were then asked to rate the service department on 14 different attributes—ranging from the attitudes of service personnel to the quality of the work performed—and then to rate their overall satisfaction with service from the dealer.

Customers were also asked about where they would go in the future for maintenance, service, minor mechanical and electrical repairs, major repairs in those same categories, and bodywork. The options listed for service were the selling dealer, another Ford dealer, "some other place," or "do-it-yourself." Finally, there were questions about overall satisfaction with the dealer sales department and the dealership in general, as well as the likelihood of their purchasing another Ford product and buying it from the same dealership.

Dealers received monthly reports summarizing customer ratings of their dealership for the most recent month and for several previous months. To provide a comparison with how other Ford dealerships performed, the reports also included regional and national rating averages. After analysis, completed questionnaires were returned to the dealership; since these included each customer's name, a dealer could see which customers were satisfied and which were not.

The nine-month survey findings disturbed her. Although vehicle ratings were in line with national averages, the overall level of satisfaction with service at FM was consistently low, placing it in the bottom 25 percent of all Ford dealerships.

The worst rating for service concerned promptness of writing up orders, convenience of scheduling work, convenience of service hours, and appearance of the service department. On length of time to complete the work, availability of needed parts, and quality of work done ("was it fixed right?"), FM's rating was close to the average. For interpersonal variables such as attitude of service department personnel, politeness, understanding of customer problems, and explanation of work performed, its ratings were relatively poor.

When Gail reviewed the individual questionnaires, she found that there was a wide degree of variation between customers' responses on these interpersonal variables, ranging all the way across a five-point scale from "completely satisfied" to "very dissatisfied." Curious, she had gone to the service files and examined the records for several dozen customers who had recently completed the nine-month surveys. At least part of the ratings could be explained by which service writers the customer had dealt with. Those who had been served two or more times by her sisters, for instance, gave much better ratings than those who had dealt primarily with Peter Ries, the service writer who had recently quit.

Perhaps the most worrying responses were those relating to customers' likely use of FM's service department in the future. More than half indicated that they would use another Ford dealer or "some other place" for maintenance service (such as oil change, lube, or tune-up) or for minor mechanical and electrical repairs. About 30 percent would use another source for major repairs. The rating for "overall satisfaction with selling dealer" after nine months was below average, and the customers' likelihood of purchasing from the same dealership again was a full point below that of buying another Ford product.

AN UNWELCOME DISTURBANCE

Gail pushed aside the spreadsheets she had printed out and turned off the computer. It was time to go home for dinner. She saw the options for the dealership as basically twofold: either prepare the business for an early sale at what would amount to a distress price, or take a year or two to try to turn it around financially. In the latter instance, if the turnaround succeeded the business could be sold at a higher price than it currently commanded, or the family could install a general manager to run the dealership for them.

George Playter, owner of a Lincoln-Mercury dealership about two kilometres away, had offered to buy FM for a price that represented a fair valuation of the net assets, according to FM's accountants, plus $125,000 in goodwill. However, the rule of thumb when the auto industry was enjoying good times was that goodwill should be valued at $1,000 per vehicle sold each year.

As Gail left her office, she spotted the sales manager coming up the stairs leading from the showroom floor. "James," she said, "I've got a question for you."

"Fire away," replied the sales manager.

"I've been looking at the customer satisfaction surveys. Why aren't our sales reps introducing new customers to the folks in the service department? It's supposedly part of our sales protocol, but it only seems to be happening about one-third of the time."

James Gable shuffled his feet. "Well, Gail, basically I leave it to their discretion. We tell them about service, of course, but some of the guys on the floor feel a bit uncomfortable taking folks over to the service bays after they've been in here. It's quite a contrast, if you know what I mean."

Suddenly, the sound of shouting arose from the floor below. A man about 40, wearing a windbreaker and jeans, was standing in the doorway yelling at Roy, one of the salespeople. Gail and James could catch snatches of what he was saying, in between various obscenities: "... three visits ... still not fixed right ... service stinks ... who's in charge here?" Everybody else in the showroom had stopped what they were doing and had turned to look at the angry man.

James looked at his young employer and rolled his eyes. "If there was something your dad couldn't stand, it was guys like that, yelling and screaming in the showroom and asking for the boss. David would go hide out in his office! Don't worry, though, Roy'll take care of the fellow and get him out of here. What a jerk!"

"No," said Gail, "I'll deal with him. One thing I've learned from working at St. Michael's is that you don't let people yell about their problems in front of everybody else. You take them off somewhere, calm them down, and find out what's bugging them."

She stepped quickly down the stairs, wondering to herself, *What else have I learned in health care that I can apply to this business?*

Condomania:
Marketing Safer Sex

Moya D. Brown,
Darren W. Dahl,
Gerald J. Gorn, and
Charles B. Weinberg

Alicia Wagner finished reading a research report by the Fowler Research Group entitled "Young Adults and CONDOMANIA" just as she started to drink her third coffee on a sunny Friday morning. Helping to distribute free condom packs at bars the previous night had taken a toll on Alicia, a community health education consultant and director of the Vancouver Health Department's Condomania project. The late night behind her, Alicia was responsible for creating a preliminary outline for the seventh campaign in the Condomania series. She was to present her recommendations for this seventh Condomania program at a meeting slated for Monday at 10:30 a.m.

Alicia had been involved with the Condomania program since its inception more than three years ago. As Condomania Chairperson, Alicia headed the Condomania programming committee, which was directly responsible for planning and implementing each of the Condomania campaigns. The committee consisted of a chairperson, the volunteer coordinator, the creativity coordinator, a program material coordinator, and a media coordination specialist. The committee met every two weeks to plan and discuss initiatives particular to upcoming Condomania campaigns.

After reading the Fowler Research Group's report, Alicia became quite concerned about the future direction of Condomania and the advertising approaches employed. At times, she felt that "selling sexual health in the context of AIDS was almost an impossible task." Condomania organizers were only able to offer the target audience the possibility of disease prevention, which might "not be a saleable product that the target audience was interested in buying," especially considering that few people really liked using condoms in the first place. Recent figures had shown a dramatic increase in the incidence of HIV/AIDS among young heterosexuals, despite attempts by public health units and others to curb this growth through preventive education.

As the sixth and most recent of the semi-annual campaigns had achieved only limited success, Alicia and members of the committee wondered if a new focus was necessary. Previous campaigns had primarily targeted young heterosexual women between the ages of 19 and 25 who lived in the Vancouver metropolitan area. In each previous campaign, a media approach involving bus advertising had been used to increase both the awareness and acceptance of condom usage. Perhaps the advertising message that Condomania had been using was beginning to wear out. Or maybe the media chosen were no longer appropriate. Some committee members felt that more emphasis should be placed on young males. Alicia also remembered looming funding issues—who would the future funding sources be, how could she secure these funds, and for what time period could they be secured?

Alicia knew she had to address these concerns before she presented a tentative outline for campaign seven at the next committee meeting. The transmission of HIV/AIDS to young adults was an escalating, challenging problem with no definite cure in sight. As she pondered these issues, Alicia thought over the current situation and began to recount the history of Condomania (see Exhibits 1 and 2).

BACKGROUND

By the end of 1996, nearly 30 million people worldwide tested positive for the human immunodeficiency virus (HIV), of whom almost 30 percent had AIDS. In North America alone, more than 1 million individuals were infected with HIV. The majority of these infections were sexually transmitted. Furthermore, an estimated 12 million North Americans suffered from a sexually transmitted disease (STD) each year, resulting in serious morbidity for many thousands of adults and children. In the U.S., approximately 25 percent of people had at least one STD by age 21.[1]

In the early and mid-eighties, public health programs battled the growth and development of STDs through information programs, one-on-one counselling, and educational efforts. A typical message presented by most of these approaches was "know the facts about HIV/STD transmission and prevent infection." An educated and knowledgeable public was thought to be the most effective way to reduce the growth in HIV infections and other STDs.

Research conducted in the late eighties indicated that most North Americans had developed a high degree of knowledge about STDs and their prevention, but many were not using this knowledge. Preventive education and preventive behaviour seemed to be two separate entities. Though people knew the importance of safe sex, most individuals were not practising it, at least not all the time.

---

[1] Douglas Kirby and Ralph DiClemente, "School-Based Interventions to Prevent Unprotected Sex and HIV among Adolescents," in Ralph J. DiClemente and John L. Peterson, eds., *Preventing AIDS: Theories and Methods of Behavioral Interventions* (New York: Plenum Press, 1994), 118.

Faced with these research findings, public health departments searched for new and more effective approaches to reducing HIV/STD transmission. One potentially promising avenue was a more comprehensive social marketing approach. No-smoking campaigns, seatbelt safety crusades, and dental hygiene programs had all successfully implemented social marketing principles in formulating and implementing broad-based behavioural change programs.[2] In each of these areas the use of marketing principles had helped health departments to identify target audiences, create effective messages, use an appropriate communications medium, and evaluate the entire process.

Increased Incidence of AIDS

Like many North American cities, HIV infection was first identified in Vancouver, B.C. in the early eighties. At that time, Vancouver was a rapidly growing city with a metropolitan population of approximately 1.6 million people.[3] The incidence of HIV infection grew dramatically with each passing year, especially among the homosexual community, due in part to a general ignorance about HIV and its transmission.

By the late eighties, the growth in infection had subsided within the Vancouver homosexual community, mainly due to a remarkable increase in condom usage. Unfortunately, an increasing number of heterosexuals, especially young women in their early childbearing years, were now being infected with HIV. These young females were being infected through vaginal intercourse rather than intravenous drug use, which was becoming a common additional method of HIV transmission in the United States. During the past year, 270 new AIDS cases had been reported in British Columbia and 688 people had tested positive for HIV for the first time (Health Canada, 1994).

This increase in HIV among young women, along with a concern over the lack of public awareness of HIV risk for women, prompted informal discussions between the Vancouver Health Department and the Women and AIDS Project. Now defunct, the Women and AIDS Project was a local AIDS service organization focusing on HIV/AIDS prevention and women.

THE "CONDOMANIA" PROGRAM—CAMPAIGNS 1 TO 5

The "Vancouver Condom Awareness Program," known as Condomania, was born five years ago out of the interaction between the Vancouver Health Department and the Women and AIDS Project. Rather than directly working on actual condom usage behaviour, this program attempted to use a social marketing approach to change the surrounding environment for this product, to increase its salience in the community, and to change how people perceive condoms. To reach a broad audience of young people, the program employed several media forms over limited periods of time (usually one to two months in duration) that conveyed an informative and provocative message. The committee believed that if the

---

[2.] Gallagher, Katherine and Charles B. Weinberg (1991), "Coping with Success: New Challenges for Nonprofit Marketing," *Sloan Management Review*, (Fall), 27–42.

[3.] Much of the growth has been fuelled by Canadians moving to British Columbia and by Asian immigration. About 16% of the metropolitan Vancouver population did not speak English as their mother tongue—approximately 44% of these people listed a Chinese language as their mother tongue (Statistics Canada, 1994).

social environment changed to become more open and accepting to public discussion of condoms and their use, individual behaviour change would follow.

The Health Department's goal was to influence behaviour via Condomania by making condoms more acceptable. The first step in influencing or changing condom use behaviour was to generate awareness among the target population. Funding was secured for a three-year project. Each year included two one-month campaigns approximately six months apart. Major components of the initial campaign and subsequent campaigns consisted of the design and production of campaign materials, advertising, focused community educa-tion, volunteer recruitment and training, and program evaluations.

Statistics from Vancouver-area blood testing (seroprevalence) studies showed that women in their early childbearing years had the highest rate of HIV infections among females.[4] This information helped Alicia identify the initial target audience for Condomania: heterosexual women between the ages of 19 and 30. Targeting these women had the twofold purpose of informing them of their risk of contracting HIV *and* educating them as to various preventive options. Since vaginal, anal, and oral intercourse put these women at risk of contracting HIV, the best preventive method (other than abstinence) would be condoms.

Alicia also felt that even though condom usage by women was to be the central element in the campaign, men also had to be included. As such, Condomania's message had to be relevant and accessible to both young females and young males. With condoms as the focus, the primary target group for campaigns one through three was women aged 19–30, and the secondary target was young men in the same age group. In campaign four, men aged 19–24 became the primary target, because data revealed little or no behaviour change in this segment. The target age group remained the same for campaigns five and six, but females once again became the primary target.

COMMUNICATING THE MESSAGE

Communication objectives for campaigns one through six were defined as follows:

- assist in making condoms more socially acceptable as a method of maintaining sex-ual health
- encourage public discussion of sexual relationships and condom use
- create positive associations with condoms
- increase condom use among the target audience by making the use of condoms more socially comfortable

Focus Groups

Initial focus groups, conducted with members of the target audience, indicated that con-doms should be perceived as fun and that any advertising copy should "leave out the heavy message about AIDS." The Vancouver Health Department's own research on effective communication showed that fear tactics were usually ineffective, especially in cases where the audience felt powerless to change their behaviour; however, humour readily increases

---

[4.] Young females aged 15 to 19 have the highest rates of the STDs gonorrhea and chlamydia of any age group (Health Canada, 1997).

one's ability to integrate and retain new information. Consequently, Alicia thought that a humorous message combined with concrete, factual information would be the most effective approach. Alicia said the name Condomania was chosen to "reflect a fun and light-hearted tone and to move away from a disease orientation because [the] target audience did not identify with disease prevention."

Advertising

Condomania organizers wanted to reach as many people in the target audience as possible and as such chose advertising as the vehicle to achieve this goal. Based on a review of other public campaigns with a focus on AIDS prevention, the committee concluded that billboards, bus interiors, and bus shelters would be the most effective communication vehicles. In reaching this decision, Alicia also considered the costs and reach associated with each promotional alternative.

In the first campaign, seven billboards, ten bus shelters, and 500 interior bus advertisements were used. The total cost of this campaign was $52,834. After the first campaign, it was concluded that for the expense of renting billboard and bus shelter space and considering the printing costs, too little exposure was achieved.

Subsequent campaigns used advertising only on the exterior and interior of local buses. Consultations with advertisers gave more clarity as to how to reach the target audience; for example, more men drive cars and are more apt to see exterior advertising (e.g., billboards), while more women ride buses. Advertising was purchased on the outside of 55 local buses for the second campaign. The transit advertising company then donated 414 interior spaces. These changes improved cost effectiveness, led to an increase in the number of advertising spaces, and enhanced visibility. Bus advertising was used for all subsequent campaigns in addition to various other vehicles, such as washroom posters and bar coasters.

One-on-One Approach

In addition to the public campaign, Alicia believed it was necessary to use a more personal one-on-one approach to address the specific issues of condom use. Each one-month campaign was two-pronged: mass public promotion using advertising and media coverage, and a condom giveaway using trained volunteers to contact their peers at local bars, nightclubs, concerts, pool halls, and sports events.

This peer-oriented approach was thought to be more credible than using health-care professionals. Volunteers were obtained from a variety of sources including local AIDS service organizations, university and community colleges, and from the volunteer base of the Vancouver Health Department. All volunteers were educated about HIV/STD transmission, condom usage, and the purpose of Condomania. Volunteers wore special "Condomania" shirts so that they could readily be identified as part of the campaign. Finding volunteers for the initial campaign was difficult, but recruitment in all subsequent campaigns had been easier. Many people were repeat volunteers and the popularity of Condomania attracted new people to the program.

Volunteer recognition was an important component of the program. After each campaign Condomania organizers held a dinner for volunteers at which they discussed and informally evaluated the campaign. Volunteer reports centred on the challenge of approaching people. However, many of the volunteers indicated that distributing condom packets was relatively easy in bar and nightclub environments.

Specially designed packets containing a major brand of lubricated condom, a 3cc packet of personal lubricant, and a cartoon strip with instructions were distributed directly to individuals in the target audience. Distribution of the condom packets was conducted at bars and nightclubs frequented by the target population. Posters, coasters, and ideas for campaign-related activities were also provided to bar and nightclub management.

Approval Difficulties

Gaining design acceptance from the transit company was no easy task. Alicia had to submit the designs for review because condoms, and the issue of AIDS in general, were perceived by the transit company to be controversial. An educational presentation was prepared in order to gain acceptance of the messages from transit decision makers. They insisted upon changes during campaigns one and two, but none of these appeared to detract from the original message. Despite initial concerns about negative public reaction, only three complaints were received during the first campaign; hardly any were reported over the course of subsequent campaigns.

Although bar owners were originally reluctant to allow Condomania to distribute sample packets of condoms in their bars, personal meetings helped to rectify the situation. Many proprietors were afraid of intruding in patrons' private lives and scaring them with a serious AIDS message. This fear made educating the bar managers during the initial meeting a primary objective of focused community education. Enlisting the participation of bars was much easier in campaigns two to six because of the success of the initial campaign.

Press Kits and Media Exposure

Each campaign also included a press kit to foster media exposure. Contained in the kits were a press release, background information, samples of the condom packets, and the campaign poster. Kits were marketed differently for each campaign in order to attract attention. Follow-up phone calls were made to radio stations, TV stations, and newspapers to set up appointments for interviews and to arrange for broadcast coverage in the bars.

According to Alicia, "the issues we wanted to promote had to be tangible, slightly sensational, and people-oriented—a good formula for television, radio and print stories."

The first campaign received extensive media exposure. All major radio and television stations and newspapers picked up the story, and only two stories (out of about 30) were negative. When the second and subsequent campaigns were implemented, the program was no longer novel and Condomania received considerably less coverage. Alicia considered hiring a celebrity to participate in bar events and act as a media spokesperson to combat declining coverage, but time and budget constraints prevented this.

Campaign Assessment

The final element of each Condomania program was the campaign evaluation. Individual campaign evaluations proved to be somewhat challenging since behaviour change was difficult to measure within a short time span. To measure and understand attitude and behaviour change, serious personal questions must be asked that often pose complex methodological problems. While exposure to the campaign could be readily measured for many media, it is next to impossible to gauge an increase in the incidence of condom use as a result of one campaign. These issues were critical, since funding of programs like Condomania often depended on fairly immediate results.

Both quantitative and qualitative approaches were used to acquire a baseline measure of HIV transmission and prevention knowledge before the campaign began, to evaluate the impact of the campaign, and to assess the level of acceptance of condoms as a form of STD prevention. A randomized pre-/post-test telephone survey was conducted with the target group, and a series of in-depth interviews were held with bar patrons after the first campaign. The telephone survey indicated a high pre-test level of knowledge and awareness of HIV transmission, although a self-serving, biased understanding of the risk associated with "risk group" (underestimating your risk) was common, as was the belief that HIV could be spread by food handlers. Alarmingly, women were identified by respondents as a low-risk group. In the post-test, of the relatively small number of people who could recall seeing the outdoor promotion only 25 percent retained the primary message. The in-depth interviews gave insight as to the attitudes behind low condom use. According to Alicia, "a belief in the existence of high and low risk groups, with the person classifying themselves in the low risk group, and the belief in 'trusting' one's partner appear to create the illusion of little or no risk." Despite some disappointing results, evaluations showed campaign one and subsequent campaigns had been somewhat effective.

Funding Issues

Inconsistent funding had been a recurrent problem for the Condomania program. Lack of funding resulted in the sixth campaign having to be pushed into the fourth year. Many times, Condomania organizers had to limit their programs due to budget constraints. This inconsistency in funding had made it difficult to plan ahead.

Alicia often considered the possibility of seeking funding outside of the government grant that Condomania received. She also knew that the ability to secure outside funding might be hampered by a number of constraints. The fact that the Condomania program was part of a municipal health department ensured that support could not be sought from any "unhealthy" sources. Corporate support from a beer company, for example, would definitely be out of the question. A possible source of support would be condom manufacturers, but the Condomania program had adopted a policy that no one specific brand of condom should be promoted.[5] Alicia wondered if this policy should be re-evaluated.

In formulating recommendations about possible new promotional strategies, Alicia reviewed information from campaigns one through six. Despite many similarities among the campaigns, there were also differences that could potentially affect her promotional strategy for the seventh campaign. To understand Condomania's present situation, Alicia spent more time focusing on the most recent (sixth) campaign.

[5.] However, Condomania was willing to accept free samples of condom brands that met government-regulated safety standards and achieved high scores on consumer tests (e.g., in *Consumer Reports*).

THE SIXTH CAMPAIGN

The sixth Condomania campaign was conducted over a four-week period during May and June. The goal was to provide a supportive message to the female target audience that would reinforce the importance of communicating with your partner, shared responsibility, social acceptability of condoms, and having positive self-esteem. The theme "You're the Most Important Reason for Using Condoms" was developed to achieve these objectives. The budget contained in Exhibit 3 outlines the resource allocations. These allocations were similar to those of previous campaign initiatives.

The advertising copy found on the bus posters highlighted the campaign theme and pictured a closeup of a female face (see Exhibit 1). The poster also featured a statistical insight on the transmission and susceptibility of STDs (e.g., "...70% of women and 50% of men with certain STDs have no symptoms"). Transit advertising was located both on the interior and exterior of the bus, and was maintained at the same advertising weight as in the previous Condomania campaigns.

The free condom packet distribution was again conducted in the bar/nightclub environment, but to reach a wider audience this campaign's packets were also distributed at fitness clubs, university campus cafeterias, outdoor parks, and Vancouver pharmacies.[6] In the pharmacy, condom packets were distributed to females between the ages of 19 and 25 when they filled their birth control prescriptions. Pharmacies were included in this community distribution as a direct means of reaching young women and to combat the widely held myth that birth control pills protect against STDs.

A total of 14,700 condom packets were distributed during the campaign. Of these, 4,800 were distributed in bars and nightclubs and 3,800 in the pharmacies.

Press coverage for the campaign was relatively successful. Coverage was achieved by 12 different media entities including newspaper, radio, and TV. However, this exposure level was down from previous campaigns. Coverage had typically been attained from 17 different media entities.

Evaluation of the campaign included a random telephone survey, questionnaires at participating venues, and the anecdotal reports of the volunteers. The phone survey sought to assess memorability and impact of the bus advertising. Results indicated that females felt the advertising "gave me a reason to use condoms" and "it gets you to think condoms are good for you." Males also scored fairly high on these statements, but were noticeably lower in scoring than females. Disturbingly, the survey also revealed that the campaign theme and posters had the lowest memorability score of all of the Condomania campaigns, and more negative comments were received than in any other campaign.

The evaluation questionnaires sent to participating venues provided mainly positive comments that reflected an appreciation of having participated in the program. All venues indicated they were willing to be part of Condomania again.

Following the sixth campaign, Alicia and her committee commissioned the Fowler Research Group to conduct an evaluation of all the Condomania campaigns, up to and including the sixth campaign (see Exhibits 4 and 5). The intent was to assess the cumulative impact of Condomania on the target audience's attitudes and behaviours. Telephone interviews were conducted with 324 young adults, 19 to 24 years of age. The sample consisted of a control group—those who had never seen the campaign—and a test group of people who

---

6. Some bar managers dropped the program because patrons were littering the establishments with inflated condoms.

had seen at least two campaigns. Differences in attitudes and behaviours were based on a comparison of these two groups. High awareness among the targeted audiences of the importance of proper condom usage, HIV/STD transmission, and Condomania in general pointed to Condomania's positive impact. While there were no differences in the percentage agreeing by respondent's age (within groups from 19 to 24 years of age), those for whom English was not their mother tongue were somewhat less likely to agree with some of the statements in the survey. For example, 85 percent of those for whom English was the mother tongue (n=241) agreed strongly that "Today, condoms are a must," but only 70 percent of those for whom English was not the mother tongue (n=83) agreed strongly with the same statement.

The Condomania program was scheduled to conclude with the sixth campaign. However, an application for additional funding to continue the program was submitted to the Vancouver Health Department. While additional funding was secured at the same level as previous projects, it was sufficient for only two more campaigns. Alicia was very disappointed because she had hoped for a longer-term commitment—the availability of future funding was uncertain at best.

THE COMMITTEE

At the last committee meeting, each member clearly stated his or her opinions about Condomania's future. Jane Schultz, the Media Coordination Specialist, argued that other promotional vehicles should be considered. She expressed the opinion that the traditional campaign format had become stale and too repetitive. Jane noted that all six of the previous campaigns had used bus advertising as the primary promotional medium, and that other vehicles such as print and radio had been used only indirectly, and not for advertising Condomania specifically. She advocated making immediate changes to the promotional strategy, fearing that repetition may now be producing wearout among the current target population. Alicia worried too that conducting a seventh campaign that paralleled the previous efforts would be redundant and provide little in the way of incremental gains in condom usage and awareness.

Jane Schultz was also concerned that the focused community education approach was being taken for granted. The free condom packets had become expected by the young female targets and the bar/nightclub managers. In contrast, the Volunteer Coordinator, Vanessa Brown, held a different view. She felt that Condomania had become a success through these strategies and that there was no need to change the program. Tampering with an effective campaign would be too risky given the social importance and success of Condomania. Moreover, she felt the basic message had to be continuously reinforced over time. Other committee members felt that behavioural change in the current primary target group had reached a plateau.

Changing the Target

Alicia wondered if campaign resources would be better used by targeting a different segment. While attitudes toward condoms and their regular use appeared to have become more positive in women, little change had been documented in men. For perspective, Exhibit 4 shows that 79 percent of women who had seen Condomania (67 percent of those who had not) strongly agreed that one should always use condoms the first time they have sex with a new partner, compared to only 65 percent of men who had seen the campaign (72 percent for men who had not seen it). Furthermore, focus groups with males aged 19–30 demonstrated a good level of knowledge, but young men did not perceive condoms as a necessity (see Exhibit 6). Alicia thought that men were perhaps being left out of the "sexual health picture."

As she gave the situation further consideration, Alicia thought that changing the targeted age group could be advantageous. Focusing the campaign on young high-school teens might help to address the problem before or as they became sexually active.[7] Alicia had reminded the committee on several occasions that the program was initially developed to address the problems of young female adults, but she also wondered if the traditional target was still appropriate.

Finally, Alicia wondered if the cartoon approach to communicating the campaign's message was still viable, especially if the decision was made to change the target segment. Susan Wong, the Program Material Coordinator, pointed out that Fowler Group research showed that both the humorous tone and focused community distribution of condoms were experiencing significant wearout. Advertising tone, mode of message communication, and actual condom distribution would certainly have to be re-evaluated if the target audience were changed. In all cases, Alicia realized that changing the promotional strategy could be costly. Since she had to work within a stringent budget, Alicia recognized the importance of gaining maximum reach for the lowest cost.

Using Radio

Alicia realized that many of the concerns voiced in the discussions with her committee were attributable to the experiences and ideas introduced during the past few campaigns. She had tried to encourage innovative ideas and new approaches throughout the program, and had allocated funds to explore them. One of these endeavours was the development of 30-second public service announcements (PSAs) to be aired on radio. The PSAs were developed to grab attention with a humorous skit about condom use.

The following is one of the PSAs, titled *"It Beats the Movies."*

Scene 1: Movie theatre

Young Man: Two tickets, please.

Ticket Taker: That'll be $22.

Scene 2: Restaurant. (Ambient restaurant noises)

Waiter: Anything else, coffee, dessert?

Young Man: Just the bill, please.

Waiter: Here you are, sir.

Young Man: (Gulp) $73!

Announcer: With the price of an evening out getting more and more expensive, some forms of entertainment are still a great value... like having sex. Sex for 2 with a condom can cost less than $2. So even if you make love 3 or 4 times a night, it's still cheaper than dinner out or a movie. But remember: use a new condom each time. Be thrifty, but don't be cheap.

---

7. According to a 1997 survey of 17-year-olds conducted by Health Canada, only 57 percent of males and 45 percent of females reported using a condom the last time they had sexual intercourse. Approximately 50 percent of Canadian 17-year-olds have had sexual intercourse (*Globe and Mail*, February 15, 1997, p. A8).

Fourteen radio stations said they would broadcast the announcement, but in the end only three radio stations aired it. The lack of airtime was likely due to two factors. The content was perceived to be controversial, and radio stations felt their audience would react negatively to the PSAs. As well, radio stations had been bombarded over the past decade by various health and social cause agencies wishing to have their messages played over the public airwaves. Nevertheless, audience data indicate that radio announcements are a viable advertising medium,[8] but to ensure airplay of the message advertising time would have to be purchased. (Refer to Exhibit 7 for airtime and print costs.)

A second initiative was the recent sponsorship of a focus group with males between the ages of 19 and 25. The focus group discussion provided an opportunity to identify male issues and attitudes. Research conducted in the past had focused on identifying the attitudes of females, so this provided a view of a different potential target segment. Comments from the focus group indicated a high level of awareness of the importance of condom usage. Discussion confirmed what the committee had learned in previous focus groups—that a male often perceives a female to be responsible for condom usage. For example, when asked if they had any hints about how to reach males their age and get people to use condoms, one focus group participant responded, "target towards the females... they're easier to convince." A young man stated, "people get more careless as the relationship goes on... you probably will have sex if you've been with her for a month or so." Some participants also said that not using a condom was acceptable when you are comfortable with your partner.

SPECIAL-INTEREST GROUPS

An additional concern Alicia needed to address was the sensitivity of the programs and the issues they involve. The use of condoms and the open approach to sexual interaction that Condomania encouraged was not appreciated by all members of society. During the last campaign, for example, packets were to be distributed at the local stadium during baseball games, but threats from special-interest groups resulted in the cancellation of that venue.

Further problems had occurred when bus posters had been submitted to the transit authority. In one campaign the message was censored because of the sexual innuendo in this ad: *Male:* "The longer you use condoms...," *Female:* "The longer you last...." Despite the rather bold lyrics of many popular songs (e.g., "I Want Your Sex" by George Michael), radio ads, too, were subject to close scrutiny by the radio station.

Alicia knew that in preparing for the seventh campaign the committee's decisions and planning had to be sensitive to all campaign issues. She felt that given the public importance of Condomania, being proactive in dealing with the issues was crucial. One committee member argued that maintaining a "manageable" level of public controversy would enhance the campaign's effectiveness.

THE PROPOSAL

Alicia glanced at her watch and was startled to see it was already 1:00 p.m. on Friday afternoon. The committee meeting to decide the future of Condomania was scheduled to begin in less than 72 hours. Though she had thought a lot about Condomania issues and con-

---

[8.] John Fowler, president of the Fowler Research Group, indicated that 67 percent of young adults (ages 18 to 25) listen to at least one hour of radio per day.

cerns, Alicia had yet to begin writing a tentative proposal for the seventh campaign. Regrettably, she recognized that a quick lunch and a long weekend of work awaited her.

The committee had raised important concerns and had some excellent ideas, but there was still no concrete plan in place. To some people, like Vanessa Brown, Condomania had been such a success that it seemed illogical to change its structure and strategies. On the other hand, Jane Schultz's arguments for changing the promotional strategies had merit and seemed to make sense intuitively. And what about the target audience? Condomania had been developed as a response to the lack of attention given to young women. If the target segment were to change, how and why would this be done? What tone should be used to communicate Condomania's message effectively to this target audience?

Realizing that her tentative plan had to include answers for the future, Alicia wondered how the upcoming campaigns would deal with the threat of special-interest groups who might not understand or agree with the Condomania message. More importantly, Alicia needed to identify how Condomania would survive in the long term. With monetary backing for only two more campaigns, Alicia knew the issue of fundraising would also be high on the minds of committee members.

EXHIBIT 1A	Bus Poster

EXHIBIT 1B	Sample Package

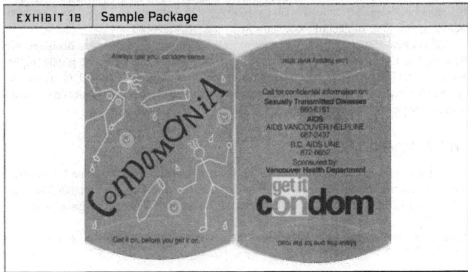

EXHIBIT 1C | Advertisement

EXHIBIT 2 | Input and Activity Measures

Campaign #	Advertising Copy	Target Audience	Dollar Budget	# of Condom Packets Dist'd	# of Paid Ads	# of Free Bus Ads	# of Participating Bars/Nightclubs	# of Volunteers
1	"Enjoy your lovelife" and "Condoms keep your love alive."	Young women & men 18-30 years, especially women	Proposed: $54,850 Actual: $52,834	13,000	12 bus shelters 500 interior bus ads 5 billboards 3,000 posters 2,000 coasters	4 spaces donated	9	40
2	Two women talking: "Remember, if he cares, he wears."	Young women & men, aged 19-30	Proposed: $51,000 Actual: $48,083	12,000 condoms 12,000 3cc Astroglide (lubricant) packets	478 interior bus ads 55 exterior bus ads 1,250 posters 4,000 condom stickers	414 spaces donated	9	40
3	Woman #1: "Boys will be boys but men will wear condoms" Woman #2: "every time."	Sexually active women & men, 19-30	Proposed: $67,512 Actual: $55,442	11,520 condoms 15,000 3cc Astroglide	2,800 washroom posters 65 exterior bus ads 267 interior bus ads 500 posters	234 interior bus ads	N/A	37
4	Guy #1: "Will she call me a jerk if I don't wear a condom? Guy #2: "She probably won't call you at all."	Men and women aged 19-24	Proposed: $48,481 Actual: $52,532	14,000	20,000 bar coasters 65 exterior bus ads 27 interior bus ads 200 posters	240 interior bus ads	15	21
5	Man: "In the heat of passion" Woman: "it's cool to wear a condom."	Women & men, aged 19-24	N/A	15,000	N/A	240	15	30
6	"You're the most important reason for using condoms."	Women, aged 19-24	Proposed: $58,500 Actual: $61,008	15,000	200 exterior bus ads 156 interior bus ads 245 posters	240	15	30

Note: In campaign 1, separate condom packages were designed for men and women. The male condom packets had the message, "In the heat of the moment … keep a cool head." The female line said, "For your pleasure … a little lubrication goes a long way."

EXHIBIT 3	Budget for Campaign 6 ("You're the most important reason")	

	PROPOSED $	ACTUAL $
Personnel		
Contractual		
Volunteer Coordinator	5,000	4,905
Creative Coordinator	3,000	1,496
Media Coordination	2,000	2,445
	10,000	8,846
Services		
Contractual		
Creative Development	7,000	8,835
Focus Group Research	0	3,638
Research Evaluation	15,000	14,525
PSA Development	0	625
	22,500	27,623
Advertising		
Contractual		
Rental of Advertising Space	8,250	6,362
on City Buses		
Materials		
Condoms	4,000	5,576
Lubricant	2,500	2,475
T-Shirts	500	421
Bus Posters	2,200	1,755
Wall Posters	1,000	862
Bar Coasters	2,500	2,078
Condom Instruction Inserts	1,000	917
Condom Packages	3,500	2,566
	17,200	16,654
Miscellaneous		
Other Expenses	1,050	1,523
TOTAL	$58,500	$61,008

EXHIBIT 4	Selected Fowler Research Data

	Females (n=163)		Males (n=161)	
	Have Seen Condomania %	Have Not Seen Condomania %	Have Seen Condomania %	Have Not Seen Condomania %
IMPORTANCE OF CONDOMS				
Agree strongly that:				
Today, condoms are a must	90	86	73	69
I always use condoms the first time I have sex with a new partner	79	67	65	72
Condoms are still necessary when you use the pill	71	63	54	61
Do *not* agree at all that:				
A condom gets in the way of good sex	54	40	27	26
The pill keeps people from getting STDs	89	81	86	75
RESPONSIBILITY FOR CONDOM USE				
Do *not* agree at all that:				
Condom usage is the responsibility of men	58	49	27	15
Condom usage is the responsibility of women	56	47	28	25
Agree strongly that:				
Condom usage is the responsibility of both partners	95	88	84	69
SOCIAL ACCEPTABILITY OF CONDOMS				
Agree strongly that:				
It is easy for me to talk about condoms with my friends	60	60	52	41
I feel comfortable talking with my partner about using a condom (of those in a relationship)	84	85	81	75
Do *not* agree at all that:				
I would be embarrassed to buy condoms	52	57	66	51
WHAT WOULD MOTIVATE CONDOM USE				
I find it easy to use condoms when...				
I'm with someone I care about	61	50	36	30
I don't know the person very well	22	22	27	31
On a one-night stand	8	16	28	26
When I consider using condoms...				
I want to protect myself from STDs	74	64	49	62
I feel caring towards my girlfriend/boyfriend	19	21	31	25
I want to satisfy my girlfriend's/boyfriend's request	–	10	11	10
I prefer *not* to use condoms because...				
It doesn't feel as good	17	25	37	41
I can't be spontaneous with lovemaking	24	23	29	15
I feel embarrassed	12	15	5	3
Don't know/no reason	28	26	17	15

EXHIBIT 5	Tracking Measures

*Q. What do you think was the main idea or the main thing
this advertising was trying to get across to you?*

UNAIDED MESSAGE COMMUNICATION

Volunteered Responses

	Campaign 6 Total Sample (n = 41) %
Practise safer sex (net mentions)	68
Use condoms	39
Practise safer sex	22
Use condoms for yourself (net mentions)	46
Protect yourself from others	29
Use condoms for yourself	12
Statistics (net mentions)	39
Beware of STDs	27

*Q. Could you please tell me what thoughts or feelings went
through your mind when you were looking at the poster?*

THOUGHTS AND FEELINGS FROM ADVERTISING

Volunteered Responses

	Campaign 6 Total Sample (n = 41) %
Catchy/like the ad (net mentions)	42
Catchy/stands out	22
You're important message (net mentions)	39
You're the most important reason/important one	20
Protect yourself against STDs	20
Statistics (net mentions)	37
Noticed/liked statistics/information	15
Shocked/surprised by statistics	15
Not catchy/don't like the ad (net mentions)	22
Not catchy/dull	12
Cartoon unprofessional/cheesy/crude	7
Geared at younger people	12

EXHIBIT 5	Tracking Measures (continued)

STYLE, MOTIVATION, RELEVANCE, AND IDENTIFICATION WITH ADVERTISING

	Average Score (+6 to +1)			
	"You're the most important reason" (n=41) Campaign 6	"In the heat of passion" (n=42) Campaign 5	"Will she call me" (n=40) Campaign 4	"Boys will be boys" (n=15)* Campaign 3
Style of Ad Scores				
Style of ad was very right for product	4.5	4.6	4.8	5.4
The ad was in very good taste	4.7	4.7	4.7	4.8
It had an appropriate tone for this topic	4.3	4.3	4.6	4.9
Motivation Scores				
The ad did not put me off using condoms	5.4	5.5	5.5	5.8
The ad made me think I should use condoms	4.7	4.7	5.0	5.1
Relevance Scores				
I did not think "who cares"	4.9	4.8	5.0	5.3
I felt the ad was relevant to me	4.4	4.6	4.1	5.0
Identification Scores				
It was aimed at people like me	3.8	4.1	3.8	4.9
Showed a situation which I could relate to	3.8	4.3	4.1	4.5
I liked the ad because it was personal and intimate	3.2	3.2	3.5	3.7

Notes: All data based on research conducted after each campaign. Scale ranges from +1 "Strongly Disagree" to +6 "Strongly Agree."

* Caution: Small sample size. Data based on 19- to 24-years-old respondents from Dec. 1992 evaluation.

EXHIBIT 6	Sample Comments from Male Focus Group

Question: Condoms—What comes to mind?

Answers: "Safe sex"

"Part of life"

"Ruins it"

"People that care"

"Wearing a condom is all about responsibility"

EXHIBIT 6	Sample Comments from Male Focus Group (continued)

Question: About condom usage?

Answers: "I hate it"

"I would rather not know about it"

"I feel fine, safer"

"It stalls the action, not natural"

"Like playing hockey with equipment on"

"Our society has made us use them because of disease"

Question: When do you decide not to use a condom?

Answers: "When it is low risk"

"After a medical test"

"When you're comfortable"

Question: How long is comfortable?

Answers: "Depends on you"

"A situation where you trust an individual, that's when you stop"

"People get more careless as the relationship goes on, it's come on let's go...I don't have anything on me...you probably will go for it if you've been with her for a month or so"

Question: Any hints about how to get people to use condoms/reach guys your age?

Answers: "Start 'em young"

"Something from the heart"

"Use everyday people"

"Need to do it in high school"

"More ads in buses...on the sides of taxis"

"Target towards females...easier to convince"

"Don't over promote it, people will get tired of it"

"Major target is women....if you're gonna sleep with him have a condom"

"If a guy our age started crying on TV about how he had AIDS, it would upset me"

Selected Group Discussion Comments (males aged 19-30):

Answers: "No one's gonna give you their true history...who cares?"

"If she sees you with one in your wallet, your chances of getting a date are pretty slim."

"As long as you're careful, and watch the women you're with, it'll be okay not to use condoms."

"It's hard to say who should suggest using a condom, if she's on the pill, I won't."

EXHIBIT 7	Print and Airtime Costs

PRINT

Publication	Rate for Black & White Ad, 4" × 5"	Circulation (Average Weekday)	Readership (Average Weekday)
The Vancouver Sun	$1,400.00	183,500	510,400
The Province	$ 860.00	156,670	498,400
The Georgia Straight	$ 468.00	100,000	498,000

The *Vancouver Sun* and *The Province* are Vancouver's two daily newspapers.

The *Georgia Straight*, a free weekly newspaper focusing on entertainment, has a wide readership.

RADIO

Radio Station	# of Listeners	# of Listeners for Evening Show, 3 p.m.-8 p.m.	Primary Listener Profile	60 seconds (cost per spot)	30 seconds (cost per spot)
99.3 The Fox	385,800	220,400	men 18-34	$ 280.00	$ 140.00
95.3 Z-FM	308,900	279,700	ages 18-34	$ 225.00	$ 150.00
101.1 CFMI	318,500	202,400	ages 24-44	$ 245.00	$ 163.00

Note: # of listeners = total audience over age 12 reached by the radio station in one week.

Kraft Canada Inc.: Kool-Aid Powdered Soft Drink

Lauren Dmytrenko
and Peggy Cunningham

It should have been a time for celebration. Kraft had just been named "Canadian Marketer of the Year" by *Marketing* magazine, and the 1998 Kool-Aid "Be Kool" summer campaign had certainly been a key step in gaining that prestigious recognition. Yet, Andrew Sneyd, Product Manager for Kool-Aid at Kraft Canada, didn't feel like celebrating when he sat down to review the latest sales figures in December 1998. Kool-Aid had been aggressively marketed in 1998, but still the sales figures were disappointing. He wondered if their current marketing strategy was appropriate for today's market. Even though Kraft had released a number of new flavours in 1998—and even a new product, Slushies—the private-label companies had continued to make market inroads. They were copying flavours and had a price advantage. With the recent grocery industry consolidation, Andrew feared they were taking control of the category. Since it was December 1998, he had to make a concrete recommendation on how to approach the 1999 season. He had to prepare for a critical meeting with Kraft's Retail Sales team regarding Kool-Aid's 1999 strategy.

PRODUCT HISTORY

Kraft Canada Inc. is one of Canada's leading food companies, marketing brands such as Kraft Dinner, Kool-Aid, Jell-O, and Post Cereals across the country.

Kool-Aid's history began in 1920, when the product was developed as a bottled soft drink syrup named Fruit Smack. The original flavours included grape, orange, raspberry, cherry, strawberry, root beer, and lemon-lime. The product Kool-Aid, as it is found in stores today, was inspired by Edwin Perkin's decision to sell concentrated beverage powder, similar to that of Jell-O, instead of offering the liquid in a bottle. The product was given the name Kool-Ade (later changed to Kool-Aid in the 1950s) and eventually General Foods purchased Perkins Products Company so that it could take a foothold in the powdered soft drink (PSD) market.

Since the 1950s, the Kool-Aid product line has expanded to include a variety of lines of sweetened, unsweetened, and sugar-free powdered beverages. (See Exhibit 1 for examples of current Kool-Aid products.) Kool-Aid's trademark symbol, the smiling jug, was introduced in print advertisements in 1954 and has since been involved in all of Kool-Aid's packaging and promotion.

Kool-Aid's current offerings include Regular (RKA), Sugar-Sweetened (SSKA), and Sugar-Free (SFKA) beverage powders. The Regular Kool-Aid requires the consumer to add a portion of sugar and water to the powder, whereas the Sweetened and Sugar-Free beverage powders simply require water. The Sugar-Free Kool-Aid is sweetened by aspartame, a popular sweetening substitute for sugar. Kool-Aid's traditional flavours include orange, grape, cherry, lemon-lime, and strawberry, while the sub-line of Kool-Aid Island Twists, introduced in 1995, includes tropical punch, orange pineapple, strawberry-kiwi, lemonade, and mango-berry. For a full listing of product sizes and national retail prices, see Exhibit 2.

Kool-Aid has always been a market leader in the powdered soft drink category due to its fun image and variety of flavours' appeal to youths. For example, in 1997 more than 48 million litres of Kool-Aid were sold in Canada; enough to fill over 128 Olympic-sized pools. However, an ACNielsen study of 1998 consumption of PSD (Exhibit 3) found that Kool-Aid was losing market share. Private labels (control labels), on the other hand, were gaining share at Kool-Aid's expense by copying flavours, undercutting Kool-Aid's prices, and leveraging power and control from recent grocery industry consolidation. Kool-Aid's competitors include other PSD producers as well as ready-to-serve juices and soft drinks and frozen concentrated beverage mixes.

1998 PRODUCT LAUNCHES

Mega Mountain Twists

To expand Kool-Aid's flavour offerings, Kraft introduced Mega Mountain Twists (MMT) for trial in the 1998 season, which began February 23. The three new flavours, Soarin' Strawberry Lemonade (SSL), Grapeberry Splash (GS), and Blastin' Berry Cherry (BBC), inspired by the consumer trend toward "fruit-blended" drinks, were all offered in Regular Kool-Aid, while GS and BBC also had Sugar-Free versions. Kraft had found that new flavours and varieties were the key driver leading to kids' requests for the product.

Fruit-blended drinks were quickly making a move into kid-oriented products, and Kraft saw the potential and need to increase variety within the Kool-Aid flavour to suit a slightly older demographic, particularly tweens aged 10–13. Ready-to-drink, ready-to-serve, and frozen concentrate beverages were all moving toward a more sophisticated product offering. The success of Kool-Aid's Island Twists flavours (which grew the line 7.2% after its launch), paired with the considerable success of MMT in the U.S. market, indicated that a launch in the Canadian market would be optimal. U.S. research found that all three of the MMT flavours exceeded beverage norms for "definitely would ask" among kids and "definitely would buy" among moms.

In an effort to continue to adapt to consumer needs, GS and BBC were offered in SFKA. Consumer complaints in the past had centred on not being able to purchase the same flavours in SFKA that were available in RKA. Such complaints were most common from parents of children with diabetes or children whose sugar intake had to be controlled.

While prices for the Mega Mountain Twist flavours remained aligned with the other Kool-Aid flavours, the packaging and promotion placed much less emphasis on the Kool-Aid man (see www.koolaid.com for an illustration of the Kool-Aid man and other Kool-Aid designs and packages). This was done in an effort to clearly differentiate the Mega Mountain Twist flavours from the regular flavour offerings by visually displaying more fruit on the packaging, and in turn hoping to enhance a quality image to parents.

In order to make room for these innovative new flavours, Kraft discontinued three flavours of RKA (Pink Swimmingo, Rock-A-Dile Red, Incrediberry) and three flavours of SFKA (Pink Swimmingo, Rock-A-Dile Red, Purplesaurus Rex). All of these flavours had been poor performers. Furthermore, given that the MMT were actually 3 SKUs (versus 1 for the regular flavours), a higher volume was achieved.

Kool-Aid Slushies

In an effort to build upon its current product line, Kraft released Kool-Aid Slushies to the Canadian market on February 23, 1998. The consumer could make the product, which is a frozen, slush beverage, in three steps:

1. **Mix**—Water is added to the sweetened Slushie beverage powder (from a 170-gram package) and mixed (exactly as one would mix Sugar-Sweetened Kool-Aid).

2. **Freeze**—Mixed Slushie liquid is frozen in containers or freezer bags for 3 to 5 hours.

3. **Serve**—Can be served immediately or, if the product was frozen for longer than 5 hours, can be thawed in the microwave.

The introductory Kool-Aid Slushie flavours were Polar Punch, Arctic Orange, and Frosted Grape. Kraft hoped to establish a foothold in the PSD category with this innovative product. No other competitor had a similar product on the market at the time of the Kool-Aid Slushies introduction, and it was hoped that it would attract both new and existing Kool-Aid consumers. Concept appeal was strong among mothers, at 61 percent, but even stronger (86%) among mothers who currently buy Kool-Aid.

Though the soft-drink powder was similar in nature to Kool-Aid mixes, the final product of the Slushie was distinctive enough that most consumers in preliminary research identified it as an incremental purchase that would not cannibalize the other Kool-Aid drinks. Because the Kool-Aid Slushie was a different usage occasion, the direct competitors to the product were popsicles and freezies. However, the Kool-Aid Slushie mix would be located in the PSD section.

Given the innovation of the Kool-Aid Slushie, foil packaging was used to make the product stand out in displays. In addition, retail sale pricing for the Slushies was $1.29

nationally, a 30-percent premium to the 135-gram SSKA. Research revealed that the price was considered to be fair given the consumer value ratings of the new product. The comparison to the SSKA was important due to the fact that the consumer's frame of reference would be with the other Kool-Aid products and not other frozen products. On a per-serving basis, the Kool-Aid Slushie retail sale price was at a premium to base frozen treats such as popsicles, and a discount versus premium frozen treats such as Juice Jets.

DISTRIBUTION

Kool-Aid is sold primarily in grocery stores. "Traditional grocery" (for example, Loblaws, Safeway, Loebs, IGA) represented 90 percent of all Kool-Aid sales in Canada.

Kraft employs a direct salesforce that has been successful in ensuring that the top five Kool-Aid flavours have distribution in more than 95 percent of grocery outlets and even the weakest flavours have over 50-percent representation. The goal for innovations such as MMT and Slushies is to achieve 70-percent distribution in less than 12 weeks. The 1998 innovations exceeded the typical 70-percent hurdle by May 1998, in time for the summer promotions.

Merchandising of the Kool-Aid brand was crucial to the immediate listing of the products during the summer season. A temporary sales crew installed more than 2,500 Kool-Aid racks in more than 3,000 Canadian grocery stores in May of 1998 in order to initiate high visibility for the Kool-Aid products. Market research showed that stores with Kool-Aid racks generated 42 percent more sales than similar stores without racks. Kraft placed high importance on the racks as they acted not only as secondary display in-store, but also created high consumer impact as a "go-to" site for the Kool-Aid "Get Stuff" (see below) program. Bright POS materials paired with the Kool-Aid rack were meant to create an opportunity for high impulse buying. They also acted as a bright reminder for moms to purchase the product before the summer season began.

Andrew wondered if Kraft would be able to maintain these important displays. The grocery industry in Canada was changing rapidly. Loblaws and Sobeys had been on acquisition sprees, with the end result being that the two retailers now controlled 60 percent of the country's grocery sales. Both retailers also featured their own house brands in many product categories. As a result, national manufacturers like Kraft were placed in a tougher negotiation position, heightening the power struggle for shelf space. This was particularly pertinent to Kool-Aid's strategy, as the number-two competitor within PSD was a controlled/private label.

In addition to traditional grocery stores, Kool-Aid was sold in Club Channels, but only in the 2.3-kg SSKA format due to the consumer need for a $5–$10 unit purchase price. Margins were lower for this channel; however, the opportunity for volume delivery was important. Costco/Price Club sales accounted for approximately 5 percent of all Kool-Aid sales in 1998.

Two other channels of distribution that were not heavily used in 1998 were mass merchandisers and drug stores—Wal-Mart, Zellers, Shoppers Drug Mart, and so on—(only 2% of sales), and foodservice (only 1% of sales). Foodservice outlets serving Kool-Aid in liquid form included Famous Players and selected restaurants. Costs associated with this channel were low due to the powder form of the beverage.

KOOL-AID PROMOTIONAL STRATEGIES

The Kool-Aid mascot and the traditional Kool-Aid smile have been the cornerstone of Kool-Aid's brand recognition over the years. Kraft has consistently used this image in its packaging and promotion, including providing communities with the opportunity to book a Kool-Aid mascot for special events. The original 1954 advertisements for Kool-Aid showed the soft drink in a large pitcher with a smiling face drawn on the surface condensation. From its continued use in promotion through the decades, the smiling Kool-Aid jug is now a highly recognized symbol in Canada. Ingrid van Leeuwen, former Associate Product Manager, Kool-Aid, Kraft Canada Inc., emphasized that "Kool-Aid and the image of the smile is synonymous with childhood and summertime fun for generations alike."

Kraft generated interest in the Kool-Aid product through kid-request and advertising more geared to mothers (80 percent of product purchases are made by mothers). Traditional television advertising geared toward mothers has featured parents serving children in seasonal settings, such as picnics and backyards, putting smiles on their faces. The "Pennies A Glass" advertising campaign, which ran until 1993, was extremely popular. It was discontinued once the audience was aware that Kool-Aid was cheap and because it offered no long-term advantage to the consumer given the low price of private-label brands. However, given that kid-request generates most purchases through parents, Kraft has attempted to retain the Kool-Aid brand as trendy and innovative.

Beyond pricing promotions (outlined in Exhibit 2 with product and price offerings), the following promotions were continued or initiated in the 1998 season in order to encourage consumer purchase.

Kool-Aid "Get Stuff" Promotion

Initiated in 1989, the Kool-Aid "Get Stuff" campaign was developed to encourage brand loyalty among kids and to provide parents with the opportunity to help kids work toward an attainable goal. Previously known as "Wacky Warehouse," the award-winning promotion had been successful in gaining nationwide recognition of the Kool-Aid brand. One study showed that 70 percent of Canada's kids were aware that they could collect Kool-Aid points to "Get Stuff."

The "Get Stuff" campaign operates using points printed on the packaging of all the Kool-Aid products. Kids and moms collect the points to redeem "prizes" from a selection of Kool-Aid items (6–10 offered each year). Most of the items are Kool-Aid branded, with an effort to follow current children's trends to make the free stuff as appealing as possible. Additional items geared toward mothers were also added, including the famous Kool-Aid pitcher and Kool-Aid cups. The attraction of such a campaign was twofold: first, mothers would be pleased to have children working toward a goal, and second, kids would be enthusiastic about having the responsibility to collect these points and get something fun in return. Other Kraft international partners (U.S., Mexico, the Philippines, etc.) quickly adapted and implemented this simple campaign in their markets due to the high impact it had.

The current Kool-Aid products offered the following point values:

- RKA pack—1 point
- SSKA canister—12 points

- SSKA pouch—3 points
- SFKA box—9 points
- Slushies—3 points

The 1998 "Get Stuff" campaign was a huge success, with Kool-Aid running out of the 1,000 Kool-Aid Indoor/Outdoor tents offered. This was significant, as 700 points were required to redeem this prize. Research showed that most points redeemed were collected over a period of a year, showing the huge influence of moms in the success of the program. Advertising for the "Get Stuff" program used to be done as five-second tags at the end of kid-focused commercials; however, these were abandoned in 1998 due to the already overwhelming success of the program at that time.

"Be Kool and Smile" 1998 Campaign

To build on the past success of the traditional Kool-Aid smile, the 1998 summer campaign for Kool-Aid created by Young & Rubicam involved using a variety of traditional and non-traditional media to splash the updated Kool-Aid smile across the country. The emphasis of the campaign was not only to help promote the new Mega Mountain Twist flavours and Kool-Aid Slushies, but also to help revitalize interest in the variety of other Kool-Aid flavours to new and current users by making the summer of 1998 a Kool-Aid summer.

Included in the campaign were the following, linked together with the tag line "Be Kool" and the Smile:

- Radio Promotions—Humorous reminder advertising aimed at mothers (reliving childhood Kool-Aid memories).
- Enhanced Kool-Aid "Get Stuff" Promotion—(as above).
- Television Advertising—Used to generate kid-request for new product offerings, with two executions, "Cruisin' Mega Mountain" (Kool-Aid man cartoon spot), and "Morse Cold" (Slushies spot where the chattering from a child's teeth were loud enough that a satellite detected his "Brain-O" as Morse code).
- In-store Sampling—Highlighting new product offerings (Slushies and MMT).
- Wall Murals/Billboards/Posters—Transit routes, superboards, high-profile buildings.
- Consumer Giveaways—Fridge magnets, posters, beach towels, water bottles, and more at common summer destinations across Canada.

Among the most original placements of the Kool-Aid Smile were in conjunction with the North Toronto Memorial Community Centre and the Royal Canadian Yacht Club, both located in Toronto. Children who visited the busy Community Centre in the summer of 1998 were greeted with a huge (colour) Kool-Aid Smile covering the bottom of the main swimming pool. The colourful Smile campaign's relationship with water continued with the sponsorship of three new Olympic-class sailboats. The Kool-Aid Smile was displayed prominently on the sails with the "Be Kool" tag line. The boats, competing in local, national, and international regattas, received significant media coverage proving to be an invaluable public relations move along with the rest of the campaign. Numerous articles (news and opinion) commented on the campaign. For example, an article entitled

"Kool-Aid smile passes mnemonic acid test" in *Strategy* (July 20, 1998) said, "Another successful aspect of the Kool-Aid campaign is its wide appeal. To a parent, it's a trusted brand, familiar and authentic brand; it has staying power. To kids, it's instant refreshment, building a new franchise with every generation."

MARKET RESEARCH AND CONSUMER ATTITUDES

To help build Kraft's promotional campaigns in 1998 and to measure their success for the 1999 strategy, a number of research results were taken into consideration. Young & Rubicam, Kool-Aid's media firm, provided Andrew Sneyd with a summary report outlining the PSD category, purchase behaviour, and consumption models (see Exhibit 4).

Tandemar tracking, qualitative research done on a reoccurring basis, evaluates advertising effectiveness. Exhibit 5 contains a summary of recent Tandemar results for moms and kids.

Insignia Marketing Research Inc. was contracted to identify consumer attitudes toward Kool-Aid and the PSD category. Insignia held eight mini focus groups in Toronto at the end of August 1998 (see Exhibit 6).

A subsequent study (Exhibit 7) about "Kids in General" also highlights some significant concerns and interests to help Kraft in planning Kool-Aid's marketing strategy.

"KOOL" INNOVATIONS: YEAR-END RESULTS

Launched under a "Tween Extreme" campaign, MMT did not generate the sales initially sought, with only one MMT flavour overtaking an existing flavour in terms of popularity (based on sales—see Exhibit 8), despite the high level of distribution. The MMT did appeal more to the kids in the age 6–12 bracket, but in general Kraft found from consumer feedback and focus groups that children ask for flavours by colour. The MMT simply added one more "red," "purple," and "pink" packet to the Kool-Aid rack. Mothers did not seem further inspired to purchase the MMT based on the change in packaging since there was no proven additional nutritional value.

Yet again, though Slushies were a new product innovation, sales for the product were not at anticipated levels. Discussion took place regarding offering an additional flavour more in line with the attributes of the product, such as Ice Blue.

Traditional Kool-Aid flavour sales remained high; however, the PSD market-share values for RKA dropped in almost every province. Concerns about nutritional value and convenience were again raised.

STAYING "KOOL" IN THE FUTURE

The breadth of issues that faced the Kool-Aid brand astounded Andrew Sneyd. He knew that Kraft would have to re-evaluate the current marketing plans and examine how they could become stronger in order to increase consumption. The profitability report (Exhibit 9), which also outlined where spending occurred for the Kool-Aid product, looked to be a good summary to provide to his co-workers to help with 1999's strategy formulation.

Andrew certainly had a lot of things to consider. For example, he had to wonder if Kool-Aid's full product offering and strategy of extending flavours had already been overused in terms of driving sales for PSD. Moreover, he asked if MMT and Slushies were really going to be a strong initiative to continue into the future. While discussions about releasing an additional flavour of Slushie, Ice Blue, had seemed to be a positive initiative given the information Kraft obtained about kids choosing by "colour," he had to worry if this wasn't just another "red" or "purple" to pick from. The importance of staying aligned with current flavour and product trends, though, was still high, especially since new flavour offerings and innovations were the key driver in initiating kid-request over the long term. Though some kids would develop preferences for certain flavours, their impulsive nature is best exploited through offering them new and fun things to try. Also, though a step had been made in the right direction to add MMT to the SFKA line, concerns about the consumer trend to more nutritious beverages had to be addressed in terms of Kool-Aid's long-term image with the consumer. In particular, parents were not moving to the SFKA line over other beverage alternatives due to concerns surrounding the artificial sweetener, aspartame.

The promotion of Kool-Aid to the correct segment while highlighting the proper values identified the necessity to stay cool to kids yet also encourage the parents to purchase the product. More emphasis on promotions and advertising directed to both the parent and the child, while creating harmony between the two, was essential. The challenge lay in the increasing consciousness of kids to stay "cool," regardless of whether it was the beverage they drank or the toy they played with. However, Andrew found that promotions had really run wild in 1998 and that perhaps a re-focus of value-adding activities would be necessary. Furthermore, the difference between having the Kool-Aid Man or the Kool-Aid Smile represent the brand had to be resolved for packaging considerations in the future. The "Face Campaign" had been quite successful in 1998 for Kraft in terms of building brand recognition (including winning *Strategy* magazine's Best Media Plan Competition for 1998), but currently the Kool-Aid packaging only featured cartoons incorporating the Kool-Aid man.

Lastly, the methods of distributing Kool-Aid and maintaining market share showed room for improvement and further innovation. As Canadian consumers looked to "one-stop" shopping to fill their needs, mass merchandising seemed viable. Andrew wondered what other distribution alternatives should be exploited. The foodservice industry also looked appealing from a cost and promotion standpoint; not only would the product be cheap to distribute due to the product qualities, but also the convenience disadvantage faced in the supermarket would be eliminated. Promotion partners could be aligned with the Kool-Aid fun and cool image, with opportunities to highlight new product innovations, such as Slushies. However, Kool-Aid would still be competing directly with other soft drink beverages such as Coke and Pepsi, in addition to other bottled fruit drinks.

With all these issues in mind, Andrew knew that there was ample opportunity for Kraft to build on the success of the 1998 Kool-Aid strategy. Having made such strides in the past year, he looked for inspiration to maintain the excitement surrounding Kool-Aid in the marketing community and to "Stay Kool" with kids and moms.

EXHIBIT 1	Kool-Aid Products

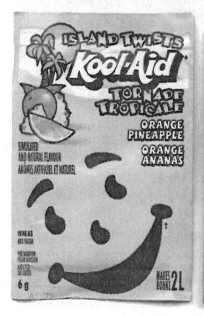

EXHIBIT 2	Kool-Aid Product Formats and Pricing

Regular Kool-Aid (RKA)

Size: Packet (6-8 grams)—makes 3 litres

Requires: 1 cup of sugar (gives consumer ability to control amount of sugar) + water

Flavours Featured: All 14 Kool-Aid flavours, including Mega Mountain Twists (MMT)

Unit Price: $0.39 per pack

Price Promotions: Featured three times for Summer 1998, selling at $0.25 per pack, or in multiples (4/$1.00, 8/$2.00)

Sugar-Sweetened Kool-Aid (SSKA)

1. *Size:* Canister (used to be 603 grams, changed to 517 grams with Kool-Aid face packaging in 1998): makes 6 litres (flexibility with serving size—re-sealable canister)

   Requires: Water

   Flavours Featured: Top 8 flavours (no MMT)

   Unit Price: $2.99

   Price Promotions: No promotions (everyday price point)

2. *Size:* Pouch (135 grams): makes 1.5 litres (no flexibility with serving size)

   Requires: Water

   Flavours Featured: Top 8 flavours (no MMT)

   Unit Price: $0.99

   Price Promotions: No promotions (everyday price point)

3. *Size:* Jumbo (2.3 kg): makes 27 litres

   Requires: Water

   Flavours Featured: Cherry and Tropical Punch

   Unit Price: $7.99

   Price Promotions: No promotions (everyday price point)

Sugar-Free Kool-Aid (SFKA)—Sweetened with Aspartame

Size: Box (9–12 grams): contain two packets, each makes 1.5 litres

Requires: Water

Flavours Featured: Top 8 flavours (including two MMT flavours)

Unit Price: $1.99

Price Promotions: No promotions (everyday price point)

Kool-Aid Slushies

Pouch (170 grams): makes 1 litre (4 servings)

Requires: Water

Flavours Featured: Arctic Orange, Polar Punch, Frosted Grape

Unit Price: $1.29

Price Promotions: Featured three times for Summer 1998, selling at $0.99 per pouch

EXHIBIT 3	National Powdered Soft Drinks Market Consumption				
	National Share Chg. vs '97	Maritimes Share Chg. vs '97	Quebec Share Chg. vs '97	Ontario Share Chg. vs '97	West Share Chg. vs '97
Total Powdered Soft Drinks	0.0	0.0	0.0	0.0	0.0
Total Kraft Powdered Soft Drinks	-2.5	-0.3	-8.2	-3.4	-2.4
Total Kool-Aid PSD	-1.9	-0.2	-3.0	-3.8	-3.1
Total Kool-Aid Unsw. PSD	-2.5	-0.4	-2.5	-3.4	-2.5
Total Kool-Aid S 93w. PSD (incl. Slushies)	0.0	0.0	-1.0	-0.2	0.8
Total Kool-Aid Slushies PSD	1.1	0.3	0.7	1.1	1.2
Total Kool-Aid Sugar Free PSD	0.1	0.1	0.0	0.1	0.0
Total Crystal Light PSD	0.0	0.0	-0.1	0.6	-0.6
Total Count Time PSD	0.0	0.0	0.0	0.0	0.1
Total Tang Flavours PSD	0.0	-0.1	0.0	0.0	-0.1
Total Quench PSD	-0.6	0.0	-8.4	-0.1	0.0
Total Lipton (Unilever Mfr.) PSD	0.5	0.0	5.4	0.4	0.3
Total Associated Brands Mfr. PSD	3.0	0.0	0.0	0.0	6.4
Total Dutch Mill PSD	0.0	0.0	0.0	-0.1	0.0
Total Neilson PSD	3.0	0.0	0.0	0.0	6.4
Total Crosby PSD	-1.8	-1.3	0.0	0.0	-3.3
Total Freshie (Dalton Mfr.) PSD	0.4	-0.1	0.0	1.2	0.0
Total Monte C (Laurentide Mfr.) PSD	0.0	0.0	0.6	0.0	0.0
Total Private/Control Label PSD	2.1	2.1	7.2	2.9	1.3

Source: ACNielsen, Calendar 1998

EXHIBIT 4	Young & Rubicam, Ltd., PSD Market & Kool-Aid Report

Category

Powdered Soft Drinks (Source: ACN–Sept. 12, 1998, latest 52 weeks)

- Total powdered soft drink volume is down 7% vs yr. ago (vya) at 2,229.4M hectolitres.
- This translates to sales of $78,606.7M (down 2% vya).
- Kraft is the leader accounting for 64.9% of the volume (down 2.9% vya) and 58.5% dollar sales (down 4% vya).

Kool-Aid (Source: ACN–Sept. 12, 1998, latest 52 weeks)

- In Canada, Kool-Aid is only available in the powdered soft drink format, whereas RTD (ready-to-drink) is available in the U.S.
- Kraft has experienced share erosion in this category over the past few years.
- Volume declines were experienced this summer and are attributed to merchandising and pricing issues.
- Kool-Aid continues to be a category leader accounting for 55.9% of the volume (down 11% vya) and 38.5% of dollar sales (down 3% vya).

Positioning

Kool-Aid (Source: Qualitative Analysis of Beverage Market, 1994)

- Kool-Aid is typically perceived to epitomize the crystal category.
- Described as child-targeted, fun, fruit-flavoured beverage.
- Kool-Aid's strengths are:
  —Brand name
  —Economical
  —Available in wide range of flavours
  —Easy to prepare
- At the supermarket level, primary competition for Kool-Aid is private label. This is true more so in the Prairies.
- RKA is generally preferred over SSKA since the latter is perceived to have too much sugar.
- SFKA consumption seems to be limited to households with dietary restrictions. Parents seem to shy from giving their children products with aspartame.

EXHIBIT 5	Tandemar Tracking Results*		

	Pre	Post	
Mom Success			
Ad Awareness	4%	41%	Significant Increase
Top-of-Mind Brand Awareness	61%	76%	Significant Increase
Value for Money	71%	81%	Significant Increase
Kid Requests	67%	80%	Significant Increase
Kid Success			
Cool	83%	94%	Significant Increase
Tastes Really Good	93%	99%	Significant Increase
Fun to Drink	86%	93%	Significant Increase
Asked Mom to Buy	34%	50%	Significant Increase

* 1998 "Be Kool" Campaign Success. Tandemar Ad Tracking: "Pre" April 1998, "Post" September 1998.

EXHIBIT 6	Insignia Marketing Research Study

Focus Group Recruiting Specifications:

- Female heads of household
- Principal grocery shoppers
- At least half per group with household of 4+ members
- Ages of children:
    - —All with at least one child under 18 years of age living at home
    - —At least 4 per group had at least one child aged 2 to 12
    - —Each group had representation of the following age ranges: 2-6 years, 6-12 years, and 13-18 years.
    - —A range of household incomes but maximum of one respondent per group with household income of $70,000+.
- Willing to do "homework" exercise (recreating a purchase experience and completing a subsequent questionnaire).

Key Reasons for Continuing to Purchase Kool-Aid Are:

- Price—as a PSD entry, it is economical relative to other beverage segments such as pop, shelf-stable juices/drinks and refrigerated entries.
- Convenience—as a PSD entry, it is very portable, has a long shelf life, and takes up little storage room.

(Continued over)

| EXHIBIT 6 | Insignia Marketing Research Study (continued) |

- High appeal of brand name to younger children—younger kids know the brand name, like the "jug man" character, like the packaging, like the product (sweet and coloured), like the variety of flavours, and enjoy making the product.

- Brand name is familiar to and trusted by moms.

The recent volume declines for Kool-Aid appear to trace to a number of different reasons rather than being the result of a single problem.

First, as a PSD, Kool-Aid has some key weaknesses versus the other multi-serve beverage segments. These could be causing consumers to move out of PSDs/Kool-Aid or at least replace a share of PSD/Kool-Aid glasses with other beverages. The key weaknesses for PSDs/Kool-Aid are:

- Poor/no nutritional value—even "bad for you" given the high sugar content and presence of artificial colours and flavours.

- Not pre-made; have to make. This reduces the convenience of PSDs relative to RTD entries. It also means that the RTD products that are in home tend to be the first in line to be consumed.

- Lack of (or consumer lack of awareness of the existence of) interesting fruit flavour combinations.

- While Kool-Aid has high appeal to young kids, the brand is seen by older kids as being for "little kids." Kool-Aid is thus not as cool to older kids. Sunny Delight appears to have been very effective in appealing to older kids, and Gatorade also appears to be viewed as cool by older kids.

Second, Kool-Aid appears to be losing ground within the PSD segment. Again, this research suggests there may be several reasons for this.

- Both RKA and SSKA are more expensive than the private label (PL) entries. While SSKA in the can delivers more reconstituted volume than PL (7L vs 6L), the similarity in the size of the cans means that consumers may not look beyond price when making price comparisons. In the case of the SSKA pouch, this is not only more expensive than the PL entry, but it makes less (1.5L versus 2.25L). In determining value, the key issue for consumers is price relative to reconstituted volume. The price difference versus PL is judged as less of an issue for RKA than for SSKA because RKA purchases appear to be more kid-driven, and Kool-Aid has high appeal to little kids.

- Unlike the PL entries, Kool-Aid has no nutritional/good-for-you communication on pack: the PL entries feature quite realistic fruit graphics, and package copy indicates that they contain Vitamin C.

- Entries like Lipton's fruit crystals appear to be appealing on flavours that interest adults, so may be bought by them for the whole family.

- Both the PL and Lipton's packages have a more adult/whole family look.

Other issues for Kool-Aid identified in this research are:

- The points program does not appear to be a strong driver on loyalty, either because of lack of familiarity with the program or because too many points need to be collected before they can be redeemed.

EXHIBIT 6	Insignia Marketing Research Study (continued)

- The choice of flavours in any one store can be limited.

- The similarity in the colour of the RKA packaging is confusing, especially for the red flavours, which is an issue for little kids who pick their flavours based on colour (and graphics).

There is no evidence in this research that RKA is losing volume to SSKA: the two products do not appear to interact significantly given that they deliver different benefits and consumers tend to prefer one or the other, or to buy both but for different uses, because of these differences in the products/benefits.

EXHIBIT 7	"Kids in General" Report Summary

1. The kid segment of the population is experiencing slower growth versus the adult segment and versus previous years. This trend is most pronounced among younger kids, with the 5–9 segment projected to decline from 2001 to 2006.

2. Kids evolve through different cognitive and social stages as they grow. Different age targets require different marketing approaches to be effective.

3. Brands cannot rely on historical activity to be relevant to kids—they need to be current.

4. Kids in 1999 are vastly different than kids of even 10 years ago.

5. From the age of about 5 on, kids have strong purchase influence across a variety of categories, including non-kid categories (e.g. cars).

6. There may be an opportunity to decrease substitutability by C/L (cost leadership) through increasing product differentiation and strengthening kid influence.

7. Kids (especially those over 5) do not go grocery shopping with their parents.

8. The Gene Del Vecchio "ever-cool" model cites: "Satisfy a kid's timeless emotional needs but routinely dress it up in a current fad or trend."

Planning Implications

1. Growth in kid brands will not come from the population trend: it must be driven by stronger marketing plans that will increase consumption. Aligning against an 8–11 bull's eye in 2000 maximizes the population trend.

2. Advertise to kids. Reassess brands with long kid advertising hiatuses. This will ensure awareness and help combat C/L.

3. Develop programs that will be able to be adapted to be relevant to different kid lifestages.

4. Based on demographic trends and the influence curve, prioritize kids as:

   Tweens 9–12   Teens 13–17   Boys and Girls 5–8

5. Invest in a continuing effort to understand today's kids.

6. Use kid-directed promotions and advertising to decrease substitutability versus C/L.

7. Design kid scale events so that the in-store portion encourages mom purchase.

8. Follow the "ever-cool" formula in managing kid brands.

EXHIBIT 8	Kool-Aid Canadian Sales (by flavour)

(Share of PSDs: 52 weeks ending December 1998)*

	1998 (%)	1997 (%)
Cherry	7.1	7.9
Grape	6.9	8.1
Orange	6.1	7.0
Lemon-Lime	4.8	5.4
Strawberry	4.5	4.8
Tropical Punch	4.4	5.0
Orange Pineapple	3.8	4.2
Strawberry Kiwi	3.2	3.8
Lemonade	3.0	4.0
MM Grape Berry Splash	2.3	0.0
Mango Berry	2.2	3.0
MM Blastin' Berry Cherry	2.0	0.0
MM Soarin' Strawberry Lemonade	1.9	0.0
Slushies		
Slushies Polar Punch	0.5	0.0
Slushies Frosted Grape	0.4	0.0
Slushies Arctic Orange	0.4	0.0

* Numbers have been adjusted to maintain confidentiality.

EXHIBIT 9 | Kraft Powdered Soft Drinks Profitability (in thousands)*

	Total Kool-Aid 6g		Regular Kool-Aid (inc. Slushies)		Sugar-Swtnd Kool-Aid 9g		Sugar-Free Kool-Aid		Crystal Light		Quench		Country Time		Tang	
	$	$/Lb	$	$/Lb	$	$/Lb	$	$/Lb	$	$/Lb	$	$/Lb	$	$/Lb	$	$/Lb
Volume (Mlbs)	5,840		800		5,000		40		250		1,000		1,600		4,000	
Gross Revenue	32,600	5.582	19,600	24.50	11,000	2.20	2,000	50.00	13,750	56.00	1,500	1.60	2,720	1.70	5,600	1.40
Variable Cost of Goods	8,260	1.414	3,840	4.80	4,000	0.80	420	10.50	2,875	11.50	800	0.60	1,120	0.70	2,000	0.50
Variable Trade (Sales)	3,230	0.553	2,320	2.90	750	0.15	160	4.00	1,025	4.10	250	0.25	320	0.20	400	0.10
Variable Contribution	21,110	3.616	13,440	16.80	6,260	1.25	1,420	35.50	9,860	39.40	660	0.65	1,280	0.80	3,200	0.80
Direct Trade (Sales)	845		96		605		144		103		0		272		40	
Net Contribution	20,265		13,344		5,645		1,276		9,747		650		1,008		3,160	
Advertising	3,000								750		0		0		0	
Media Production	600								140		0		0		0	
Coupons	20								150		0		200		0	
Consumer Promotions	1,500								800		0		200		0	
Consumer Spending	5,120		3,075		1,725		320		1,840		0		400		0	
Controllable Margin	15,145		10,269		3,920		956		7,907		650		608		3,160	
Overhead	3,700		1,500		2,000		200		900		600		500		1,600	
Income from Operations	11,415		8,769		1,920		756		7,007		60		108		1,560	
% of Operating Revenue	35.1%		44.7%		17.5%		37.8%		51.0%		3.3%		4.0%		27.9%	

Note: Consumer spending on Kool-Aid is not "format specific." It is allocated to formats on % Gross Revenue.

*Numbers have been adjusted to maintain confidentiality.

Braun's Bicycle & Fitness

Hugh Munro

Robert Braun, one of the four Braun family members who own and operate Braun's Bicycle & Fitness in Kitchener, Ontario (www.brauns.com), had just returned from a trade show in Toronto. There, he had met with Monica Reid of Emerge2 (www.emerge2.com) to discuss Braun's future marketing plans. Buoyed partially by the positive response at the trade show, but mostly by his enthusiasm and passion for his family's business, Robert was visibly excited about Braun's success to date and its future opportunities. At the same time, Robert expressed some concerns about the future pace, scope, and direction of the business, particularly in light of its growing e-commerce presence. "We are a small business that has managed to survive and grow successfully but at a controlled pace. We have an opportunity to build and leverage the Braun's brand but don't have real deep pockets. The key is making the right moves at the right pace."

BACKGROUND

Bicycle Industry

Worldwide, the bicycle industry is heavily trade dependent, with a high degree of country-specific product identification and specialization. Brand names dominate in the sale of medium- to high-end products, with an estimated 85 percent of sales occurring under a manufacturer's brand. Bike sales in North America are dominated by imports coming primarily from China, Mexico, and Taiwan. (Additional information on the global bicycle industry is available at www.bikecrawler.com and www.bicycleretailer.com)

The bicycle retail structure in the U.S. consists of mass merchants, specialty stores, and sporting goods retailers (Exhibit 1A), with mass merchants representing the largest market share and lowest average retail price per bike; specialty stores represent the highest price per bike. Rationalization in the specialty bicycle segment of the market has been evident as the number of specialty retailers in the U.S. declined from 7,000 in 1998 to 6,000 in 1999.

The product sales mix of bicycle specialty stores includes mountain, BMX, road, and hybrid bikes; bicycle components and accessories; clothing; and repair and service (Exhibit 2). Gross margins for specialty stores run between 34 percent for bikes and 45 percent for clothing, equipment, and hard goods. The financial structure for a typical specialty bike retailer is presented in Exhibit 3.

Canadian Bicycle Industry

The Canadian bicycle market has a structure that's very similar to the U.S. market (Exhibit 1B). Imports, mostly from Taiwan, China, and the U.S., accounted for 46 percent of the 1.76 million bike sales in 1999, translating into a $500-million industry from bike sales alone. Parts and accessories contributed another CND$120 million to the industry in 1999. Shipments by domestic parts producers are estimated at less than CDN$20 million.

Three major companies—Procycle Inc., Victoria Precision, and T.I. Raleigh of Canada—represent well over 80 percent of domestic production. Smaller firms like Rocky Mountain Bicycle are generally more specialized assemblers, serving a regional market or a specialized market niche. Manufacturers in Europe, Japan, and Taiwan are expected to concentrate even more on technical developments as worldscale volume production shifts to low-cost countries such as Malaysia, India, and China. Canadian volume manufacturers will experience competitive pressures from these imports as well as the continued influx of U.S.-manufactured bicycles. Specialty manufacturers in Canada will have to continue to focus on the higher-end, technically advanced offerings (www.strategis.ic.gc.ca/SSG/sg01103e.html).

At the consumer level it is estimated that 55 percent of Canadians (age 18+) engage in bicycling (Exhibit 4A), although there is a difference in participation levels by gender and age (Exhibit 4B). Almost 52 percent of Canadian households own one or more adult bicycles and there are more than 10 million adult bicycles in the possession of Canadian consumers. Increased emphasis on personal fitness and recreational activities in North American society combined with an aging population suggest a positive impact on the future of cycling in Canada. Bicycle penetration is highest in Alberta and Quebec, where 59.1 and 56.4 percent, respectively, own one or more bicycles. According to recent surveys, more than 54 percent of cyclists ride more than 50 times a year, and recreational use is by far the major reason for purchasing a bike.

BRAUN'S BICYCLE & FITNESS COMPANY

Background

Braun's Bicycle & Fitness is a 75-year-old, family owned, specialty retail business operating out of a single location in Kitchener, Ontario. Started by Gordon and Grace Braun in 1925, ownership and management still rests with family members Willard, Mae, Roger, and Robert. Recently the fourth generation of the Braun family got involved in the business as Robert's daughter was hired for occasional work in the retail store.

By most standards, Braun's is a relatively small operation. It employs 10 to 20 people (some on a seasonal basis) in its 16,000-square-foot retail facility. Prior to its move into e-business, Braun's business exemplified that of many other successful small retail establishments. Its sales of bicycles and accessories were limited to customers within one hour's drive of the Kitchener store. A key ingredient to its success is the company's strong customer-service orientation that contributes to solid, loyal relationships with its retail store customers. These customers reflected a rather broad spectrum from 30-year-olds to 65-year-old parents and grandparents. Like most retail establishments, the business had to inventory and own every item sold. Sales were also subject to local economic, seasonal, and weather fluctuations.

Braun's currently sells more than 2,000 bikes per year. They carry a range of name brand models of bikes from medium to high end, although they typically stock and show medium-range recreational bikes. It can be very challenging to stock bicycles, especially in the high-end range, where each model comes in different sizes and can be paired with different components. Braun's also displays components and accessories for bikes, bicycle-specific clothing, and car racks. They also organize and advertise cycling tours through the store. In 1996, Braun's was recognized as the Retailer of the Year from more than 6,000 businesses in the Kitchener-Waterloo area.

The company has had a Novell network for about eight years and currently has 14 computers networked. Sales, ordering, record keeping, and inventory control are completely automated at Braun's. Of the 14 stations, 4 have Internet access and are authorized for use mainly by staff in purchasing, sales, and management. These personnel use e-mail for supplier/customer correspondence and the Internet for product research. Nevertheless, all employees may receive and send customer-service-related e-mail. E-mail is checked three times per day and the messages are distributed appropriately.

Braun's Involvement in E-Commerce

It was in 1995 that Braun's management decided to experiment with the Internet. At first, this was understood to be an attempt to be innovative—or, at least, to appear to be innovative within the local market. Spokes Plus was Braun's first attempt at a Web presence and was initially merely an "electronic business card." This site was followed by Club Tread Monthly Specials and the Club Tread Reports, both offshoots of Braun's Club Tread concept, a "customer loyalty program" or discount buying club for subscribing customers. In 1996, Braun's Online was introduced, with further upgrades following in 1997. Today, Braun's Online is the automated version of Braun's Bicycle & Fitness.

Braun's Online offers a product search engine, online shopping capability including product selection (shopping basket software), secure credit card transactions, a real-time shipping calculator, and a real-time currency exchange calculator. More than 1,500 products and services are offered online (visit www.brauns.com for a complete list). This site was recently awarded the "Best of Online Shopping" in its category by Ballantine, and voted one of the Top 10 online cycling shop sites by online users.

The design of the Braun's Online Web site has brought significant benefits to the company. Braun's has moved from being a single-location, community-based retail operation to a business selling its products in more than 50 countries. This global reach has helped to expand supply capacity but also has served to round out demand that is normally subject to seasonal and weather fluctuations. In addition, more of the orders are being directly shipped from suppliers, reducing Braun's inventory carrying costs and financial risk. The geographic breakdown of Braun's Internet sales for the last 19 months is provided in Exhibit 5.

Because it's Canadian, Braun's Online has a currency exchange advantage over many countries where Braun's now sells. Braun's has capitalized on this advantage by installing shipping calculation software that operates behind the customer interface. In the past, the manual processing of customer inquiry, quotes, and submission/response was very time-consuming. With complete online, real-time automation, response time is more or less immediate. This also encourages impulse buying and, in retail sales, the factor of "buying when excited" can be significant.

Braun's, however, is not unique in offering online sales as a specialty bike store. As more stores have adopted e-commerce sites, competition has shifted from known local players made up of biking enthusiasts running small retail operations to more sophisticated global players using the Net to expand their reach and offerings. For example, an online B2B (business-to-business) exchange (www.icongo.com/www/zoneManager/zone0.cfm) exists to facilitate online commerce between buyers and sellers.

Another example of online competition, Bikeshop.com, Inc. (www.bikeshop.com) was launched nationally across the U.S. on April 1, 2000, with the objective of providing a unique retail experience that would combine the best the Web and physical retailers have to offer: an unlimited selection of bicycles available through 24/7 shopping from the convenience of one's home, and the full assembly and post-sale service provided by a national network of quality bicycle dealers. The site was supported through 550 physical dealers in all 50 states and focused primarily in the medium- to premium-priced market. DCC, the world's leading designer, manufacturer, and marketer of branded bicycles, represented the majority owner of Bikeshop.com. However, despite the conceptual appeal, Bikeshop.com was terminated in the first half of 2001.

Issues Facing Braun's

Robert was beginning to recognize that e-business also had its unique issues and challenges. The expanded product-market scope of Braun's business changed the customer base and also the competitive landscape. Prior to selling online Braun had a very good feel for its customer base through its direct local contact. It prided itself on this customer intimacy and used it to govern its business activities. With the expanded product and geographic market scope of the online business, the profile of Braun's customers was becoming less clear.

Braun's was also experiencing a channel conflict with some suppliers. While Braun's sourced product from around 100 suppliers, the number was shrinking because of competition and consolidation. Of these suppliers about 15 preferred that their dealers not sell online, so as to preserve assigned market boundaries. While many suppliers from Japan and Taiwan supported online sales through Braun's, many U.S. manufacturers were building their own direct relationships with buyers online and therefore were less receptive to retail dealers moving online with the same products. Robert estimated that about 25 percent of Braun's product mix was not being sold online because of supplier restriction.

A different but every bit as important issue for Braun's was building its brand in this expanded market space. Braun's Online was becoming well known for its expertise in cycles in general, and in certain product categories sold its own private brand including unicycles and clothing. In fact, Braun's was considered to be the largest retailer of unicycles in North America. It was also building a brand presence with its customized online solutions for car racks. Finally, Braun's had extended its offer of cycling tours to online customers to give them the opportunity to put their purchases to use. They even provided a CD of photos from the tour to capture the experience for participants.

Robert was positive about the activity and sales that were generated from the online site (Exhibit 6). Online sales currently represented close to 10 percent of the store's annual revenue. Of the approximately 1,100 online orders over the past 19 months, 40 were sales of bicycles, many to enthusiasts who were comfortable buying without the usual test run. Because of the limited floor space in the showroom, Robert had begun to use the Web to test the sales viability of new products. He had recently adopted the policy that if a product did not sell online then it likely would not be put in the store.

He was also pleased that they were seemingly able to maintain excellent customer service over the Internet. Based on an average volume of 75 e-mails a day, Braun's staff had been able to meet their policy of responding to e-mails within hours of receiving them. Based on the customers' shocked reactions at their prompt replies, Robert believed that this service offered value to online customers.

Robert believed that the things that they were doing, they were doing well. The issue was how to leverage this very positive momentum to build the brand on a much larger scale. The catch was that Braun's budget for communications was quite modest, at just over $100,000 per year. To date, communications have consisted of listings in the Yellow Pages; newsletters for club members (approximately ten issues per year); and radio, newspaper, and direct mail advertising. Braun's Web site was listed in the Yellow Pages, in newsletters, on its promotional clothing, and in the literature for the loyalty program. Some information on Internet sales and how purchasers heard about Braun's Online are provided in Exhibit 7. Much of Braun's current communications activity seemed to be focused on reinforcing relationships with existing customers. Robert felt that a more aggressive and creative approach was needed to build more traffic for their online retail business.

Robert also recognized that an increase in online retail activities would necessitate changes to Braun's organizational structure. Internet-related expenses (e.g., e-commerce rental fees from Emerge2, dial-up access, Internet secure fees, cross-promotions, and webmaster services) were approximately $50,000 per year. The expanded product scope was already taxing existing personnel, and the addition of a full-time product development person was being considered. The increased Web activity may also require the support of a call centre to handle customer inquiries and service. Braun's current online experience was signalling that not only would additional capacity be required, but also the company would need a revamping of many of its business processes.

THE DECISION

Following his meeting with Monica at the trade show, Robert was still very enthusiastic and excited about the challenges ahead. Although Braun's had had success in its online sales, he wondered if this was the primary vehicle for future growth. The closure of Bikeshop.com concerned Robert and made him question how competitive their Web site was. Although using the Web site to test out new products helped to minimize inventory costs and financial risk, Robert wondered if this was the most viable strategy, and what effect it would have on the composition of the in-store customers and the product sales mix. He was also concerned about Braun's ability to maintain the same quality of online customer service if the volume grew. Robert recognized that the decisions he made could significantly alter the scope and nature of the family business.

EXHIBIT 1A | **1998 U.S. Bicycle Retail Structure**

	Market Share	Average Retail Price Per Unit
Mass merchants[1]	60%	$100
Specialty stores[2]	30%	$355
Sporting goods retailers[3]	10%	$260
Total units sold (1998)	16,100,000	
Total retail value (1998)[4]	$5.6 billion	

[1] Includes Wal-Mart, Toys 'R' Us, Kmart, Target and Sears Roebuck & Co.

[2] Includes bicycle stores that sell only bicycles and related parts and accessories. May be one store or multiple store operations.

[3] Includes The Sports Authority, Champs Sports, Jumbo Sports, Sport Mart.

[4] Includes bicycle sales as well as related parts and accessories.

EXHIBIT 1B | **Canadian Bicycle Retail Structure**

	Market Share
Mass merchants[1]	65%
Specialty stores[2]	27%
Buying groups[3]	8%
Total units sold (1999)	1.76 million
Total retail value (1999)	$500 million

[1] The largest mass merchant being Canadian Tire.

[2] This segment would include stores such as Braun's.

[3] This segment would include groups of specialty stores that purchase en masse to buy through volume and increase their buying power.

EXHIBIT 2	Product Sales Mix–Specialty Retail Bicycle Stores

Category	Percentage of Sales
Mountain bike	13
BMX bike	14
Hybrid bike	13
Road bike	8
Total bikes	**48**
Repair and service	21
Clothing, components and accessories	31
Total nonbike	**52**
Grand total	**100**

EXHIBIT 3	Average Financial Structure–Specialty Bicycle Store

Sales	100%
Cost of goods sold	57.7%
Gross margin	**42.3%**
Staff & wages	11.8%
Occupancy costs	6.8%
Owner's salary	5.3%
Other expenses	12.9%
Profit before tax	**5.5%**

EXHIBIT 4A	Five Highest Participation Rates in Physical Activities by Canadian Adults

Activity	Participation Rate (Total)	Women	Men
Walking	86%	92%	79%
Gardening, Yard Work	75%	72%	78%
Swimming	57%	58%	57%
Bicycling	55%	50%	60%
Home Exercise	50%	56%	45%

| EXHIBIT 4B | Five Highest Participation Rates in Physical Activities by Canadian Adults, by Age |

18-24		25-44		45-64		65+	
Walking	83%	Walking	86%	Walking	88%	Walking	82%
Swimming	74%	Gardening	77%	Gardening	84%	Gardening	65%
Social dancing	74%	Swimming	65%	Bicycling	47%	Home exercise	41%
Bicycling	69%	Bicycling	63%	Swimming	47%	Swimming	30%
Jogging	67%	Social dancing	53%	Social dancing	45%	Bicycling	23%

| EXHIBIT 5 | Braun's Online Sales by Geographic Region May 1999 to November 2000 |

Geographic Region	Number of Individual Sales	Total (%)
Canada	142	12.8
United States	779	70.5
Europe	96	8.7
Asia	59	5.3
Other	30	2.7
Total	1106	100.0

| EXHIBIT 6 | Braun's Online Activity Log: May to August 2000 |

Month	Hits (millions)	Page Views	User Sessions	Avg. Session (minutes)	Transactions	Revenue
May	1.23	149,058	42,410	7:04	36	$10,415
June	1.16	157,588	38,659	7:39	59	$13,101
July	1.20	171,853	42,974	7:18	67	$16,675
August	1.05	137,868	37,229	7:37	25	$6,784

EXHIBIT 7	Sales by Hear-About-Us: May 1999 Through November 2000

Hear-About-Us	Number of Sales
Amazon	1
On a Sign	1
Newsletter	3
Canadian Internet Mall	4
Newspaper	4
Brochure	5
TV	5
HotBot	7
Other Online Mall	10
AOL	11
Friend	13
Excite	15
Infoseek	15
Magazine	16
Lycos	18
Link from Other Braun's Site	19
Other Search Engine	77
AltaVista	77
Yahoo!	124
Unknown	676
Total	**1,101**